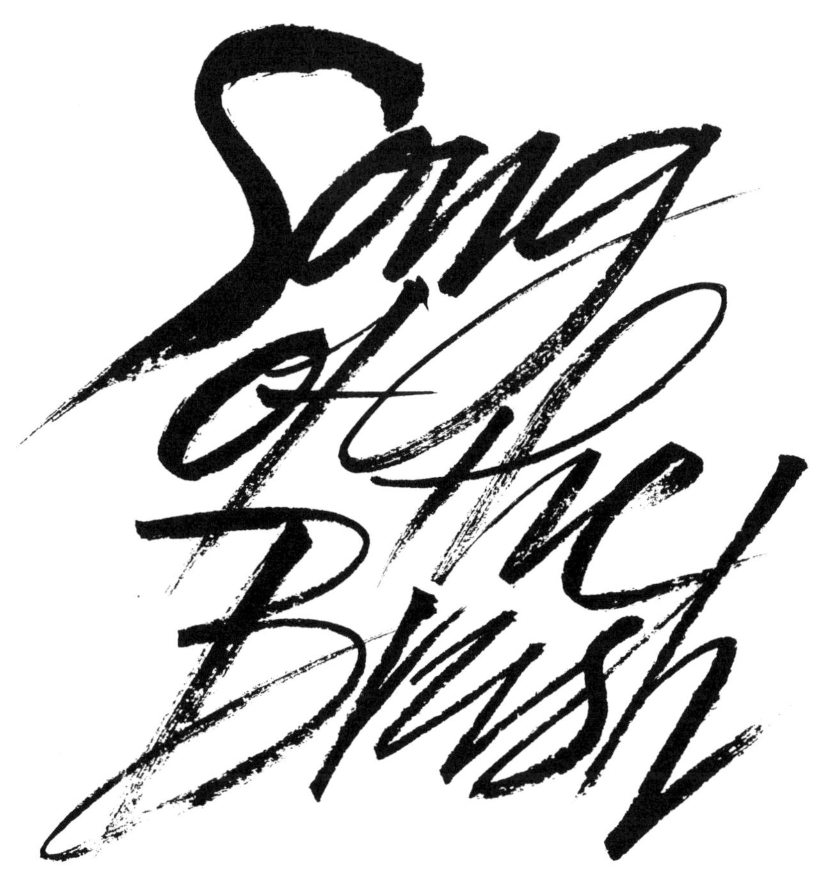
Song
of the
Brush

AF478491

Edited by
John M. Rosenfield

Song of the Brush
Japanese Paintings
from the Sansō Collection

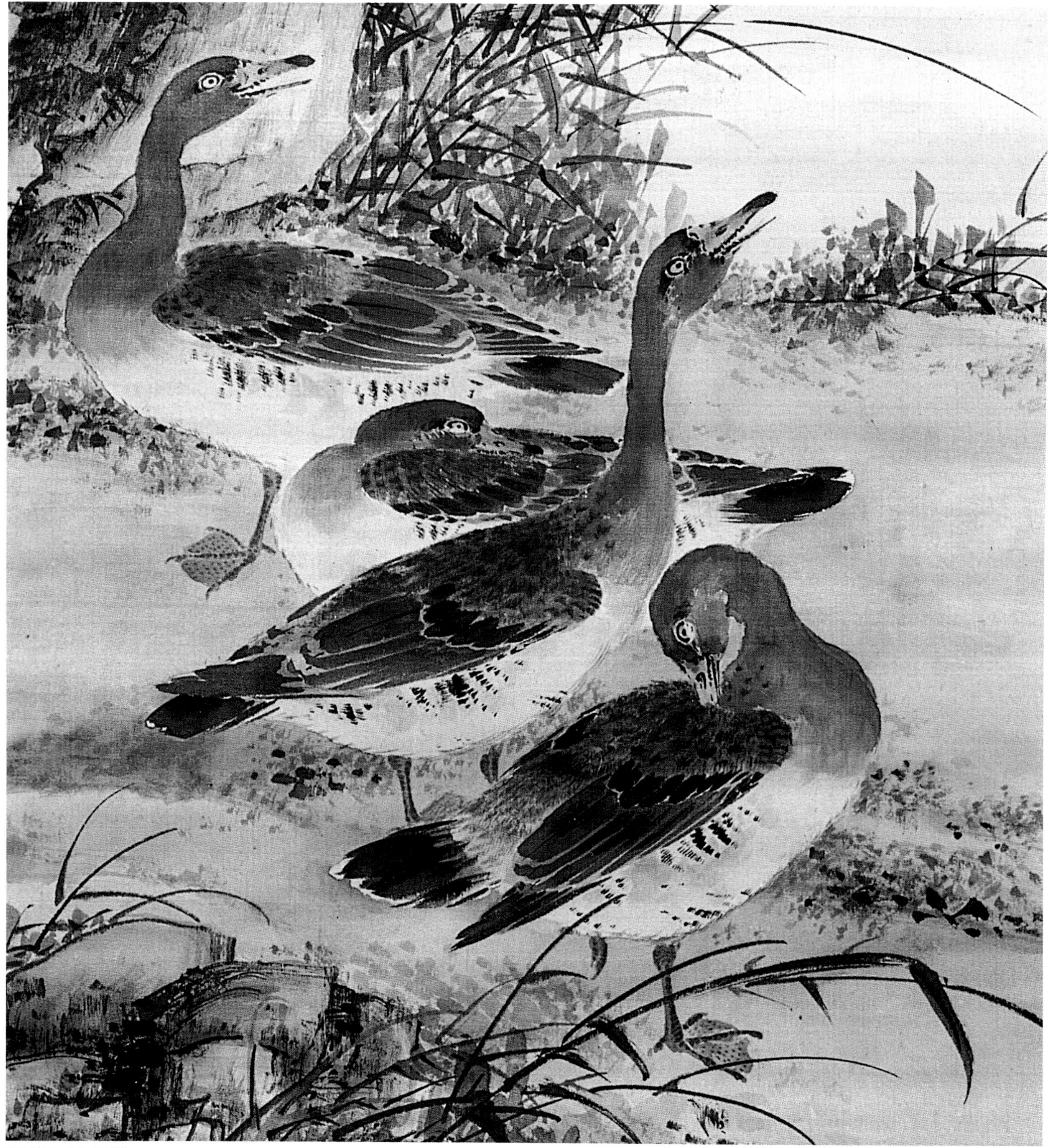

Detail (See entry no. 53)

Preface by
Henry Trubner

Essay by
Peter F. Drucker

Contributions by
William J. Rathbun
Fumiko E. Cranston

Assisted by
Catherine A. Kaputa
Rita Lee

Translation by
Fumiko E. Cranston
unless otherwise indicated

Seattle Art Museum

Participating Institutions

Japan House Gallery
New York
September 20—November 4, 1979

Fogg Art Museum
Harvard University
November 28, 1979—January 13, 1980

Denver Art Museum
February 9—March 23, 1980

Asian Art Museum of San Francisco
The Avery Brundage Collection
April 9—May 25, 1980

Seattle Art Museum
September 25—November 23, 1980

This catalogue was made possible by support from the National Endowment for the Arts.

Copyright ©1979 by the Seattle Art Museum

Library of Congress Cataloging in Publication Data

Seattle. Art Museum.
 Song of the brush.

 Exhibition catalog.
 Bibliography: p.
 Includes index.
1. Water-color painting, Japanese—Kamakura-
Momoyama periods, 1185-1600—Exhibitions.
2. Water-color painting, Japanese—Edo periods,
1600-1868—Exhibitions. 3. Sansō Collection—
Exhibitions. I. Rosenfield, John M. II. Rathbun,
William Jay. III. Cranston, Fumiko E. IV. Title.
ND2071.S36   1979   759.952′074′019777   79-19922
ISBN 0-932216-02-1
ISBN 0-932216-03-X pbk.

To preserve the beauty of the scrolls, we have reproduced portions of the silk borders. Because of their hand-mounted qualities, these borders make some of the paintings appear askew.

Nancy Roberts
Publications Manager

Pamela Diedrichs
Editor

Printed in the United States of America

Preface and Acknowledgments

The Seattle Art Museum takes great pride in presenting "Song of the Brush," a special exhibition of Japanese paintings from the fourteenth to the nineteenth centuries from the Sansō Collection. The show will be exhibited in five major museums and galleries in the United States. This first public showing of a major portion of this distinguished private collection focuses on three important schools of Japanese painting: Suibokuga (ink painting) of the Muromachi (1333-1568) and Momoyama (1568-1603) periods; Zenga, or paintings by Zen Buddhist monks of the Edo period (1603-1867); and paintings by masters of the Nanga or literati school, flourishing in the eighteenth and nineteenth centuries. The exhibit also includes selected paintings from other schools of the Edo period.

This group of rare and fine Japanese paintings could not have been brought to the American public without the cooperation and generous support of the lenders and of the National Endowment for the Arts. When the present writer first proposed the exhibition, the collectors, husband and wife, responded with enthusiastic endorsement and deep interest. They wish to remain anonymous, but nevertheless deserve highest praise for their discriminating taste, for their devotion to Japan and its culture, and for their willingness to share their collection with the general public. They travel frequently to Japan, keenly study Japanese history and social institutions, and have a wide circle of friends among Japanese scholars and government and business officials. The Sansō Collection, with its emphasis upon those aspects of Japanese culture that express an intimately personal, individualistic search for beauty and spiritual insight, bears the unmistakable imprint of the collectors' own tastes and personalities. The concluding essay, "A View of Japan through Japanese Art," by Peter F. Drucker, the distinguished scholar of management, both in the public and private sector, has been chosen by the collectors as best exemplifying their thoughts. The organizers of the exhibition are honored to be able to include Dr. Drucker's contribution in the catalogue.

The Seattle Art Museum is especially grateful to our colleagues in the other institutions who have joined with us in bringing the Sansō Collection to the American public: Rand Castile, director of the Japan House Gallery, and Maryell Semal, assistant director; Seymour Slive, director of the Fogg Art Museum, John Rosenfield, curator, and Fumiko E. Cranston, research assistant in the Oriental Department; Thomas E. Maytham, director of the Denver Art Museum, and Ronald Otsuka, curator of Oriental Art; and René-Yvon Lefebvre d'Argencé, director and chief curator of the Asian Art Museum, San Francisco, and Yoshiko Kakudo, curator of Japanese Art. We extend to each of them our warmest thanks and appreciation.

The organization of the exhibition and the writing of the catalogue have required the cooperation and expertise of many individuals at the Seattle Art Museum and at the Fogg Art Museum, Harvard University. This truly cooperative effort has been greatly assisted by the collectors themselves, who provided much valuable documentation and background material pertaining to the paintings.

John M. Rosenfield, Abby Aldrich Rockefeller Professor of Oriental Art and Curator of Oriental Art at the Fogg Art Museum, undertook the difficult task of editing the entire manuscript, coordinating the work of the younger scholars listed below, and combining the various parts into a unified publication. He was greatly assisted by Katharine O. Parker, who copyedited the manuscript and Marie Carden, who typed it.

William J. Rathbun, curator of Japanese Art at the Seattle Art Museum, has been responsible for the organization and circulation of the exhibition. He also shared with this writer and John Rosenfield the responsibility of selecting the paintings in the Sansō Collection to be included in the exhibition. In addition, Mr. Rathbun wrote the entries for the paintings of the Nanga school, his own principal field of specialization, and worked closely with the Seattle Art Museum's very able publications staff, Nancy Roberts, publications manager, and Pamela Diedrichs, editor, in the publication of the catalogue.

Fumiko E. Cranston, research assistant in the Oriental Department of the Fogg Art Museum, undertook the difficult and time-consuming task of reading all the seals and signatures, translating the inscriptions, and assembling bibliographical data on each work of art. Mrs. Cranston wishes to acknowledge the assistance of Professor Nakata Yūjirō and Professor Edwin A. Cranston; however, without Mrs. Cranston's selfless and exacting scholarship and extraordinary abilities in these difficult aspects of connoisseurship, this catalogue would not have been possible. Unless otherwise indicated, all translations from Chinese and Japanese sources are based on her work.

Catherine A. Kaputa, formerly a member of the Asian Department of the Seattle Art Museum who now resides in New York City, drafted the entries for the ink painting section. Having spent two years in Japan as a graduate student in Japanese painting of Harvard University, she is particularly well qualifed to contribute to this portion of the catalogue. Rita Lee, who joined the Seattle Art Museum's Asian Department in December, 1978, as curatorial assistant, willingly accepted the task of writing the entries for the final section of paintings by diverse artists. Hiro Kawasaki, of the faculty of Evergreen State College in Olympia, Washington, generously shared his knowledge of the history of Japanese literati painting; he prepared entries and contributed to entries. W. J. R. Dreesmann of the Asiatic Department of the Museum of Fine Arts, Boston, gave valuable assistance in the preparation of the section on Zen painting.

We are greatly endebted to Paul Macapia, Seattle Art Museum photographer, who made all photographs for the catalogue, including those of seals and inscriptions. Jo Nilsson of the museum's Photo Slide Library, and Elizabeth de Fato, museum librarian, rendered invaluable assistance to this project, as did Deborah Stuteville, Asian Art Department secretary, and her successor MaryAnn Dosch. Museum Registrar Gail Joice McKeown and her able staff, together with William J. Lahr, shipping supervisor, have been responsible for packing, shipping, and security arrangements; to them goes our deep gratitude.

Henry Trubner
Associate Director for Curatorial Affairs
Seattle Art Museum

Chronology

Japan	China
Muromachi Period (1333-1568)	**Southern Sung Dynasty** (1127-1279)
Momoyama Period (1568-1603)	**Yüan Dynasty** (1280-1368)
Edo Period (1603-1867)	**Ming Dynasty** (1368-1644)
Meiji Period (1868-1912)	**Ch'ing Dynasty** (1644-1912)

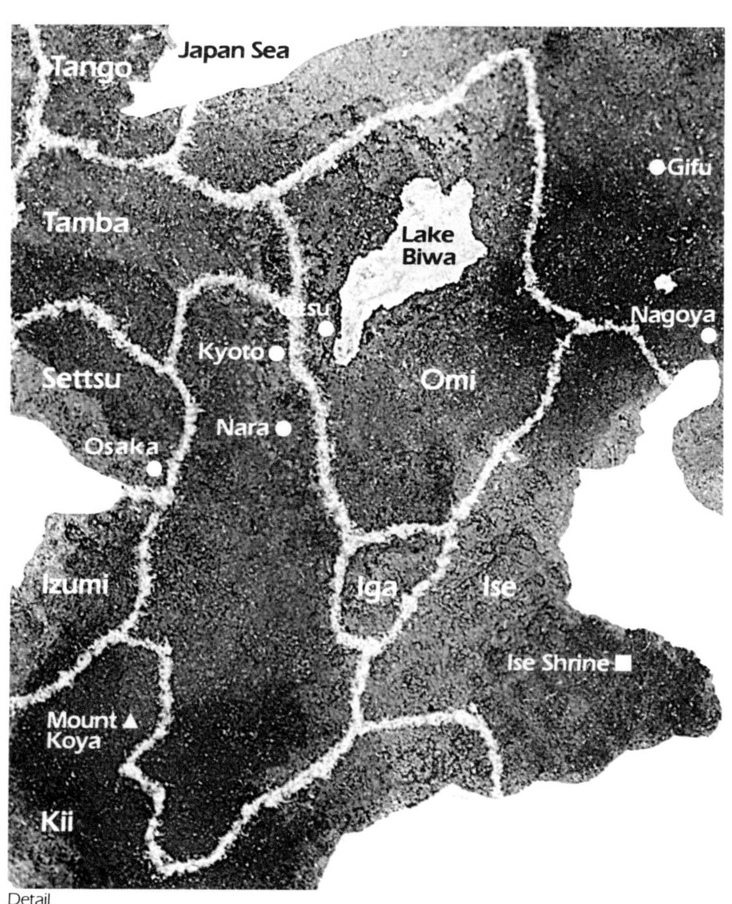

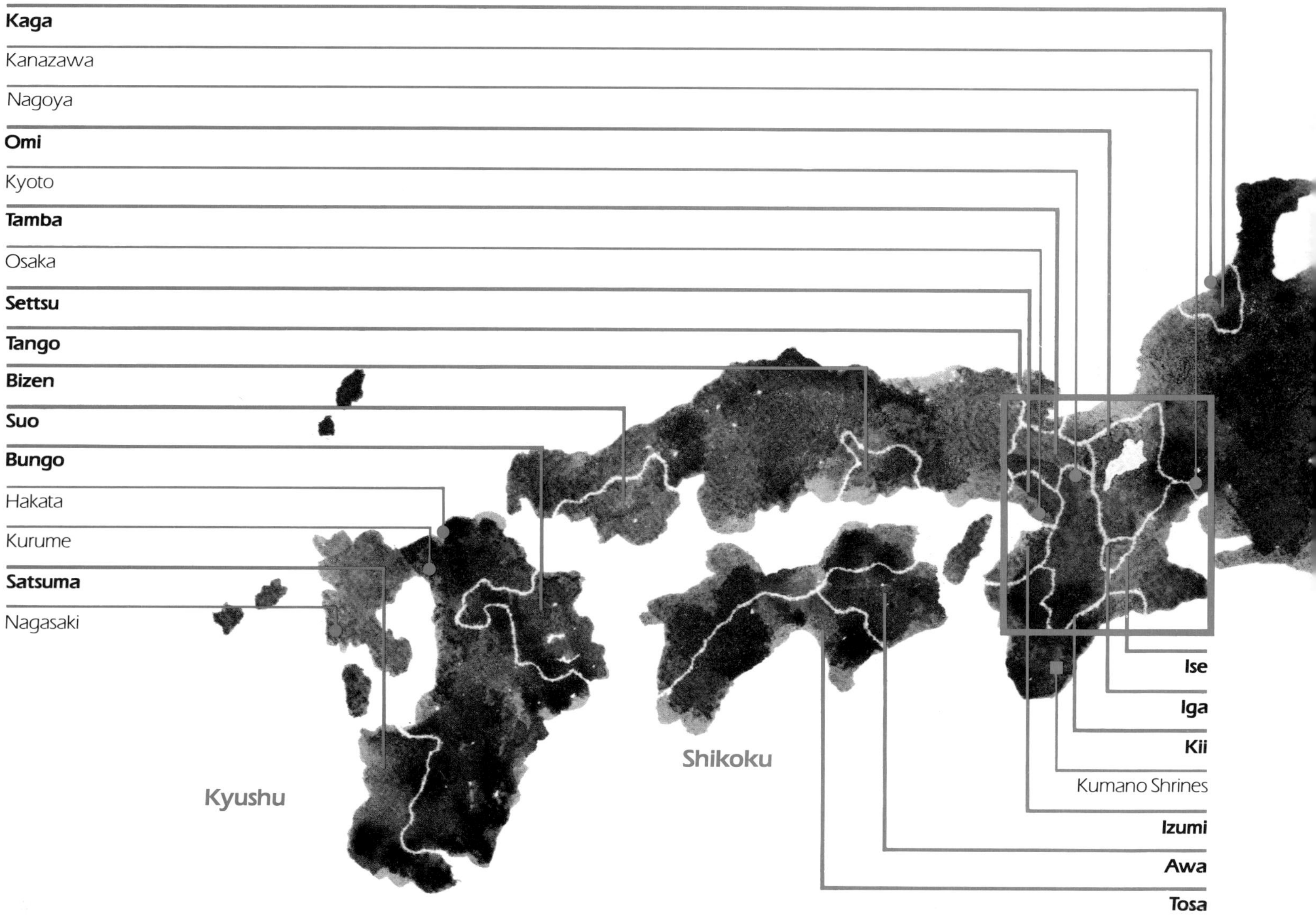

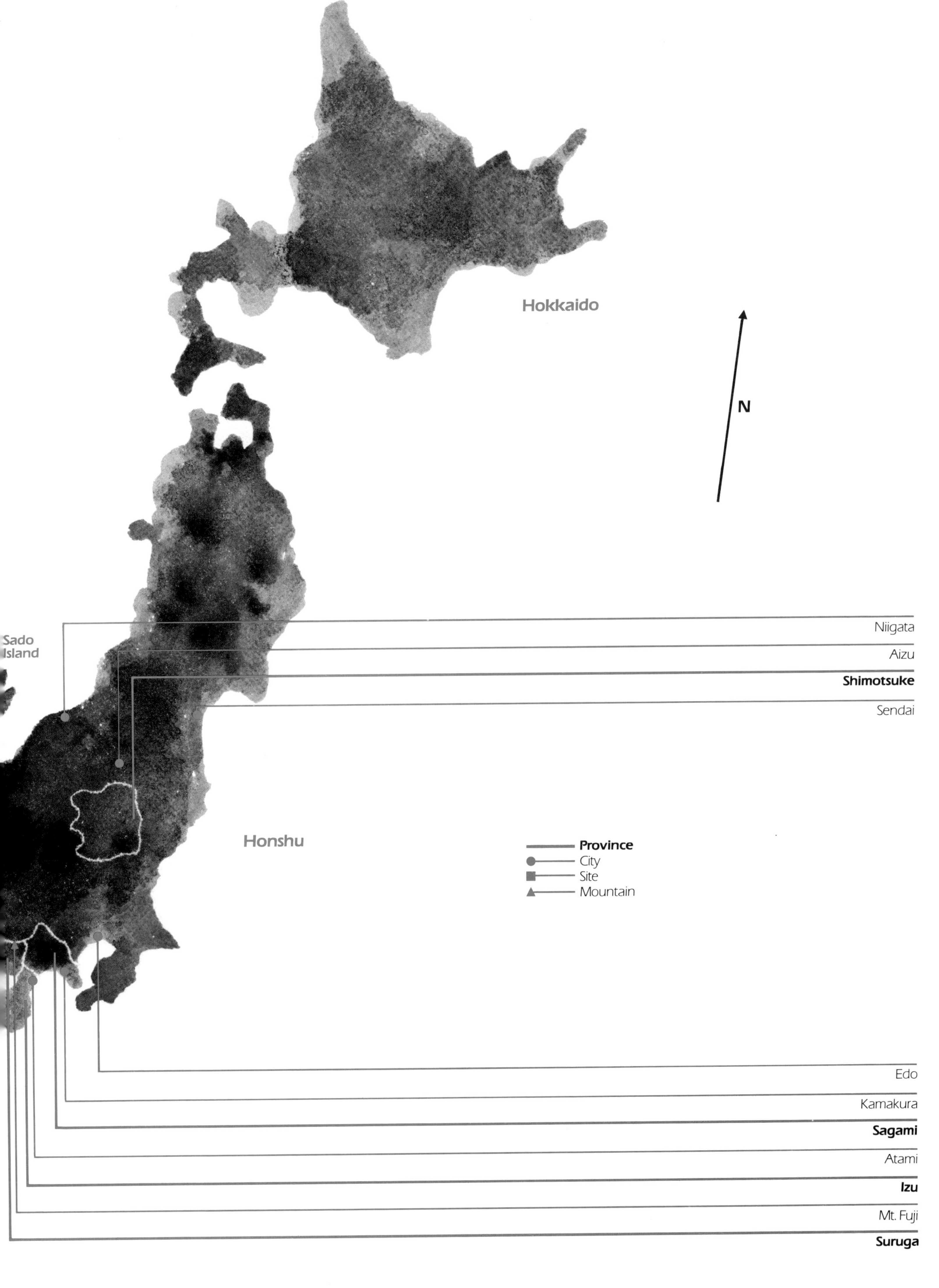

Hokkaido
N
Sado
Island
Niigata
Aizu
Shimotsuke
Sendai
Honshu
Province
City
Site
Mountain
Edo
Kamakura
Sagami
Atami
Izu
Mt. Fuji
Suruga

Contents

***Reproduced in color**

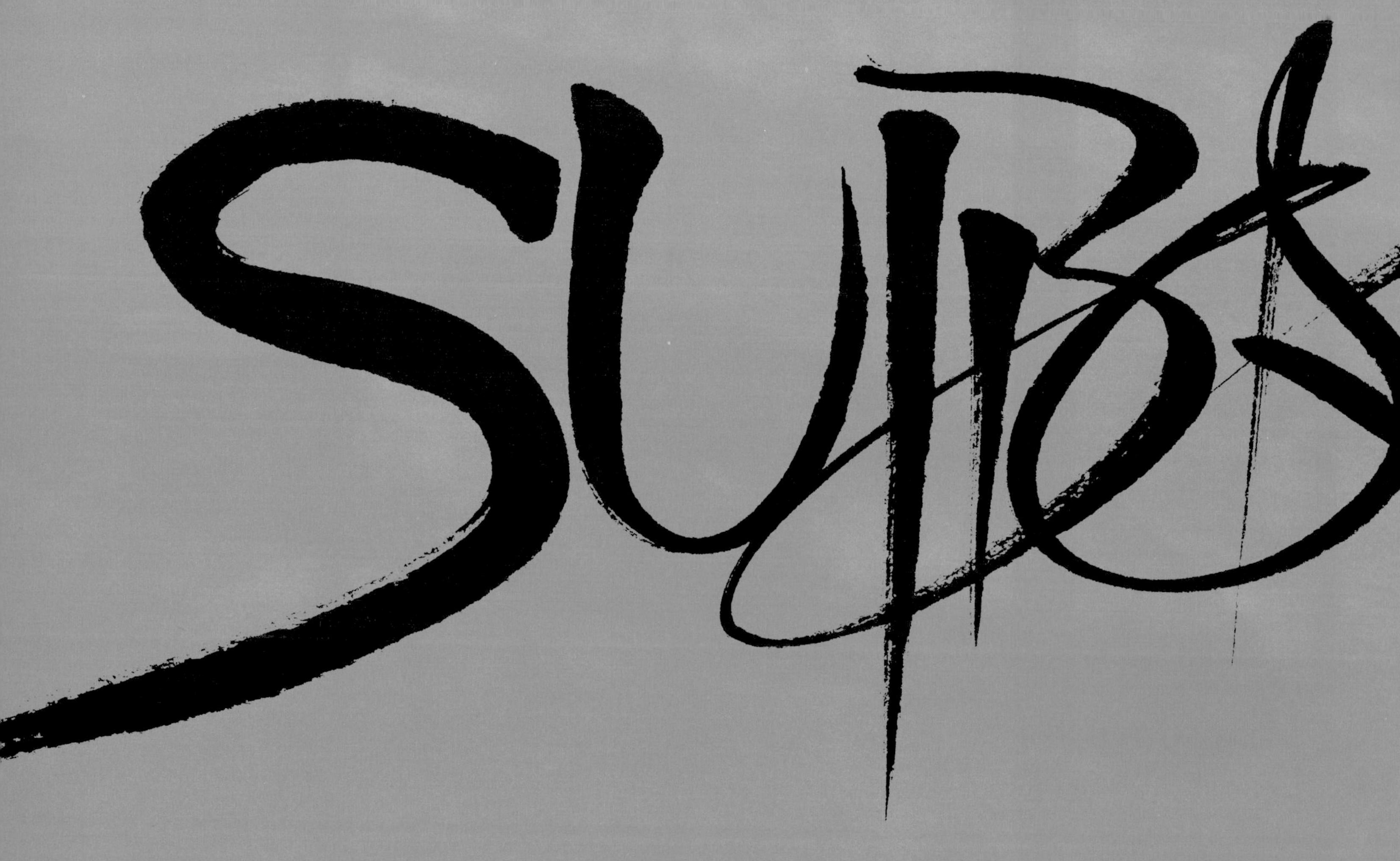

Part I

Suibokuga: Ink Paintings from the Zen Monastery

If the term renaissance is used to denote an artistic and cultural flowering from old but dormant roots, then Japan's Muromachi period (1333-1568) was the setting for a Japanese renaissance of unparalleled vigor. This renewal was rooted in China of the Sung dynasty, and particularly in the art and culture of the Southern Sung (1127-1279), the fragile and doomed remnant left under Chinese rule after the conquest of northern China by the warlike Tatar nomads from inner Asia.

The original focal points of the Japanese renaissance were the great Buddhist monasteries of Kyoto and Kamakura, which, like the fourteenth- and fifteenth-century churches of Rome and Florence, received lavish patronage from the governing elite. The main monasteries of Kamakura and Kyoto were called the Gozan (Five Mountains), a term first used to describe the leading Ch'an monasteries in the vicinity of the Southern Sung capital of Hangchou in China. The cultural movement that grew from these sanctuaries in Japan is often called the Gozan bunka.

From the Japanese Buddhist clergy came the outstanding artists of the Muromachi era, inspired by the ideal of a lost classic age of Sung China, an era far closer to them in time than was the antiquity of Greece and Rome to the Italian renaissance. The analogy between Japan and Italy should not be overdrawn, however, nor the use of the term renaissance abused; the two contemporary cultures, half a world apart, differed in fundamental ways, such as language, religion, and social customs. Nonetheless, in the fifteenth century both cultures saw the emergence of secular art from a matrix of religious symbolism; both saw the decline of a system of ancient hieratic religious imagery that had previously dominated their arts; both heralded the emergence of the secular values upon which so much of modern culture is based.

The Japanese renaissance bore many fruits, such as the Nō theater and the tea ceremony. Most important to us are the suibokuga, literally water-ink-pictures, done with brushes and monochromatic inks upon paper or mounted silk. The development of ink painting in Japan was closely allied with the rapid growth of the Meditation sect of Buddhism (called Ch'an in Chinese, or Zen in Japanese), which became the dominant ideology of the ruling military clans and, eventually, of most educated Japanese. In the early Middle Ages, ink painting was done by monks living in Zen monastery compounds that were lavishly supported by the military regime. The paintings were part of a larger set of aesthetic values which influenced the austere and abstract art of the monastic gardens, and a bold and assertive style of calligraphy. Those who admired the ink paintings also patronized the Nō theater, another extremely abstract art form, and participated in the ceremonial drinking of tea. In the last decades of the Muromachi era, the tea ceremony became a preeminent aspect of Japanese high culture, unifying the diverse elements of Gozan literary and artistic life.

The works of twenty-one masters of ink painting are represented in the Sansō Collection. The great majority of these artists were Zen Buddhist monks, and their biographies, with few exceptions, are exceedingly obscure. As monks, they had embarked on a career leading to the exalted spiritual condition of Buddhist enlightenment; they sought not to assert the self but rather to submerge the ego in the condition of selflessness. Consequently, they left little concrete record of their careers, and modern scholarship has been obliged to extract biographical data from extremely scattered and fragile evidence: from the inscriptions on their paintings, and the dates of those who wrote them; from references in contemporary diaries; from the partly apocryphal histories of Japanese painting written in the seventeenth and eighteenth centuries; from old catalogues of the collections of monasteries and the ruling shoguns (military dictators). One of the most important sources of information is the art itself; the style of the paintings often indicates the artistic and cultural ambience in which the artists worked.

To give a sense of the human realities from which early Japanese ink paintings arose, we composed the biography of a hypothetical monk painter of the fifteenth century, a man we call Baisetsu, who was born around 1425 and died around 1510. In creating this fictitious biography, we tried to avoid both romanticizing and excessive detail, and sought to combine data from a number of documented lives to present a typical pattern of training and development in the Gozan atmosphere.

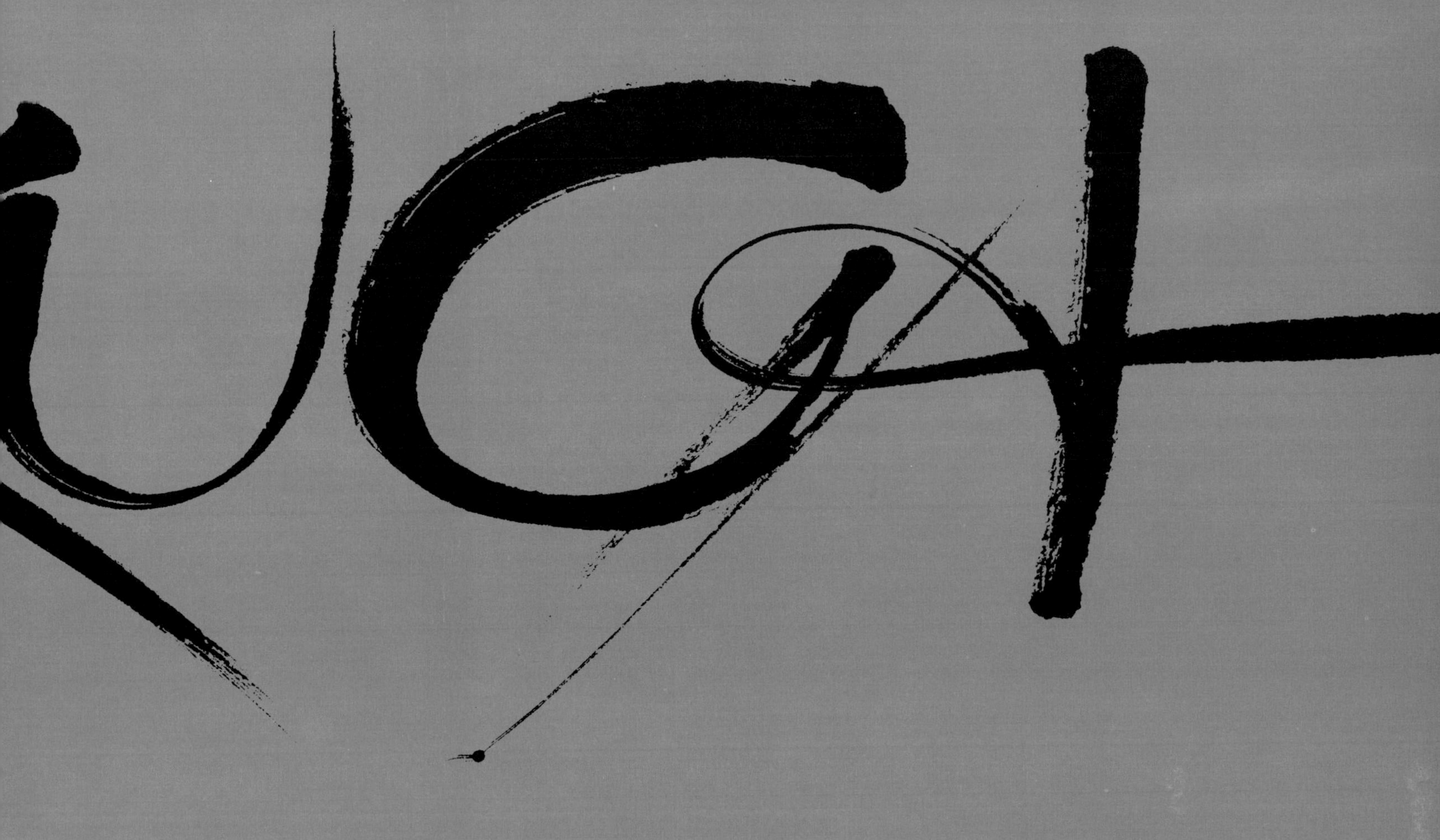

Baisetsu was the third son born to a low-ranking samurai who had been assigned the income from rice fields in a small valley in the rugged hills of Suruga in eastern Honshu. The Ashikaga shogun gave this fief as a reward to Baisetsu's grandfather, who had fought valiantly in the dynastic succession struggles of the 1350s. The family had become ji-samurai, agrarian as well as military in its profession.

Our painter-to-be was taught the martial arts of swordsmanship, archery, and the care of horses by the father and the family retainers. When he reached the age of twelve or thirteen he was sent, as were his elder brothers before him, to a neighboring Buddhist temple to begin his formal education under the local priest. In the first year, he was taught the Japanese kana syllabaries and was introduced to Chinese characters. He memorized the short prayer that comprises the Heart Sutra, and learned to copy it faithfully in Chinese characters. He also studied the Kannon Sutra and Buddhist instruction books for children. In his second year, he began to study Confucian classics such as the **Book of Rites,** the **Analects,** and the **Book of Poetry,** as well as Chinese military manuals. During his third and last year, he was introduced to such Japanese classics as the great fictional works—**Tales of Ise** and **The Tale of Genji,** the poetry anthologies—the **Manyōshū** and the **Kokin Wakashū,** and the ancient annals of Japan—the **Nihon Shoki.**

When his elder brothers had completed this rudimentary education, they took up duties supervising the rice crops and roads and improving their martial skills. During his three years, however, Baisetsu had so impressed the priest by his aptitude for study and by his mastery of the various styles of Chinese writing that the priest arranged for him to enter a large Zen Buddhist monastery near Gifu to study with his own revered teacher. Thus, at the age of seventeen years, Baisetsu became a novice monk. He was given the tonsure and a supply of simple, coarse robes and sandals, and initiated into the regimen of austerity and self-denial that he would follow for the rest of his life. Each day, regardless of the weather—the freezing cold of midwinter, the bone-chilling dampness of early spring or the suffocating humidity of late summer—he was awakened by the temple drum before the first light and began his day with meditation and morning ceremony. With the other novice monks, he would sleep in the Zendō, the meditation hall, and on certain days they would all leave the monastery to practice the ancient Buddhist custom of begging for food and other gifts from the neighborhood. Their diet was vegetarian and plain. The younger monks worked long hours tilling the monastery gardens, preparing food in the kitchens, and sweeping the ceremonial halls and temple grounds.

The young painter was given advanced training in the spiritual and intellectual disciplines of Zen. In the company of the other novices, he was shown how to fold his legs, hold his body upright, control his breathing, concentrate his mind for long hours and chant in unison basic Zen prayers. Sometimes the ordinary routine of the monastery ceased for periods of a week or more so that the monks could undergo the more intense discipline of a sesshin, where they remained seated in meditation for up to sixteen hours.

Baisetsu was assigned to a rōshi (senior monk) who lived in one of the monastery's numerous subtemples, and once or often twice a day, the novice would come to the rōshi's chambers for an interview. In an early interview, the rōshi gave him his first kōan, the enigmatic proposition used as a meditation text in Zen temples of the Rinzai tradition. Many of the kōan were of ancient vintage, having been developed in the Ch'an Buddhist communities of T'ang China. Some were of a semihistorical character: What is the meaning of Bodhidharma's coming from the west? Others were more philosophical in character: One who has realized his own original nature escapes from birth-and-death. When the light of your eyes falls to the ground how will you escape? The propositions were often paradoxical or illogical: What is the sound of one hand clapping? The student's responses could well be of the same character.

Baisetsu's old teacher possessed hanging scrolls with bold calligraphy written in Chinese by the teacher's own master, a man who had studied in Kamakura with one of the great Chinese Zen monks brought to Japan in the late thirteenth century. The calligraphy texts were rather like the kōan, assertive but enigmatic statements of Zen doctrine, and the young Baisetsu spent many hours deciphering them and discussing their meaning. Baisetsu's teacher kept a portrait painting of his master, given to him when he left his master's tutelage thirty years before. On each anniversary of the master's death, the old priest would hang the portrait between paintings of a plum and of a bamboo, and recite sutras in the teacher's memory. The old monk also had a pile of blackened paper rubbings made in China from engravings of T'ang and Sung calligraphies which he loaned to the acolyte. Baisetsu carefully copied their rich and flowing writing styles as he began to write his own verses in Chinese.

By the time he had reached his twenty-first year, the young painter had impressed the elders of the monastery with his seriousness and abilities. He was especially honored when his rōshi gave him the religious epithet Baisetsu—plum, snow—taken from one of the calligraphies of his old teacher. The elders also arranged for him to enter one of the great Zen monasteries of Kyoto, Tōfuku-ji, located in the hills southeast of the city. His life in the great monastery did not differ greatly from the one he had left except in two respects: There were more activities in the new monastery, and all sermons and text readings were given in Chinese. At Tōfuku-ji, Baisetsu joined several hundred novices from all parts of the country. Like a small army, the tonsured youths in black robes would sit for hours, rank upon rank, in the vast Zendō. They were also sent to the numerous subtemples where they received advanced instruction from the senior monks.

Because of his quick mind and clear precise hand, Baisetsu was assigned to work several hours a day in the monastery's department of administration, first as an attendant, then as a clerk. There he helped maintain the registry of names of resident monks, kept account books of temple land holdings and income, and copied out religious texts.

Several monks worked in one small room in the department of administration painting the pictures required by the monastery and its branch temples for various rituals: portraits of the temple patriarchs, scrolls depicting the Death of Sākyamuni, and episodes from the legendary history of the Zen sect in China. They also painted landscapes, portraits of the White-Robed Avalokiteśvara (Byaku-e Kannon), often used in funeral services for parishioners of the temple, and pictures of birds, orchids, bamboo, and plum blossoms. The paintings with secular themes were often taken into the city to be shown at literary gatherings organized by the shogun or other high-ranking members of the military or the court aristocracy. Senior monks from Zen monasteries around the capital would attend these gatherings and inscribe appropriate poems directly on the paintings in the empty spaces deliberately left by the artists.

Baisetsu was intrigued by these painters. He already possessed many of their artistic skills. He was a calligrapher of long standing; he could control the flow of ink from his brush onto paper, and he had a good eye for the balanced compositions and lively line quality of his written characters. He was also familiar with Chinese poetry and the complex nuances and overtones of meaning in paintings taken from poetic themes. One of the monk painters he befriended drew some simple pictures for him to copy: Bodhidharma in meditation, a branch of flowering plum, a kingfisher poised on a branch. In the moments of leisure from his monastic training and his duties as a clerk, Baisetsu would copy these models over and over until he had mastered them. Because of his evident talent as a painter, he was given permission to assist the monk painters whenever his clerical duties were light.

His life soon settled into a routine pattern of long hours of meditation and spiritual training, coupled with his routine clerical tasks and his work as a painter. There were, however, distractions. In the office of administration, Baisetsu noticed the contributions made to the monastery by its patrons among the leaders of the military government. He often heard the rumors of political intrigue that swept through the brotherhood of monks, tales of disaffection and possible rebellion by the powerful daimyo (feudal lords). He also began to notice some of the monks slipping quietly through a side gate of the monastery at night to visit the wine shops and brothels of the Shimabara district; others seemed to be caught up in homosexual attachments.

Even though Baisetsu, when he became a monk, severed his worldly attachments and "quit the family," he experienced terrible grief over the death of his parents and guilt that he was absent when they died. His native district had been swept by an epidemic of smallpox that killed many of his relatives. During the same summer, a series of typhoons destroyed the rice crops in the Kyoto area, the capital and its monasteries suffered from a severe food shortage, and the poorest of the townspeople died of starvation. He nearly died of pneumonia during one bitter winter, and of undulant fever during a summer when the atmosphere over Kyoto was like a humid cauldron; still he survived.

By the time Baisetsu was in his thirties, he had been fully ordained. His superiors recognized his deep religious understanding and placed him in charge of a temple in western Japan, where he had relatively light duties: teaching local children, supervising the activities of two other monks, and conducting public readings of sutras, funerals, and public ceremonials on the birth and death anniversary of Sakyamuni. Although he frequently offered private counsel to parishioners, he had ample time for study and, best of all, for painting.

While living in this remote temple, Baisetsu was suprised to receive a short visit from the monk painter whom he had befriended at the Kyoto monastery. The man had been appointed to one of the rare official trade missions organized by the shogunal regime to travel to Ming China, and was enroute to Hakata, the port of embarkation. In the previous century private missions were sent out once or twice a year, but now, in Baisetsu's time, official missions were organized only once a decade, and membership in them was greatly prized. The missions brought Japanese swords, fans, brocades, gold ingots and other metals and minerals, to trade for Chinese cultural goods—ceramics, lacquerware, temple fittings, paintings, textiles, and books. Zen monks played an important role in these delegations because of their mastery of the Chinese language and their familiarity with the objects to be obtained.

The following year, upon his return from China, Baisetsu's friend stopped once again at his temple and showed him copies of famous Chinese pictures, and sketches of the landscape around Hangchou and Peking. Baisetsu, stimulated by his friend's enthusiasm and new knowledge, began to experiment with landscapes painted on long handscrolls.

The local daimyo had lived in Kyoto and observed how the Ashikaga shoguns had collected works by the Kyoto Zen monk painters. He was thus delighted to discover a man of such talent in his district. He built a fine, small building at a corner of the temple grounds where Baisetsu could live and paint. In return, the artist made a portrait of the daimyo and gave him a landscape handscroll which the lord proudly showed to his visitors.

Next, Baisetsu was transferred to a temple not far from Ise, east of Kyoto. While traveling to it, he stopped at Tōfuku-ji, his old monastery in the capital. He was invited to stay in the official hostel for visiting abbots, a signal honor. He was also invited to attend a literary gathering at the shogun's villa within the Hana no Gosho. For the first time, Baisetsu actually observed the religious and literary elite of the capital, about fifteen men, gathering to drink tea, to discuss literary matters, and to admire a new painting and inscribe poems on it. The painting was a rainswept landscape by his artist friend, and he was startled when the abbot of Tōfuku-ji invited him to inscribe a poem on it. He thought a moment, dipped a brush in the ink and, writing over a low table, excited the gathering by composing a poem in Chinese that caught the spirit of the painting, the mood of the season, the motion of natural forces, and the sense of transiency of living things.

Three days later, Baisetsu received a letter from the curator of the shogun's collection, inviting him to see the shogun's treasures of Chinese painting which had been handed down by five successive heads of the military regime. For a few hours, in the soft light of a room in the shogun's private retreat, he closely studied perhaps a dozen original works by the Sung masters whose names he had heard for two decades: Mu-ch'i, the Ch'an monk painter; Hsia Kuei, the great landscapist and member of the court academy; the emperor Hui-tsung, a brilliant painter who died tragically at the hands of the Jurchen Tatars; the monk Wu-chun Shih-fan, a great Chinese prelate and amateur painter with whom many Japanese monks and Chinese Ch'an masters studied; Lian K'ai, the court academician who became a Ch'an devotee and developed a style of highly simplified figure painting. Most startling of all was Yü-chien's long landscape handscroll in the haboku (broken-ink) technique.

It is impossible to describe the profound impact these Chinese originals made on the mind of the monk painter who had waited twenty years for this unique moment. His eye was fully prepared to appreciate the subtle orchestration of grays and blacks in Mu-ch'i's monumental painting on silk of gibbons in a pine tree. He marveled at the radical simplicity of Liang K'ai's brushwork in his painting of the poet, Li Po. Baisetsu compared Hsia Kuei's stormy landscape with his friend's painting and realized the greater unity of expression and power of brushwork in the Chinese work. He was deeply moved by the clumsy, almost childlike paintings of Wu-chun, for he knew that Wu-chun had been the most influential thinker and prelate of his age. He exclaimed over the broken-ink landscapes of Yü-chien, noting how the image had been dissolved into amorphous areas of splashed ink and drawn into focus by a few deftly placed details.

For the rest of his life, Baisetsu retained these impressions in his memory. He had been given the privilege of seeing the great works of Sung ink painting which had profoundly influenced the imagery of all Japanese Zen monk-artists. At his next post, near Ise, he described these works to the young monks who came to study painting with him, and sought to recreate effects he had seen. Although he was nominally in charge of a local temple, he persuaded another monk to attend to the main public functions while he concentrated his energies on his paintings. Again, his work came to the attention of the regional daimyo, who, feeling his independence of the rapidly weakening central regime in Kyoto, wished to assert himself in cultural matters as well. The daimyo arranged for Baisetsu to be comfortably and properly housed, and invited his friends and retainers to visit the temple. Some of the visitors commissioned the painter to do their portraits.

Baisetsu's old artist friend from the Kyoto monastery had advanced in the Zen hierarchy, and became the abbot of the great Kyoto temples Kennin-ji and Nanzen-ji. Such appointments at the end of a man's career were usually honorific in character; a celebrated monk might become the abbot of four or five major monasteries for short periods of time. In the 1460s, Baisetsu was invited several times to return to Kyoto, but he refused. He knew the political tensions in the capital had grown. The shogunal regime became weak and ineffective while the regional lords grew increasingly independent and assertive. It was only a matter of time before civil war broke out, as it did in the Ōnin rebellion of 1467. Baisetsu felt he was better off in his rustic temple under the protection of his local lord than in one of the huge monastic compounds in the capital. In addition, Baisetsu was puzzled that men who were not Zen monks were beginning to excel as painters in the Southern Sung tradition. They were given posts of honor in the shogun's court and circle of companions, and they even executed large landscape paintings on sliding screens for Zen monasteries. He himself had painted landscapes on screens; assisted by his younger acolytes, he had enlarged the compositions he normally employed for hanging scrolls to ornament the screens of a large meditation chamber; but he felt uneasy doing so. He was troubled because no precedent for that kind of mural-scale imagery existed in the Southern Sung tradition. He had been trained to think of ink painting as a personal, intimate art form, closely linked to poetry. These ink paintings were shown on special occasions, and not left on permanent view. While Baisetsu mused on the fact that he seemed to have become as much a professional painter as a Buddhist monk, he continued to spend many hours in meditation and remained vegetarian and frugal in his habits. He thought of himself as a loyal follower of the tradition of the Chinese monk painters, Mu-ch'i and Yü-chien.

Local youths, attracted by his reputation as a painter, came to apprentice themselves to him. He executed painting models for them to copy, criticized their efforts, and spent long hours discussing Chinese poems. He was somewhat dismayed by the younger generation's seeming lack of discipline. He had not begun to paint until he was well into his thirties, but these boys believed they could be artists without mastering the Chinese classics or submitting to the iron discipline of long hours of seated meditation. They were what some of the old Zen prelates scornfully called bunjin-sō (monk litterateurs). Baisetsu had been called one himself, but even as he became increasingly interested in painting and poetry, he had never doubted his loyalty to his Buddhist calling. He remembered reading a passage from a sermon given by Musō Soseki (1275-1351), one of the most influential of Japan's early native-born Zen thinkers:

What is that which we call the [Buddhist] "Law"? It is the Truth inherent in all its perfection in every living creature. The sage possesses it in no greater measure than does the ordinary man. Enlarge it and it will fill the universe; restrict it and it can be contained in a fraction of an inch…Everything the world contains—grass and trees, bricks and tile, all creatures, all actions and activities—are nothing but manifestations of this Law. Therefore is it said that all phenomena in the universe bear the mark of this Law. If the significance of this were only grasped, then even without the appearance in this world of a Tathāgata Buddha, the enlightenment of man would be complete*…

By these criteria, pine trees and rocks were no less sacred a theme for a Buddhist painter than was the Bodhisattva Kannon. Moreover, if Kannon and pine trees shared the same degree of sanctity, the same style of painting could be used to depict either subject. Baisetsu felt this identity between religious and secular content but he doubted that any of his young students ever would.

Baisetsu died early in the sixteenth century, as the country became increasingly drawn into the vortex of civil war. The struggles virtually destroyed the social basis upon which the cultural achievements of the great Japanese Zen monasteries had been based, but the influence of the Japanese renaissance would be felt for centuries to come.

*Sources of Japanese Tradition, vol. I. de Bary, William Theodore (ed.) (New York, 1958), p. 260.

1

Orchid and Rocks

Hanging Scroll
Ink on paper
29.0 x 38.1 cm

Seal
Tesshū

Tesshū Tokusai
Active 1342–died 1366

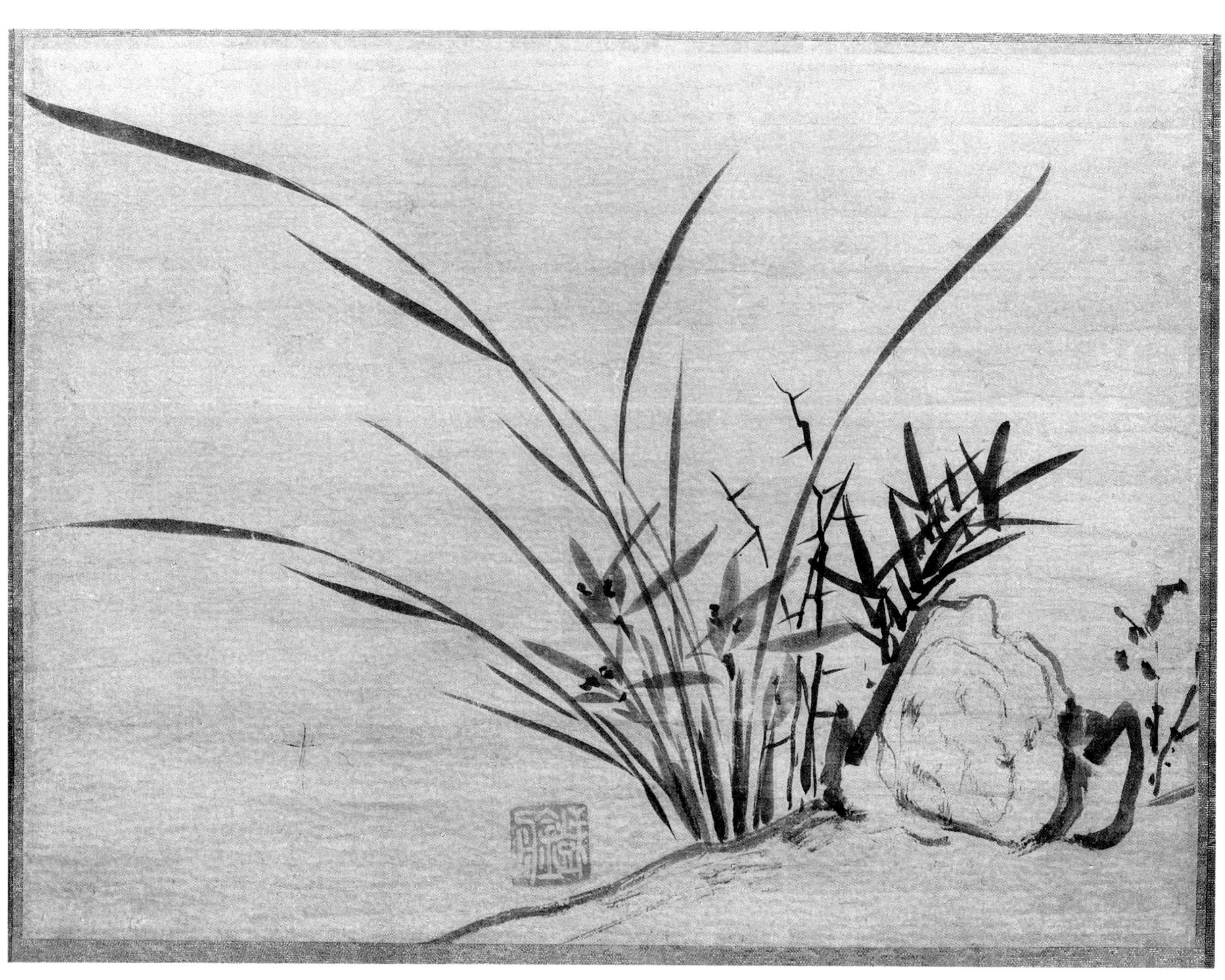

Detail

The austere, straightforward quality in this painting arises from its symbolic content. Among Japanese Zen Buddhists of the early Middle Ages, the orchid had become an emblem of such ideals as purity and nobility of character, incorruptibility, and loyalty. It was, however, one of several similar motifs from the natural world—bamboo, chrysanthemum, blossoming plum, wild geese—that expressed a wide range of meanings which had originated in Chinese poetry and secular painting but which were later given Buddhist spiritual overtones.

The five elements of the composition are lined up along the diagonal slope of the ground: a large clump of orchids, three thorny brambles, a small bamboo, a pair of rocks, and a nondescript plant. Dominating the composition are the long and undulating leaves of the orchid, which fan outward to fill the page and offset the concentration of pictorial elements to the right. Of the three surviving orchid paintings usually attributed to Tesshū, this one is the most informal and was the most rapidly executed. The artist, rather than emphasizing volume or three-dimensionality in the objects, concentrated on brushwork. To define the rocks, for example, he used broad wet strokes to establish the sides of the rocks, and a rather dry brush with its hairs splayed open to define the surface forms.

Tesshū was one of the earliest of the prominent Japanese Zen bunjin-sō, monks who excelled in the arts of painting, poetry, and calligraphy. His ecclesiastical status was high, as was his reputation for religious discipline and intellectual power. He began his Zen training in Kamakura under the eminent Zen master Musō Soseki (1275-1351), and later, during his twenties, he made a pilgrimage to China. During Tesshū's extended stay on the mainland, he was honored, according to tradition, with the Buddhist title of Yüan-t'ang Ta-shih (Great Master of Perfect Penetration) by the Yüan Emperor Shun-tsung (reigned 1322-1341). After his return to Japan in 1343, he held a number of important positions in Zen temples, including an appointment in 1362 as the abbot of the influential Manju-ji monastery in Kyoto.

During his long apprenticeship in Chinese literature and painting, Tesshū must have become closely familiar with the orchid pictures of Hsüeh-ch'üang P'u-ming, a monk painter active in the mid-fourteenth century in the Ch'an communities around Suchou when Tesshū was studying there. The works of the two men are strikingly similar; both attempted to bring plant forms into an orchestral relationship that is highly stylized and yet retains the qualities of natural shapes: undulation, thorniness, weathered irregularity, and the sense of growth or movement in the wind. P'u-ming's paintings, however, are more dramatic in their composition, more complex in the number of floral elements, and more atmospheric in their treatment of pictorial space. Tesshū, arising from Japan's national traditions, worked in a more two-dimensional manner. His paintings are less atmospheric and they bring the objects depicted closer to the spectator, traits that were to find a more developed stage of expression in the orchid paintings of Gyokuen Bompō (no. 2) two generations later.

As a poetic and cultural emblem, the image of the orchid came from deep within the Chinese literary tradition. The primary source of its significance was the classic poem **Li Sao (On Encountering Sorrow)**, composed in south China in the beginning of the third century BC and attributed to the statesman Ch'ü Yüan. In the minds of later generations, Ch'ü was the righteous and loyal minister who had been slandered and sent into bitter exile, and who recorded in the **Li Sao** his lament at injustice and misrule. Part of the literary culture of educated persons throughout East Asia for centuries, the **Li Sao** contains the following famous passage:

The age is disordered in a tumult of changing;
How can I tarry much longer among [my enemies]?
Orchid and iris have lost all their fragrance;
Flag and melilotus have changed into straw.

(Translated by David Hawkes)

So powerful was the expressive content of tne **Li Sao** that, even in Japan a millennium after the poem was written, an image of an orchid alone was sufficient to bring those emotions back to the viewer's consciousness. However, on one of Tesshū's surviving orchid paintings, now in the Randag Collection, the monk Gidō Shūshin (1325-1388) likened the flower to Ch'ü Yüan himself. The **Li Sao** is also mentioned in Gyokuen Bompō's inscription on his own orchid painting shown here (no. 2).

Published
Japanese Ink Paintings, Shimizu, Yoshiaki and Wheelwright, Carolyn (eds.) (Princeton, NJ, 1976), no. 31.
Muromachi Suibokuga, Matsushita, Takaaki (Tokyo, 1960), pl. 6.

References
Ch'u Tz'u, The Songs of the South, Hawkes, David (Oxford, 1959), pp. 21-34.
Kaō, Minchō, Kanazawa, Hiroshi, Nihon Bijutsu Kaiga Zenshū vol. 1 (Tokyo, 1977), pls. 16, 17.
Kokka, no. 77 (February 1896), pp. 55-56.
Museum, no. 98 (May 1959), pp. 20-22.

2

Orchids, Bamboo, Rocks, and Thorn Bushes

Hanging Scroll
Ink on paper
90.2 x 38.1 cm

Signature
Gyokuenshi (at end of inscription, from left to right)

Seals
Chisokuken
Gyokuen

Gyokuen Bompō
1348–ca 1420

Although only a half-century or so separates Bompō's orchid painting from that of Tesshū Tokusai (no. 1), and though the two men were indirectly linked, the differences in these two paintings are striking. Above all, the differences reveal the degree to which the old Chinese tradition of orchid painting had been affected by the native Japanese sense of two-dimensional design. Where the older painting shows the flower close at hand in a direct and straightforward manner, the newer one shows it more removed, thereby creating a unified visual effect with a more conscious artistic motif. In Bompō's lyrical, highly abstracted image, the long leaves of the orchid create harmonic curves and countercurves, undulating only slightly into depth and imbuing the picture with a rhythmic, almost musical character.

Gyokuen Bompō, the archetype of the Zen monk with strong literary and artistic interests, depicted orchids and rocks almost exclusively; approximately thirty orchid paintings by him are listed in old records. Today, over twenty examples are assigned to Bompō, including eight in the United States. Even though all share the same limited vocabulary of motifs—rocks, grasses, orchid leaves and flowers, and thorn bushes—they exhibit great variety. Each painting in the series is carefully composed around its own formal principle. In this example, the orchids emerge laterally from a cleft between two rocks; "flying white" strokes texture the solid rocks, which are well integrated with the flowering orchid plant rather than separated from it. The powerful vertical thrust of the long center blade reaches into the inscription to integrate the two elements of Bompō's work. The poem in praise of the orchid reads:

Having grown old, I can only vainly fondle brush and
blank paper and cannot compose a poem.
Although I have not yet read the **Li Sao,** I have fortunately
encountered the most beautiful of all flowers,
Difficult to praise in a single word.

Gyokuenshi

The Li Sao is an ancient, melancholy poem attributed to the statesman Ch'ü Yüan (ca 343–277 BC) in the chaotic era of Chinese history called the period of the Warring States. The poem employs the orchid as a complex metaphor for the beauty and meaning of life, as well as for political loyalty (see no. 1). Bompō, however, dissociates himself from the **Li Sao** and praises the orchid in its own right. Bompō was not only a gifted artistic and literary personality; he formed important associations with a number of key religious and political figures. For more than a decade, Bompō was jisha, the personal attendant, to Shunoku Myōha (1311–1388), a nephew of the influential Zen leader Musō Soseki (1275–1351). Bompō's name appears in the diary of Gidō Shūshin, one of Musō's most respected disciples. His connection with the shogun Yoshimochi (1386–1428) seems certain, for Yoshimochi attended Bompō's inaugural ceremony as the abbot of Nanzenji in 1413. Bompō held the abbacy of several Zen monasteries as well as other ecclesiastical positions during his lifetime, and his inscriptions appear on such prominent paintings of the period as the celebrated **Catfish and Gourd** by Josetsu. The last years of Bompō's life are veiled in mystery; he died in exile after being banished from Kyoto in 1420 though the circumstances of his departure are unclear.

The ancient tradition that claimed Bompō to be a disciple of Tesshū Tokusai is unlikely, given the known dates of the two men. Bompō, however, was probably inspired by the older master's work and shared his interest in Chinese orchid painting, especially that of P'u-ming. Moreover, Gidō Shūshin, Bompō's teacher, had been a friend of Tesshū. Literary documents indicate that Bompō began to paint orchids fairly early in his career, but, judging from the seals he used on them, the surviving works can all be dated to the last two decades of his life. Although students of Bompō have been able to distinguish three different styles of painting and composition, they have not been able to determine any stylistic growth or development among them. This painting is closest in brush technique to works in the Cleveland Museum of Art and the Fujii Collection in Nishinomiya, Japan.

Published
Shin-hakken: Sengo Mikōkai Meihin-ten, Nihon Keizai Shimbun (ed.) (Tokyo, 1962).

References
Japanese Ink Paintings, Shimizu, Yoshiaki and Wheelwright, Carolyn (eds.) (Princeton, NJ, 1976), no. 34.
Kokka, no. 690 (September 1949).

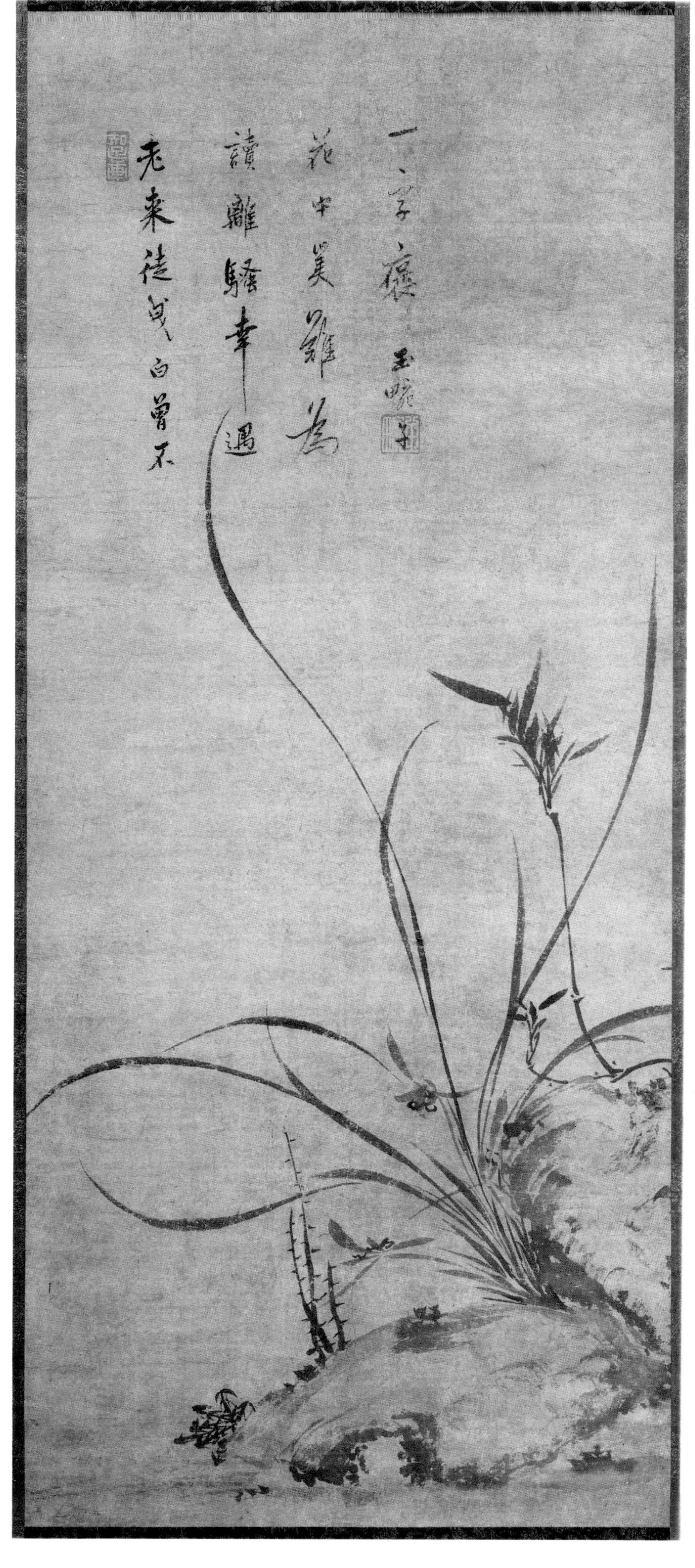
一字癡
花中美難為
讀離騷辛遇
老來徒爾白曾不

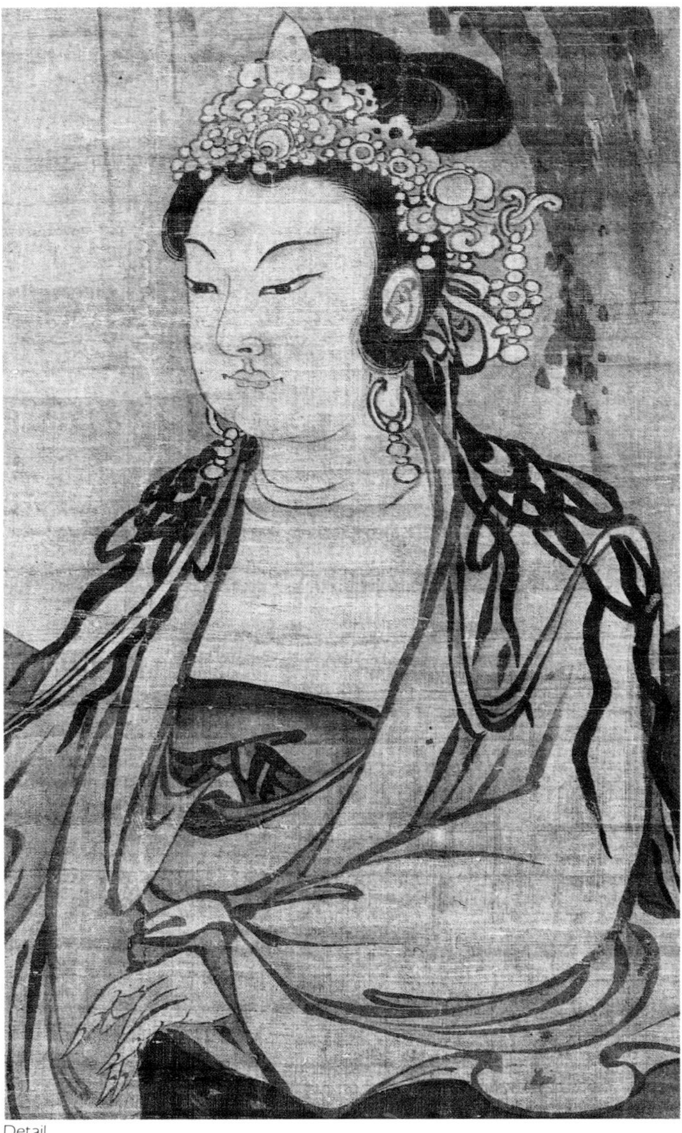

Detail

Attributed to
Isshi
Active first quarter of the fifteenth century

3

The Byaku-e
(White-Robed) Kannon
(See color plate no. 3)

Hanging Scroll
Ink on silk
95.6 x 49.5 cm

Seal
Undecipherable

The Buddhist deity most frequently depicted in Japanese Zen ink paintings was Avalokiteśvara (Kannon), embodiment of compassion and mercy, shown in one of his many guises—in a feminized form, dressed in a white robe. The rocky setting is a cave overlooking the sea on Potalaka, the island-mountain off the south coast of India thought to be Avalokiteśvara's abode on earth. Potalaka, however, was also identified with numerous other places: the Potala temple in Lhasa, capital of Tibet; the P'u-t'o sanctuary on an island near Ningpo on the south China coast; and at the towering Nachi waterfall at Kumano in Japan.

In this painting, one of the most authoritative and magistral examples of the theme to be found outside of Japan, the goddess is seated in a rocky niche beneath an overhanging cliff that is festooned with looping vines and a cascading waterfall. The image was created through strong contrasts of light and dark established by the gradual application of ink washes over the silk, and by the assertive, linear outlines. The composition's cohesiveness is due to the strongly geometric and harmonic shapes that underlie the forms of the robe, halo, rocks, and waves.

Because its seal impression is partially obliterated and cannot be deciphered, the painting can be attributed only on the basis of its style, a complex task for the work bears affinities to several different stylistic currents in Japanese ink painting. The most convincing resemblances, however, are to pictures of the White-Robed Kannon that have been attributed to an obscure monk-painter named Isshi, who, according to the **Honchō Gashi** and other traditional biographic records, may have worked both in Kyoto and Kamakura in the early fifteenth century. The outlines of the robes here resemble the strong catenary curves seen in paintings of the Tōfuku-ji school, especially in the work of Ryōzen (active ca 1350s) and Sekkyakushi (early fifteenth century); but the density of the composition and its assertive textures also have affinities to the Kamakura school, especially in the paintings of Chūan Shinkō (no. 4), who belonged to the generation following Isshi. As Yoshiaki Shimizu concluded in his detailed study of the Sansō painting: if the attribution is correct, this work is an important document of the growth of painting outside of the imperial capital in the first half of the fifteenth century.

Published
Japanese Ink Paintings, Shimizu, Yoshiaki and Wheelwright, Carolyn (eds.) (Princeton, NJ, 1976), no. 2.

References
Journey of the Three Jewels, Rosenfield, John M. and ten-Grotenhuis, Elizabeth (New York, 1979), nos. 52, 53.
Koga Bikō, Asaoka, Okisada (Tokyo, 1912), pp. 541-543.
Kokka, no. 479 (October 1930).
Shōkei, Nakamura, Tanio, Tōyō Bijutsu Sensho vol. 9 (Tokyo, 1970), figs. 18, 28.

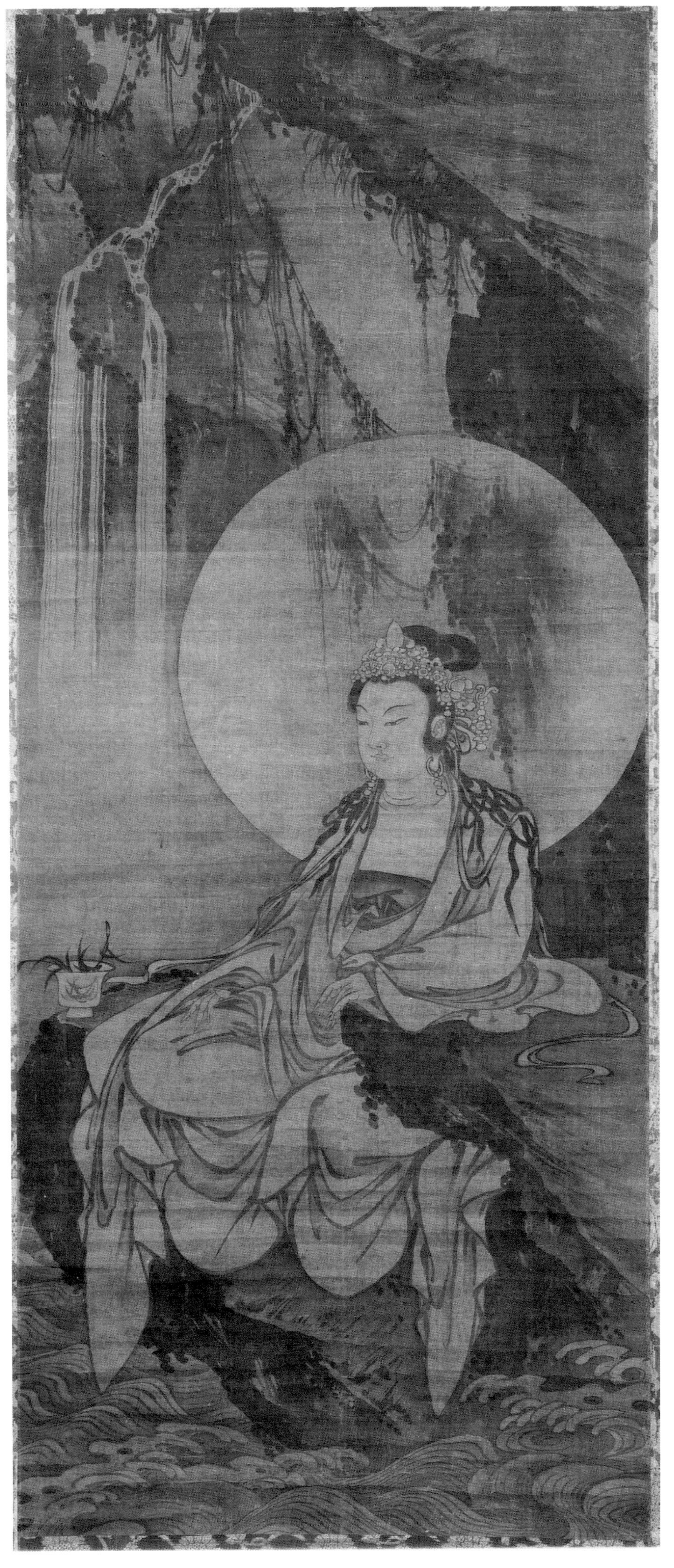

This remarkable triptych from Kamakura, painted in a most assertive and self-confident mode, demonstrates two important aspects of medieval Zen Buddhist art: the mixture of secular and religious values, and the unmistakable influence of Chinese professional painting of the Ming period. In the center of the triptych is the bodhisattva of compassion, Kannon, shown in a mysterious setting before the vast and infinite sea. She is flanked by two of China's most celebrated classical poets, T'ao Yüan-ming (365-427) and Li Po (701-762), in highly descriptive, naturalistic landscapes. Despite the differences in setting, the three paintings were most likely created as a single unit; they share the same decisive, conceptually powerful mode of composition and brushwork that is an outgrowth of the one employed in the White-Robed Kannon attributed to Isshi (no. 3).

As with the Isshi painting, these three scrolls, lacking signature or seals, can be assigned a date and likely place of origin only on the basis of their resemblance to other works. In this case, however, the point of reference is very close: paintings of the monk Chūan Shinkō, to whom a small corpus of about ten other works has been assigned. Chūan's biography has survived only in fragments. He lived in Kamakura in Seirai-ji, a subtemple of the major Zen monastery of Kenchō-ji. He is also said to have been the teacher of the well-known Kamakura monk painter Kenkō Shōkei, who was active in the last quarter of the fifteenth century, thereby pushing his master's date probably back to the middle decades of the century.

Among the paintings attributed to Chūan Shinkō are a pair, now in the Kumita Collection, that depict Li Po in the same mountainous, misty landscape settings as seen in the Sansō triptych. Bearing apparently authentic seals, these paintings share many stylistic traits with the Sansō works: the highly linear mode of depicting water, the peculiar reserved light boundary line on the rocks under Li Po, the same densely textured composition and abstracted mountain forms. However, slight differences suggest that, either the painter of the Sansō triptych was the same person in a more advanced or mature stage of his career, or, more likely, that he was an extremely gifted student of Chūan Shinkō whose figure style was more unified, and whose mastery of the brush was more fluent and less tentative than that found in the Chūan Shinkō oeuvre. The close affiliation of the two groups of paintings, however, is truly remarkable.

Iconographically, the two classical Chinese poets are shown virtually as attendants of Kannon. Li Po is seated before a waterfall on Mount Lu, the subject of one of his most celebrated poems; T'ao Yüan-ming, in his country retreat along the foot of the same mountain, stands by his beloved yellow chrysanthemums. Such religious and secular motifs had long been combined in the arts of the Japanese Zen monasteries. One of the most salient early examples is a triptych entitled **Shussan Shaka** (Śākyamuni Leaving the Mountains). Both the central painting and the scrolls of blossoming plum branches which flank it are inscribed by the second abbot of Tōfuku-ji, the famous Hakuun Egyō (1223-1297). Hakuun's poems reinforced the overt symbolic meaning that grew out of the union of the ascetic figure of the Buddha and the blossoming plum branches: that spiritual and metaphysical significance pervades the splendors and the beauty of this world. Through this union of religious and poetic themes the status of the poet was greatly enhanced, and indeed, throughout the Muromachi period, poets such as these two, or Su Tung-p'o and Po Chu-i, were depicted as men to be admired. They were not shown in a portrait-like guise but in an allegorical one, as men of virtue and spiritual insight; except for certain iconographic traits, such as Li Po's waterfall or T'ao Yüan-ming's chrysanthemums, their images were interchangeable.

Stylistically, the Sansō triptych is the product of two Chinese traditions: the Southern Sung mode that was faithfully transmitted through numerous generations in Japan long after the fall of the dynasty in 1279; and the Chinese revival of that style in the Ming period by professional painters and members of the court academy. Yoshiaki Shimizu, in his brilliant analysis of the Sansō paintings, found in them stylistic elements surviving from Japanese ink painting of the fourteenth century, especially from the circle of Takuma Eiga (active 1312-1316), and he concluded that the triptych, and indeed the early phases of the Kamakura school of ink painting, were conservative and provincial in character. However, it is also possible to see in the Sansō triptych reflections of contemporary Chinese modes, especially the semiprofessional Che school of suibokuga named after the province of Chekiang, where the Southern Sung ink painting style had flourished. Several paintings by Tai Chin (1388-1462), the leader of the Che school in his day, bear an uncanny resemblance to the composition and execution of the paintings of the poets in the Sansō triptych. Most accessible to American scholars is Tai Chin's painting **The Hermit Shu Yu Resting by a Stream** recently acquired by the Cleveland Museum. Another close analogue is the Freer Gallery's painting by the little-known Wang Shih-ch'ang (fifteenth century), **Scholar's Abode in the Mountains**. The remarkable composition of Kannon, seated frontally, small in scale, against a seascape that is highly abstract in design, and comparable to a braided rug provides further evidence of influences from contemporary China in the Sansō triptych. Nothing quite like it existed in the Southern Sung mode but a strong parallel may be found in such Ming paintings as one in a private Japanese collection that depicts an immortal on the back of a tortoise in the ocean, wrongly attributed to the Yüan painter Chao Yung, son of Chao Meng-fu. Stylistically, the ink painters of eastern Japan were behind the times when viewed from the perspective of Kyoto, but for reasons that are not yet entirely clear, they seem to have had direct contacts with the Chinese mainland, and they were aware, not only of Ming ink painting, but of flower-and-bird painting as well.

Published
Japanese Ink Paintings, Shimizu, Yoshiaki and Wheelwright, Carolyn (eds.) (Princeton, NJ, 1976), no. 6.
Kokka, no. 797 (August 1958).

References
Koga Bikō, Asaoka, Okisada (Tokyo, 1912), pp. 795-799.
Mindai Kaiga-shi Kenkyū: Seppa, Suzuki, Kei (Tokyo, 1969).
Parting at the Shore: Chinese Painting of the Early and Middle Ming Dynasty, 1368-1580, Cahill, James (New York and Tokyo, 1978), pl. 12.
Ryōkai, Indara, Kawakami, Kei, Suiboku Bijutsu Taikei vol. 4 (Tokyo, 1975), pl. 84.

Attributed to
Chūan Shinkō
Active mid-fifteenth century

4

Triptych
The Byaku-e (White-Robed) Kannon (center)
Li Po (left)
T'ao Yüan-ming (right)

Hanging Scrolls
Ink on coarse silk
117.3 x 54.9 cm each

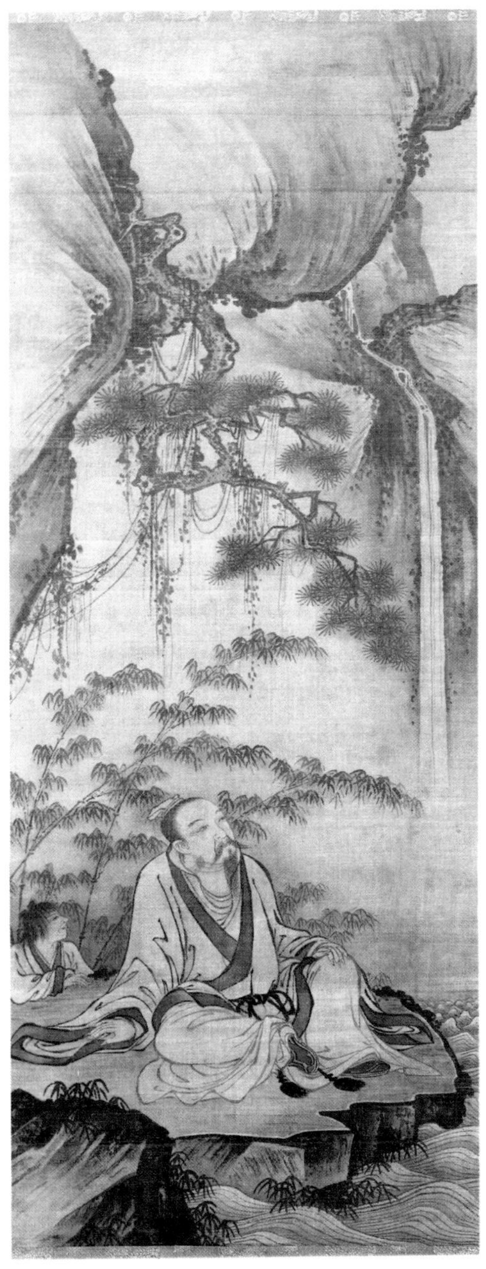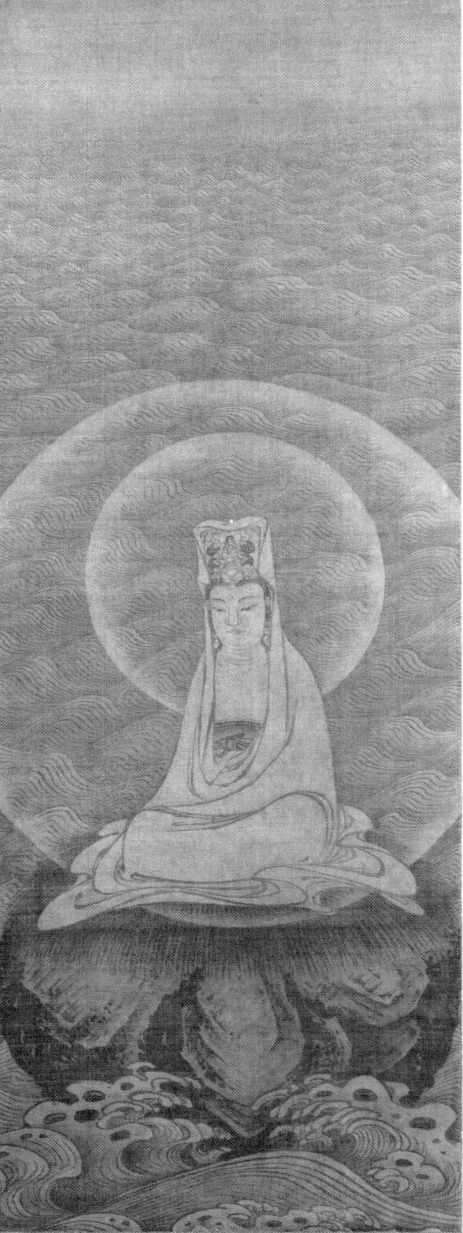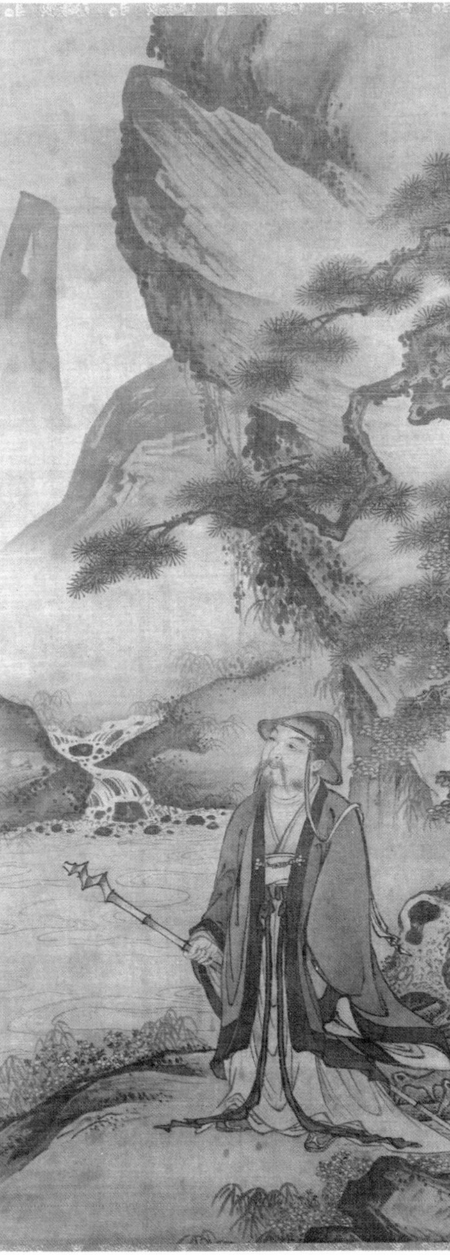

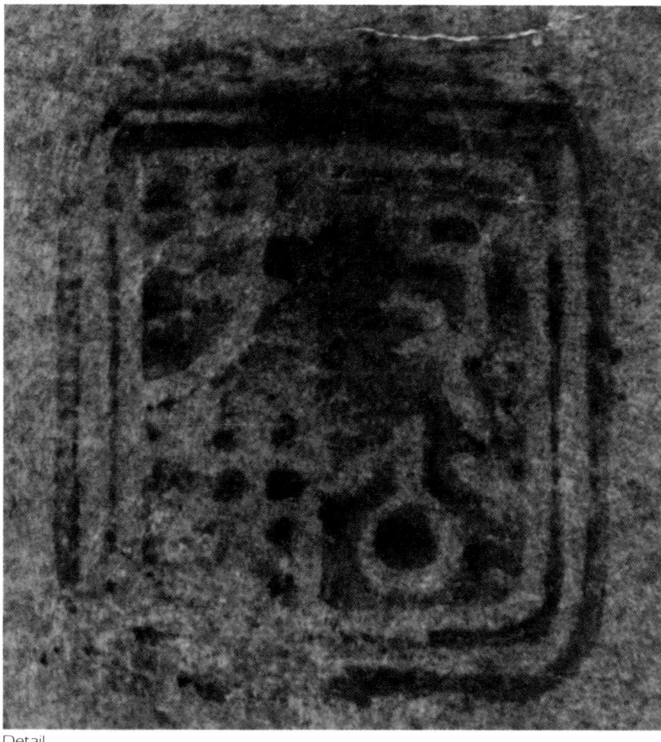

Detail

Bokushō Shūshō
Active ca 1484-1506

Landscape

Hanging Scroll
Ink on paper
60.8 x 30.4 cm

Seal
Bokushō

Japanese ink painting of the late fifteenth and early sixteenth centuries was dramatically influenced by the personality and work of a single man, Sesshū Tōyō (1420-1506). Although he remained a Zen monk throughout his adult life, Sesshū brought a strong sense of individual assertiveness and stylistic invention to an artistic idiom that had hitherto been more restrained. This painting is by a close associate of the master in his later years, the monk and poet Bokushō Shūshō. Nonetheless, although it is the oldest of many works in the Sansō Collection that document the range of Sesshū's influence, it does not reflect any of Sesshū's dynamic personal styles. It is pervaded instead by the calm lyricism of the Southern Sung manner which Sesshū, although he had admired and emulated the compositions of Hsia Kuei and Li T'ang, nonetheless executed in a far more energetic and assertive manner.

Bokushō's biography, by no means free from uncertainties, has been assembled from a few clues gleaned from the seventeenth-century **Honchō Gashi,** from four paintings bearing his seal, and from his inscriptions on paintings by Sesshū and Sessō Tōyō. In addition, he wrote a long inscription on a fine Yamato-e portrait of a certain Sue Hiromori, a samurai who was closely related to the Ōuchi family, Sesshū's last patrons.

The Sansō picture well represents Bokushō's character and attainments as an artist, for it couples high poetic sensibility with slightly amateur effects. It was built up with soft touches of the brush: the initial strokes were thin, wet washes of irregular contour; the last ones were thick black strokes that defined the foliage, boats, and buildings. Although the painting is somewhat worn and faded, it retains the sense of an intimate, misty mountainous setting so characteristic of the style of the Southern Sung Academy. The large scale of the human figures, however, makes the landforms appear even more intimate, and even miniature, in effect. Unnaturalistic scale relationships appear in the other Bokushō painting in the United States, a haboku (broken-ink) landscape in the Burke Collection in New York. The very difficult idiom of haboku, a rapidly executed and highly abstracted painting technique (no. 10), had greatly intrigued Sesshū, who modeled his haboku paintings upon the work of the Southern Sung master Yü Chien (active in the thirteenth century). Haboku was thus one of the outstanding traits of the Sesshū school; Bokushō inscribed a haboku painting now in the Masaki Collection, Osaka, by the enigmatic Sessō Tōyō, probably a member of Sesshū's immediate circle.

The name Bokushō was most likely the gō (artist's name) of the monk poet, Issan Shūshō, who had served as abbot of Nanzen-ji and also (in 1484) of Sōkoku-ji in Kyoto. He spent most of his career in Suō in the western end of Honshu (modern Yamaguchi prefecture), where Sesshū had established his famous atelier-hermitage, the Tenkai Togarō. His connections with Sesshū are recorded in one of the most touching and intimate documents in the history of Muromachi ink painting: the inscriptions on the very sober, conservative landscape by Sesshū now in the Ōhara Collection in Okayama. On this landscape, one of the very last works from Sesshū's brush, Bokushō wrote a tribute to Sesshū implying that the master had already died and that Bokushō was aware of his own impending death. In 1507, another member of Sesshū's circle, the monk Ryōan Keigo (1425-1514) passed through Suō en route to Ming China, called on the master, and learned to his sorrow that both Sesshū and Bokushō had died. He found the Ōhara landscape in Sesshū's atelier, and wrote upon it his own inscription in honor of both men.

Published
Ryūsen Shūhō: Mayuyama Seventy Years, vol. 2 (Tokyo, 1976), pl. 400.
Sesshū, Nakamura, Tanio, Nihon Bijutsu Kaiga Zenshū vol. 4 (Tokyo, 1976), fig. 36, p. 131.
Sesshū, Shimada, Shūjirō, exhibition catalogue, Kyoto National Museum (Kyoto, 1956), pl. 55.
Sesshū, Sesson, Tanaka, Ichimatsu and Nakamura, Tanio, Suiboku Bijutsu Taikei vol. 7 (Tokyo, 1973), pl. 32.

References
Bokushō Bokuga Sansui ni Tsuite, Miyake, Chōsaku, Nihon Bijutsu Kyōkai Hōkoku no. 13.
Japanese Art: Selections from the Mary and Jackson Burke Collection, Murase, Miyeko (New York, 1975), no. 35.
Kokka, no. 767 (February 1956).
Kokka, no. 618 (May 1942).
Kokka, No. 385 (June 1922).

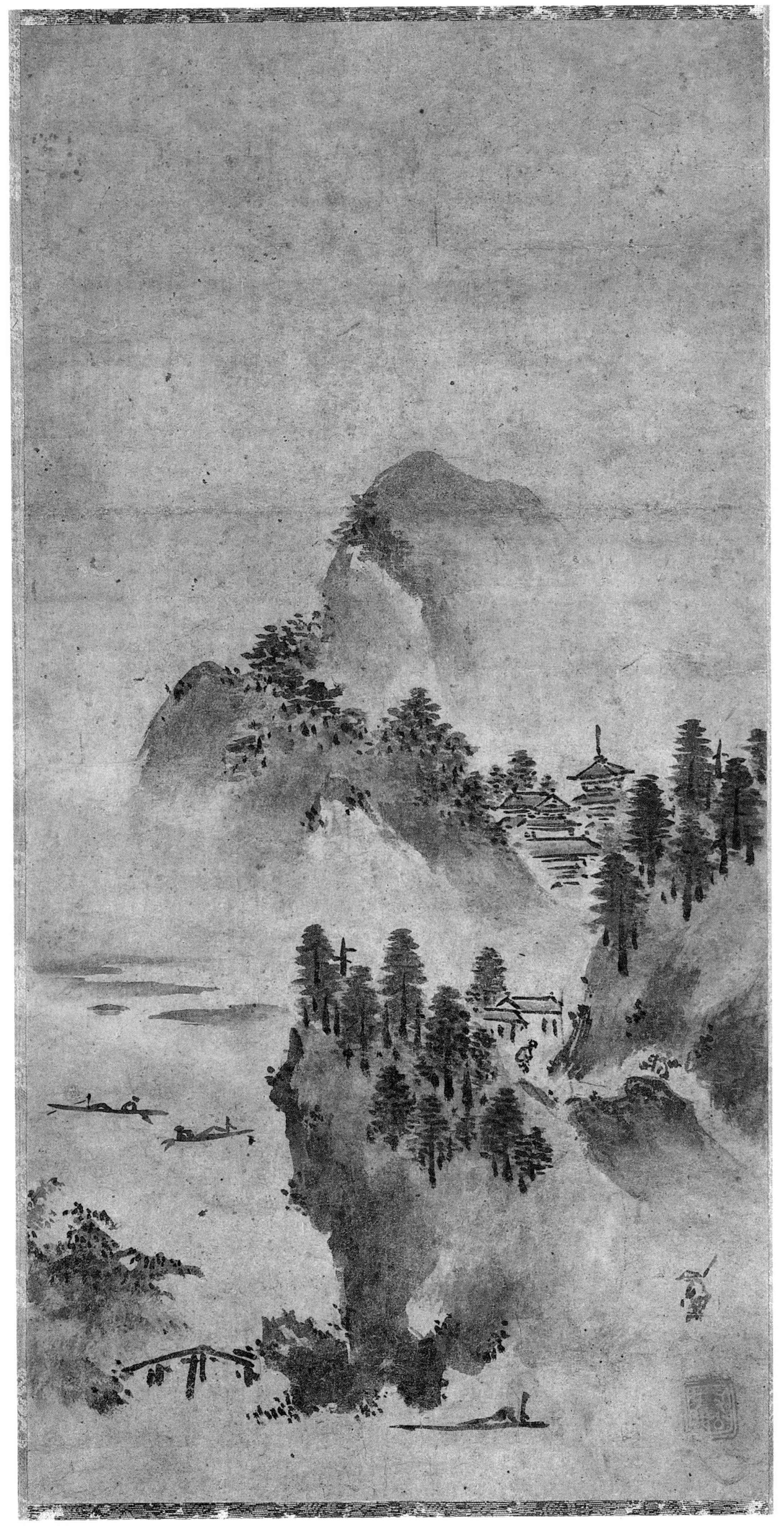

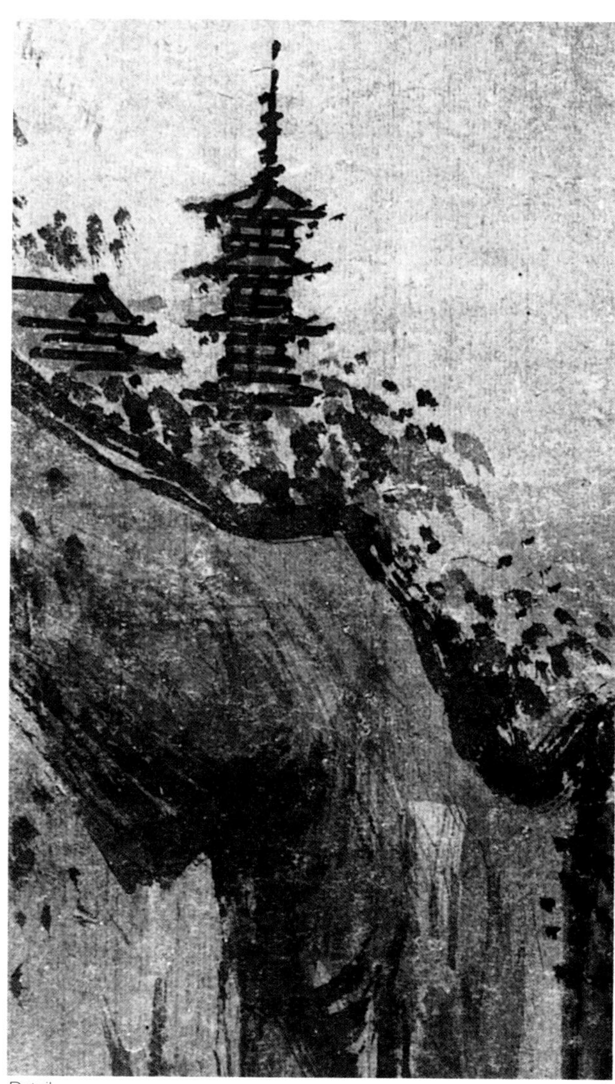

Detail

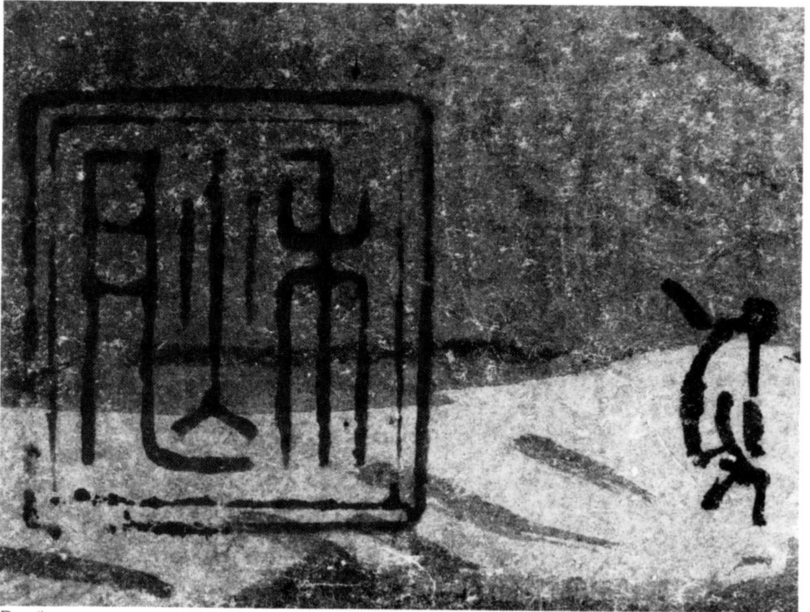

Detail

Seal of
Shūgetsu Tōkan
Ca 1440-1529
Early sixteenth century

6

Mountain Temple

Hanging Scroll
Ink on paper
88.9 x 40.5 cm

Seal
Shūgetsu

The seal impression in the lower left corner of this large and impressive landscape is the mark of the monk Shūgetsu, Sesshū's most accomplished painting disciple. The authenticity of the seal, and hence of the attribution itself, is open to question; in fact the corpus of works to be safely assigned to Shūgetsu is still small and much debated. Nonetheless, the painting is an extremely effective expression of the Sesshū style done within a few decades of the master's death in 1506. It is also an example of the idiom of the topographic landscape, the descriptive representation of specific places, which Sesshū brought to a prominent role in Japanese ink painting. Sesshū's spectacular **Amanohashidate** of ca 1501-1505 is probably the most famous example, but in his oeuvre and those of his followers may be found many other efforts in this idiom: views along the Yang-tze River and of the celebrated Ch'an monasteries of the Hangchou region, views of Mount Fuji and its environs, or the well-known panoramic landscape of the Kyoto monastery of Tōfuku-ji. The painting of the Hsi-hu, the West Lake of Hangchou, inscribed with the names of temples and bridges and a date equivalent to 1496, is attributed to Shūgetsu.

Shūgetsu's biography is preserved in only the barest details. The son of a samurai from Satsuma at the southernmost tip of Kyushu, he was ordained a Zen monk in 1462 and came into the orbit of Sesshū, who around 1464 began his lifelong association with the Unkoku-an in Suō, in the western end of Honshu. An unsubstantiated tradition claims that Shūgetsu accompanied Sesshū to Ming China in 1467; however, far stronger evidence suggests that Shūgetsu went there in 1496. Apart from the close resemblance between their paintings, one of the most concrete documents of Shūgetsu's relationship to Sesshū is a self-portrait that the master, then aged 71 years, painted and presented to Shūgetsu; the original is lost, but a copy was made by Kanō Tanyū in the 1670s.

The Sansō landscape possibly represents the Ch'an temple complex on A-yu-wang-shan (Mount Aśoka), a celebrated pilgrimage site near Hangchou. According to tradition, the Liang Emperor Wu Ti (502-550) built a pagoda there to enshrine relics of Aśoka (272-232 BC), third emperor of the Indian Mauryan dynasty and known throughout the Buddhist world as the first great royal patron of the faith. In time the sanctuary became a major center of Ch'an Buddhism, and during the Sung and Yüan periods, many Japanese monks came there to study.

Although this painting retains many traits of the idealized landscapes typical of Japanese ink painting until the late fifteenth century, the cluster of temple buildings at the base of the cliff and the prominent pagoda up above form a configuration that is usually identified as A-yu-wang-shan. A review of the many topographic landscapes of this kind in Japanese ink painting will show that even though the individual landscape compositions were more or less standardized, the names were varied. For the Japanese, the thought that such a painting depicted a famous Chinese sanctuary was more important than the fidelity of the painting to the site itself.

This composition is divided into three distinct areas separated by bands of mist: the foreground road with temple structures and a grove of pine trees; the middle ground cliff with a waterfall coming from the right; and the cloud-shrouded peaks that tower over all. The sense of height of the mountains and pagodas is enhanced by the tiny scale of the figures on the path in the foreground.

One of the most distinctive features of this painting is the nōtan, the harmony and balance of the tones of black, white, and gray. When seen under soft lighting, as though in the deep recess of a temple hall with tapers burning nearby, the painting comes to life and acquires depth, tension, and the sense of the brooding, awesome presence of great mountains that characterizes the finest landscape paintings of China and Japan.

References
Sesshū, Nakamura, Tanio, Nihon Bijutsu Kaiga Zenshū vol. 4 (Tokyo, 1976), pls. 56, 59, 60.
Sesshū, Sesson, Tanaka, Ichimatsu and Nakamura, Tanio, Suiboku Bijutsu Taikei vol. 7 (Tokyo, 1973), pls. 63-68.

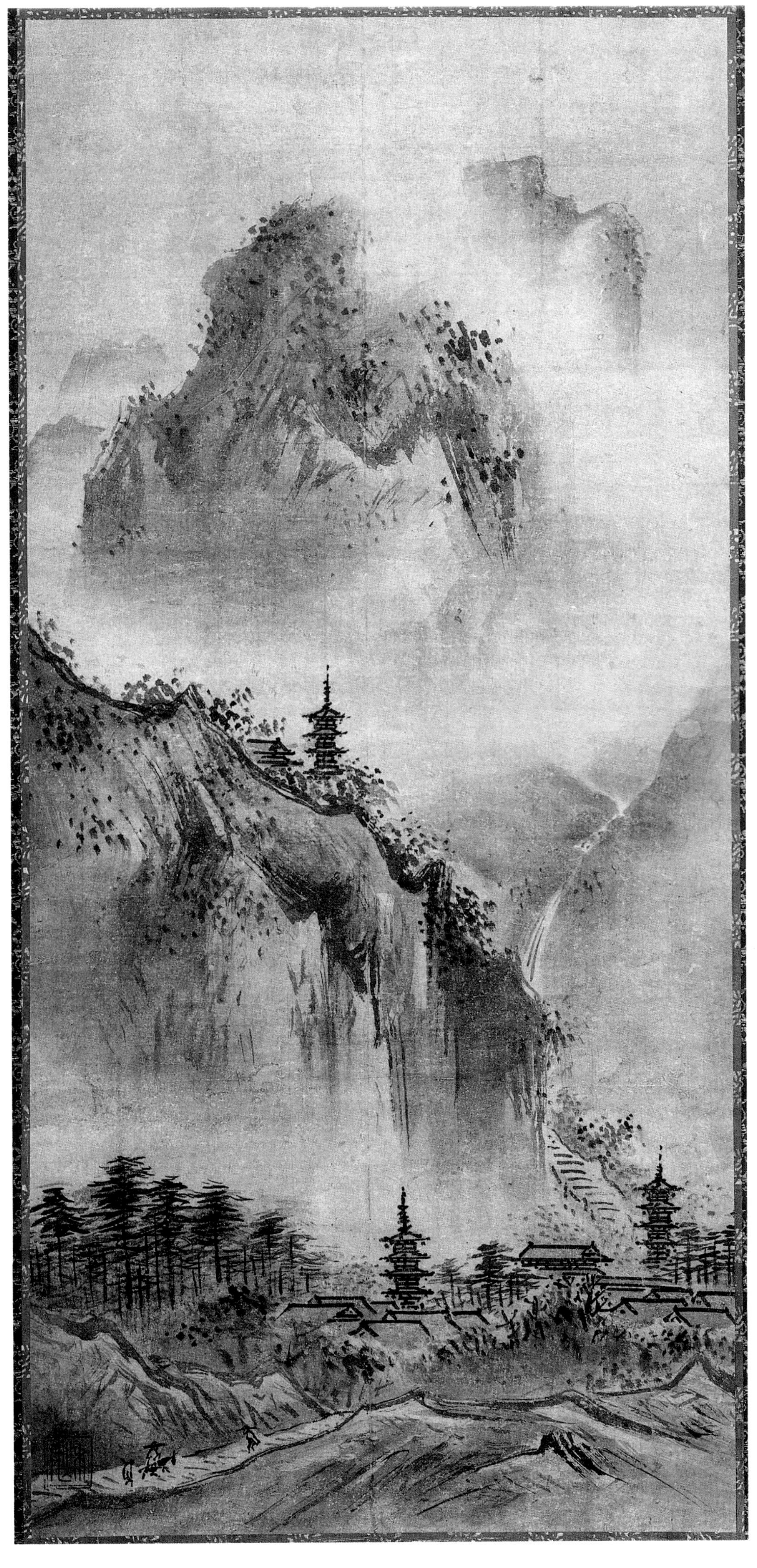

Nyosui Sōen
Active ca 1490-1500

7

Willows by the Ferry

Hanging Scroll
Ink on paper
39.5 x 29.6 cm

Signature
Sōen

Seals
Nyosui
Settō

Nyosui Sōen, the painter of this haunting and dreamlike landscape was according to old tradition the favorite disciple of Sesshū. When Sōen left the master's tutelage at Unkoku-an in Suō in 1495, Sesshū gave him the famous haboku landscape now in the Tokyo National Museum. Above it, Sesshū inscribed the oft-quoted account of his trip to China nearly thirty years before, and ended with the advice that Sōen should seek instruction from the works of Japanese masters like Josetsu and Shūbun.

Indeed, the Sansō painting by Sōen owes more to the lyrical, intimate mood of early and mid-fifteenth century Japanese ink painting than it does to Sesshū's more assertive techniques. The empty middle ground and melancholy air are traits of the Shūbun style that were ultimately derived from Yüan-period Chinese painting, particularly that of Ni Tsan (1301-1374). In the foreground, two willows crisscross in a graceful ballet of forms. Small human figures activate the rural scene: at the left a ferryman poles a flatboat with two travelers, while a solitary man patiently waits under the thatched hut and two peasants approach. Broad strokes of wet ink define the sandbars and the mountain peaks in the distance; finely hatched lines of gray ink establish the bands of mist and impart a shimmering effect rather like a mirage.

Only a few facts about Sōen's life are documented. A native of eastern Japan, of Sagami province near the modern Odawara, he became a Zen monk at Engaku-ji in Kamakura, but later went to study under the aging Sesshū at Unkoku-an. He returned to Engaku-ji in 1495 where he was a relatively prolific monk-painter. Few of his works are dated or inscribed. Although he too attempted the haboku technique, which Sesshū had pioneered, his paintings lack the dynamic thrusts that are hallmarks of Sesshū's paintings. Sōen's artistic temperament was gentle, quiet, and lyrical; he frequently worked on a small scale, depicting self-contained, intimate landscape scenes.

Published
Hokusō-ha, vol. 1, Nihonga Taisei vol. 3 (Tokyo, 1931), pl. 143.
Masterpieces of Asian Art in America, exhibition catalogue (New York, 1970), pl. 52.
Sesshū, Sesson, Tanaka, Ichimatsu and Nakamura, Tanio, Suiboku Bijutsu Taikei vol. 7 (Tokyo, 1973), pl. 69.
Shimbi Taikan, Tajima, Shiichi, vol. 3 (Kyoto, 1900), pl. 24.
Suiboku-ga, Tanaka, Ichimatsu and Yonezawa, Yoshiho Genshoku, Nihon no Bijutsu vol. 11 (Tokyo, 1970), p. 199.
Zaiga Hihō, Shimada, Shūjirō (ed.), vol. 2 (Tokyo, 1969), pl. 11.

References
Koga Bikō, Asaoka, Okisada (Tokyo, 1912), pp. 704-706.
Muromachi Suibokuga, Matsushita, Takaaki (Tokyo, 1960), pls. 45, 46.
Sesshū, Shimada, Shūjirō, exhibition catalogue, Kyoto National Museum (Kyoto, 1956), pl. 60.

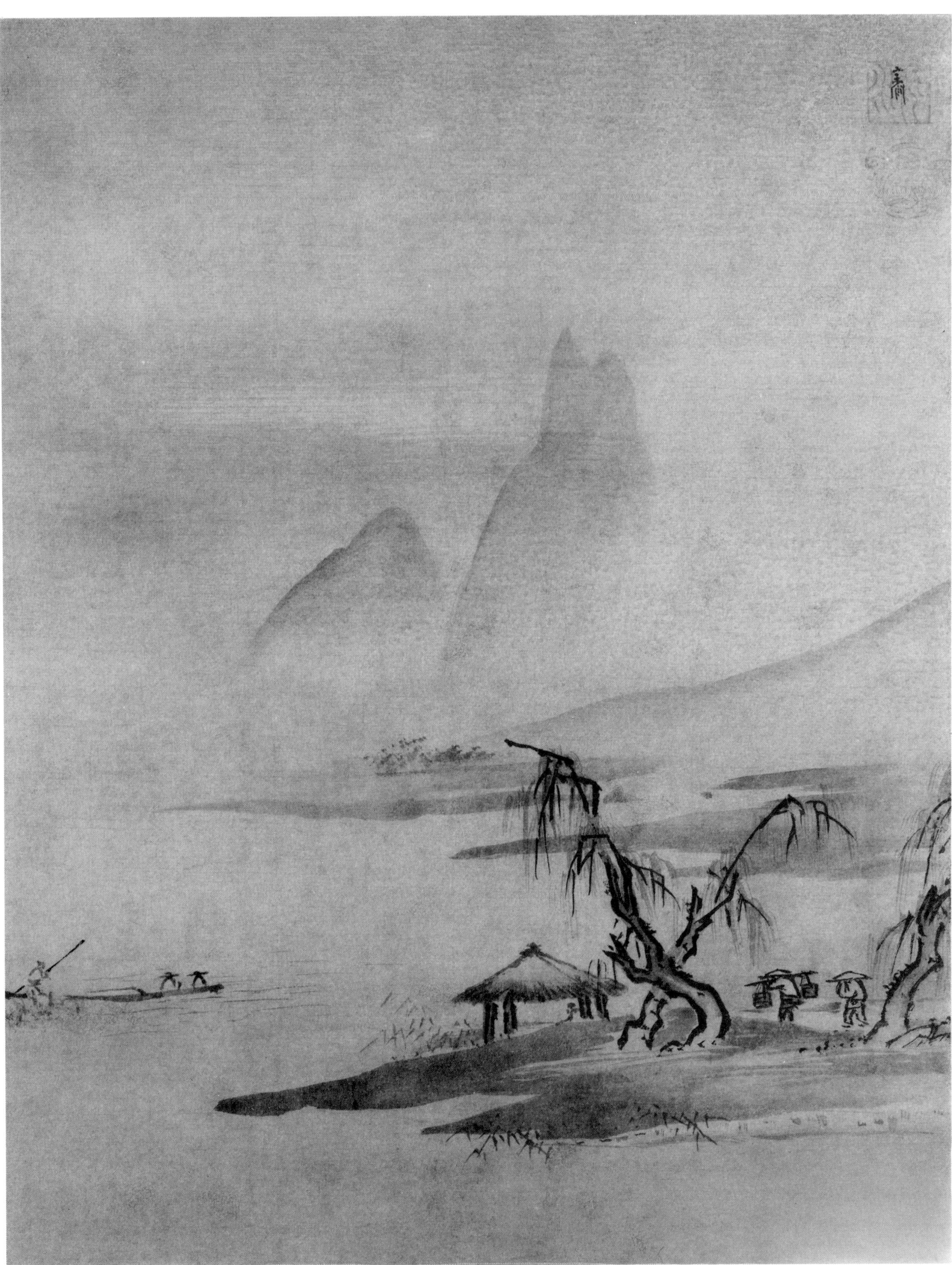

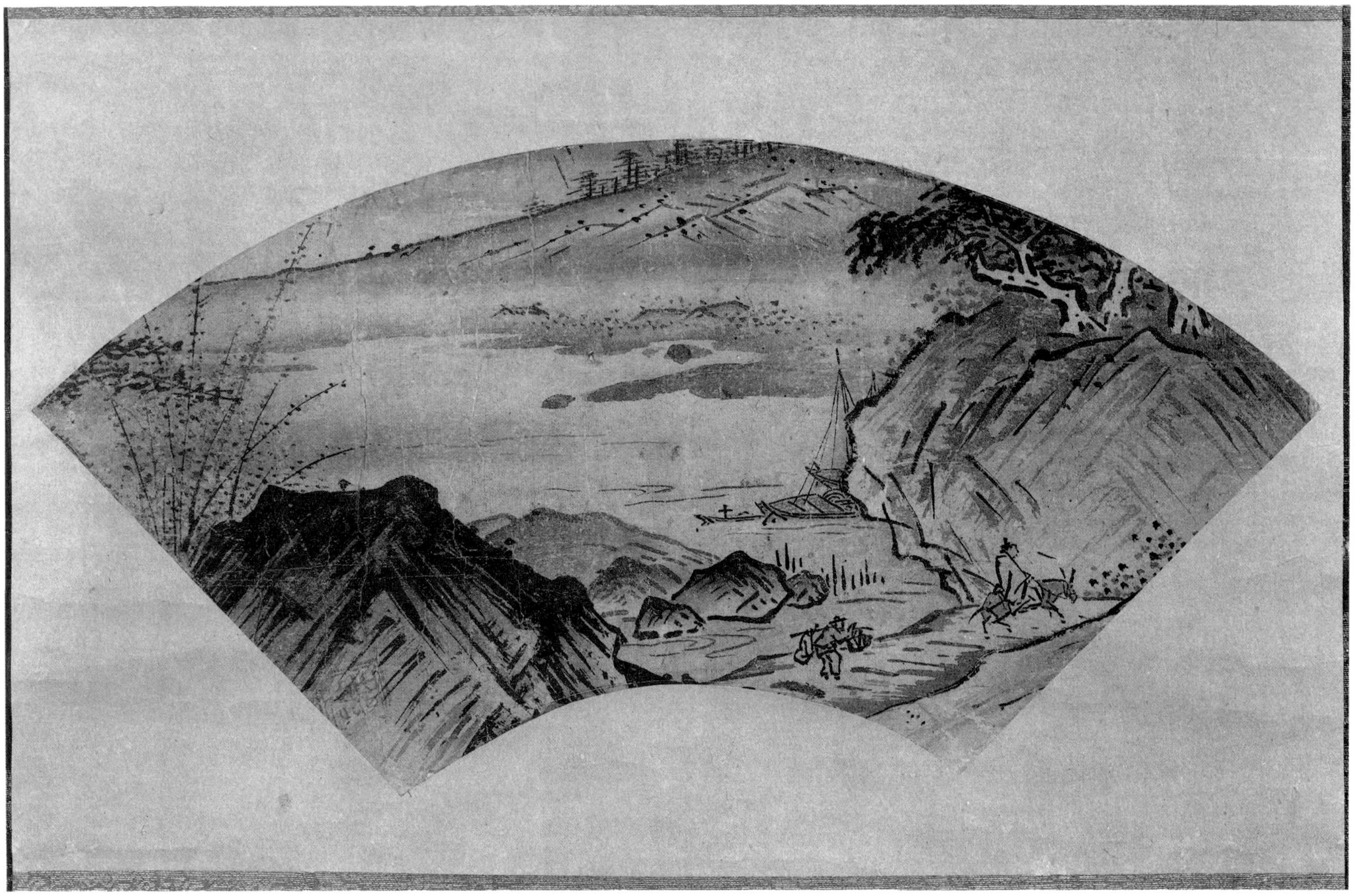

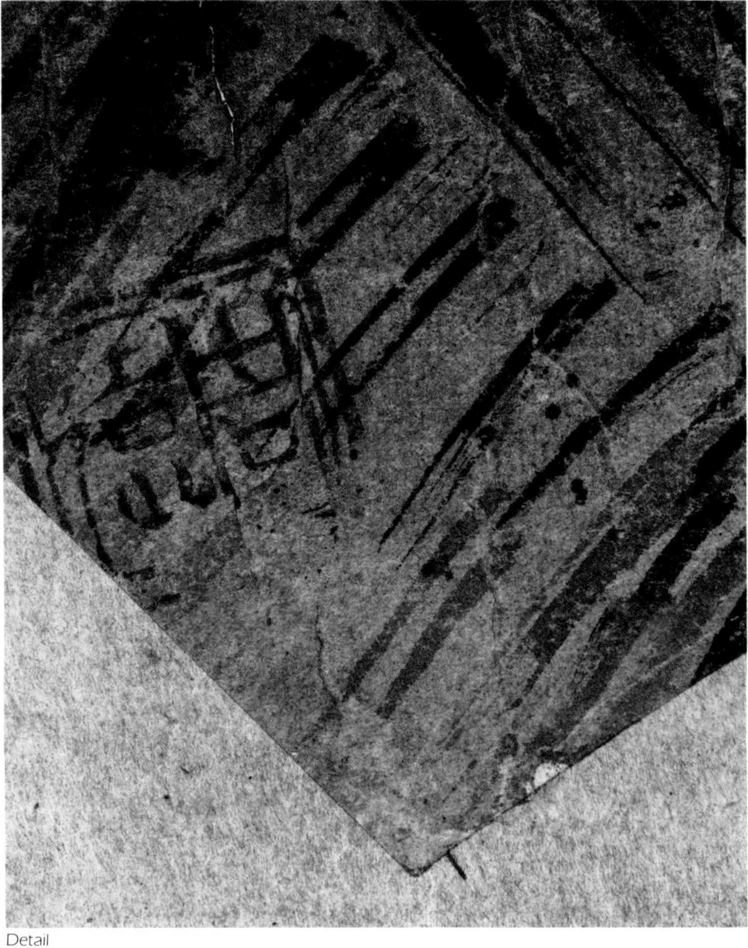

Detail

Seal of
Ikei Shūtoku
Active 1539-1540

8

Landscape

Hanging Scroll
Mounted fan painting
Ink on paper
28.9 x 45.5 cm

Seal
Shūtoku

Judging by style alone, the painter of this remarkable, tiny landscape must have been a contemporary or a close follower of Sesshū. The seal at the lower left corner is that of Shūtoku, a name employed by as many as three different monk-painters of the fifteenth and sixteenth centuries. One of these men, however, is said to have lived in Sesshū's painting atelier, the Tenkai Togarō at Unkoku-an in Suō, after the master's death in 1506. That Shūtoku experimented with Sesshū's haboku style and also with his linear, academic manner, derived from the Southern Sung academy is seen in this fan. The Sansō painting is from the hand of an extremely accomplished artist, and thus the attribution to the shadow-like Shūtoku is quite plausible.

The composition and mode of painting in the Sansō fan are close to those found in Sesshū's celebrated "long handscroll" of 1486, now in the Mōri Collection, which he painted while living at Unkoku-an. All the traits of Sesshū's shin (regular) style—the strongly linear definition of forms, the hatchet strokes of the modeling in the rocks, the active movements of the man on the donkey followed by his servant—are present in the fan.

Although tiny in size, this landscape has an extraordinary sense of amplitude. The housetops and distant hills suggest a deep spatial recession; the careful asymmetric balance imparts a sense of the harmony between the realm of nature and the realm of human affairs. Even though each of its features can be traced back to a Chinese prototype, this painting remains profoundly Japanese in the nuances of its expression.

The composition was probably fan-shaped from the beginning, but the awkward location of the seal makes it likely that the picture has been carefully trimmed. The paper is too heavy to have been used as a fan; moreover, there are no folds or traces of the struts to which it would have been affixed had it been employed as a folding fan. In all probability, it was mounted on a screen or in an album. Fan-shaped paintings, usually round or oval, were common in Southern Sung ink painting, but the Japanese preferred the format of the folding fan, which they had used for centuries.

References
Bijutsu Kenkyū, no. 53 (June 1936), pp. 16-22.
Japanese Art: Selections from the Mary and Jackson Burke Collection, Murase, Miyeko (New York, 1975), no. 39.
Japanese Ink Paintings, Shimizu, Yoshiaki and Wheelwright, Carolyn (eds.) (Princeton, NJ, 1976), no. 21.
Koga Bikō, Asaoka, Okisada (Tokyo, 1912).
Nihon Kaiga-shi Ronshū, Tanaka, Ichimatsu, "Tōshun Gasetsu" (Tokyo, 1966), pp. 401, 403, 439n.
Sesshū, Sesson, Tanaka, Ichimatsu and Nakamura, Tanio, Suiboku Bijutsu Taikei vol. 7 (Tokyo, 1973), pls. 81, 82.

Seal of
Ikei Shūtoku
Active 1539-1540

9

Mountain Landscape with Travelers

Hanging Scroll
Ink, light color, and gold pigment on paper
26.4 x 21.8 cm

Seal
Shūtoku

Like the preceding fan painting (no. 8), this essay in the Sesshū style bears a seal reading Shūtoku, and is generally accepted as a work of the monk by that name who succeeded the master in his painter's retreat, the Tenkai Togarō. The fan painting and this mountain landscape closely resemble one another, for they share common derivation from Sesshū's shin (regular) style as seen in the Mōri Collection scroll. The mountain landscape, however, is considerably more abstract; light washes of gold pigment were brushed into the strongly planar cloud bands—a decorative, somewhat antinaturalistic effect that began to appear in Japanese ink painting in the last decades of the fifteenth century.

Also appearing in the mountain landscape is a distinctive method for depicting leaves in repeated patterns of small ovals or trefoil forms, a stylistic device that was not employed in Southern Sung ink painting but that nonetheless appears in Chinese literati painting of the fifteenth century. These schematic formulas used to depict leaf forms, together with the drawing of the houses in simplified outlines, first appear in Japanese painting in the work of Sesshū, in the Mōri long scroll, for example, or in the landscapes of the four seasons on silk in the Ishibashi Collection. When and how Sesshū came into contact with the mature Chinese wen-jen (literati) painting is not at all clear. He did not refer to it in his writings, and for the most part he remained loyal to the techniques of the Southern Sung ink painting tradition.

The composition of this painting, in both two-and three-dimensional terms, is extremely sophisticated. A series of opposing diagonal movements provides passage along the foreground path, through the rustic village, and back to the viewing pavilion set at the cliff's edge. The bands of haze continue the recession through the ranks of mountain peaks, but the tall, vertiginous peaks in the middle ground are painted in such detail that they appear to contradict the sense of spatial recession and to flatten the composition. The human figures also contribute to the ambiguous spatial relationships; they do not diminish as they are placed farther back into pictorial space. Effects of this kind appear in Chinese literati painting, but they are not uncommon in the work of sixteenth century Japanese ink painters, who shared the desire to imbue a landscape with an expressive mood rather than to define logical spatial relationships.

Published
Muromachi Suibokuga, Matsushita, Takaaki (Tokyo, 1960), pl. 56.

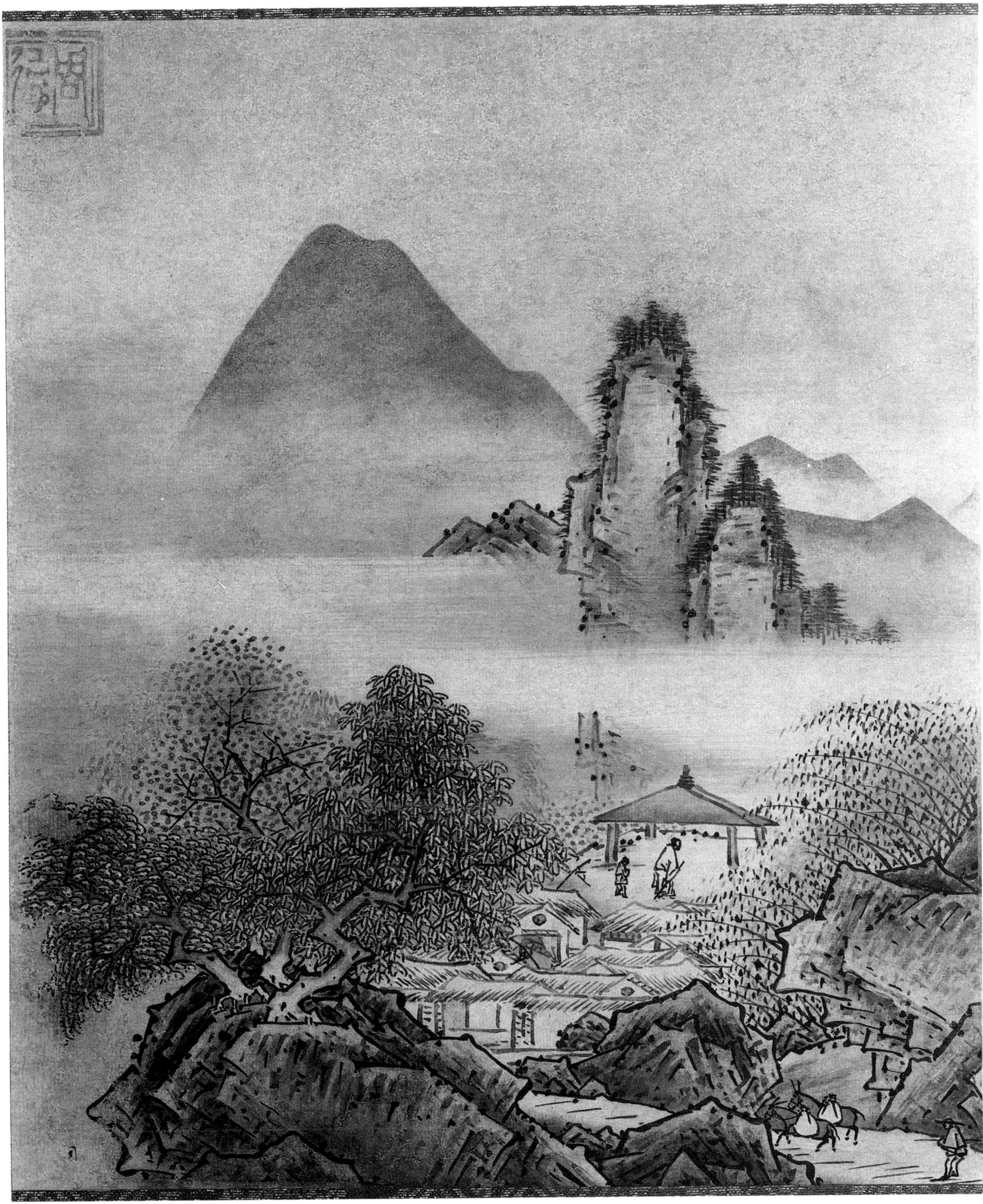

10

Haboku (Broken-Ink) Landscape

Hanging Scroll
Ink on paper
25.0 x 41.6 cm

Seal
Eii

Unkei Eii
Active early sixteenth century

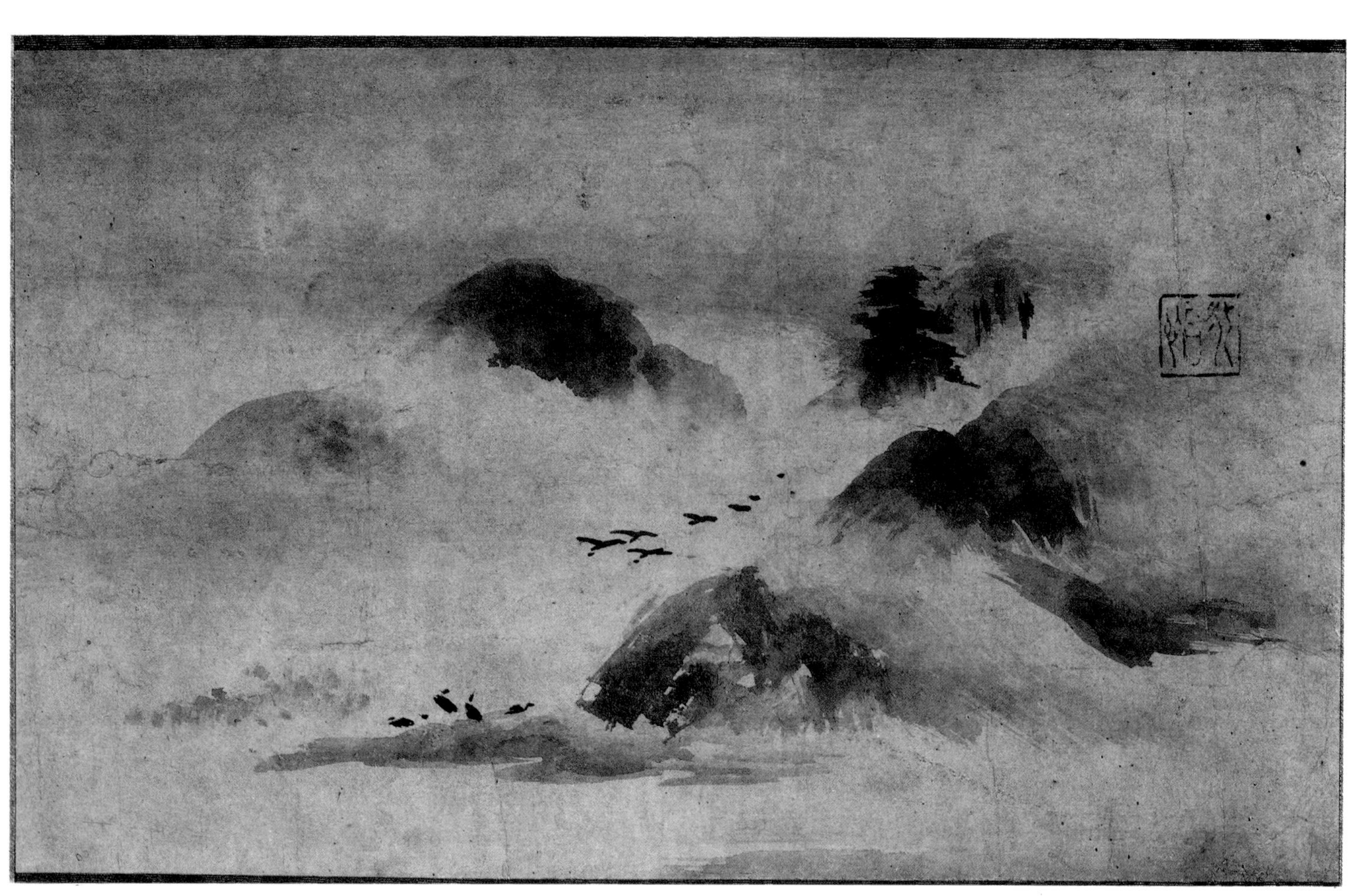

Detail

Rapidly brushed tones of black ink establish the most generalized shapes of rounded mountains, trees, and sandbank. The painter defined much more carefully the black ink silhouettes of flying geese descending toward the sandbank, awaited by those already standing on the ground, and added the well-defined form of a large conifer tree in the background to the few precise clues of recognizability in this abstract, subtle, and evocative essay in haboku (broken-ink) painting.

The haboku idiom had appeared in South China in the thirteenth century, and appealed greatly to visiting Japanese Zen Buddhists, who took examples back with them. The style, however, was by no means limited to Ch'an or Zen circles in either country. Probably the best-known Chinese practitioner of the broken ink technique was Yü-chien (active in the thirteenth century), a monk affiliated with Mount T'ien-t'ai in Chekiang. The painter of this Japanese exemplar of haboku was probably a Shingon monk, Unkei Eii (see also no. 11). Surviving from his brush is a section of a landscape handscroll copied from a lost original by Yü-chien, one of the **Eight Views of the Hsiao-Hsiang District,** a classic theme in Southern Sung ink painting. Moreover, Japan's most accomplished master of the technique, Sesshū Tōyō, reproduced a haboku landscape by Yü-chien among the Southern Sung fan paintings that he copied. This particular mode of painting thus had a strong identity among Japanese ink painters of the late fifteenth and early sixteenth centuries, and Yü-chien was considered its classical source.

In particular, the followers of Sesshū energetically practiced the broken-ink technique; fine examples have survived from the brushes of Shūgetsu, Bokushō, and Shūtoku as well as of Sessō Tōyō and Tōshun. A haboku painting similar in format and conception to the Sansō work bears the signature as well as the seal of Unkei; it also contains the same softened and rounded landforms and the rather simple and blunt accents in black ink that were essential to create a coherent illusion.

Published
Suibokuga, Osaka Municipal Museum (ed.), exhibition catalogue (October 1964), no. 90.

Reference
Sesshū, Sesson, Tanaka, Ichimatsu and Nakamura, Tanio, Suiboku Bijutsu Taikei vol. 7 (Tokyo, 1973), pls. 94, 95.

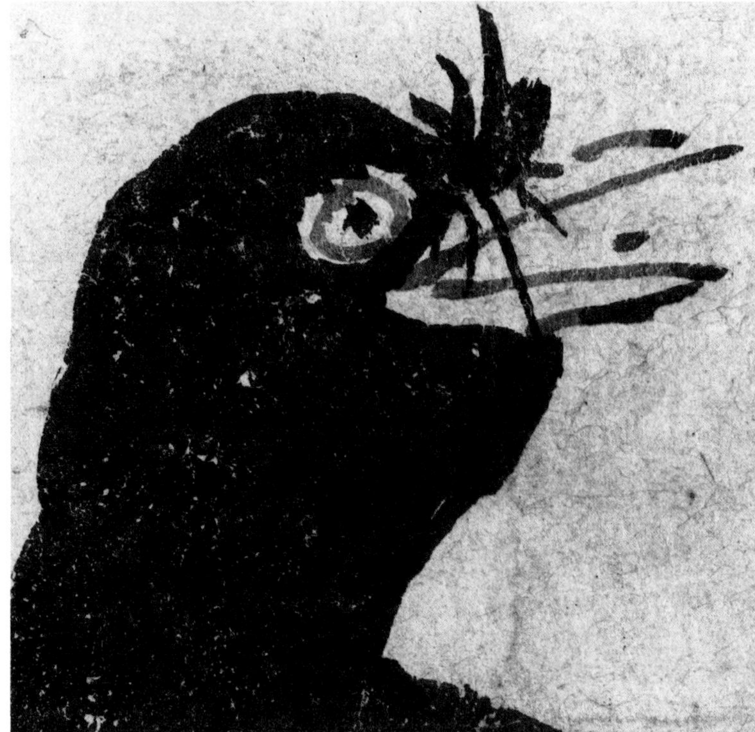

Detail

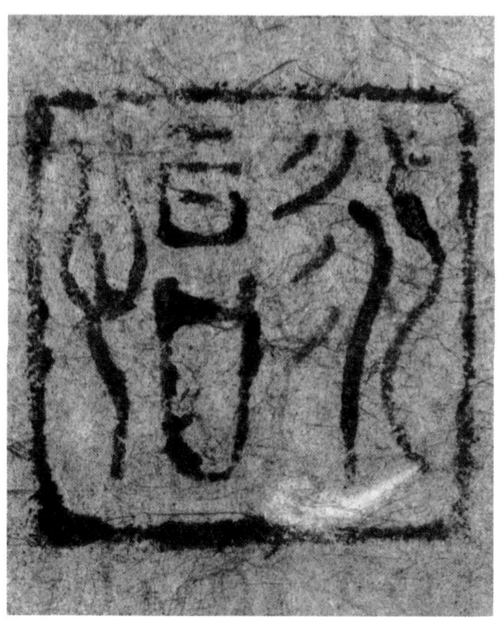

Detail

Unkei Eii
Active early sixteenth century

11

Myna Birds

Hanging Scroll
Ink on paper
78.7 x 35.5 cm

Seal
Eii

The Zen monk painters of both China and Japan delighted in close-up depictions of birds painted rapidly and with a minimum of detail, capturing their characteristic gestures and attitudes. This pair of myna birds, though painted by a monk affiliated with the more traditional Shingon school of Buddhism, is imbued with energetic liveliness, as though the bird in the rear is calling out, while the other one looks ahead in self-satisfaction. The loose, free application of the ink gives the painting a feeling of spontaneity, almost of improvisation, but the differences in tonal values and spatial relationships have been carefully worked out. Deep black ink tones were used to define the bodies of the birds and the tall thorny brambles in the background. More diluted ink shades were applied in diagonal thrusts to form the side of the jutting rock face. The untouched whiteness of the paper suggests a great sense of ambient space, and the similarities in shape and accent between the birds' claws and the thorns above greatly enhance the unity of the painting.

This painting has no signature but the seal gives the name Eii; this seems to have been the monastic name of a certain Unkei Eii who was considered a follower of Sesshū and an adept of the haboku style (no. 10). He was also said to have lived in the great Shingon monastery atop Mount Kōya, evidence of the degree to which the modes of ink painting, once closely identified with the Zen Buddhist community, had spread to other parts of the Buddhist establishment. The Seinan-in of Mount Kōya possesses a Buddhist triptych bearing Eii's seal and painted in ink alone, very much in the Kanō style; another painting, however, also with his signature and seal and now in the Tokiwayama Bunko Collection, depicts a flower basket in a highly detailed fashion derived from Ming academic painting. The stylistic range of the Unkei paintings demonstrated the growing virtuosity and professionalism of Japanese suiboku masters.

Published
Birds, Beasts, Blossoms, and Bugs: The Nature of Japan, Stern, Harold P. (New York, 1976), no. 15.

References
Koga Bikō, Asaoka, Okisada (Tokyo, 1912), pp. 713-714.
Muromachi Suibokuga, Matsushita, Takaaki (Tokyo, 1960), pls. 49-51.

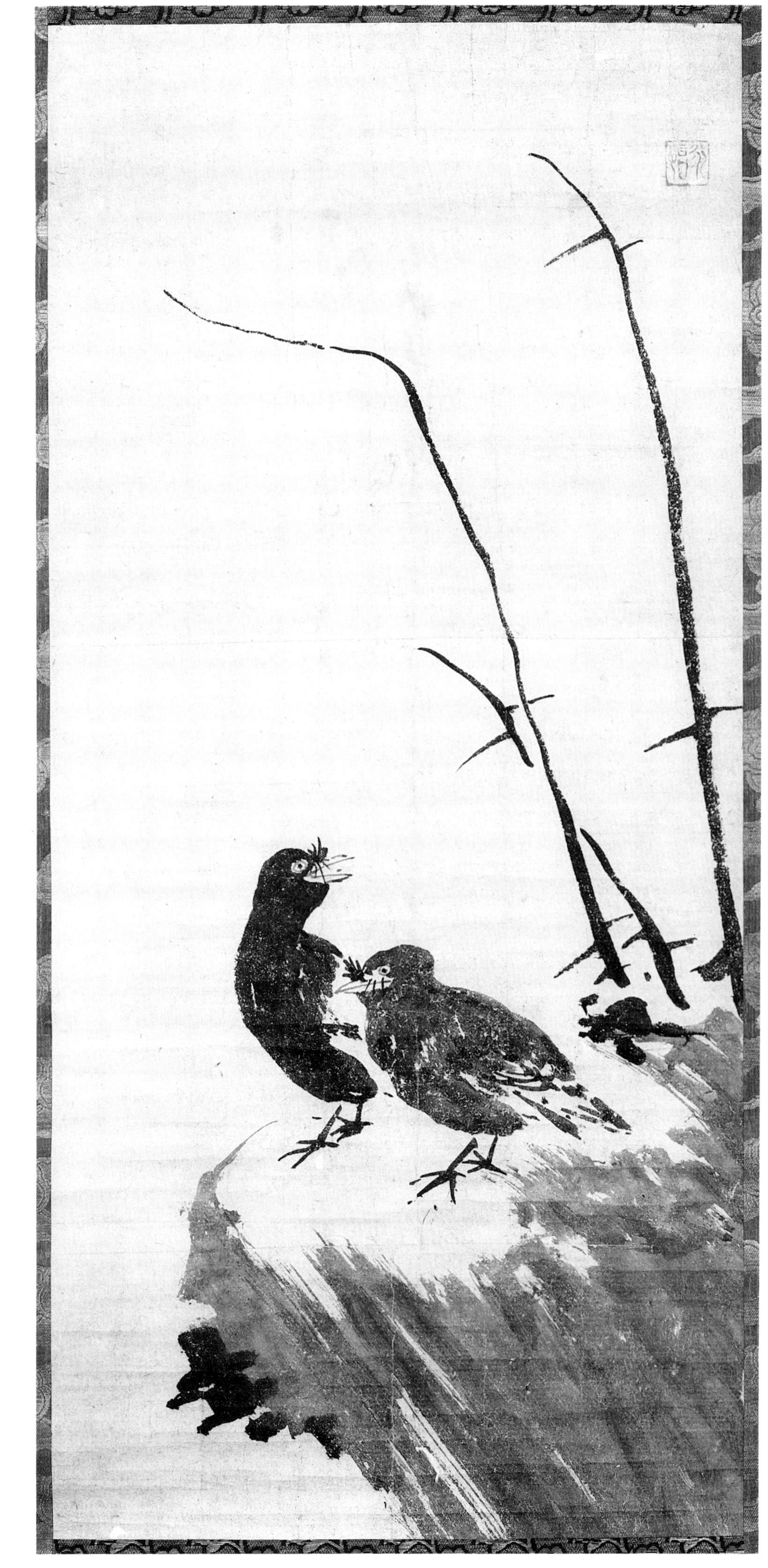

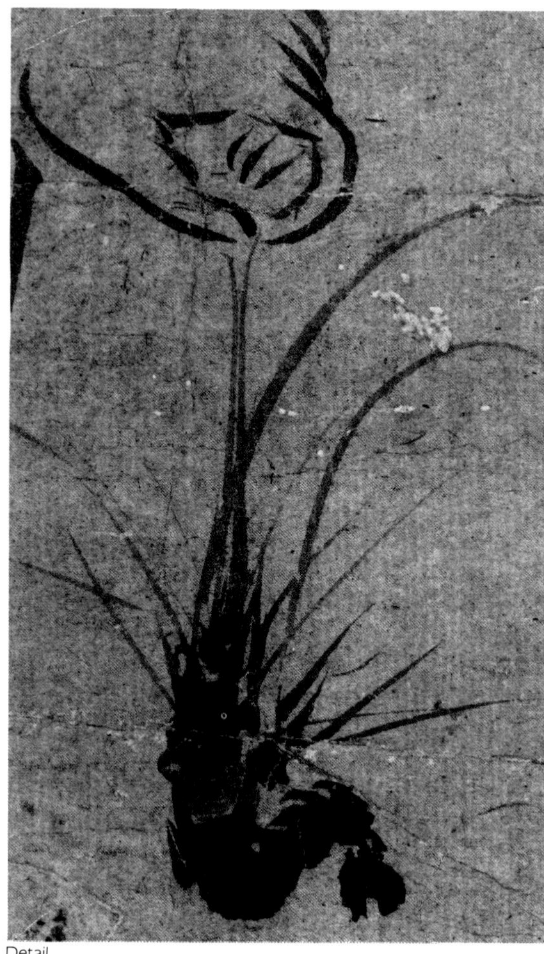

Detail

12

The Monk Kensu (Hsien-tzu)

Hanging Scroll
Ink on paper
59.9 x 24.7 cm

Seals
I-lung I-she
Yü Hsien Chih Yin
Yüan-chang
Yōgetsu

Yōgetsu
Active late fifteenth century

Inscription
Yü Ch'eng-hsien (dates unknown)

This painting depicts the semilegendary Chinese monk Hsien-tzu of the late ninth century. Very much like Pu-tai (no. 26), Hsien-tzu was an itinerant Ch'an Buddhist who wandered from village to village, living along the riverbanks and gathering shrimp and clams to eat, hence his nickname, Kensu (Hsien-tzu, in Chinese), or clam. Because devout Buddhists were forbidden to kill sentient creatures for food, Hsien-tzu was seriously violating customary behavior by eating such things. His action, however, was in keeping with other activities recorded in Ch'an Buddhist legends—the burning of Buddhist statues, the shredding of sutras, or the killing of a kitten by the T'ang monk, Nan-chüan—intended to demonstrate the folly of traditional distinctions between the sacred and the nonsacred. Although the monk depicted here was described as a wandering, lackadasical fellow, he had been a disciple of Tung-shan Liang-chieh (807-869), one of the founders of the Ts'ao-tung (Sōtō in Japanese) sect of Ch'an Buddhism.

The inscription above the painting is a Chinese style poem with the signature and seals of a certain Yü Ch'eng-hsien, probably a fifteenth-century Chinese or Korean. Although it gives no simple explanation of the theme, it does establish the philosophical premise by which seemingly eccentric Zen Buddhist behavior was inspired: ultimate reality is ultimately indefinable, and, with limited human verbal abilities, can be suggested only by a word such as void, or emptiness; moreover, only through intuitive means can a person grasp the grandeur and profundity of this reality and experience Buddhist enlightenment. A simple monk or even a peasant, living in intimate harmony with nature, is more likely to attain enlightenment than the most learned and bookish of scholars.

Zen believers say the origin [of all things] is emptiness.
An enlightened one like you—is there another?
Cold or hot, just one plain robe is enough.
Every day, carrying nets, you accompany fishermen.

(Translated by Ann Yonemura)

The seals used by the man who inscribed this poem are themselves instructive of the strongly Chinese intellectual atmosphere for which such paintings were created. The seal at the upper right reads I-lung I-she, "a dragon at one time, a snake at another," a proverb taken from the Taoist philosopher Chuang-tzu, suggesting the mutability and instability of the world. The seal on the lower left reads Yüan-chang, and is probably the inscriber's hao (artistic name), or gō in Japanese.

This painting by Yōgetsu presents the monk purposely eyeing his catch. The expressive face is defined by a controlled line which fluctuates from broad to thin, from angular to curved. Although the facial features are highly simplified—the eye and the mouth are each defined by a single stroke—they convey the monk's spiritual intensity. His profile shows the body of a stooped and aged man; a forceful curvilinear movement travels in a broad arc over his back into his raised left arm and hand, and abruptly drops down to the shrimp, whose tail ends in a twist. The robe is defined by thin, wet washes of gray ink, accented at the folds.

A seal impression reading Yōgetsu at the left edge of this work identifies the painter. Sketchy records indicate that a monk painter of that name was born in southern Kyushu, in Satsuma province as was Shūgetsu (no. 6), but spent much of his life at Kasagi-dera, a rural Shingon temple southeast of Kyoto. He is recorded as having been a follower of both Shūbun and Sesshū, but the few paintings attributed to him show no traces of influence from Sesshū. Either his paintings are closer to the Shūbun style, or, as in this work, they reveal knowledge of fourteenth-century Japanese ink painting, such as those by the master Kaō. Surviving from Kaō's brush is a well-known painting of Hsien-tzu, now in the Tokyo National Museum, which has much of the same warm and fluid brush style of the thirteenth-century Chinese painter, Liang K'ai.

Published
Japanese Ink Paintings, Shimizu, Yoshiaki and Wheelwright, Carolyn (eds.) (Princeton, NJ, 1976), no. 8.

References
Koga Bikō, Asaoka, Okisada (Tokyo, 1912).
Kokka, no. 213 (February 1908).

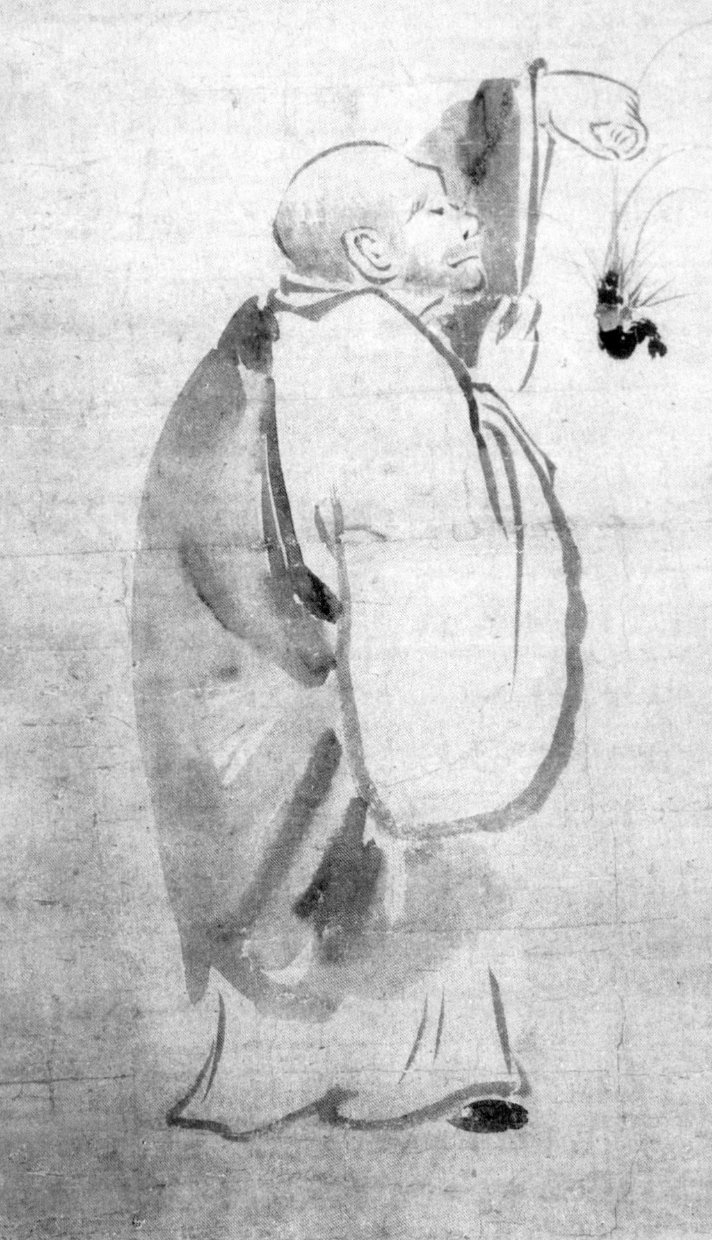

禪家曾說本
來空解脱必
君有執同窓
暑逸于惟一
衲日持綱署
伴漁翁
守笙憲

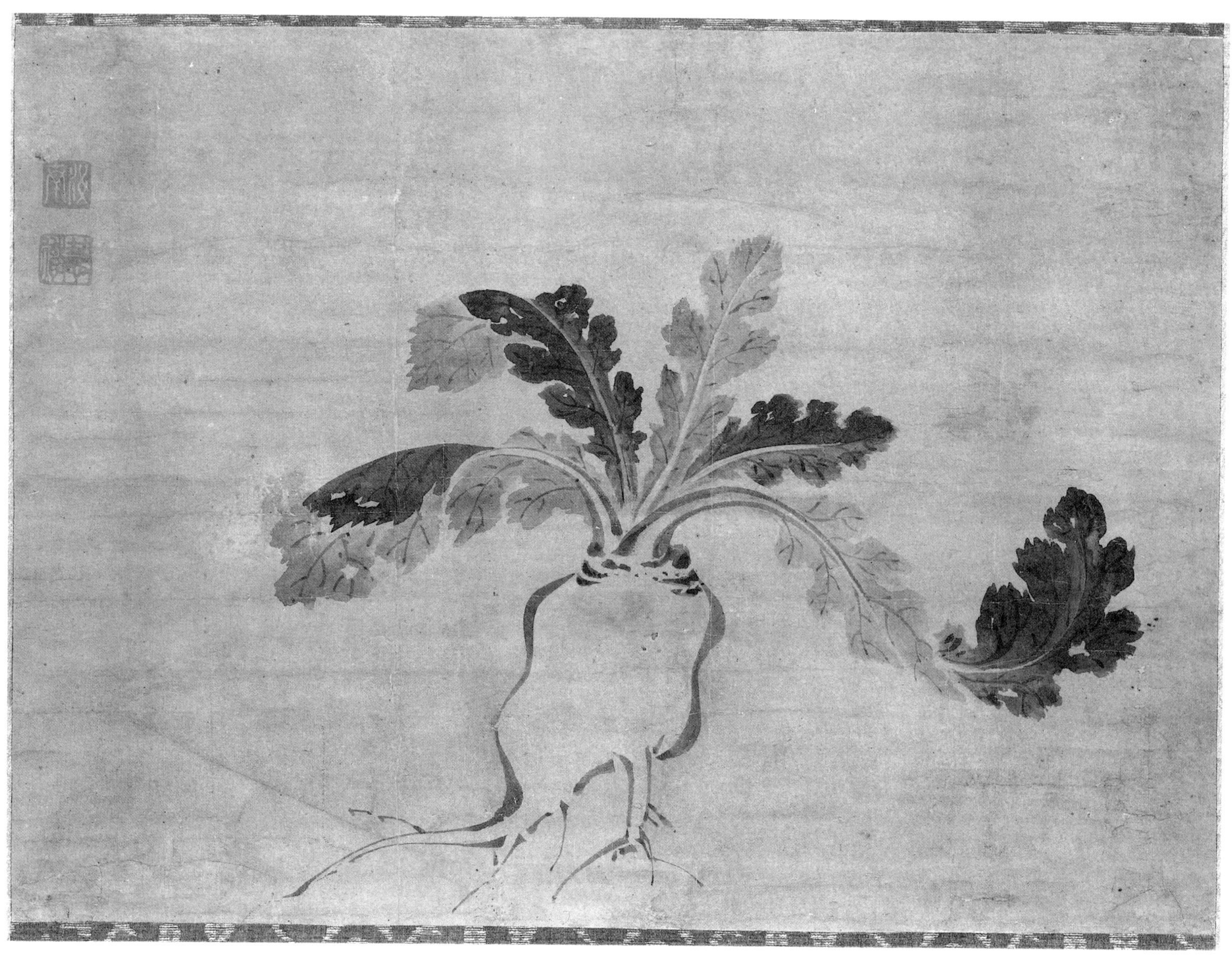

Jonan Etetsu
1444-1507

13

Radish Plant

Hanging Scroll
Ink on paper
33.8 x 45.4 cm

Seals
Jonan
Etetsu

Although unsigned, this painting bears two seals reading Jonan and Etetsu, the name of a little-known Zen monk who held brief tenure as the one hundred and eighty-third abbot of the influential Tōfuku-ji monastery in Kyoto. Contemporary records barely mention Jonan Etetsu, and this simple painting of a radish (daikon) is the only known example of his work. However, like many Zen ecclesiastics, Etetsu may have painted as an avocation. An inscription by him on a haboku (broken-ink) landscape attributed to Sesshū suggests that he came into the orbit of this famous late fifteenth-century master and may have been a follower.

Etetsu's depiction of a solitary radish with squat misshapen body and lush foliage is thought to have been modeled after a painting by the thirteenth-century Chinese master Mu-ch'i which was once in the Sōkoku-ji monastery in Kyoto. This painting may be the **Radish,** now preserved in the Imperial Household Collection in Tokyo, that bears the same four-character inscription that was recorded in the **Onryōken Nichiroku,** the daily journal of the Sōkoku-ji subtemple where it was kept. The shapes of both radishes are virtually identical, suggesting that the Chinese painting in the Imperial Collection, or a similar one, served as Etetsu's prototype. As a work associated with Mu-ch'i, the painting no doubt was a highly revered model for fifteenth-century Zen ink painters. A similar painting, by the sixteenth-century monk painter Sesson, bore a long inscription by a fellow monk. A number of vegetables and fruits associated with Mu-ch'i—**Six Persimmons, Chestnut** and a long handscroll with vegetables and fruits in the National Palace Museum in Taiwan—attest to the importance of still-life subjects in his oeuvre. The radish theme, with the humble character of the plant and the worm-eaten areas of the leaves, is very much in keeping with the Zen Buddhist regard for the importance of everyday experience and the awareness of the transiency of all living things.

Etetsu's **Radish** is, at first sight, a very simple painting, but its technique and conception are quite different from the **Radish** attributed to Mu-ch'i. Etetsu's radish is sharply delineated with black contour lines. The tap roots stretch out and anchor it firmly. Around the neck, heavy black lines ring the root— they are totally absent in the Mu-ch'i painting—and provide a sharp break between the radish and the feathery, curving leaves. The play of black ink and light washes in the leaves and their central ribs offsets the heaviness of the painting's lower half and lifts the whole into a dance-like movement. Although Jonan Etetsu was not a professional painter, he was thoroughly proficient and, indeed, original in his use of brush and ink.

Published
Japanese Ink Paintings, Shimizu, Yoshiaki and Wheelwright, Carolyn (eds.) (Princeton, NJ, 1976), no. 36.
Kobijutsu, no. 40 (March 1973), pp. 107-108, 112-114.
Muromachi Suibokuga, Matsushita, Takaaki (Tokyo, 1960), no. 38, p. 117.
Ryusen Shūhō: Mayuyama Seventy Years, vol. 2 (Tokyo, 1976), pl. 405.
Sesshū, Shimada, Shūjirō, exhibition catalogue, Kyoto National Museum (Kyoto, 1956), unnumbered item.

References
Mokkei, Gyokkan, Toda, Teisuke, Suiboku Bijutsu Taikei vol. 3 (Tokyo, 1973), pls. 69, 70.
Sesshū, Sesson, Tanaka, Ichimatsu and Nakamura, Tanio, Suiboku Bijutsu Taikei vol. 7 (Tokyo, 1973), pl. 117.

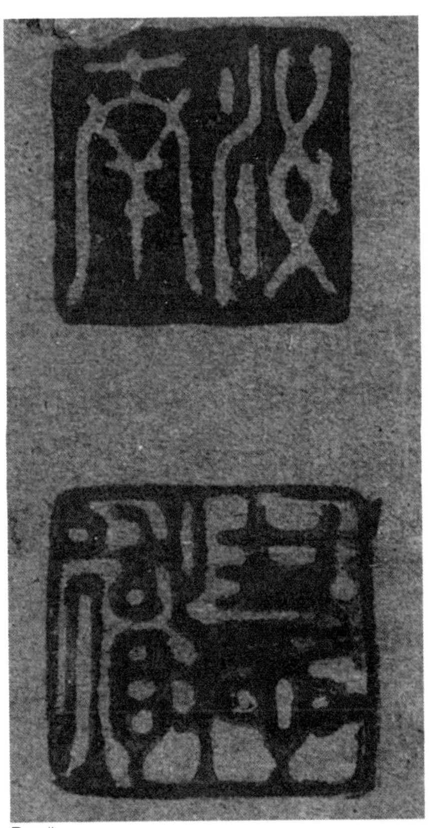

Detail

14

Precipice

Hanging Scroll
Ink on paper
72.4 x 10.2 cm

Seal
Fusō Shūkō

Shūkō
Late fifteenth–early sixteenth century

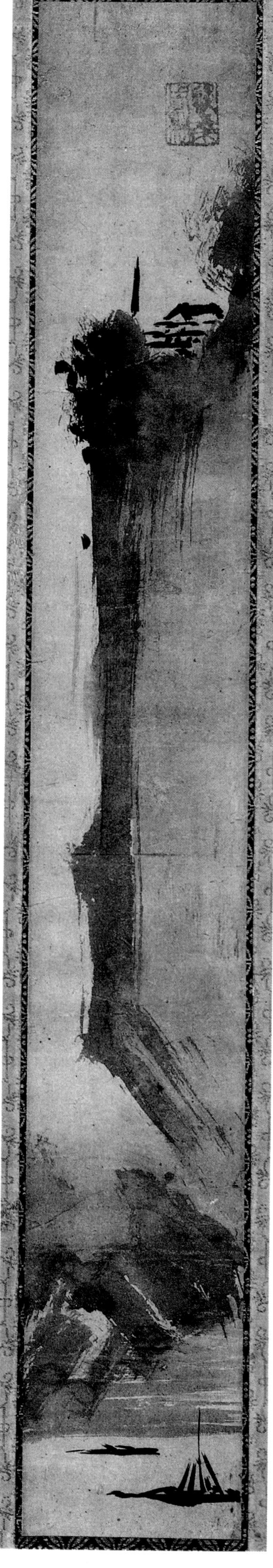

A mere ten centimeters in width, this painting with its unusually narrow format, maximizes the powerful, vertical drop of the mountain cliff. The steep rock face is simply yet powerfully executed; one broad downward sweep of gray-black ink divides the central part of the composition and then abruptly turns to the right with brush hairs splayed. The suggestive haboku (broken ink) technique delineates a rocky embankment precariously placed underneath the abutting cliff. Two boats calmly ply the water in front, seemingly undisturbed by the dynamic tension created by the towering cliff landmasses. At the crest nestles a group of houses roughly drawn in deep black ink. Swirls and dabs of rich ink wash near the edge of the cliff suggest lush foliage, though one dab of ink is suspended in midair like a meteor hurtling down the cliffside.

The extremely narrow confines of this scroll are unusual among extant early hoso jiku (narrow scroll). Narrow paintings like this one were made for display in the tokonoma, or rectangular alcoves of tea rooms, where the paintings' small, slender dimensions harmonized well with the low, narrow, spatial dimensions found in tea houses. Moreover, the abbreviated, evocative painting technique imparts the calculated simplicity and understated austerity of tea ceremony aesthetics.

Identified here by his seal, the artist Shūkō was a monk who lived at Tōnomine, the Shinto-Buddhist shrine erected in memory of Fujiwara no Kamatari (614-669) in Nara prefecture. Two seals commonly appear on his works: one, Fusō Shūkō (Shūkō of Japan), that appears on this work, and the other, Tōkai Shūkō (Shūkō from east of the sea) that indicates that he journeyed to the Chinese mainland. According to some records, Shūkō accompanied Sesshū on his trip to China in 1486, and excelled in the haboku landscape technique of which Sesshū was fond during his later years. Close relationships can be made with the loose brushwork and bold simplified forms of Sesshū's celebrated haboku landscape in the Tokyo National Museum, dated in accordance with 1495; thus, it is possible that Shūkō studied under the master, or at least, had first-hand contact with his haboku works.

Only a handful of Shūkō's works are extant: a painting of Mañjuśri at Chion-ji; a monkey in the Museum of Fine Arts, Boston; a hawk in the Freer Gallery of Art, Washington, D.C.; and the long, narrow painting, **Sparrows and Bamboo,** in a private Japanese collection.

Published
Meisaku Suiboku-ten, exhibition catalogue, Osaka City Museum (October 1964), no. 118.
Muromachi Suibokuga, Matsushita, Takaaki, exhibition catalogue (Tokyo, 1960), no. 28.

References
Koga Bikō, Asaoka, Okisada (Tokyo, 1912), pp. 638-641.
Kokka, no. 163 (December 1903), pp. 121, 130-131.
Sesshū, Sesson, Tanaka, Ichimatsu and Nakamura, Tanio, Suiboku Bijutsu Taikei vol. 7 (Tokyo, 1973), pl. 78, p. 199 (seal).

15

Bunson
Active late fifteenth or early sixteenth century

Inscriptions
Shōun Seisan (died 1517)

Triptych
Bodhidharma Crossing the Yang-tze River on a Reed, Flanked by Myna Bird and Heron

Hanging Scrolls
Ink on paper
Center scroll 64.3 x 9.8 cm; flanking scrolls 64.3 x 8.9 cm each

Seals
Center, Seisan (?), Shōun, Bunson
Flanking, Seisan (?), Bunson

As does the large triptych attributed to Chūan Shinkō (no. 4), these three tiny paintings of approximately the same date demonstrate the fusion of expressive values taken from Zen Buddhism and the Chinese literary tradition. Whereas the Chūan Shinkō paintings reflect the advent of stylistic influences from contemporary Ming China, this triptych remains faithful to the Southern Sung classic tradition. The innovations of men like Liang K'ai and Mu-ch'i have been preserved in the abbreviated formulations of Bodhidharma's robe and in the sensitive painting of the two birds, each poised in a remarkably life-like manner.

The painter, identified by his seals as Bunson, is not clearly documented in early sources; however, the monk who wrote the three inscriptions, Shōun Seisan, is known as an accomplished poet in Chinese who modeled his verses on those of Su Tung-p'o. A native of Ise, he traveled widely during his early years and studied for a while at Tōfuku-ji in Kyoto. Later, he went to Kamakura, to Kenchō-ji, where he died in 1517. If these indications are relevant to the Sansō triptych, they might be used to place the painter, Bunson, in eastern Japan. Closely related to Bunson's myna bird painting is one by Nyosui Sōen (active ca 1490–1500), one of Sesshū's most devoted pupils, who spent his last years in Engaku-ji monastery in Kamakura (no. 7).

The central painting depicts the legendary patriarch of the Zen sect, Bodhidharma, crossing the Yang-tze River on a reed. With his robe gathered over his hands for warmth, the bearded monk stands tip-toe on the single reed, the movement of the lower hem of his robe suggesting his motion as he crosses the water. According to Zen legend, his miraculous crossing took place not long after Bodhidharma had arrived in China from India and had been received by the Emperor Wu of the Liang state. Their initial interview had been unsuccessful, and the Indian monk stealthily departed, crossing the Yang-tze to make his way north. He then settled at the Shao-lin temple on Mount Sung, where, in a prodigious display of determination and self-discipline, he meditated before a stone cliff for nine years.

The inscription, written from left to right in Chinese above the Bodhidharma painting, possesses a number of double meanings and is awkward to translate:

In the morning, the western sky [India],
At evening, east of the sun [Japan].
His robe the color of snow;
Wind propels the single reed.
Chanting five-syllable verses from the
Lankāvatāra [sūtra]
Standing erect in the spume of breaking waves.

Reverently inscribed, with the burning of incense,
by the Buddhist disciple, the monk Seisan

To the right, the painting of the heron shows the bird poised on a rocky outcropping, staring into the water in wait for an insect or minnow. The inscription in Chinese, written by Seisan, contains a play on the word goisagi, which means heron as well as the fifth court rank; it also has a Japanese political connotation whose meaning is still puzzling.

In the ancient and sacred Engi reign [901–922],
The feathered tribe flourished,
Summoned and appointed to the Fifth Rank.
Now the sacred era is long past;
And only the blue heron
Remains on the old river bank.

To the left is the painting of a myna bird, also on a river bank. The poem above the bird is an adaptation of one by the Chinese poet Wang Ch'ang-ling, and refers to the jealousy between two sisters, ladies in the court of the Han emperor, Ch'eng Ti. It may be translated:

It sees something and starts up,
Its cage is thinner than gauze.
The sunlight of the Chao-yang Palace
Is no match for the cold crow.

The poem by the eighth century Wang Ch'ang-ling on which Seisan's inscription was based may be translated:

Even a colorless cold crow
Received the sunlight of the Chao-yang Palace.
It seems that my beauty
Is no match for it.
I cannot win the Emperor's favor.

References
Gozan Shisō-den, Uemura, Kankō (Tokyo, 1912), pp. 368–369.
Koga Bikō, Asaoka, Okisada (Tokyo, 1912), p. 815.

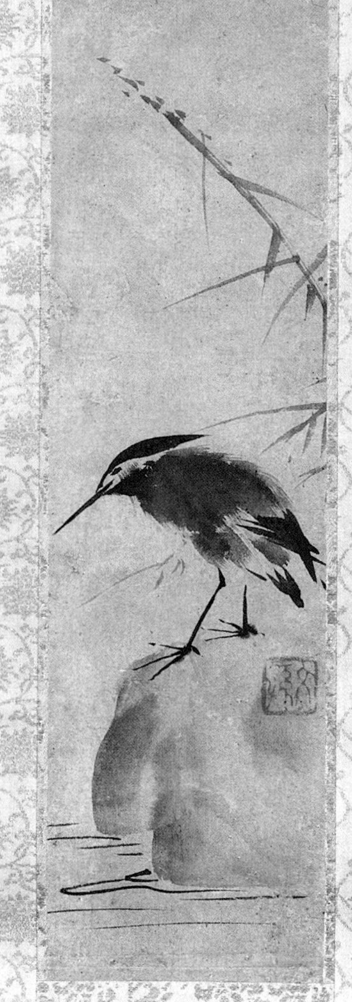
昔延禧聖代喚汝署五位ゝゝ謂羽族盛者也
今此吾聖逾遠叮佇旧江邊碧鶴鶲而已
吟梯伽五言句聲有立浪花中
朝西天芳日本七条雪一葦風
法孫比丘清三禁雪拜榿
觀物呉起鬟莠於紗
昭陽日影不及寒鴉

16

Bird on a Thorn Bush

Hanging Scroll
Ink on paper
96.3 x 45.6 cm

Seal
Chiyū

Chiyū
Late fifteenth century

A bird perched on a thorn bush—apparently a wagtail—looks down past a boulder into a stream. Next to the bird a graceful reed with feathery leaves rises to the very top of the painting. The bird and the rock are painted in a loosely brushed technique that alternates black areas with white space, as on the bird's neck, and with light grays, as in the rocks. The reed, the thorn, and the blade of grass below the bird are painted with a stiff brush that creates varying ink values by changing the pressure on the paper.

The inscription on the cloth which wrapped this painting reports, without additional documentation, that it was originally part of a triptych. If so, the center piece, which has been lost, might have been Bodhidharma or Kannon, who were traditionally flanked by birds on both sides (no. 15). The only other work that bears the Chiyū seal is a bird painting in a private Japanese collection.

The wrapping cloth further states that the lost center painting was the work of Nōami (Shinnō) (1397-1471) and the two side paintings, the work of Nōami's grandson, Sōami (1485-1525). This was apparently the tradition handed down in the Hinohara family in Tokyo in whose collection the two paintings were for many generations; but the ascription of these paintings to the august names of the Ami painters, grandfather and grandson, cannot be sustained by modern scholarship. Not only do no stylistic grounds exist for this attribution, but no record of any of the members of Nōami's group indicates they employed a seal reading Chiyū.

Remarkably the identity of Chiyū has not been discovered. Chiyū obviously had access to fine original paintings, Chinese or Japanese; the quality of the brush strokes in the plumes of grass and the foreshortened bird bespeak much practice with the brush, and much insight into the basic character of this imagery. Possibly, he was a well-established painter of the last part of the fifteenth century who, for unknown reasons, chose to use a special seal engraved with the characters Chiyū for these paintings rather than use one of his standard seals and artist names.

References
Muromachi Suibokuga, Matsushita, Takaaki (Tokyo, 1960), pl. 60.
Sesshū, Shimada, Shūjirō, exhibition catalogue, Kyoto National Museum (Kyoto, 1956), no. 50.
Sesshū, Sesson, Tanaka, Ichimatsu and Nakamura, Tanio, *Suiboku Bijutsu Taikei* vol. 7 (Tokyo, 1973), pls. 39, 74.

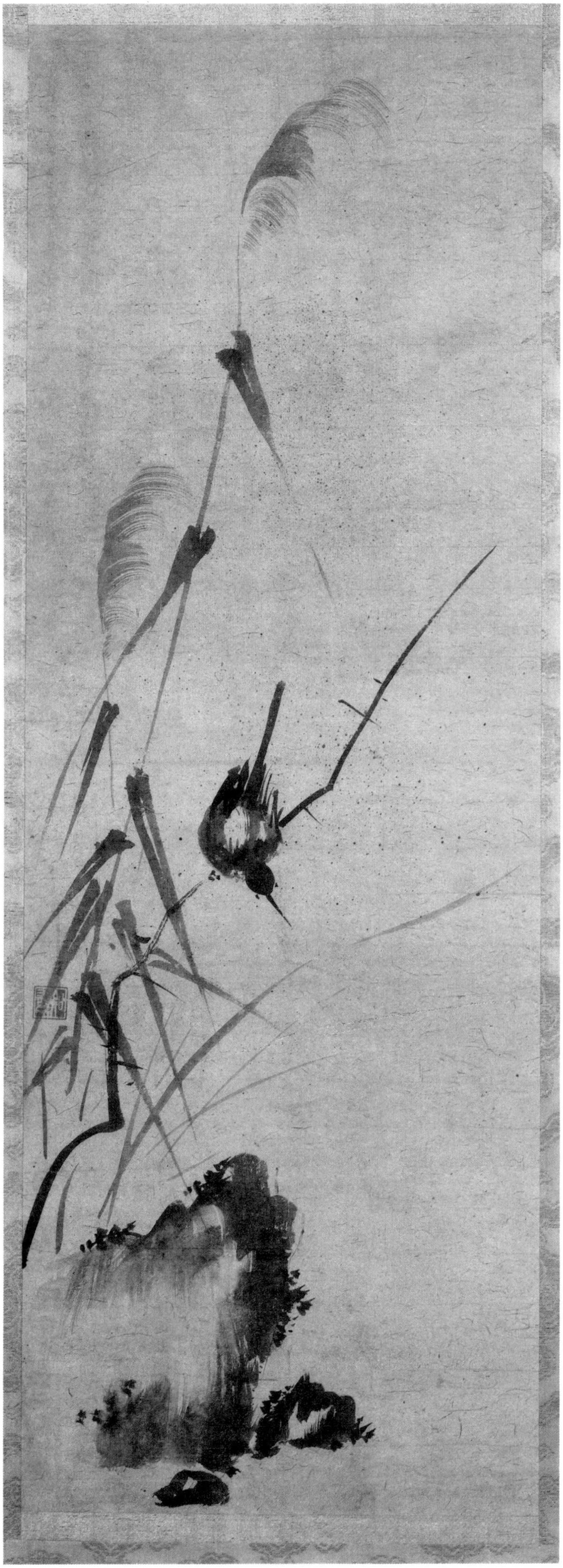

Detail

Artist unknown
Early sixteenth century

17

Diptych
Wild Geese and Reeds

Pair of Hanging Scrolls
Ink on paper
93.7 x 43.0 cm each

Seals
Shūtoku (seal altered)
Tōsetsu

The motif of waterbirds—geese, ducks, herons, and kingfishers—exerted special appeal for the monk painters of China and Japan. The extremely broad range of symbolic suggestion was drawn from Chinese nature symbolism and ancient Buddhist traditions which viewed the migrant bird as an emblem of transmigration from one existence to another. Most artists, however, were absorbed by the purely artistic problems of showing the birds in flight, at rest, floating in the water, or feeding in grass and reeds.

This pair of paintings depicts one goose in the process of landing while another turns its head and seems to call out. Painting roughly and rapidly in heavy black ink washes, the artist succeeded in capturing the birds' feathers in their characteristic shapes—outspread in the flying wings, soft along the down of the chest—with a minimum of specific detail.

The authorship and original intention of these paintings are extremely obscure. Each picture bears two old seal impressions. One seal, which has been altered, has been read Shūtoku, the name of a monk painter associated with Sesshū, Ikei Shūtoku (nos. 8, 9). The seal obviously has been carved with the intention of its being read Shūtoku, but unsuccessfully, as the first character is defective. Contrary to some scholarly opinion, the first character cannot be read as Yō either, and so the reading Yōtoku is impossible. Furthermore, the toku element may also have been altered, making the evidence of authorship in this seal quite uncertain. The second seal, Tōsetsu, appears in the **Koga Bikō** under the heading of Ikei Shūtoku, but its authenticity cannot be confirmed.

Stylistically, the paintings belong in the early sixteenth century and could well have been done by one of Sesshū's many followers. The rough vigor and self-confidence in the paintings is not out of keeping with other works in the Sesshū tradition, such as the bird paintings by Sōen or Shūgetsu.

References
Kaō, Mokuan, Minchō, Tanaka, Ichimatsu, Suiboku Bijutsu Taikei vol. 5 (Tokyo, 1974), pls. 41, 42, 74, 75.
Koga Bikō, Asaoka, Okisada (Tokyo, 1912), pp. 710-712.
Nihon Shoga Kottō Daijiten, Ikeda, Tsunetarō (ed.) (Tokyo, 1915), pp. 758-759.
Sesshū, exhibition catalogue, Yamaguchi Prefectural Museum (Yamaguchi, 1973), no. 52.
Sesshū, Sesson, Tanaka, Ichimatsu and Nakamura, Tanio, Suiboku Bijutsu Taikei vol. 7 (Tokyo, 1973), pls. 65, 66, 73.
Shoki Suibokuga, Kanazawa, Hiroshi, Nihon no Bijutsu no. 69 (February 1972), pl. 121.

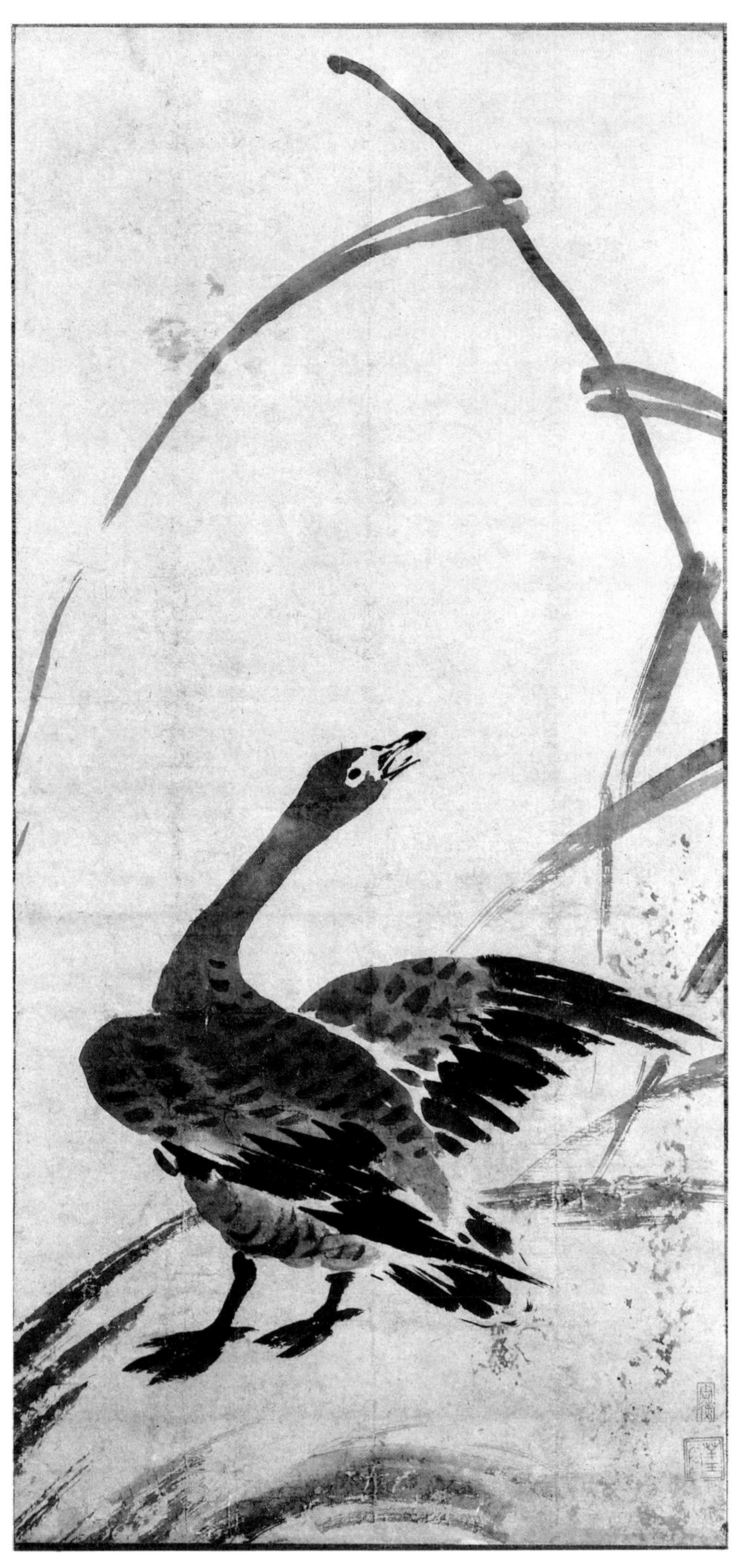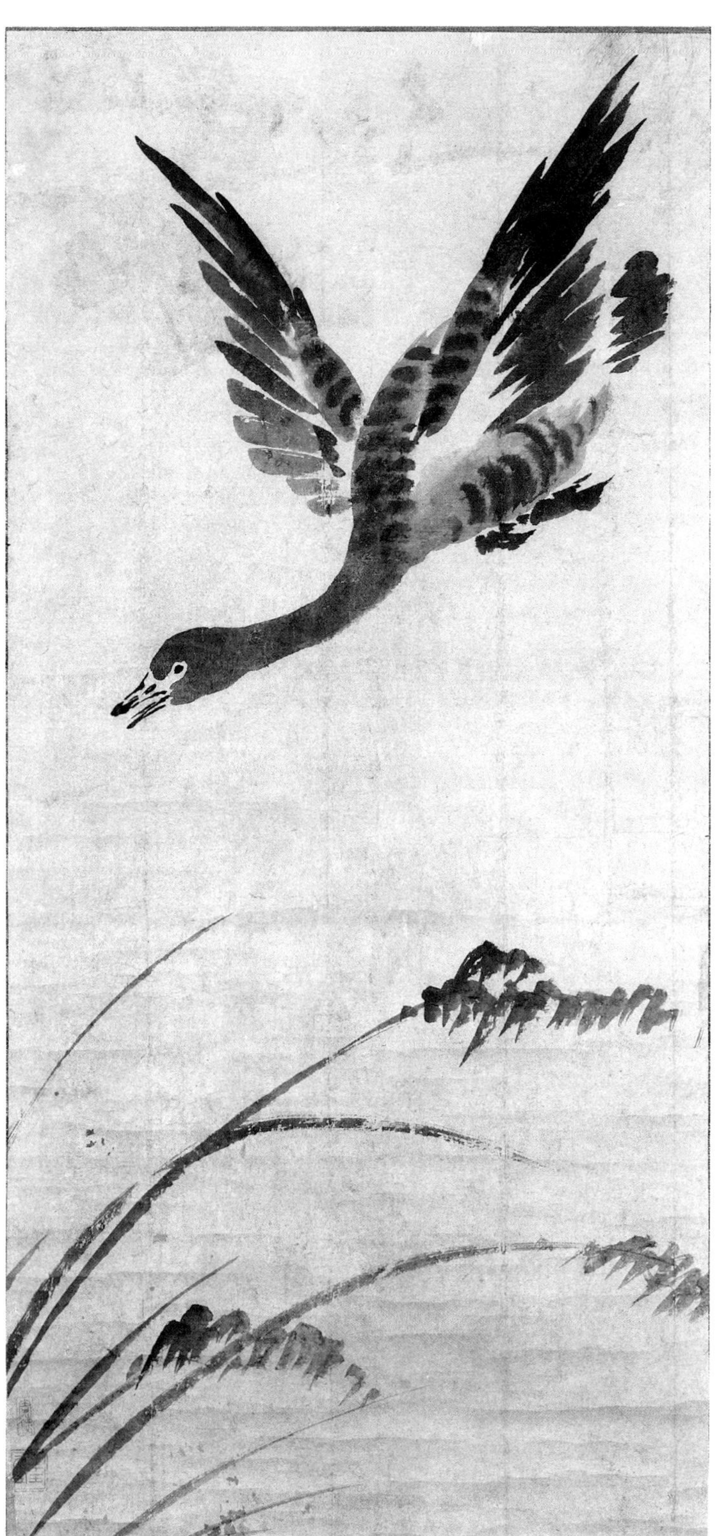

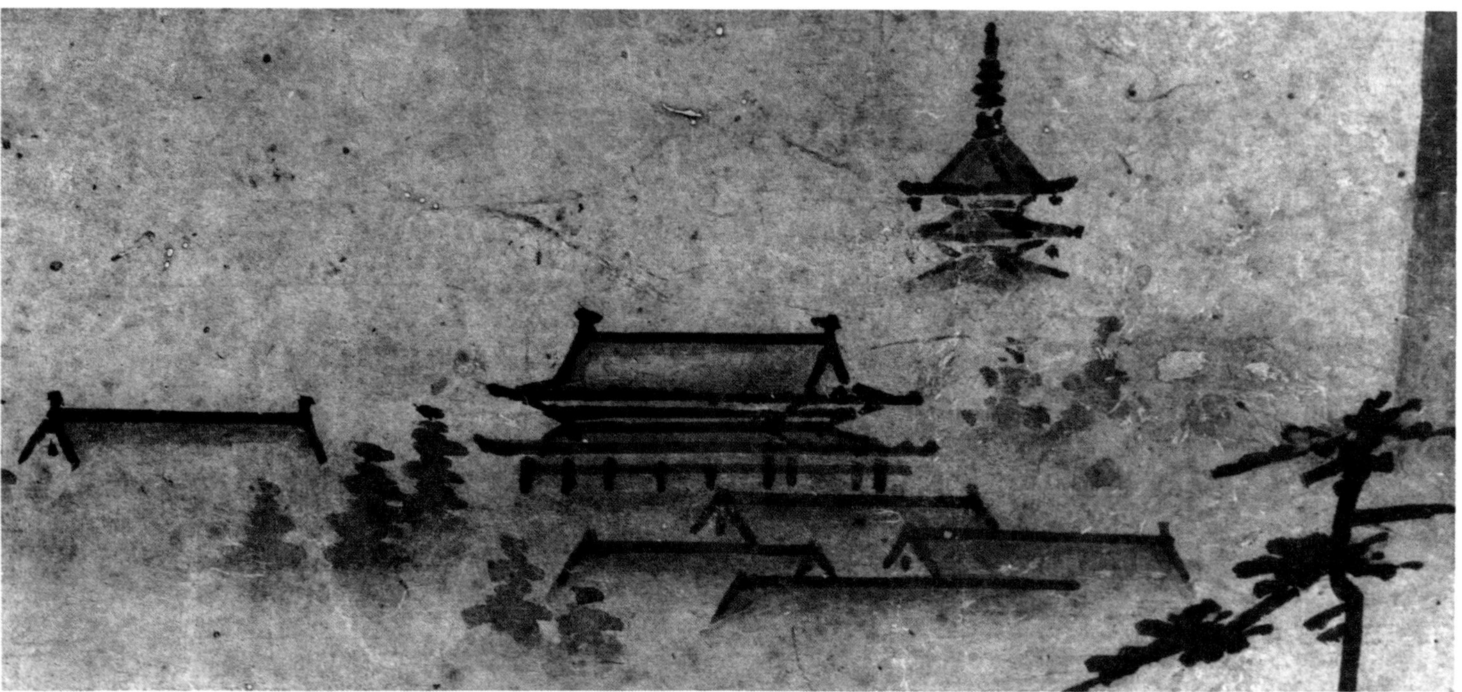

Detail

Kantei
Active late fifteenth century

18

Spring Landscape

Hanging Scroll
Ink on paper
47.1 x 31.2 cm

Seal
Kantei

Dwarfed by immense rocks and pine trees, a scholar and his attendant pause to admire the mist-shrouded vista. Although the scale of the human figures is reduced when compared to the grandeur of the landscape, the plum branch carried by the servant suggests that the scholar represents the eleventh-century poet-recluse Lin Ho-ching, who was well known for his love of plum blossoms. In the middle ground, a low bridge connects two points of land; behind the water passage, partially obscured by a low-lying fog bank, a tall pagoda marks a temple complex.

Kantei's economical painting style and simplification of the landscape into a restricted number of graphic forms produce a dramatic and unified visual image. The bold, angular form of the large foreground rock with its rich ink texturing provides a dramatic entry into the painting. (This portion of the painting, however, has been considerably abraded and retouched.) The towering pines form a strong vertical movement leading to a curiously-shaped mountain pinnacle at the right. The empty space in the center of the large expanse of water emphasizes the profiles of the poet and his servant.

Until recently scholars thought that Kantei was used as a pseudonym by the Daitoku-ji monk painter Bokkei, an assumption recorded in the seventeenth-century **Honchō Gashi.** Modern scholarship, however, has established that Kantei probably belonged not to the Zen sect, but to the ancient Ritsu (Vinaya, or Monastic Discipline) order, and lived in its headquarters at Tōshōdai-ji in Nara. Matsushita Takaaki established the stylistic character of Kantei as a semiamateur painter of high sensibility active perhaps two generations after Tenshō Shūbun (ca 1414-1463), the man credited with bringing Japanese suiboku landscape painting to its maturity. Matsushita noted two likely sources of Kantei's landscape style: the paintings in the Shinju-an at Daitoku-ji attributed to Soga Dasoku (active mid-fifteenth century), the first artist in a sequence of men who considered themselves part of a Soga school of ink painting (no. 61); and paintings of the Oguri school founded by Oguri Sōtan (1413-1481), one of Shūbun's most distinguished pupils.

In the Sansō landscape of Kantei, the clear-cut division of the composition into a tripartite sequence of well-defined elements is characteristic of the Shūbun style, but the brushwork differs from the more detailed and descriptive Shūbun mode by delineating forms in a simpler fashion. A gray ink wash applied with a rather dry brush defines the mountains; long, parallel strokes of ink are added to model the surfaces. Black ink dots representing low foliage or grass are generously applied over the terrain to animate the scene. Kantei uses a mode of atmospheric perspective typical of Shūbun followers to portray the gradual diminution in visibility of trees and mountains as they recede into the mist.

On the reverse side of the painting directly behind the seal are the characters for "spring" and "one," which have bled through to the front of the painting. Because it was customary to illustrate the spring landscape first in a series of paintings of the four seasons, the designation "one" would be superfluous. Thus, this painting must have been part of a larger group of eight or even twelve paintings containing two or three cycles of landscapes depicting the four seasons.

Published
Japanese Ink Paintings, Shimizu, Yoshiaki and Wheelwright, Carolyn (eds.) (Princeton, N.J. 1976), no. 17.
Kokka, no. 810 (September 1959).

References
Kobijutsu, no. 27 (September 1969), pp. 85-88.
Nara Hōgen Kantei, Hasumi, Shigeyasu, Nihon Bijutsu Kyōkai Hōkoku no. 38 (Tokyo, 1935), pp. 1-7.

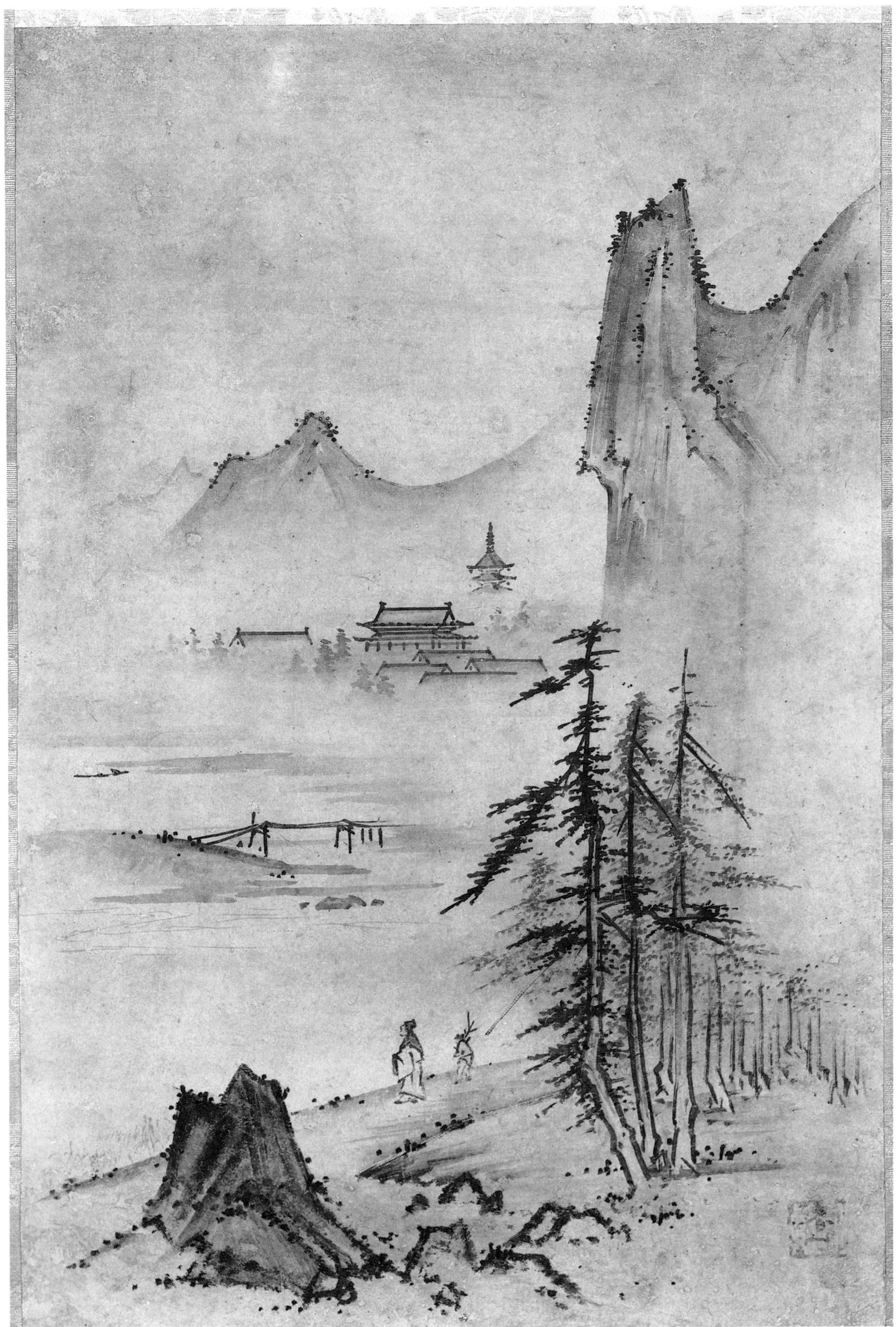

Kantei
Active late fifteenth century

19

Diptych
Blossoming Peach and Sparrow; Peonies and Butterfly
(See color plate no. 19)

Hanging Scrolls
Ink and pale color on paper
48.4 x 31.7 cm each

Seals
Kantei

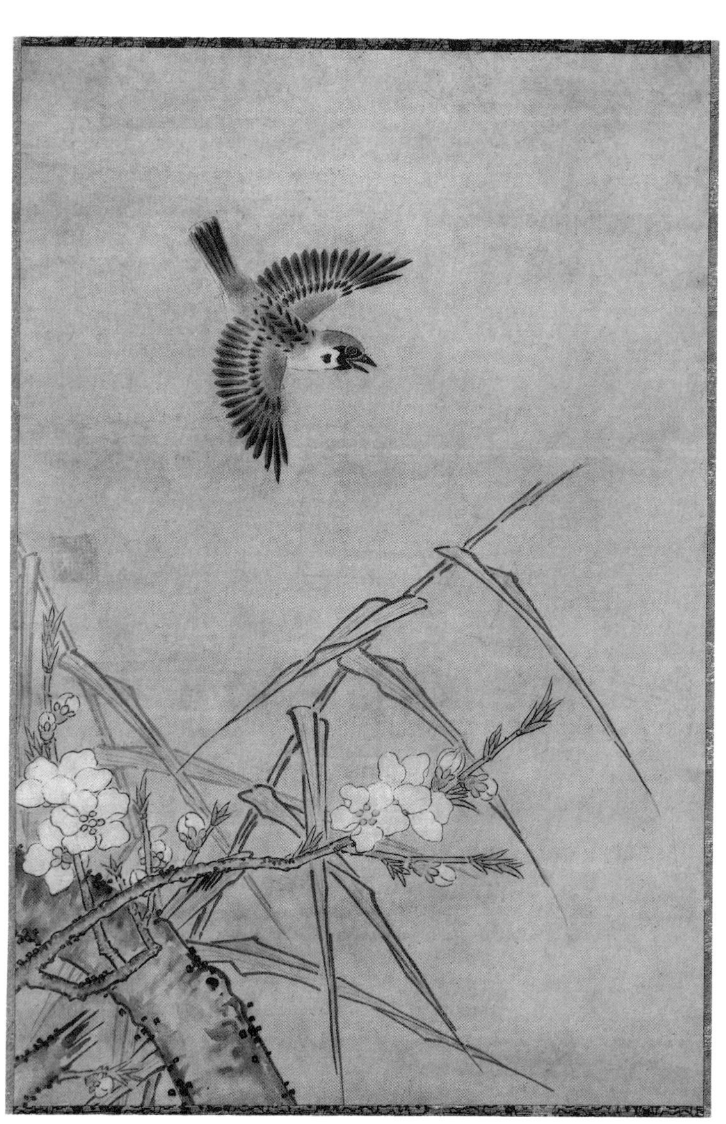

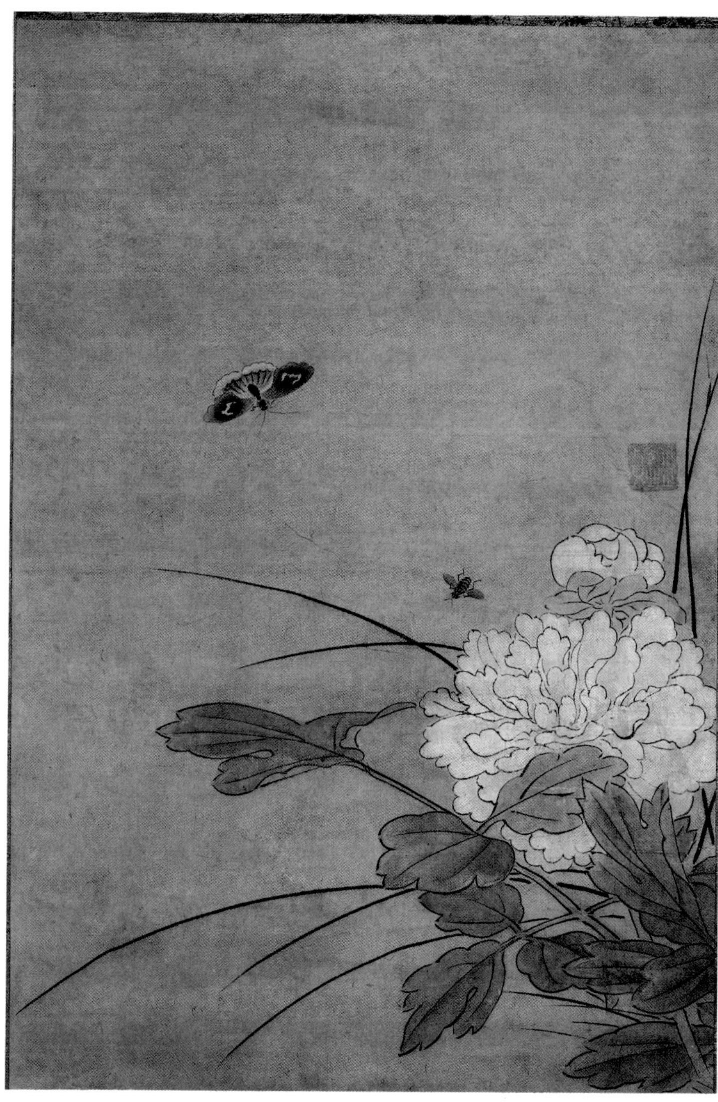

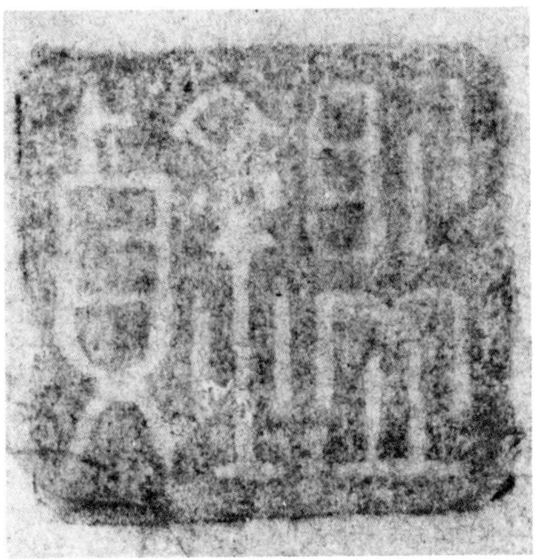

Detail

This pair of finely colored flower-and-bird paintings differs greatly in style and intention from the starkly simplified ink landscapes which comprise the bulk of the Kantei oeuvre (no. 18). Nevertheless, it was not unusual for late fifteenth- and sixteenth-century Buddhist monk painters who were experts in suibokuga to experiment with the colorful style of flower-and-bird painting then current among professional and court artists in Ming China. Examples have come from the members of the short-lived Oguri school (official painters to the shogunate), as well as from such prominent figures as Kenkō Shōkei (active 1478-1506) and Sesson (ca 1504-ca 1589), but there are many excellent works with the seals of little-known men.

These paintings, bearing the seal of Kantei along with a certificate of attribution by the late Edo-period connoisseur and painter Kanō Seisen-in Yasunobu (1796-1846), have generally been accepted as part of the Kantei oeuvre. Much of their great appeal lies in the relationship between the abstract beauty of the formal elements and the representation of living forms. For example, the butterfly and honey bee are portrayed from an overhead point of view in a flat two-dimensional fashion in order to capture their symmetrical body markings, whereas the peony blossoms are described through crisp, lilting brushwork in rhythmic arcing patterns. The sparrow has also been flattened; the feathers of its wings have been arrayed like the ribs of a fan.

It is not known whether these two paintings were originally intended to be a self-contained unit, or the flanking panels of a triptych with a representation of a Buddhist figure such as Kannon or Bodhidharma as the central piece (see nos. 4, 33). However, they were a pair as early as 1848, the date of the Seisen-in certificate, they were recognized and exhibited as a pair at the opening of the current Tokyo National Museum building in 1937. At that time, however, they were attributed to the painter Bokkei who was presumed to be using the name Kantei as a pseudonym, a practice recorded in the seventeenth-century Honchō Gashi.

Published
Hokusō-ha, vol. 1, Nihonga Taisei vol. 3 (Tokyo, 1931), pl. 156, p. 39.
Ink Painting, Matsushita, Takaaki, Arts of Japan vol. 7 (Tokyo, 1974), pl. 107.
Jidai Kachō, Iso, Hiroshi (Kyoto, 1977), pls. 98, 99.
Matsuura Hakushaku-ke Zōhin Nyūsatsu Mokuroku, Tokyo Bijutsu Kurabu (October, 1931), pl. 43.

References
Kokka, no. 810 (September 1959).
Nara Hōgen Kantei, Hasumi, Shigeyasu, Nihon Bijutsu Kyōkai Hōkoku no. 38 (October 1935), pp. 1-7.

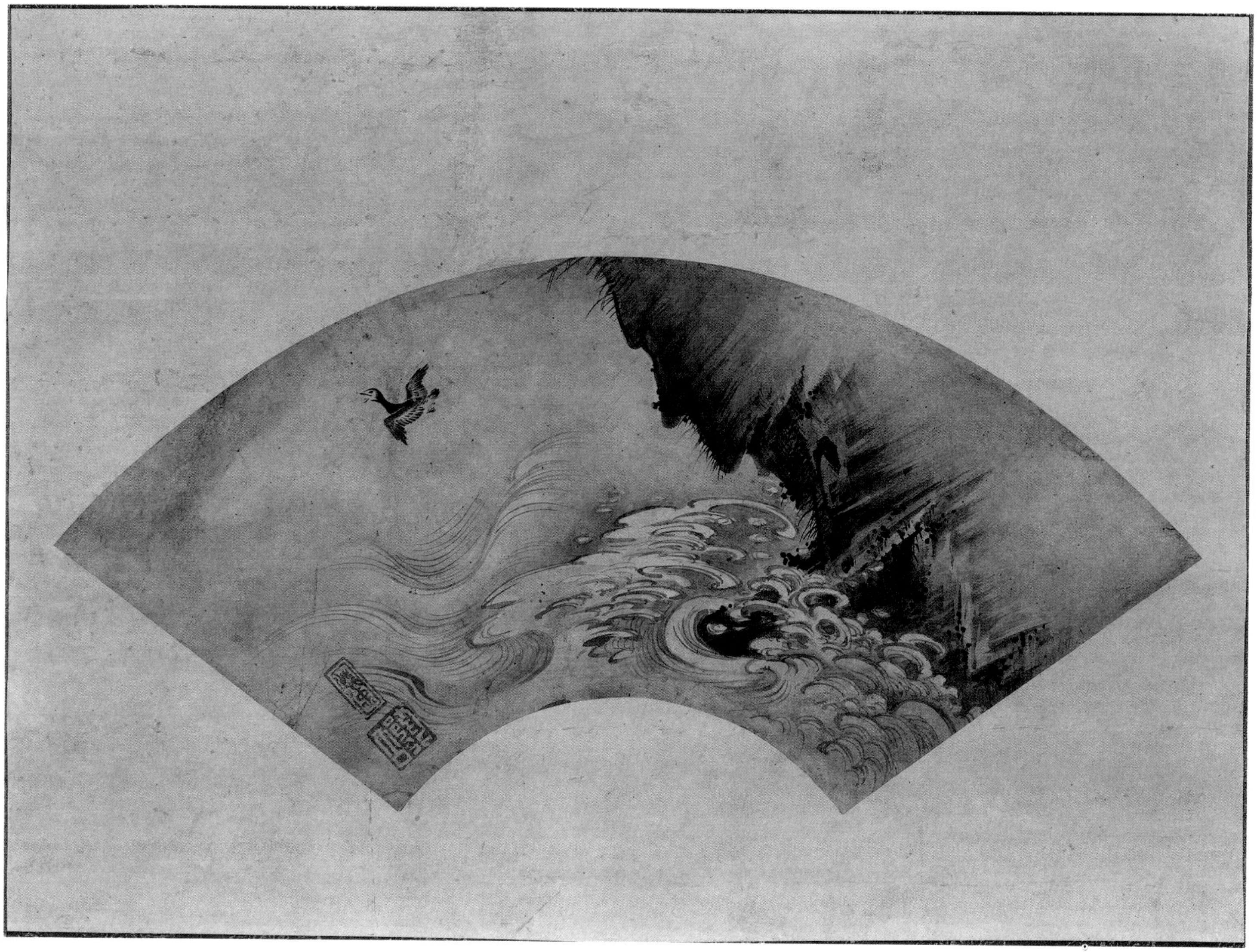

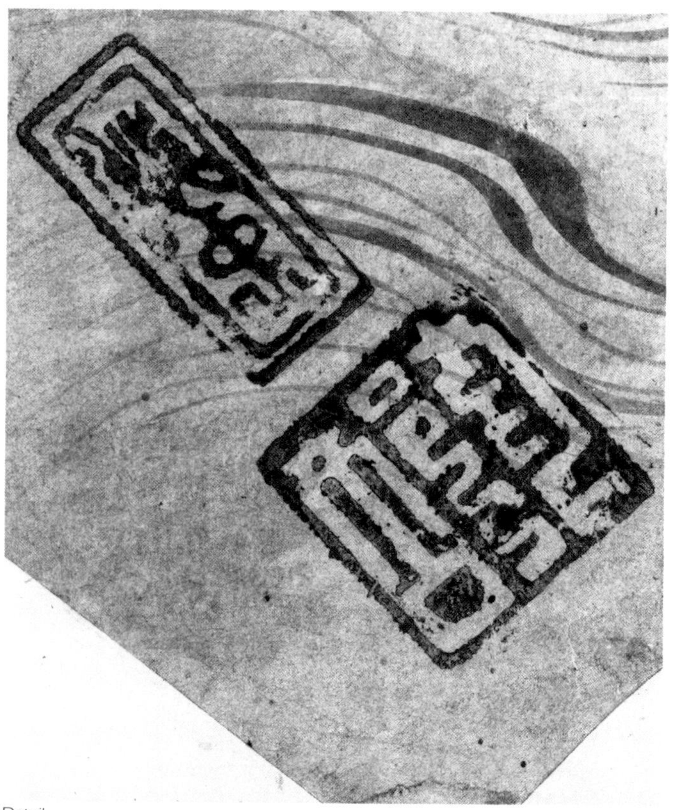

Detail

Shikibu (Ryūkyō)
Active mid-sixteenth century

20

Waves and Waterfowl

Hanging Scroll
Mounted fan painting
Ink on paper
24.1 x 52.1 cm

Seals
Terutada
Ryūkyō

In midair above a violent surf a waterfowl, probably a duck, cries out as it flies away from a treacherous, serrated rock cliff. The lighthearted quality of the duck with its open wingspan and stretched neck contrasts strongly with the turbulence of the waves crashing against the embankment. The artist utilized particularly attenuated, hook-like profiles for the waves; gray washes describe the spume, and the bare white of the paper creates the foaming crests. Deep gray-black inks and "axe-cut" brushstrokes define the cliff's deeply fissured surface.

The rendering of the duck stems from Ming flower-and-bird models, though Shikibu has imbued the bird with a lively, expressive nature not found in Chinese prototypes. Parallels can be found in post-Sesshū school works for Shikibu's rendering of the waves and rocky cliff. A painting in the Nezu Museum in Tokyo, **Waves Crashing against a Rock** signed by Sesshū, though clearly done by a follower, is remarkably close to this painting, and it is likely that Shikibu's work was based on a similar model.

Although a few large-scale works bear Shikibu's seal—the landscape screen in the Asian Art Museum of San Francisco, and the well-known pair of screens depicting monkeys registered as an Important Cultural Property in Japan—the intimate fan format was Shikibu's real metier. This small fan painting exhibits great economy and cohesion in design. The emphatic overhanging cliff at the right is balanced by the two seals at the lower left, the boiling surf by the flying duck. Finally, the quacking duck provides a light touch that offsets the formal and stylized rocks and waves.

A large number of extant paintings bear Shikibu's seal, but nothing is known of the painter. Even his name is surrounded by controversy. Some Japanese scholars assign him to Kyoto around 1510; others, more plausibly, place him in Kamakura forty years later. All the paintings bearing his seal are of high quality; but the identity of the painter remains obscure.

Published
Japanese Ink Paintings, Shimizu, Yoshiaki and Wheelwright, Carolyn (eds.) (Princeton, NJ, 1976), no. 37.
Zaigai Hihō, Shimada, Shūjirō (ed.), vol. 2 (Tokyo, 1969).

References
Koga Bikō, Asaoka, Okisada (Tokyo, 1912), pp. 795-799.
Kokka, no. 461 (April 1926), pp. 100-106.
Kokka, no. 43 (April 1893), pp. 135-136.
Muromachi Suibokuga, Matsushita, Takaaki (Tokyo, 1960), pls. 95-97.

21

Fisherman and Windswept Coast
(See color plate no. 21)

Hanging Scroll
Ink and slight color on paper
27.3 x 78.6 cm

Seals
Sesson
Shūkei

Sesson Shūkei
ca 1504–ca 1589

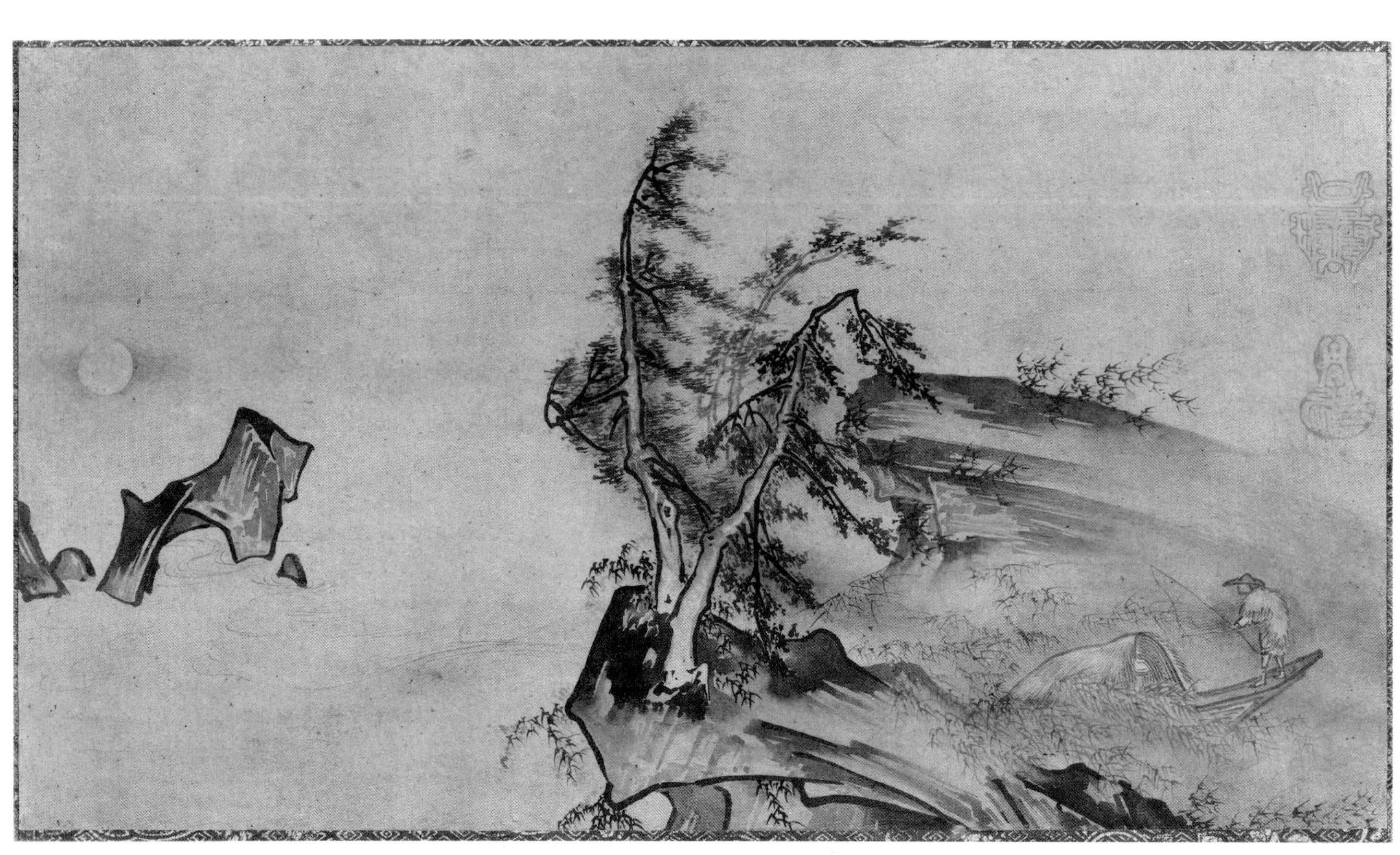

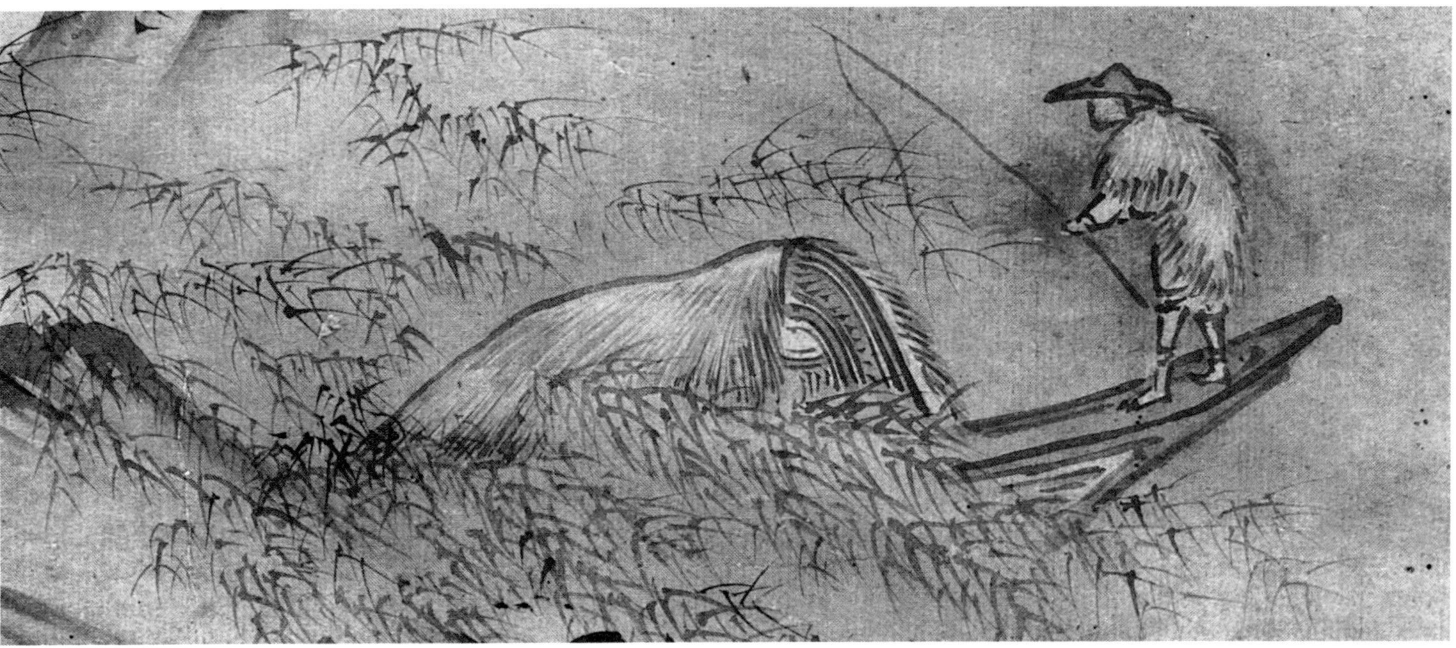

Detail

Sharp contrasts in mood create a mysterious sense of unreality in this painting, one of the finest examples of the work of Sesson Shūkei outside of Japan. At the left, a low-hanging moon rises over an expanse of water that eddies around a series of irregularly shaped rocks. The tranquil mood of this passage abruptly changes to stormy turbulence in the right-hand portion of the painting. Strong gusts of wind tug the limbs of the trees on the foremost outcropping; the rocks appear transmuted into volatile forms through sharp, knifelike strokes of heavy black ink. Seemingly oblivious to the storm, a solitary fisherman in a raincoat made of straw clasps a fishing pole.

This sort of theatricality in which contrasting moods are successfully orchestrated into a pictorial unity is a hallmark of Sesson's oeuvre. In his work Sesson distilled the compositional elements, brush techniques, and aesthetic values of Muromachi ink painting; but in style and artistic temperament, Sesson stands out as a marked individual. Although certain elements such as the graphic contour lines, slashing texture strokes, and close-range "intimate" viewpoint show Sesson's indebtedness to Southern Sung masters like Ma Yüan and Hsia Keui, his dramatic interpretation of the style is far removed from these sources. The foreground rocks, for example, cannot be explained in terms of early Chinese prototypes. Moreover, Sesson's works show little trace of the rigid compositional geometry that characterizes the contemporary Japanese disciples of Chinese painting, the Kanō school.

Rather than settling in Kyoto, the capital and center of culture, the monk Sesson led a peripatetic existence traveling among various provincial towns in northern and central Japan. His early training and painting activity is unknown; he may have been self-taught, and developed his highly personal style by studying Chinese paintings and the works of Japanese masters like Tenyū Shōkei and Sesshū. His adoption of the character "snow" from Sesshū's name indicates his admiration for the earlier master. In 1542 Sesson wrote a painting treatise called **Setsu monteishi (Instruction to His Disciples),** in which he emphasized the importance of fluid brushwork and dramatic utilization of dark tonal values.

Sesson's earliest extant paintings date from the mid-1540s, when he was under the patronage of the powerful lord of Aizu castle, Ashina Moriuji (1521-1580). Today, scholars attribute about sixty paintings to Sesson, and divide his oeuvre into three periods of artistic activity roughly corresponding to his residence in the provincial towns of Hetare, Aizu, and Tamura. Scholars believe the Sansō Collection landscape was executed during Sesson's middle period, when he resided in Aizu, though Japanese scholars disagree as to whether the painting falls into the first part of this period (1542-1562) or into the second half (1563-1572). Because the same tripod seal reading "Sesson" appears on an album depicting **The Eight Views of the Hsiao and Hsiang Rivers,** several Japanese scholars posit that Sesson executed the two works in the early part of his middle period, ca 1542-1546. However, Yoshiaki Shimizu in his comprehensive analysis of this painting, argues that Sesson created the Sansō landscape during the second half of the middle period; in this painting, brushwork and ink wash orchestrate the form and volume of the landscape elements more fully than in the Hsiao-Hsiang album.

Instructive comparisons can be made with one of Sesson's most famous works, **Wind and Waves,** in the Nomura Collection in Kyoto. Like the Sansō painting, this work combines a seascape view and a partial view of a rocky coastline placed diagonally at the corner edge. Through vigorous brushwork and dramatic ink tonalities, both paintings create a vivid impression of the storm-swept coastline characteristic of northern Japan, where Sesson lived.

The strong horizontal format and sense of incompletion at the left may indicate that this painting originally may have been a handscroll later cut down and mounted as a hanging scroll.

Published
Japanese Ink Paintings, Shimizu, Yoshiaki and Wheelwright, Carolyn (eds.) (Princeton, N.J. 1976), no. 26.
Matsuzawa-ke Zōhin Nyūsatsu Mokuroku, Tokyo Bijutsu Kurabu (Tokyo, 1919), no. 8.
Museum, no. 281, special issue on Sesson (August 1974), pl. 11, p. 25.
Ryūsen Shūhō: Mayuyama Seventy Years, vol. 2 (Tokyo, 1976), pl. 411.
Sesson no Geijutsu, Homma Bijutsukan, exhibition catalogue (Sakata City, Yamagata prefecture, 1968), no. 26.
Sesson to Kantō Suibokuga, Nakamura, Tanio (ed.), Nihon no Bijutsu no. 63. (August 1971), pl. 25.

References
Sesshū, Sesson, Tanaka, Ichimatsu and Nakamura, Tanio, Suiboku Bijutsu Taikei vol. 7 (Tokyo, 1973).
Sesson, special exhibition, Tokyo National Museum (July 1974), nos. 2, 15, 19, 33.

Detail

Attributed to
Kanō Sanraku
1559-1635

Inscription
Tanhan (?) Genhan (ca late
sixteenth-early seventeenth century)

22

Two Wagtails

Hanging Scroll
Ink on paper
60.0 x 32.9 cm

Seals
Ji (?)
Genhan
Shuri
Mitsu (?)

Two wagtails gambol by the water. One, perched at the edge of a grassy slope, peers intently into the river near a growth of water grasses. The other braces its wingspan overhead, holding a stationary position while it calls out to its mate below. To the left, a light breeze jostles long slender reeds.

Underneath the flying bird, a poem reads:

What does the inquisitive wagtail see?
The other one is in flight,
And a light breeze stirs the sand.
In search of its original state,
It flew far south of the Ch'ing River.
There are not many that have traveled
Even as far as the Yellow River.

(Tanhan [?])

The poem imbues this seemingly playful depiction of two birds by the river with a deeper Zen import. A common theme in Zen literature is the religious adept's search for the true nature of reality, and more directly, for the realization of his own innate nature. The poet uses the birds' long journey to various rivers in China as a metaphor for the seeker's quest for enlightenment.

The painter executed the grassy knoll in the foreground in the new tarashikomi technique—applying dabs of fresh ink over a first layer of wet ink. Consequently, the ink dries in soft, random ink patterns, creating an interesting abstract design which suggests the texture and volume of the embankment. The tarashikomi technique was perfected in the early seventeenth century by the painter Tawaraya Sōtatsu, who used it in both his ink and his color works to articulate form and surface values.

Sanraku is best known for large-scale screens painted in vivid colors on a gold background in the dramatic Momoyama style; for example his famous peony fusuma paintings in Daikaku-ji outside of Kyoto, executed around 1620. However, other works show Sanraku's versatility in various styles—his screen, **Battle of the Carriages,** in the detailed Yamato-e style in the Tokyo National Museum, and his hanging scroll of Chung K'uei in the Muromachi ink-painting tradition in the Museum of Fine Arts, Boston.

Kimura Nagamitsu, Sanraku's father, and a low-ranking samurai, studied painting under Kanō Motonobu. Sanraku's talent as a painter impressed the military leader Toyotomi Hideyoshi, who arranged for Sanraku to study under Motonobu's grandson Eitoku, the leading painter of the day. Sanraku distinguished himself as one of Eitoku's ablest pupils, and was adopted by Eitoku as a son.

Although no clear documentation exists, Sanraku must have assisted Eitoku on such important commissions as those for the Azuchi castle, the Osaka castle, and the Jurakudai palace. The **Honchō Gashi** records that Sanraku worked with Eitoku on the large ceiling painting of a dragon at Tōfuku-ji in 1588. When Eitoku fell ill after partially completing the work, he entrusted Sanraku with the work's completion.

Following Eitoku's death in 1590, Sanraku worked on many important painting commissions for the Fushimi castle, for the Shōshinden of Daikaku-ji, and for Tenkyū-in of Myōshin-ji in Kyoto. In contrast to other Kanō family members, who set up ateliers in Edo (the modern Tokyo), to serve the new Tokugawa regime, Sanraku headed the school's Kyoto branch and remained loyal to the Toyotomi family until the fall of the Osaka castle in 1615.

In this painting, on the other hand, Sanraku seems to have been experimenting with the abstraction of natural forms. The clearly articulated foreground rocks that often grace his works are lacking here. In the Daikaku-ji peony paintings, for example, sharp-edged, crystalline boulders provide a firm structure linking the peony bushes. The foreground rock in this painting has no linear structure; rather, wet gray ink washes, pooled in the tarashikomi technique, form a soft, spongy earthen slope. The tall grasses and the embankment on the other side of the river are also executed in pliant gray ink tones, with the growths of moss and grasses in the foreground providing the only dark accents in the landscape.

In contrast to the abstraction of the landscape forms, the birds are crisply described. The plump wagtail peering down seems about to topple into the water. This downward movement is stabilized by the bird's long, stiff tail, which sets up an opposing compositional movement to the tall marsh grasses, and to the bird hovering in the sky.

According to the inscription on the back of the painting, the inscriber, Genhan, was a monk connected with Myōshin-ji in Kyoto and a contemporary of Sanraku. This name, however, does not appear in temple documents or in other records of the late sixteenth or early seventeenth centuries.

Published
Birds, Beasts, Blossoms, and Bugs: The Nature of Japan, Stern, Harold P. (New York, 1976), no. 18.

References
Bijutsu Kenkyū no. 52 (April 1936), pp. 19-26.
Bijutsu Kenkyū no. 40 (April 1935), pp. 1-10.
Kanō Sanraku, Sansetsu, Doi, Tsugiyoshi, Nihon Bijutsu Kaiga Zenshū vol. 12 (Tokyo, 1976), pls. 15, 25, 27, 28, fig. 12, p. 106.
Shoki Suibokuga, Kanazawa, Hiroshi, Nihon no Bijutsu vol. 69 (February 1972), pl. 90.

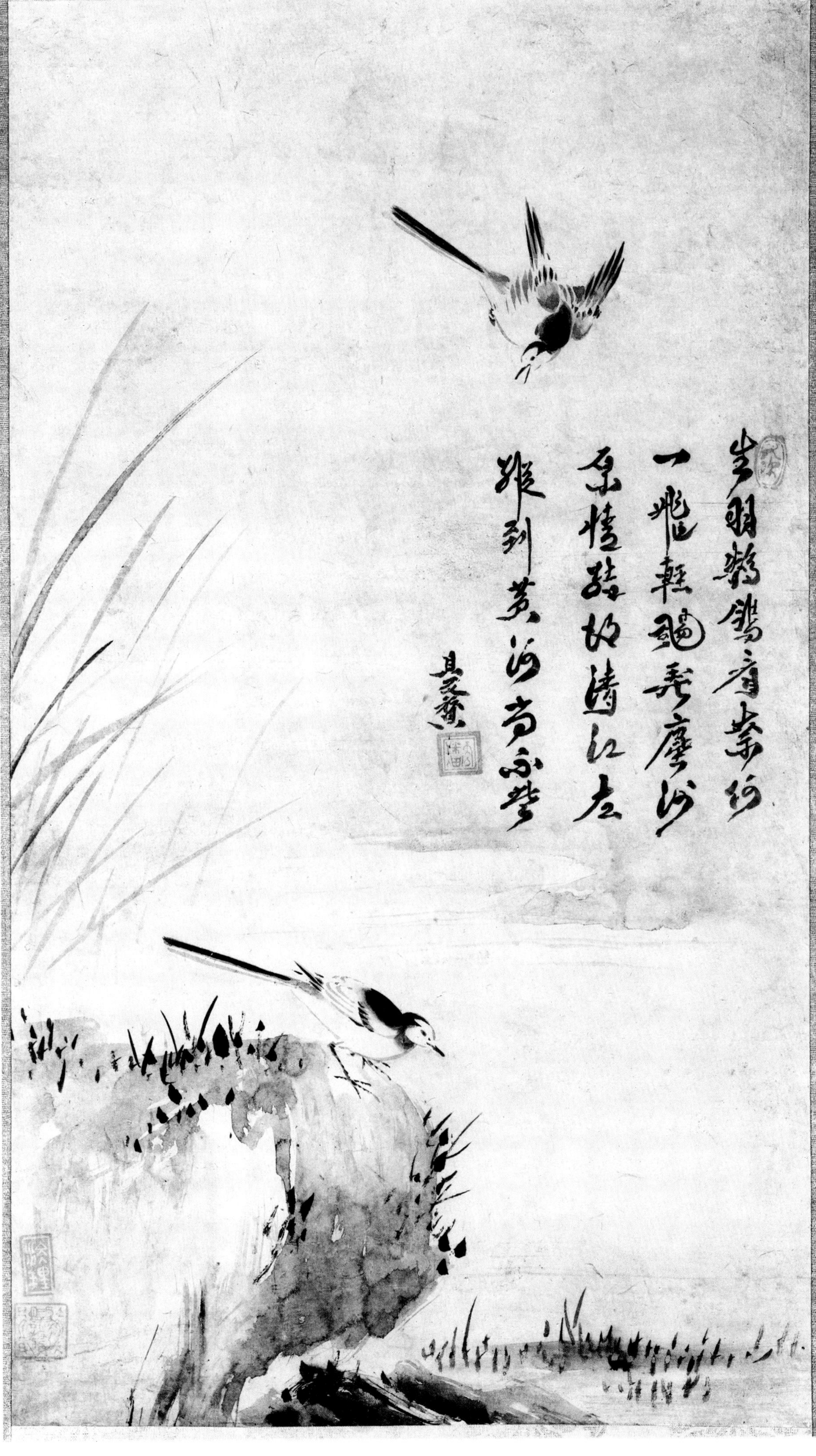

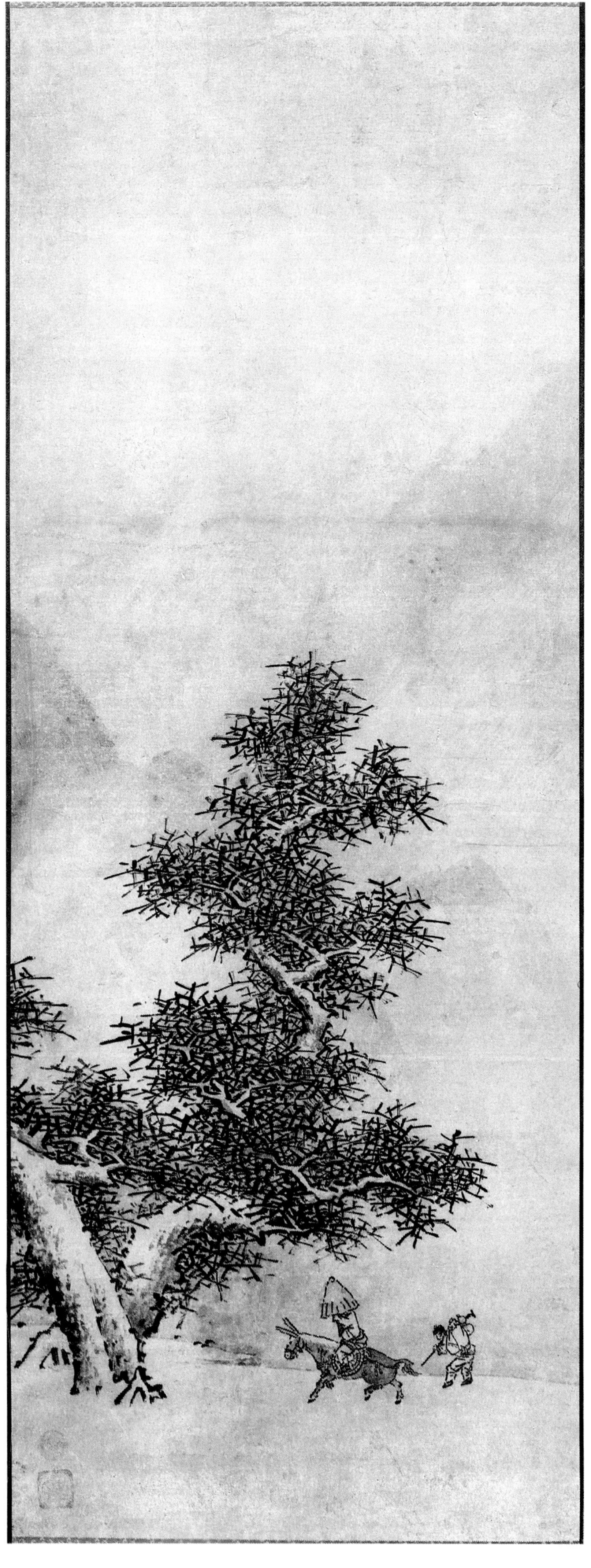

Donkei Tōshitsu
Died 1668

23

Travelers in a
Winter Landscape

Hanging Scroll
Ink and slight color on paper
113.9 x 42.1 cm

Seals
Donkei
Tōshitsu

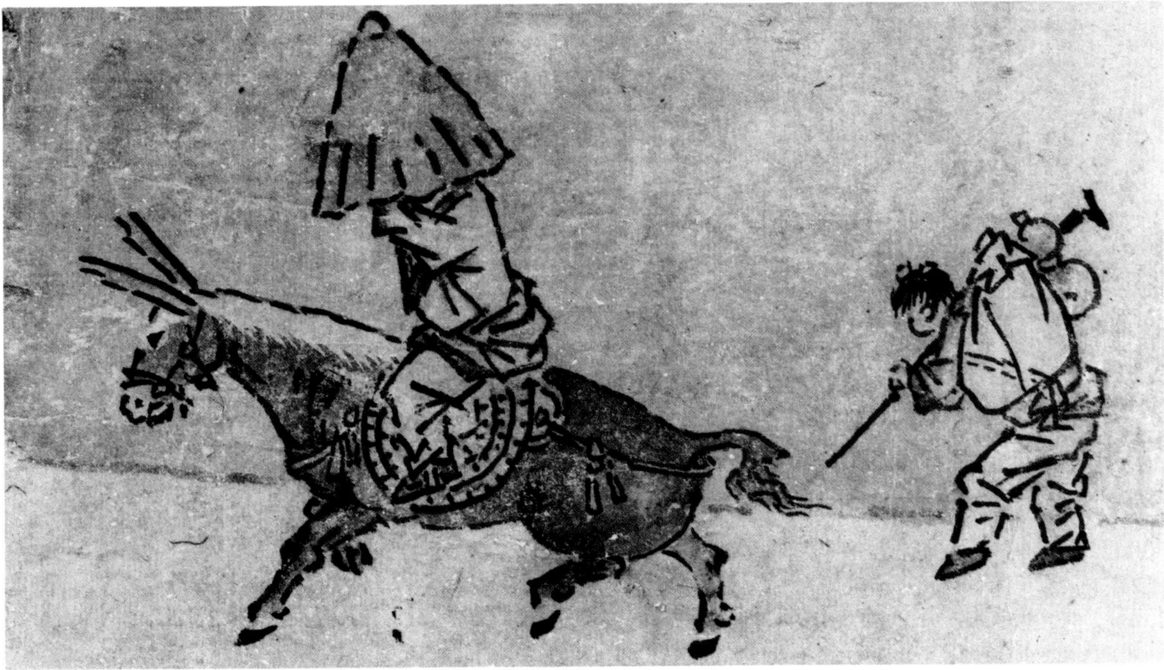

Detail

Half hidden by a straw umbrella, a man rides a donkey through strong gusts of swirling snow. A short distance behind him, a boy servant is struggling with a heavy load. The dense, spiky branches of a mammoth tree form a protective overhang for the travelers. Only the shadowy silhouettes of conical mountain forms are visible in the background, yet the painting vividly conveys the rawness and isolation of nature in winter. One can almost feel the bitter cold gusts, and hear the sound of the wind whistling through the trees.

This painting closely resembles the **Winter Landscape** by the famous thirteenth-century Chinese artist, Liang K'ai. This work, long considered one of Liang K'ai's finest and most important works, has an impressive history in Japan. It was in the private collection of the Ashikaga shoguns by the fifteenth century, and is today preserved in the Tokyo National Museum.

Although the two paintings share several compositional features such as the large barren tree and approaching travelers, the painting modes are quite distinct stylistically. Fine, detailed brushwork and modulated ink washes carefully describe forms in Liang K'ai's masterpiece. In contrast to Liang K'ai's more subdued vision, a dramatic quality permeates Tōshitsu's work. The incisive jet black brushwork of the trees provides a graphic contrast to the bare, suggestive depiction of the surrounding landscape in which the solid shapes of mountains and land are dissolved in wind and snow. Tōshitsu executed the figures in an abbreviated, highly angular style with crisp, broken contour lines.

Scholars know almost nothing about the life of Tōshitsu, a member of the Unkoku school, which flourished under its founder Unkoku Tōgan in the late sixteenth and early seventeenth centuries. Tōgan called himself a descendant of the influential master Sesshū Tōyō (1420-1506) and developed a style of ink monochrome painting based on the earlier master's style. Tōshitsu is clearly indebted to Tōgan for such compositional features as contrasting dense pictorial areas with broad areas of blank space, and contrasting areas of dark tonal values with light ones. Tōgan also often imbued natural forms with a larger-than-life appearance through exaggeration of features as did Tōshitsu with the tree branches in this work.

By the second half of the seventeenth century, when Tōshitsu was active, the Unkoku school was considered old-fashioned. Although the prestige of this school had diminished by the second generation, it did not affect the quality of this work. It is a minor masterpiece by an artist of considerable talent.

References
Koga Bikō, Asaoka, Okisada, vol. 2 (Tokyo, 1912), p. 905.
Kokka, no. 877 (April 1965), pp. 24-29.
Kokka, no. 828 (March 1961), pp. 129-139.
Kokka, no. 827 (February 1961), pp. 83-89.
Kokka, no. 826 (January 1961), pp. 36-42.
Kokka, no. 820, special issue on Unkoku-ha (July 1960), pp. 266-269.
Kokka, no. 551 (October 1936), pp. 287-291.

Kusumi Morikage
Active last half of the seventeenth century

24

Pine Trees and Fishing Village

Hanging Scroll
Ink and pale color on paper
93.2 x 55.2 cm

Seal
Kusumi

Three out-of-scale pine trees sit regally on the foreground bank, behind them clusters a group of thatched Japanese-style fishermen's cottages; small fishing boats with thatched roofs are tied up at the shore. An expansive body of still water fills the middle ground and extends to the distant hills and background mountains; small sailboats traverse its quiet surface. Soft washes of blue were added to both the farther range of mountains and the rocky knoll in the foreground.

Although dating from the last decades of the seventeenth century, this painting is a faithful exemplar of what the Japanese considered their own classical mode of ink landscape. In the work of Shūbun's followers in the third quarter of the fifteenth century appears the same combination of stylistic elements from earlier Chinese ink painting: the starkly simplified silhouettes of pine trees and mountains, and the mood of idyllic tranquility from Southern Sung academic painting; the empty middle ground and deep diagonal recession from the Ni Tsan mode of Yüan landscape that adds a tinge of melancholy.

Although this painting was once afflicted with mold, or foxing, and has been considerably washed, it retains its basic aesthetic integrity. It is said to be one of a pair with a similar landscape in another American private collection; in all likelihood, it belonged to a set of landscapes of the four seasons or of the twelve months.

For the critic and historian, the painter of this work, Kusumi Morikage, is one of the most challenging masters of the late seventeenth century. A deeply conservative and careful student of classical ink painting, as in this work, he was also innovative and rebellious. These elements are present even in the few events of his biography that scholars clearly understand. Morikage was born in the Kaga fief along the Japan Sea, and came to Edo to study under Kanō Tanyū, official painter of the Tokugawa shogunate. Tanyū's painting atelier was the most illustrious one in the mid-seventeenth century. Morikage soon distinguished himself as a talented disciple, assisting the master in many important painting commissions. He even married one of Tanyū's nieces. The circumstances of Morikage's break with Tanyū are unclear, though scholars speculate that Morikage's independent temperament may have been incompatible with the rigid discipline and adherence to authority that characterized the Kanō ateliers. In any case, Morikage left Tanyū's circle and probably went to Kyoto as an independent painter.

In 1675, he was summoned to Kanazawa by the head of the Kaga clan, one of the few documented events of the remainder of his life. One tradition holds that he executed pottery designs for the Kutani kilns located near Kanazawa. According to one confirmed document, he was banished by the government to Sado Island, where he died. Other sources indicate that he spent time in Kyoto during his later years, devoting himself to the study of the tea ceremony.

Morikage's innovative and independent spirit appears in his paintings of rural, peasant life. Inspired, perhaps, by the growing taste for genre painting that was to manifest itself in Ukiyo-e, he often depicted peasants tilling the fields, tending farm animals, and threshing rice. Moments of relaxation after a day's hard work also captured Morikage's imagination—one of his most famous paintings depicts a peasant family with their cotton robes opened in partial undress enjoying the cool evening breeze under a trellis of calabash gourds. A poetic, romantic quality pervades this work and reveals Morikage's deep personal identity with country life.

References
Chion-in, Shōhekiga Zenshū vol. 8 (Tokyo, 1966), pp. 102-103, 113 (fig. 9), 132-133.
Morikage; Itchō, Kobayashi, Tadashi and Sakakibara, Satoru, Nihon Bijutsu Kaiga Zenshū vol. 16 (Tokyo, 1978), pls. 4, 28, 34, p. 123 (seal and signature).
Museum, no. 24 (March 1953), pp. 18-25.
Nihon Bijutsu Kōgei, no. 131 (September 1949), pp. 5-19.
Traditions of Japanese Art, Rosenfield, John M. and Shimada, Shūjirō (Cambridge, MA, 1970), no. 81.

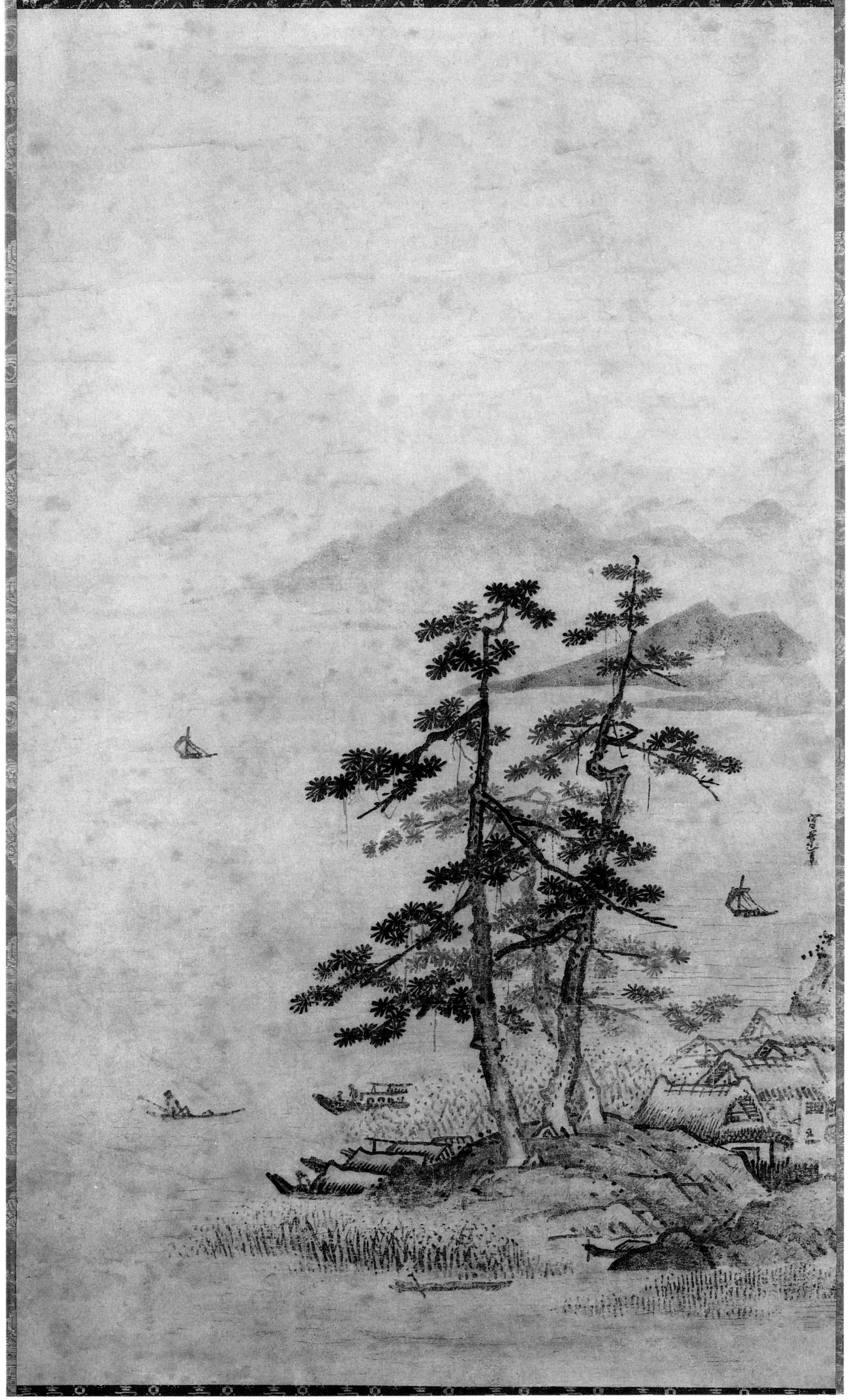

Part II

Zenga: Zen-Inspired Ink Paintings of the Edo Period

When the ambitious military adventurer, Oda Nobunaga (1534-1582), overthrew the last Ashikaga shogun, he also destroyed the power of many of the old monasteries in the Kyoto area. Nobunaga's successor, Toyotomi Hideyoshi (1536-1598), then broke up religious orders that were too big or powerful, and tried to put all sects under strict government control. The Tokugawa family, who established their rule in 1603 and maintained it until 1867, practiced a form of enlightened absolutism that was hostile to religious enthusiasm. Although the government and the new military aristocracy tolerated and even supported many Buddhist sects and Shinto shrines, the philosophical basis of the new regime was secular and Confucian. Priests still received official titles and honors, but they were excluded from participating in matters of state, and from leadership roles in higher education.

The Kanō family of artists had become the official painters to the Ashikaga shogunate during the Muromachi period (1333-1568). Successors to the Ashikaga shogunate continued the official recognition, and for nearly four hundred years, until the end of the Edo period in 1867, the Kanō family maintained its status as the nation's leading official painting school. The increasingly secular nature of the ruling classes influenced painting almost immediately, and although the Kanō artists were nominally loyal to the ideals of the Zen-inspired Southern Sung painting, they were also influenced by Chinese court paintings of the Ming dynasty (1368-1644). This painting reflected the regime's strong Neo-Confucian and anti-Buddhist bias. The triumph of the new class of military rulers—Nobunaga, Hideyoshi, the Tokugawa clan—ushered in a period of unprecedented ostentation and luxury in architecture and decorative painting. The austerity of the Zen monk artist had become old-fashioned.

This new sense of ostentation and pomp may still be seen in the Nijō Castle, the official residence and office of the shogunate in Kyoto, or in the enormous rococo mausoleum built in Nikkō, north of Edo, for the first Tokugawa shogun, Ieyasu (1542-1616). In painting, this taste was expressed in the colorful, ornate, gilded screens of the Kanō painters, or the more subdued Kyoto decorative school of Honami Kōetsu (1558-1637) and Tawaraya Sōtatsu (active ca 1600-1636).

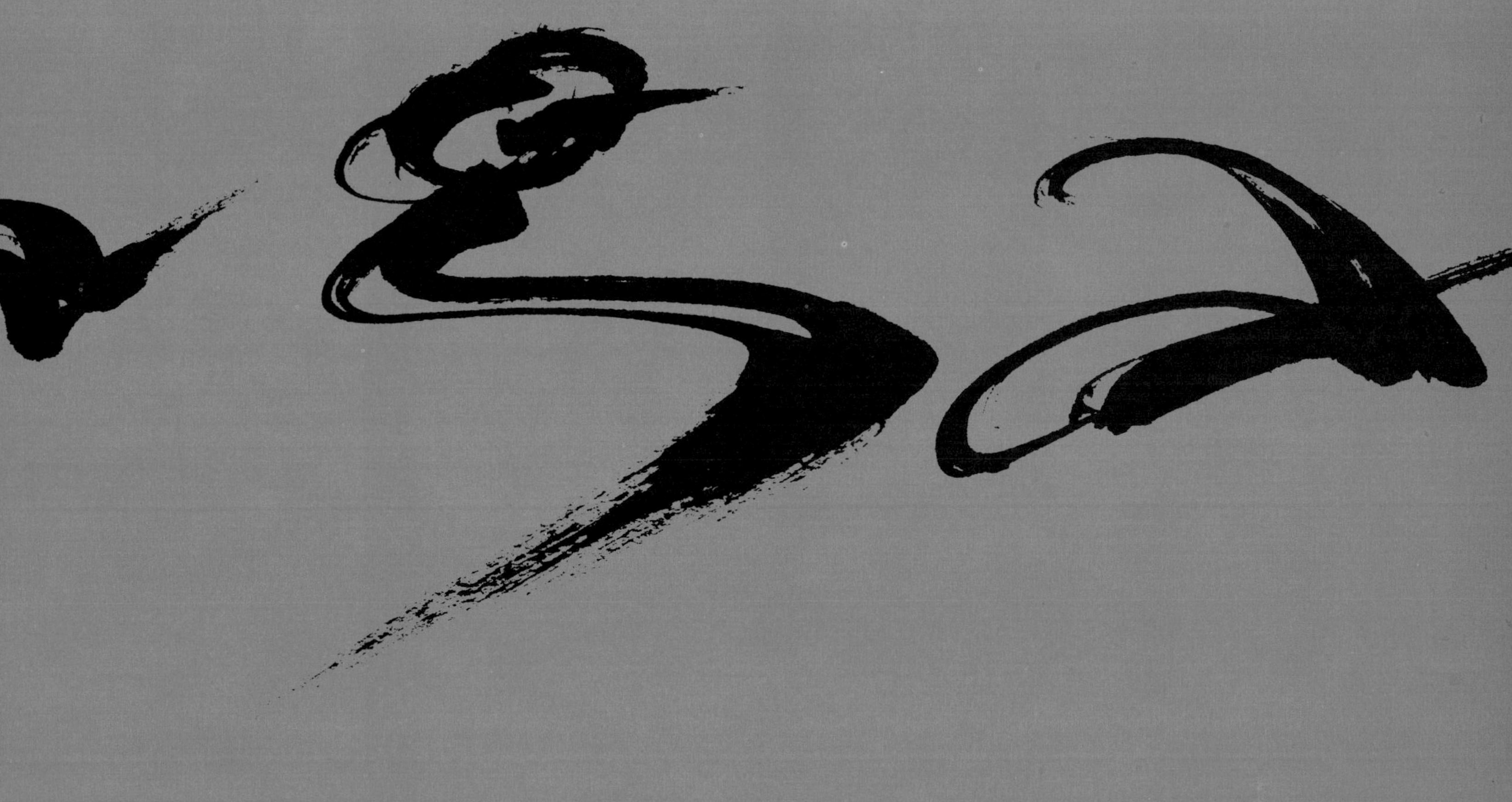

A countermovement arose to retain the spiritual and human values and customs long associated with the Zen tradition: austerity and self-denial in daily life, the regular practice of meditation, the devotion to the tea ceremony, the pursuit of ink painting. A number of Kyoto Zen monks, most of them associated with Daitoku-ji and its abbot, Takuan Shūhō (1573-1645), had resisted the efforts of the Tokugawa regime to bring the Zen community under its control. Takuan, who had allied himself with the Emperor Gomizunoo, another rebel against the new order of Japanese society, was forced into exile in northeast Honshu until he agreed to cooperate with the shogunate and was commissioned to open a Zen monastery in Tokyo, the eastern capital. Takuan and his circle had continued the tradition of the Zen monk painter, but their imagery was self-consciously primitive. They, and the courtiers who admired and emulated their painting, avoided the finesse and the elegant stylistic traits of the earlier monk artists; they sought instead a primal expression of Zen Buddhist values.

Throughout the Edo period, the tradition of the unsophisticated self-taught painter and calligrapher remained an important element in Japanese cultural life. Most of the men who practiced this style were in fact Zen monks and their work is referred to as Zenga. These monks were usually attached to small temple-hermitages in remote, rural areas. The Zenga mode, however, also appealed to monks of other Buddhist sects, to Shinto priests, and to courtiers with unconventional taste. Because its roots remained in Chinese Zen Buddhism, the Zenga mode attracted painters of the literati movement, whose ideological roots were also Chinese. Ikeno Taiga (nos. 39-41) in particular was deeply moved by Hakuin Ekaku (nos. 28-32) and his followers. Taiga is said to have kept in contact with them throughout his life. The rough bravura of the Hakuin style left an indelible trace upon Taiga's painting and calligraphy.

The works of the Zenga tradition, rough and self-consciously opposed to established canons of taste, were not esteemed by either traditional Japanese collectors and connoisseurs, or by the first Western students of Japanese art. However, the growing taste for modern expressionism in the West created a basis of understanding by which the work of a Hakuin might be understood. Modernism in the West, a rebellion against the established taste of the nineteenth-century salons and academies, made possible an insight into Japanese Zenga, a tradition which, far earlier, had denied the values of the Kanō and Tosa academies. In a semiapocryphal story set in Paris of the 1960s, Pablo Picasso stormed out of an exhibition of Japanese ink paintings because he thought that the works of Sengai (nos. 33-36) were a hoax; he thought, surely, Sengai could not have painted them without having seen Picasso's work first.

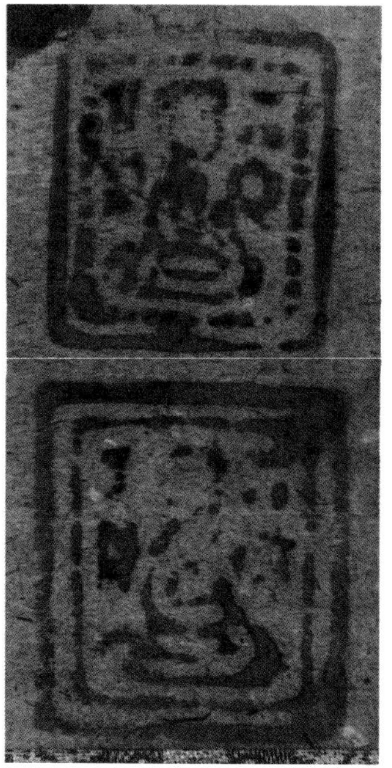

Detail

Konoe Nobutada
1565-1614

25

Kitano Tenjin Wearing a Chinese Robe

Hanging Scroll
Ink on paper
74.0 x 21.0 cm

Seals
Illegible but considered as Nobutada's seals

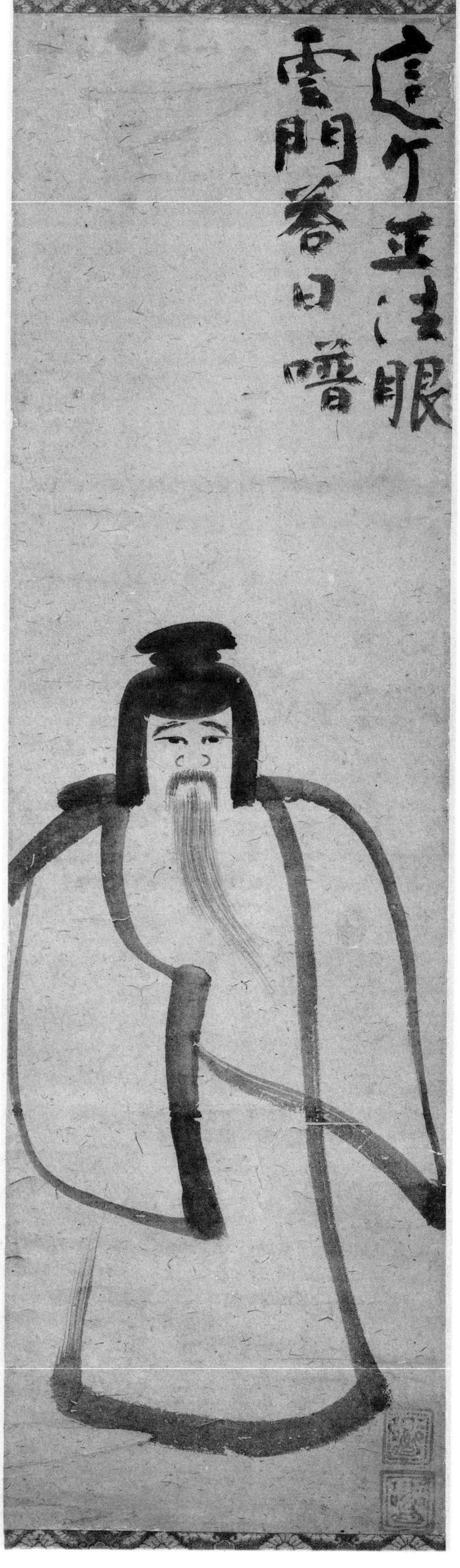

The great courtier, Konoe Nobutada, who served successively as Minister of the Left, Minister of the Right, and Regent, was also one of the three master calligraphers of the early Edo period (the other two were Shōkadō Shōjō and Honami Kōetsu). Member of one of the ancient hereditary aristocratic families who traced their roots back into the Heian period, Nobutada is said to have painted a picture of Tenjin (Sugawara no Michizane, 845-903) every morning as his daily devotional exercise; hence the designation of these pictures as Nikka Tenjin (the Daily Tenjin). Dozens of extant versions show the same figure; they vary only in size, the present painting being one of the smaller ones. Each one bears a different inscription, seemingly suited either to the occasion or to the person for whom the painting was intended as a gift.

The story of Tenjin was known to every educated Japanese of the period and, indeed, is still known to every Japanese today. The great scholar Sugawara no Michizane rose to become Minister of the Right, even though he was not a member of the Fujiwara family that dominated the imperial court of his day. The Fujiwara conspired against him, and had him banished to Kyushu, where he died in exile. Shortly thereafter, plagues visited first Kyushu and then the nation. Finally, in 942, the daughter of the priest of a Shinto shrine in Kyoto had a vision which revealed to her that all the calamities were the work of Michizane's wrathful spirit, who could be appeased only by a shrine built in his memory. The Tenjin Shrine still stands in the Kitano district in Kyoto, and branch shrines can be found all over Japan. Gradually, Michizane became the Shinto tutelary deity of learning and scholarship. In addition, he was credited with having helped introduce Zen to Japan. According to Zen apocrypha, Michizane, in his exile in Kyushu, miraculously flew to China, where he was instructed by the great Zen sage of the Sung period, Wu-chun Shih-fan. In an equally miraculous return to Japan, he brought the Zen teachings back with him.

Devotion to Michizane was widespread in Japan in Nobutada's time, especially among scholars, calligraphers, and poets, whose patron saint Tenjin had become. Nobutada may have been drawn to his daily prayer-painting by more than religious zeal. The parallel between Michizane's fate and his own life must have been obvious to him. Like Michizane, Nobutada was an all-powerful minister, but, just as Michizane and his emperor had been dominated, humiliated, and finally destroyed by the Fujiwara, so Nobutada and the imperial court were humiliated by the new military regime of the Tokugawa family. Nobutada worked to prevent the Tokugawa from completely subjugating the emperor and the imperial house. He unsuccessfully opposed the marriage of a Tokugawa daughter into the imperial family, a marriage which, when it occurred, ensured that future rulers would have Tokugawa blood and be dominated by the Edo regime. It was precisely through such marriages that the Fujiwara had ensured their control over Heian-period emperors; and it was because of his opposition to the Fujiwara that Michizane incurred their wrath and was ultimately destroyed. The Daily Tenjin was thus clearly both manifesto—in a form that could not be suppressed or even censured—and prayer for vindication.

Nobutada's Tenjin breaks new ground in Japanese painting. Although Tenjin paintings were plentiful in the Muromachi period, they showed the deity either in formal and elaborate Chinese monk's costume or in ceremonial Japanese court robes. Nobutada employed the reductionist Zenga style in his Tenjin version, for he, like the Emperor Goyozei, was attached to the rough natural simplicity of Zen taste, and not to the colorful gilded screens which the military men commissioned from the Kanō painters for their new castles and mansions. Nobutada's Tenjin, a rough outline done in a few sweeping strokes, employs distinct ink contrasts between the black of the cap, for instance, and the lighter gray of the garment's downward lines. Into this figure, which has the calligraphic character of an ideogram, Nobutada then painted, with the simplest strokes, a human face of strong character. The eyes are indicated with the barest minimum of lines—the upper lid and eyeball—yet convey considerable humanity and warmth. Nobutada's Tenjin has nothing of the supernatural in him; he is a man, of wisdom, of compassion, and of serenity. Judging by the other surviving Nobutada Tenjins, this painting may originally have been wider on both sides; the other versions have a few centimeters of blank paper on either side of the garment. The inscription, which reads in the Zen manner from right to left, alludes to the sayings of a celebrated monk of the T'ang period, Yün-men Wen-yen (862-949), whose insights were collected into a series of laconic responses to kōan-like questions:

The eye of the true Dharma?
Unmon answered, "As usual."

Published
400 Years of Zen Painting, Okabe, Hisashi, exhibition catalogue (London, 1976), pl. 2.

References
Bokubi, no. 207 (January 1971), pp. 2-36.
A History of Zen Buddhism, Dumoulin, Heinrich (New York, 1963), pp. 108-110.
Kanei no Sampitsu, Haruna, Yoshishige (Kyoto, 1971), pl. 26, pp. 150-163, 212-213.
Kokka, no. 408 (November 1924), p. 301.

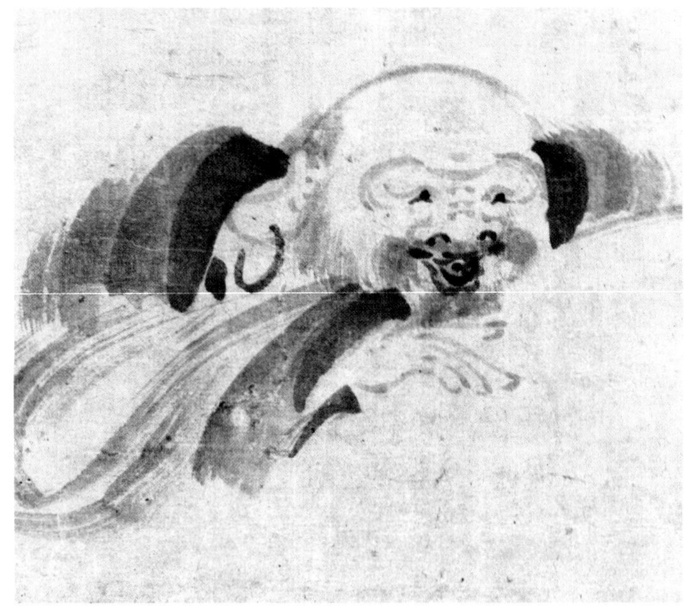

Detail

26

Hotei (Pu-tai) Peering over his Bag

Hanging Scroll
Ink on paper
64.5 x 30.5 cm

Fūgai Ekun
1568-1654

The origins of Hotei (Chinese: Pu-tai) lie in half-historical, half-legendary accounts of Ch'i-tzu, a Chinese monk of the tenth century, who wandered the countryside of Chekiang province, delighting people with his simplicity, his good humor, and his comical appearance. He had a rotund belly and an equally rotund bag in which he carried a random assortment of useless things: feathers and odd rocks, half-gnawed chicken bones, and dried flowers. He claimed, moreover, to be an incarnation of Maitreya, the Buddha of the Future. As a popular deity he became one of the twelve gods of good fortune bringing gifts to children and luck to merchants in speculative ventures. He also became a favorite subject for Zen monk painters. Like the poets Han-shan and Shih-te (Japanese: Kanzan and Jittoku), he became an emblem of innocence and simplicity, of the approach to enlightenment through everyday experience, and of a life without wordly cares.

The portly figure of Hotei is here amply suggested by his capacious bag over which he peers, an impish grin spreading across his full, round face. With characteristic brevity the artist has set down the salient features from which the viewer can instantly recognize the intended images: the bald Hotei, his bag, and his staff. The stubby arcs bracketing his face describe his shoulders and imply the presence of a robed figure behind the bulging bag. The weight of these insistent curves is countered by the sweeping expanse of the bag and the slender line that encloses it. In a manner reminiscent of a haboku landscape (no. 10), the impressionistic depiction of the figure is given focus and unity by emphasizing such details as the fingers and the grin.

The Zen monk Fūgai Ekun played an important role as a transition figure in Japanese religious as well as artistic history. A native of Kōzuki province north of modern Tokyo, Fūgai started religious training in his home district but became, apparently at a fairly early age, abbot of Seigan-ji, an important and powerful temple not far from the present resort town of Atami, southwest of Tokyo. At an uncertain date and under obscure circumstances, he left the temple and officialdom and became an itinerant missionary who often lived in caves, hence his popular name Ana Fūgai (Cave Fūgai), by which he is also distinguished from another and later Fūgai, the Zen priest and Nanga painter, Fūgai Honkō (1779-1847). Ana Fūgai did not, however, withdraw from the world. On the contrary, he sought to spread Zen doctrine to the common people, and he painted most of his pictures for them. Apparently he would give pictures to all who called on him, or came to him for advice and solace. His fondness for the Hotei motif reflects the similarity of his own chosen role to that of his Chinese predecessor.

As here, he often painted on coarse, rustic paper. Repeating the same images over and over again, he attained great fluency in a limited range of themes. His calligraphy is extremely eccentric and difficult to read, with overtones of the ancient "flying white." His inscription here reads, from right to left:

Who, in this world, can discuss [him]?
Abundant good fortune is greater than the size of his body,
What is this old guest laughing at?
He is the only one on the road.

Published
Bokubi, no. 104, special issue on Fūgai Ekun (January 1961), p. 65 (seal and signature).
Bokubi, no. 101, special issue on Fūgai Ekun (October 1960), pl. 54.

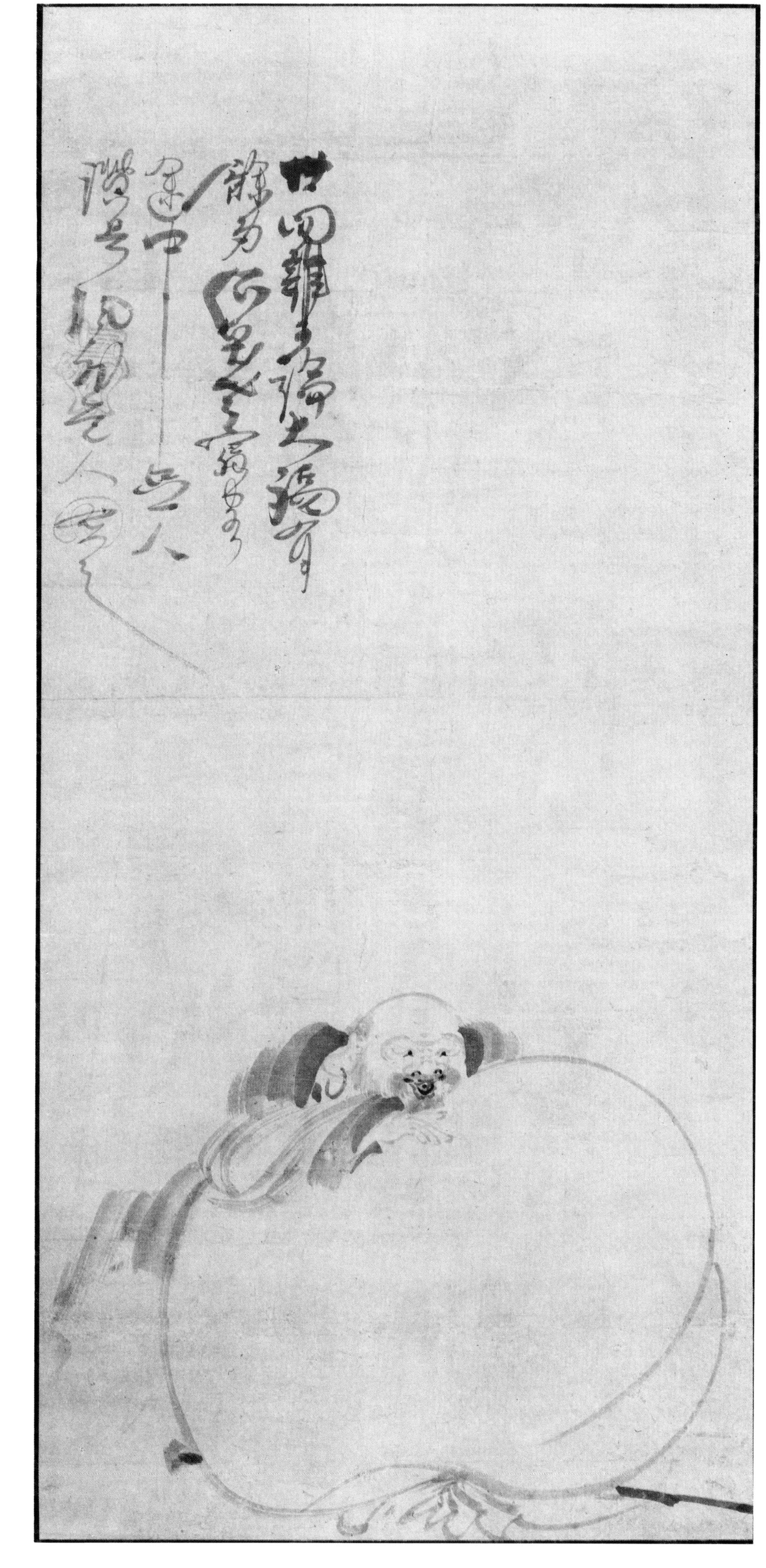

27

Bodhidharma Crossing the Yang-tze River on a Reed

Hanging Scroll
Ink on paper
80.1 x 31.9 cm

Signature
Fūgai

Seal
Fūgai

Fūgai Ekun
1568-1654

Depicting the same prominent Zen legend that appears in the Bunson tryptich (no. 15), Fūgai represents Bodhidharma in a dramatically simplified manner. All the elements in this painting are traditional, including, for instance, the bangles around the saint's ankles. The garment which actually defines the figure is drawn with simple lines: one stroke from the top of the cap to the front flap; another from the clavicle across the chest to a point in front; and three auxilliary strokes, one to define the opening for the face, one to give the garment and the figure three-dimensionality; and one, at the bottom, to give a hint of an undergarment. Within each stroke are strong contrasts in ink tonality, from the heavy wet ink of shoulder and cap to the hairline strokes near the feet, to the alternating stroke of the outermost line in front. Piercing eyes dominate the face—a characteristic of Fūgai's paintings of Bodhidharma—and seem to follow the beholder. They are shaded by heavy brows, done in a simple almost totally straight stroke that extends the brow far down into the cheek. The expression is one of power and total concentration.
Fūgai's life and career spanned two different worlds. His origins were in the late Muromachi and the early Momoyama eras and their cultures and societies. He was apparently trained in traditional Muromachi painting styles. There are extant from his hand a small number of landscapes and flower-and-bird paintings executed in a somewhat simplified, but still recognizable, style of the leading Kyoto master Sōami (1485-1525). We do not know if they represent an early stage in his career, or if Fūgai continued occasionally to paint in a more sophisticated style all his life. His more typical work, his Zenga paintings of Hotei and Bodhidharma, still show strong traces of Muromachi ink painting.
The eccentric style of his calligraphy, although legible, is strongly pictorial in character. The inscription here, reading from right to left, refers to Bodhidharma's visit to Nanking and the Liang kingdom and his northern flight to the Shao-lin-tse. The inscription reads:

Moving dragon-clouds choose to cover the country of Liang,
When he wants to ask the reason, the violent thunder roars,
Lightly flies and stops at the Shao-lin-t'ai.

With the inscription, Fūgai painted this.

References
Bokubi, no. 146 (March–April 1965), pl. 39.
Bokubi, no. 104, special issue on Fūgai Ekun (January 1961), pls. 101, 105-107, 109, pp. 63-68.

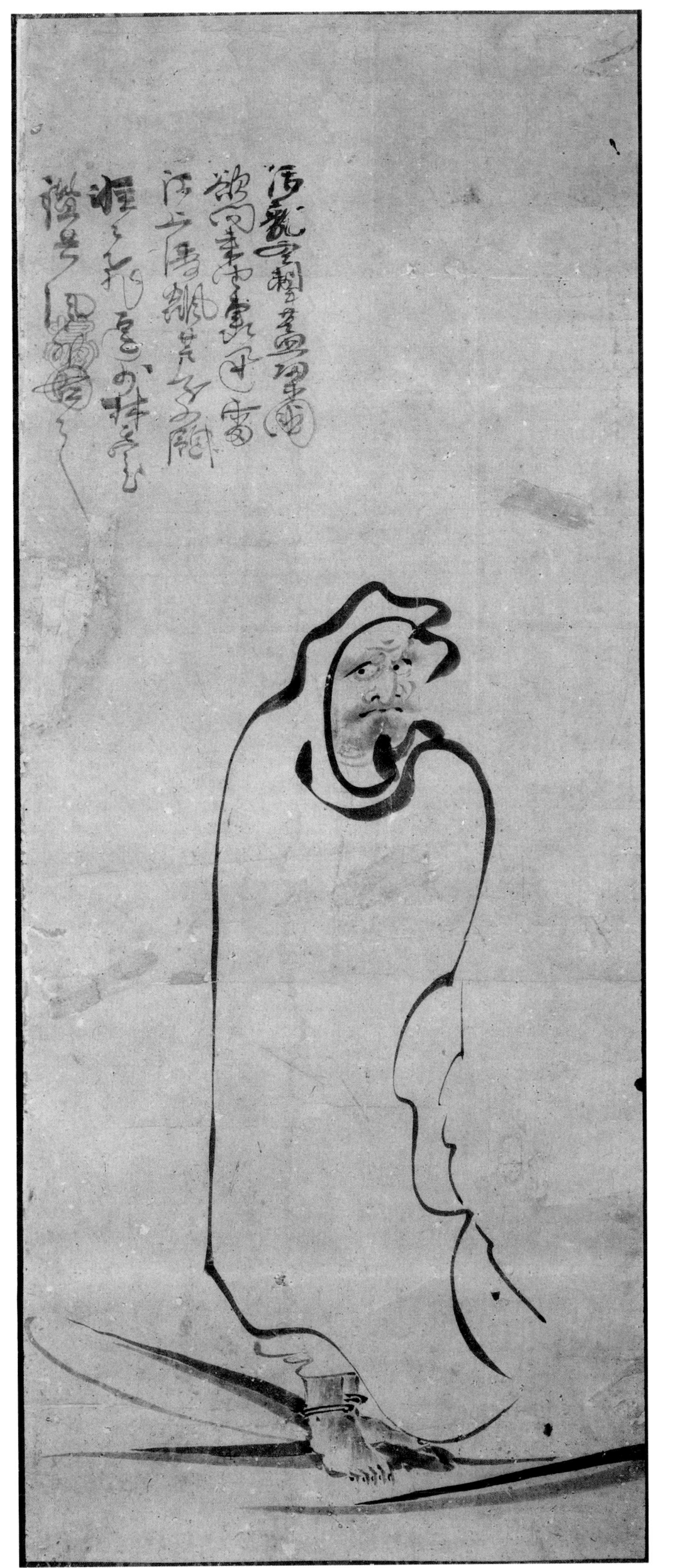

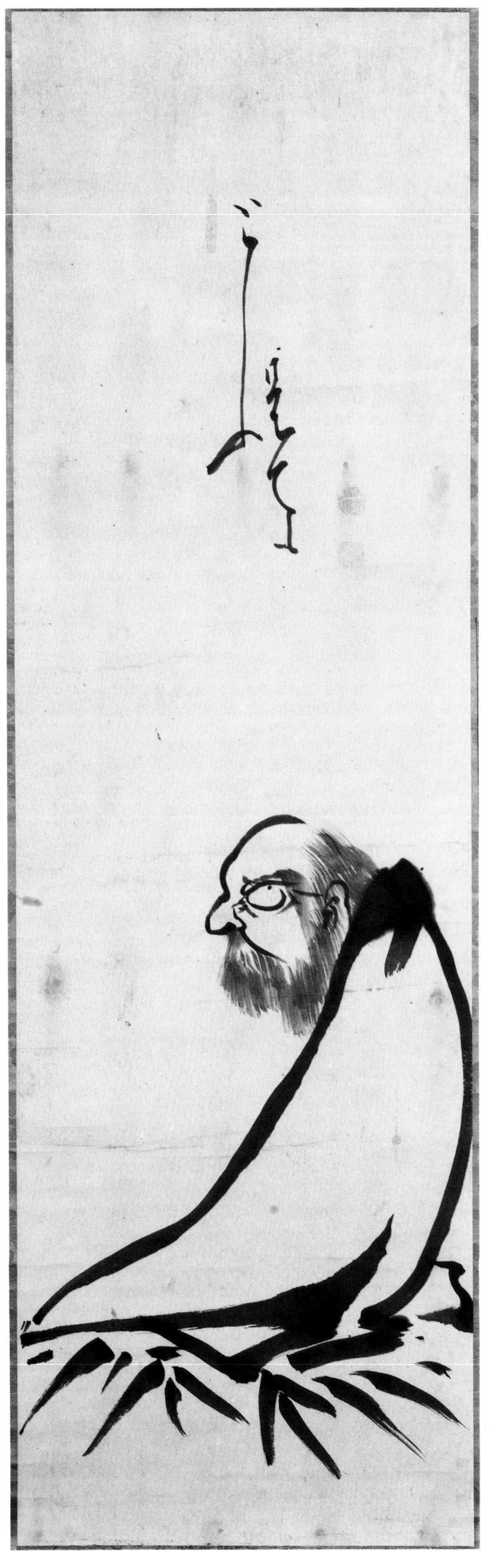

Hakuin Ekaku
1685-1768

28

Bodhidharma Seated on Grass

Hanging Scroll
Ink on paper
92.0 x 27.2 cm

Seals
Kokani
Hakuin
Ekaku

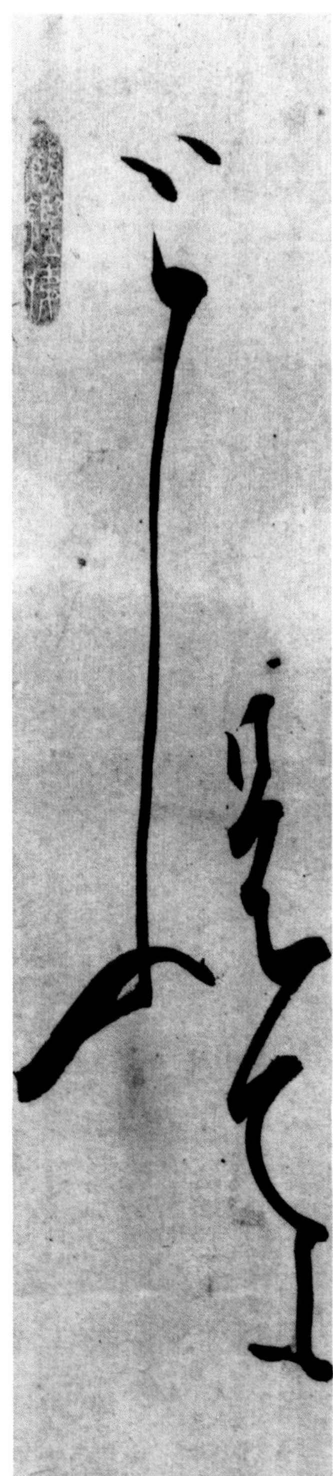

This image of Bodhidharma, shown in profile seated on a mat of loosely strewn grass, is the earliest of the three Hakuin paintings of the First Patriarch included in the Sansō exhibition. Done when the artist was in his sixties, it was composed simply and directly, like a Chinese character. Fewer than a half-dozen strokes of the brush outline the body of the patriarch; another dozen strokes indicate the mat of loose grass. The oversized head is defined chiefly by the single line of the forehead and nose, as well as by the bulging eyes. The beard, demonstrating the patriarch's Indian origins, is strongly emphasized; Chinese Zen Buddhists frequently characterized Bodhidharma and also Śākyamuni as a red-bearded, blue-eyed Western barbarian.

The seat of grass is a symbol that Bodhidharma shares with other Buddhist deities in the Zen tradition. It was derived from an episode in the legendary biography of Śākyamuni, when Indra, the lord of the Vedic gods disguised as a grass-cutter, gave freshly cut grass to the Buddha-to-be when he sat down for the meditation that was to lead to his enlightenment. Not only Śākyamuni, but Avalokiteśvara (no. 4) as well, sat upon a grassy seat. The use of the motif for the First Patriarch indicates his increasingly exalted status. Hakuin's paintings of Bodhidharma stress the patriarch's spiritual and psychological energies, his fiery discipline and enormous intellectual strength. The paintings also manage to capture the ironic or paradoxical feature in the Chinese Zen characterization of the saint; he is a most human and fallible mortal as well.

The inscription above the patriarch, one that Hakuin frequently used, is written with a supreme sense of artistry and restraint in a small, carefully controlled passage of hiragana:

dō mitemo (no matter how you look at it, … [this is Bodhidharma]).

Its meaning, only hinted or suggested in this fragmentary sentence, is that the Buddhist Law, or dharma, no matter how you look at it, is embodied in the First Patriarch.

The seal used by Hakuin at the beginning of the inscription (Kokani) has strong doctrinal significance, for it was taken from one of the celebrated short responses of the T'ang Zen master, Yün-men (died 949). He often uttered cryptic aphorisms or exhortations in answer to questions or dramatic situations. The seal can be translated: **ko** (turn around), **kan** (look back, or examine oneself), **i** (shout).

References
Bokubi, no. 102 (November 1960), pls. 19, 21.
Bokubi, no. 90 (September 1959), pl. 26.
Bokubi, no. 78 (August 1958), pls. 24, 63.
Bokubi, no. 77 (June-July 1958), pls. 85, 111, 143, 144.
Hakuin, Takeuchi, Naoji (Tokyo, 1964), pl. 323.

Detail

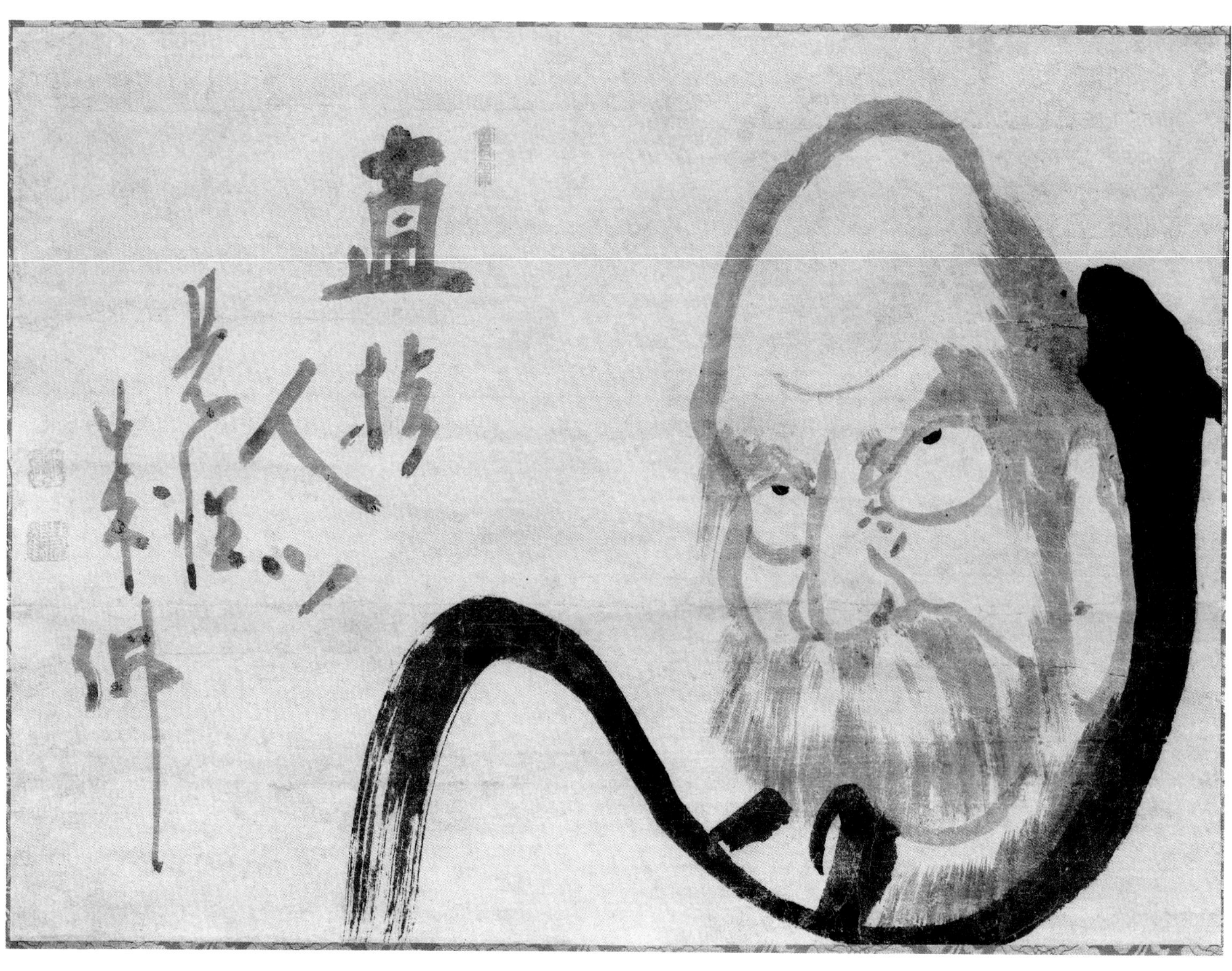

Hakuin Ekaku
1685-1768

29

Bodhidharma

Hanging Scroll
Ink on paper
55.4 x 73.5 cm

Seals
Rinzai Shōshū
Hakuin
Ekaku

Detail

Like a Byzantine image of the Pantocrator, the great head and staring eyes of Bodhidharma suggest an immensely energetic, all-powerful being. At this late moment in a centuries-long chain of portrait-like images, the legendary First Patriarch of Zen Buddhism in China and Japan has been converted into a superhuman entity, and yet the sunken cheeks and the expression of slight whimsy in his eyes also suggest the ironical Chinese descriptions of Bodhidharma as a broken-toothed old Hindu. The sense of Promethean energies that emanate from this image, however, are really those of the painter himself, for Hakuin Ekaku was one of the most decisive and deeply inspired figures in the religious and cultural history of the Edo period.

Hakuin's extraordinary biography is easily accessible to Western readers through the writings of Heinrich Dumoulin and Philip Yampolsky. Briefly, the Zen master was born in 1685 in the tiny village of Hara in Suruga province in eastern Honshu, and even though he traveled widely during his lifetime, he remained loyal to his native village. He resisted involvements with the great political, commercial, and cultural centers of eighteenth-century Japan: Edo, Nagoya, Osaka, Kyoto, and Nagasaki. Instead, he concerned himself with the spiritual and material well-being of the peasants and villagers of his native region, and also of the hundreds of monks and laymen who came to him in his later years to hear his sermons, receive his counsel and instruction, and, possibly, to obtain a drawing or calligraphy from his brush. Hakuin's childhood traumas and religious visions are described in his autobiography (the **Itsu made-gusa**), his epistles, and a chronicle by his disciple, Tōrei (died 1792). In his fifteenth year he became a monk at the Zen temple of Shōin-ji in his native village, and began the quest that led ultimately to his attainment of enlightenment after a long period of angya (wandering in extreme poverty from teacher to teacher), questioning (the Great Doubt), and nervous breakdowns. A serious and scholarly student of Zen practice and doctrine, he fixed his attention on the kōan and later used them in his own teaching. Painting and calligraphy came to play an important role in the later stages of his life, when he found they were an effective means of concentrating his own attention and that of other people on serious symbolic and doctrinal issues.

Hundreds of paintings and calligraphies survive from the last three decades of Hakuin's life. While a wide range of themes are depicted, the constant repetition of certain motifs afforded Hakuin the opportunity to perfect sharply concise, visually compelling images without using the highly sophisticated techniques of the professional painter. The Hakuin paintings in the Sansō Collection clearly demonstrate that the aesthetic sensibilities of this master were highly developed, but in a personal and innovative form.

Images of the First Patriarch were among Hakuin's most favored subjects. He was especially fond of the type shown here, a close-up view with an enlarged head and neck, and the hands obscured beneath the robe. Here he seems to have begun by painting the head and beard in pale gray ink, and then adding the sweeping calligraphic stroke of the robe. He pressed his brush firmly at the top of the neck and then, in one dramatic sweep of the hand, defined the robe, ending in a trailing edge of the split hairs of the brush.

Hakuin added the inscription, carefully and in congruence with the design of the image of the old saint. It contains the last line (jikishi ninshin; kenshō jōbutsu) of a famous four-line stanza attributed to Bodhidharma. While scholars have recently determined that it was probably composed, not by Bodhidharma, but by someone during the T'ang period, nonetheless it summarizes basic concepts of Zen Buddhism:

A special transmission outside the scriptures;
No dependence upon words and letters;
Directly pointing at the mind of man;
Seeing into his own nature, man attains Buddhahood.

Published
Hakuin Meihin-ten, Takeuchi, Naoji, exhibition catalogue, Niigata Art Museum (Niigata, 1975), pl. 15.

References
Bokubi, no. 90 (September 1959), pls. 43, 58, 70, 71.
Bokubi, no. 77 (June-July 1958), pls. 30, 31, 154.
Hakuin, Takeuchi, Naoji (Tokyo, 1964), pls. 312-319.
A History of Zen Buddhism, Dumoulin, Heinrich (New York, 1963), p. 67.
The Zen Master Hakuin: Selected Writings, Yampolsky, Philip B. (New York, 1971).

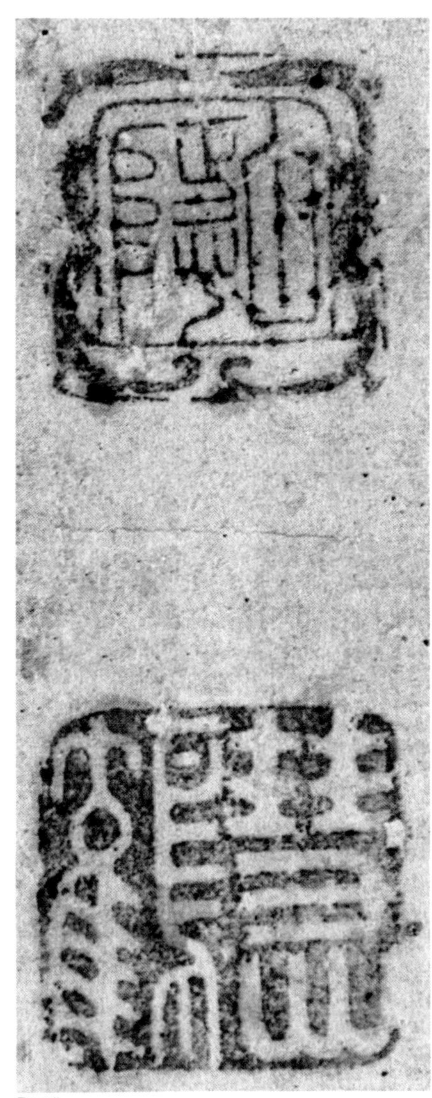

Detail

Hakuin Ekaku
1685-1768

30

Meditating Bodhidharma

Hanging Scroll
Ink on paper
101.4 x 27.2 cm

Seals
Rinzai Shōshū
Hakuin
Ekaku

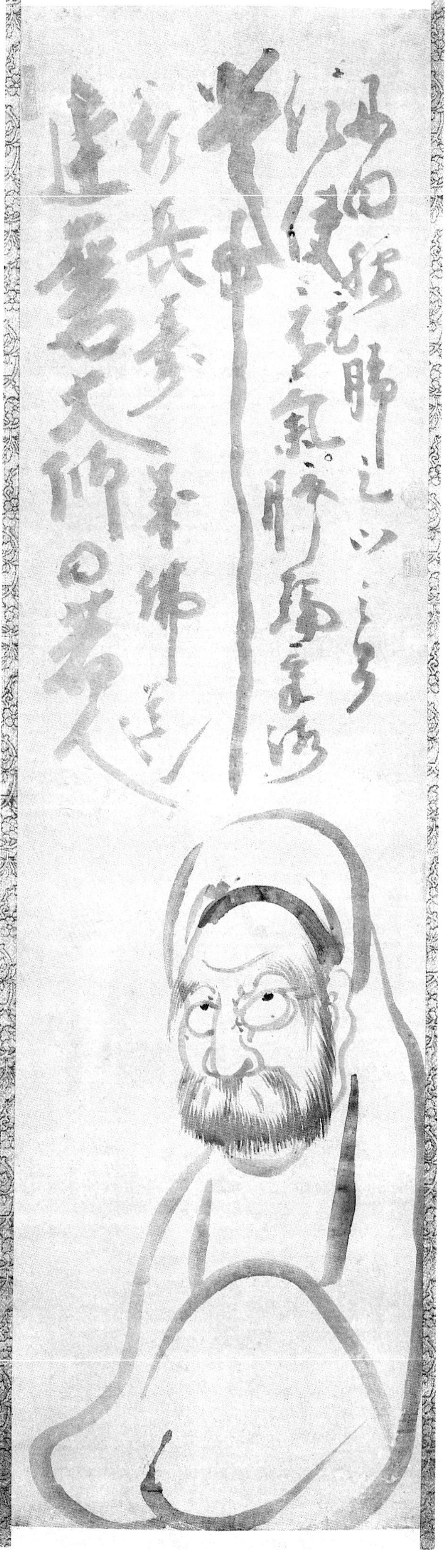

This half-figure image of Bodhidharma was painted in soft gray ink and the inscription above it is perfectly unified in composition and execution. Hakuin's text, unusual among his dozens of paintings of the founder of the Zen sect, affirms the importance of seated meditation, the fundamental physical and psychological experience of all Zen adepts:

Bodhidharma, the Great Master, said: "If a man desires long life and the attainment of Buddhahood, he must
constantly concentrate his vitality in the part of the abdomen below the navel."

This is the latest of the three Hakuin paintings of Bodhidharma in the Sansō Collection. The few lines suggest, rather than define, a body sitting on the floor, the legs and arms barely indicated. Only the face is fully articulated, with the same aquiline nose, the same arched eyebrows, the same fold across the forehead that characterize all of Hakuin's Bodhidharmas. The beard, however, was established by a rough wet brush with the hairs split apart, imbuing the image with a quality of thoughtfulness and repose that make it an outstanding example of Hakuin's many portrayals of Bodhidharma.

References
Bokubi, no. 78 (August 1958), pl. 21.
Bokubi, no. 77 (June-July 1958), pls. 100, 168.
Hakuin, Takeuchi, Naoju (Tokyo, 1964), pls. 326, 327.

31

Rice Threshing Mill

Hanging Scroll
Ink on paper
32.5 x 41.4 cm

Seals
Kokani
Ekaku
Hakuin

Boldly painted in silhouette is this karausu, a cantilever device pushed by the foot in order to hull rice in a round mortar of stone or wood. Hakuin's brush, heavily charged with black ink, imbued the image with the direct vigor and energy of a great Chinese character. The inscription, however, was written in a wiry, eccentric mode of calligraphy typical of Hakuin's work in his sixties. The context adds an ironic, unexpected twist entirely characteristic of Japanese Buddhist modes of thinking in the Rinzai (Chinese: Lin-chi) tradition to which Hakuin belonged.

Even in this highly abstract image, Zen adepts of Hakuin's time would have recognized a reference to a semi-legendary episode in the life of Hui-neng (638-713), the Sixth Patriarch of the Chinese Zen tradition. The barely literate Hui-neng had worked at the most humble tasks in the rice threshing room of the East Mountain Monastery in Hupeh province; even so, he possessed the highest degree of insight and, after much controversy, was chosen to succeed the Fifth Patriarch, Hung-jen (601-674)—events described in the Sixth Patriarch's **Platform Sutra.**

Hakuin's inscription, however, refers not to those events but to a brothel, the Naraya, in Otsu city—the pilgrimage and crossroads town a day's journey northeast of Kyoto—and makes a quasi-vulgar comment:

Coming to
The Naraya in Otsu,
One also learns
To pound a mortar.

This irreverent play on images brings to mind the activities of the flamboyant monk, Ikkyū (1395-1481), who openly violated the rules of monastic behavior in his eating, drinking, and sexual affairs. He intended to dramatize the hypocrisy of monks who adhered superficially to rules of propriety but who denied the deeper meanings of the faith. A saintly man like Ikkyū indulging purposely in unsaintly activities demonstrates the Buddhist conception of nonduality by which the enlightened vision sees a fundamental unity lying behind the appearance of great distinctions, such as the sacred and the profane, truth and falsehood, beauty and ugliness, and ethical and unethical behavior. Nowhere in Hakuin's biographies or writings is there evidence that he himself actually engaged in carnal activities. His poem, however, which has the distinct flavor of a folk song in its 7-5-7-5 metrical structure, establishes that a visit to the Naraya brothel is a suitable response to a reference to Hui-neng's biography.

References
Bokubi, no. 102 (November 1960), pl. 41.
Bokubi, no. 90 (September 1959), pl. 49.
Bokubi, no. 77 (June-July 1958), pl. 82.
Hakuin, Awakawa, Yasuichi (Kyoto, 1956), pl. 19.
A History of Zen Buddhism, Dumoulin, Heinrich (New York, 1963), pp. 82-83.
The Platform Sūtra of the Sixth Patriarch, Yampolsky, Philip B. (trans.) (New York, 1967).

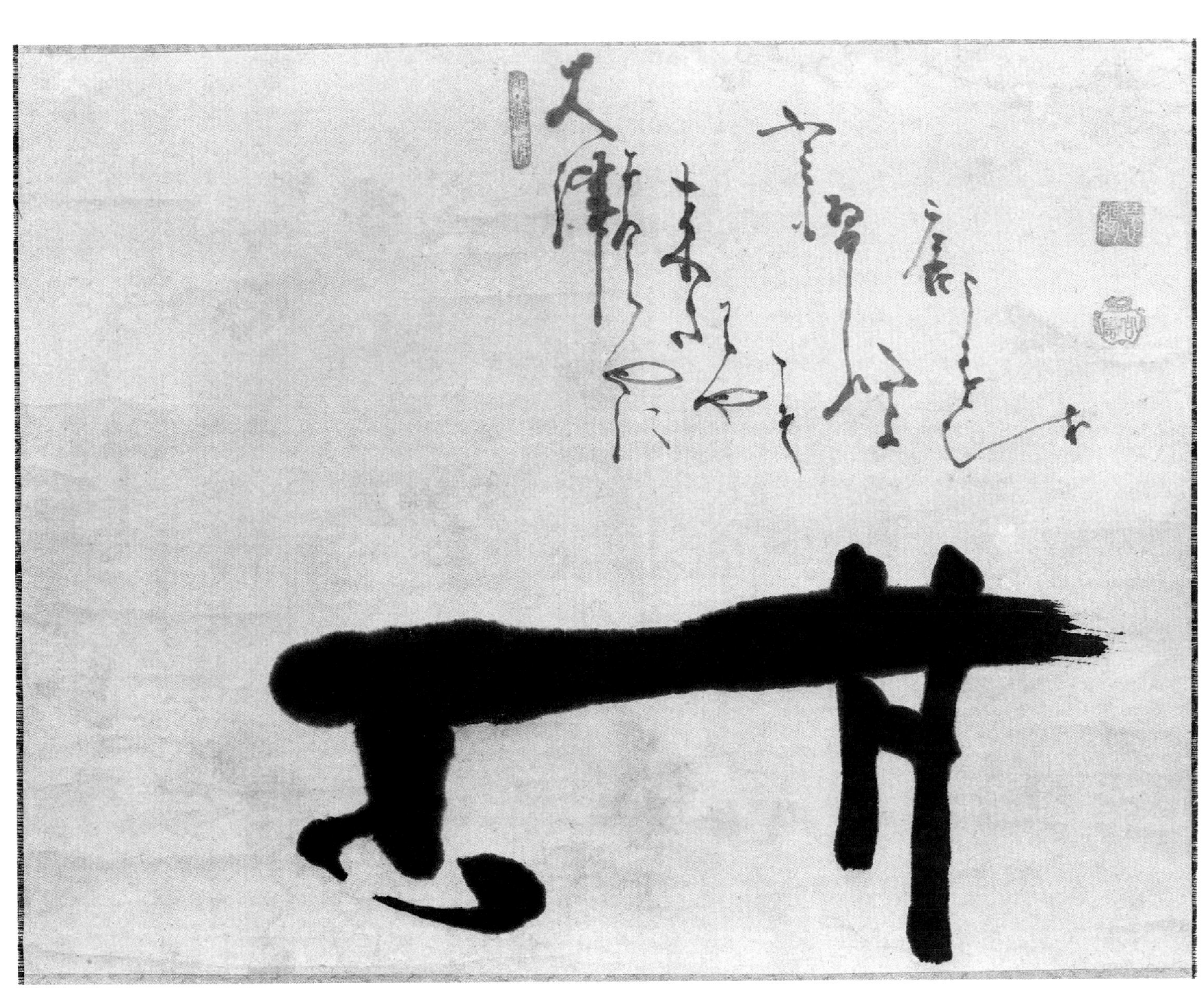

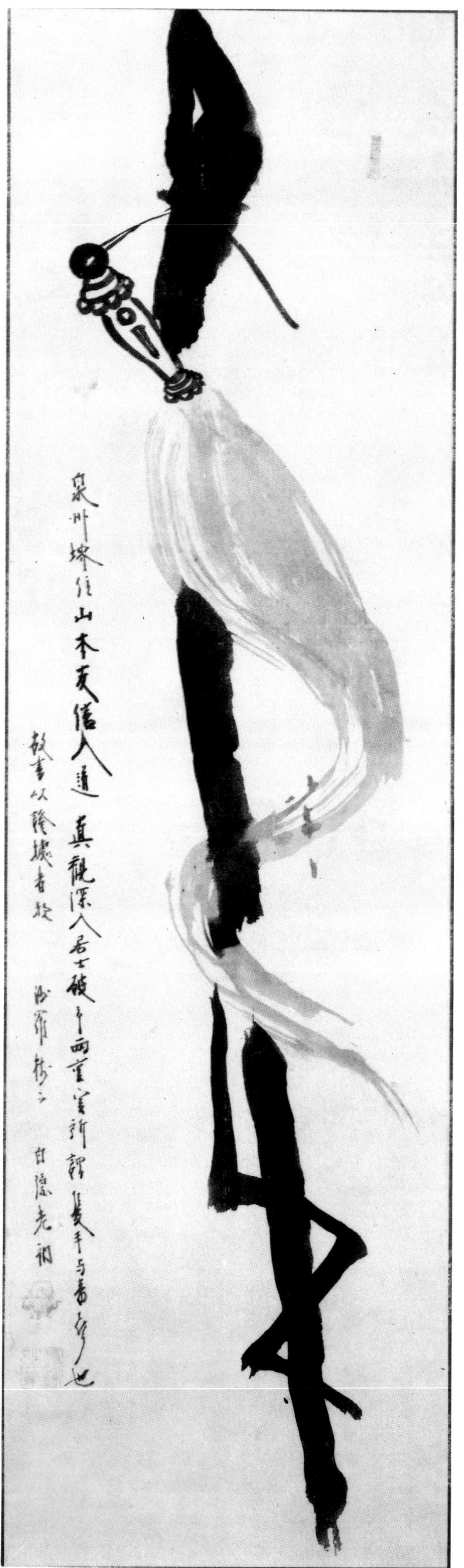

Detail

Hakuin Ekaku
1685-1768

32

Monk's Staff and Fly Whisk

Hanging Scroll
Ink on paper
126.4 x 36.4 cm

Seals
Rinzai Shōshū
Hakuin
Ekaku no shō

Judging by the seals, this work must date from the 1760s, the last phase of Hakuin's career. It is an example of a certificate issued when a Zen student monk had completed his training under a roshi (senior master). The inscription, written by Hakuin in a careful, legible manner, may be summarized as follows:

The nyūdō (initiate) Yamamoto Tomonobu of Sakai in
Senshū (Izumi, east of modern Osaka), a sage of true
vision and insight, solved the double kōan, the
so-called sekishu onjō (the sound of one hand).
Therefore I have written this as a signed certificate.
Beneath the śal tree.

The old monk Hakuin

This painting is one of dozens of similar painted certificates that have survived from Hakuin's brush. It depicts a long flowing fly whisk made of white horsehair in a wooden handle and tied to a crooked wooden staff. Both objects serve as emblems of legitimacy in a monk's process of graduation from the tutelage of his master; both have symbolic and historic overtones of great richness. The staff plays a prominent role in the legendary history of the Chinese Zen sect. The monk Yün-men (died 949), for example, one of the most celebrated masters of the T'ang period, used his staff to strike his student novices and to symbolize basic Zen concepts. On one occasion he referred to his staff in a lecture on Buddhist epistemology, saying that some Buddhists say the staff is unreal or illusory but that he sees it as a thing in itself. The staff is a staff. "My staff has transformed itself into a dragon and swallowed up the universe! Where are the mountains, the rivers, and the great world?" Other monks in his tradition used the staff as a graphic symbol of the doctrine itself, whereas the fly whisk served as a talisman handed down from master to pupil. The pioneer Japanese Zen monk, Eisai (1141-1215) brought back to Japan a fly whisk and rice bowl, as well as a staff and begging bowl, given to him by his Chinese Zen teacher when the latter granted him his seal of enlightenment.

The man, Yamamoto Tomonobu, to whom the Sansō Collection certificate by Hakuin was issued remains unidentified. The document notes, however, that he had successfully responded to the most difficult kōan of Hakuin's tradition, invented by Hakuin himself. In full, it reads:

Ika naru ka kore sekishu no onjō.
(What is the sound of the clapping of a single hand?)

Published
Hakuin, Takeuchi, Naoji (Tokyo, 1964), pl. 506.

References
Bokubi, no. 90 (September 1959), pl. 49.
Bokubi, no. 79 (September-October 1958), pls. 61, 62.
Bokubi, no. 78 (August 1958), pls. 16, 44.
Bokubi, no. 77 (June-July 1958), pl. 29.
Two Zen Classics: Mumonkan and Hekiganroku, Sekida, Katsuki (trans.) (New York and Tokyo, 1977).
Zen Dust, Muira, Isshū and Sasaki, Ruth Fuller (New York, 1966).
The Zen Master Hakuin: Selected Writings, Yampolsky, Philip B. (New York, 1971), pp. 163-166.

Detail

33

Suigetsu (Water-Moon) Kannon

Hanging Scroll
Ink on silk
85.8 x 32.0 cm

Signature
Fūsō Saisho Zenkutsu Jikūko Gai

Seal
Sengai

Sengai Gibon
1750-1837
Dated in accordance with 1830

As in the paintings by Isshi and Chūan Shinkō (nos. 3, 4), the Bodhisattva of Compassion is seated in meditation at the edge of the ocean. Here the deity gazes at the partial reflection of the moon in the water, as the waterfall behind her plunges to the earth. Sengai's painting, in contrast to the older ones, is sketch-like. Absent are the careful modulation of ink washes and the calligraphic handling of line quality. This painting is far simpler in composition and brushwork, and yet it is artistically one of the most sophisticated and complex works in Sengai Gibon's entire oeuvre. Dated in accordance with 1830, when Sengai was in his seventy-ninth year, it testifies to the remarkable mental and physical prowess of a man of such advanced age.

When Sengai Gibon died in 1837, at the age of eighty-seven, he was one of the most honored and revered Buddhist prelates in Japan. He had twice been the abbot of Shōfuku-ji monastery in Hakata, the oldest Zen monastery in Japan, founded in 1195 by the monk Myōan Eisai upon his return from China. During his abbacy, Sengai succeeded in rebuilding the temple halls, restoring records, and refurbishing the monastery grounds. He retired as abbot in 1811, at the age of sixty-one, and began only then to devote himself to painting and calligraphy. His interest in those arts, however, can be traced back to his years of training under the monk, Gessen, at Myōki-an near modern Yokohama. For thirteen years, Sengai studied with Gessen, and after the master's death, sought a suitable place to settle. A former student of Gessen invited him to Shōfuku-ji in the far western part of the country, where he eventually established himself.

During the long, twenty-five-year period of his semiretirement when he lived in Kyohaku-in at Shōfuku-ji, painting and calligraphy were a primary means of instruction. He produced hundreds of pictures and poetic or doctrinal inscriptions. Apparently obtaining one of his works became something of a sport among Japanese collectors, as he complained in an inscription on a landscape painting of Tōki-an, where he had studied with Gessen as a young man:

This play of mine with brush and ink
Is not to be taken as calligraphy or drawing.
Yet in the hands of common-minded people,
It becomes calligraphy and painting.

(Translated by Daisetz Suzuki)

Although Sengai's work lacked the deep emotional intensity of Hakuin's—indeed it often has a lighthearted, playful quality—Sengai nonetheless saw his painting and calligraphy as an important means of communicating Zen Buddhist values. On this work, for example, Sengai's inscription clearly states a devotional message, and also affirms his own position in the Japanese Zen tradition:

The Bodhisattva, like the moon
Is pure and refreshing;
Traveling freely through the realm
Of the Absolute Void,
Purifying the hearts of all
Sentient beings.

[Dated] tenth month of Bunsei Kanoe-tora [1830]
[Signed] Fusō Saisho Zenkutsu Jikukō Gai
(painted by (Sen) Gai, who resided at the first Zen cave (i.e. temple) in Japan)

References
Bokubi, no. 114 (January 1962), pl. 31.
Sengai, Furuta, Shōkin (Tokyo, 1966), pl. 38.
Sengai, the Zen Master, Suzuki, Daisetz (London, 1971).
Sengai Zenji Bokurin-satsu, Onshi Kyoto Hakubutsukan (ed.) (Kyoto, 1931), pls. 15, 23.

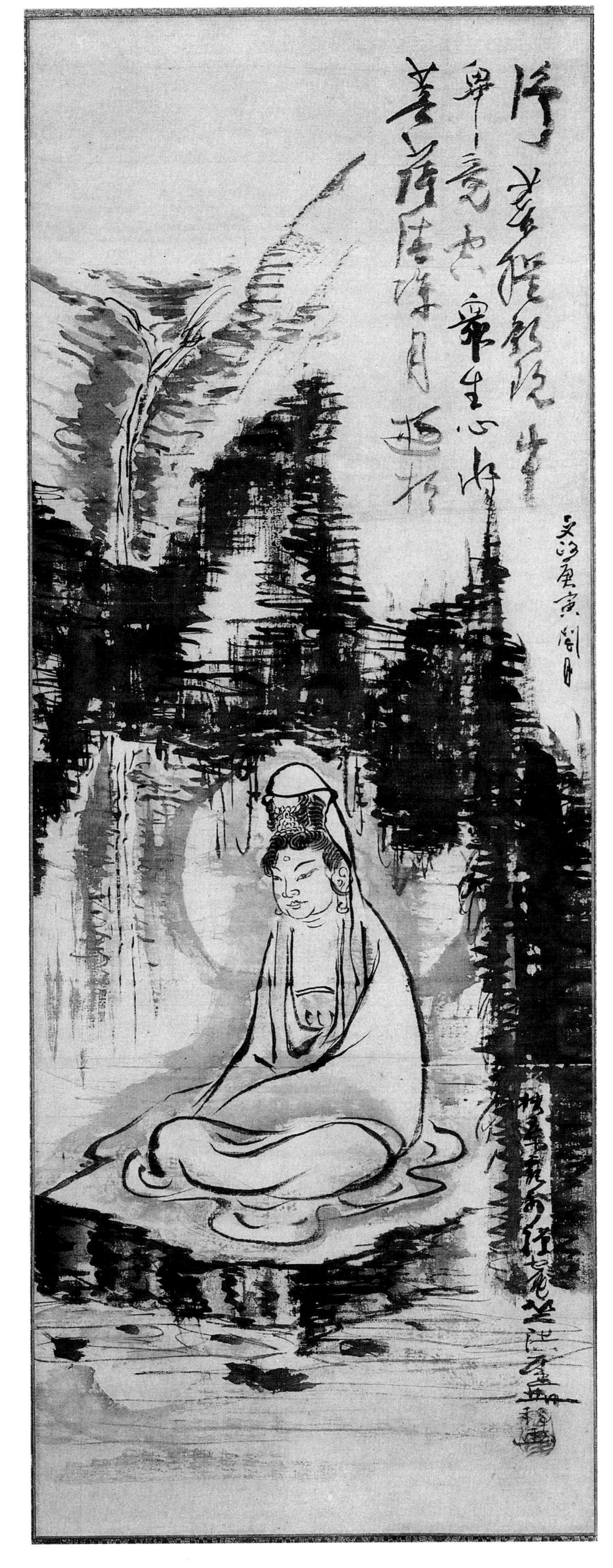

Detail

34

The Hakozaki Hachiman Shrine

Hanging Scroll
Ink on paper
34.5 x 56.5 cm

Signature
Gai Bosatsu

Seal
Sengai

Sengai Gibon
1750-1837
Dated in accordance with 1830

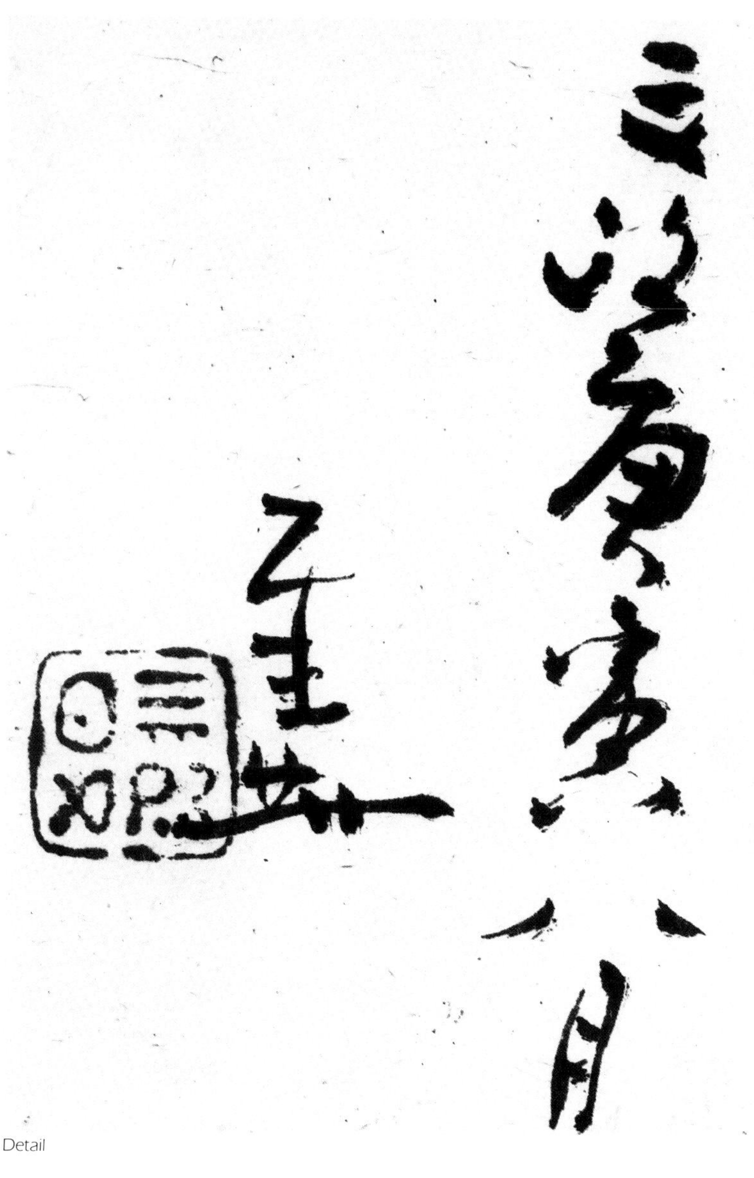

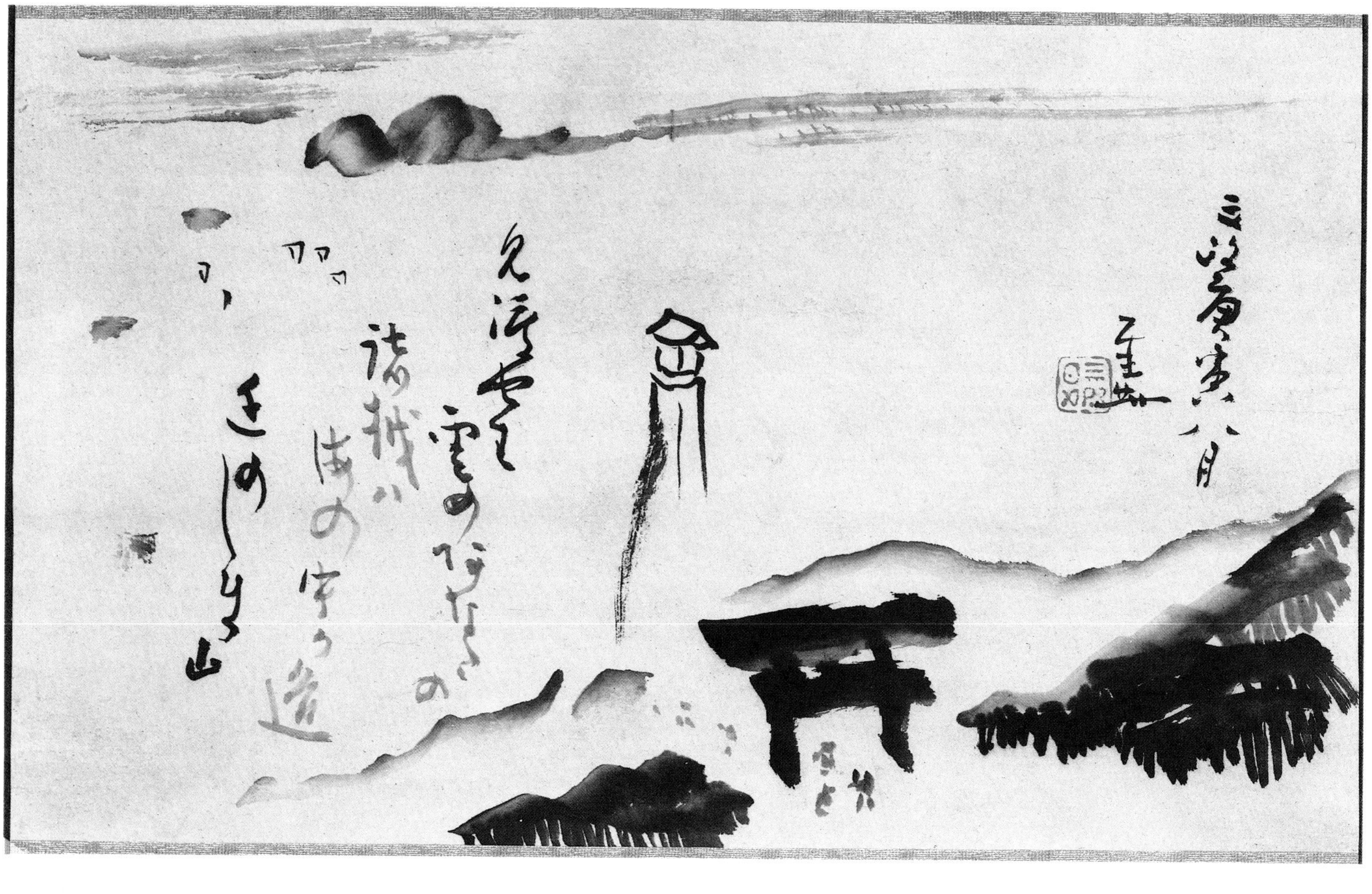

A lighthouse still stands off the beach that Sengai painted in 1830, when he was seventy-nine years old. The torii, the ceremonial entrance gate to the Hakozaki Hachiman Shinto Shrine, is also there; but just below it now stands one of the biggest petroleum refineries in Japan. The spit of sand ending in the massive rock in the middle ground of this painting is now the busy airport of the industrial city of Fukuoka. When Sengai painted it, however, the place was not an idyllic wilderness. Even then, Hakata (the present city of Fukuoka) was one of Japan's busiest ports and a commercial center. It was the main southern port of the Inland Sea and the gateway to Japan's second island, Kyushu, and second only to Osaka as a center of trade.

Sengai delighted in painting topographic landscapes—descriptive views of specific sites in Japan. His oeuvre is filled with dozens of examples: a view of Mount Kōra in Kyushu, near Kurume; a view of the ruins of Dazaifu, the ancient seat of power of the imperial government in Kyushu, located near Usa; the waterfall of Mount Rai; the great Kiso Gorge near Sarashina in central Honshu; or the waterfall at Shiraito (no. 35). We must also remember that in the 1830s, Japan's taste for topographic landscapes had reached its peak in the woodblock prints of Katsushika Hokusai (1760-1849) and the landscape cycles of Andō Hiroshige (1797-1858) just beginning to appear on the market. Sengai's fascination with the genre reflected his own great mobility. Although he traveled widely throughout his life, most of his landscapes focused on the environs of his main residence, Shōun-ji monastery near Hakata, or in the vast region comprising the foothills of Mount Fuji.

Most of Sengai's landscape paintings were endowed with a sacred or philosophic meaning. In this work, Sengai chose to see the Hachiman Shrine as the gateway to China, for he depicted it as though he were looking out to sea, and stated in his poem:

When looking into the distance
Morokoshi [ancient Cathay], lying beyond the clouds,
Is a nearby island mountain
Midway in the sea.

[Dated] eighth month of Kanoe-tora [1830]
[Signed] Gai Bosatsu

The scene was painted with very few strokes, even for the economical Sengai. Three lines denote the shore; a few heavy strokes of ink represent strands of trees between which the massive torii asserts itself. The lighthouse in the center and a roughly shaped rock in the middle ground, with the far shore of the bay in back, are hinted at rather than executed; and few triangles symbolize people in front of the torii—all that was required to create a recognizable landscape.

References
Bokubi, no. 110 (August 1961), pl. 70.
Sengai, Furuta, Shōkin (Tokyo, 1966), pl. 76.
Sengai Zenji Bokurin-satsu, Onshi Kyoto Hakubutsukan (ed.) (Kyoto, 1931), pls. 28, 70.

35

The Waterfall at Shiraito

Hanging Scroll
Ink on paper
85.1 x 27.6 cm

Signature
Gai Bosatsu

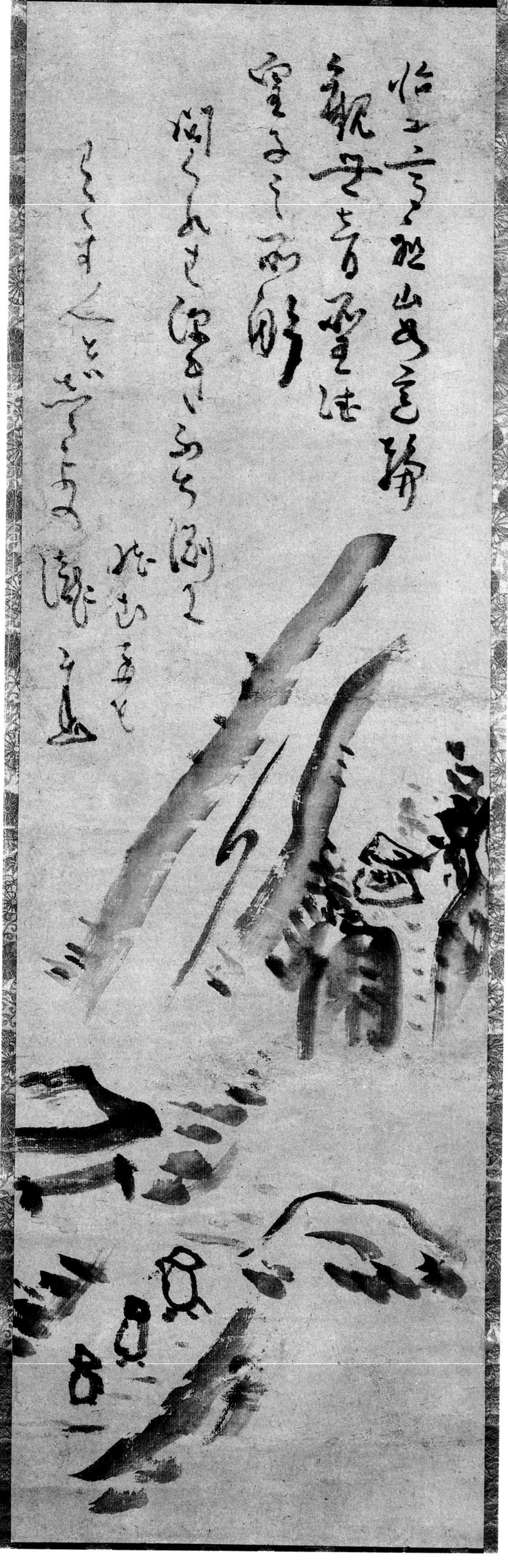

Like Sengai's landscape of the Hakozaki Hachiman Shrine (no. 34), this painting depicts a well-known site—the great waterfall at Shiraito along the western slopes of Mount Fuji, near Fujinomiya in Shizuoka prefecture. However, this painting is far more direct and childlike in its presentation; the mountain-climbing pilgrims in the foreground, for example, have been reduced to elemental shapes, as have the buildings behind them and the landforms above. Rarely has the need of the Zenga masters to return to primal forms in their painting been so clearly indicated, or with such authenticity of expression and form. At first glance, it is hard to imagine that this painting was done by one of the most knowledgeable and important persons in the Japanese Zen community of his day; upon further reflection, it would be hard to imagine that it could have been done by anyone with lesser insight.

The inscription, reading from right to left, has been somewhat abraded and is difficult to interpret. It refers to Shōtoku Taishi (574–622), the imperial prince who helped establish Buddhism as a state creed in Japan and who came to be revered as an incarnation of Bodhisattva Kannon. In the legendary biographies of the deified Shōtoku, he flew on his horse to Mount Fuji during his twenty-seventh year; this may account for his association with the Shiraito waterfall.

The enlightened Prince Shōtoku is the Kō-so-zan Nyoirin Kannon.

When I came to inquire
Who is the man who ferries
The boat to the deep pools,
No one knew
But the waterfall at Shiraito.

[Signed] Gai Bosatsu

This poem does not appear in Sengai's collected waka, the **Sutekobune,** and is still somewhat obscure in meaning.

Although it is clearly authentic and bears Sengai's kaō (cipher), this painting was not stamped with Sengai's seals. Scholars suppose that several paintings of obviously high artistic and personal importance, but lacking seal impressions, were not intended as gifts for callers and friends but as works to be retained by the artist himself.

References
Bokubi, no. 110 (August 1961), pls. 69, 75.
Sengai, Furuta, Shōkin (Tokyo, 1966), pl. 82.
Sengai Zenji Bokurin-satsu, Onshi Kyoto Hakubutsukan (ed.) (Kyoto, 1931), pls. 24, 26.

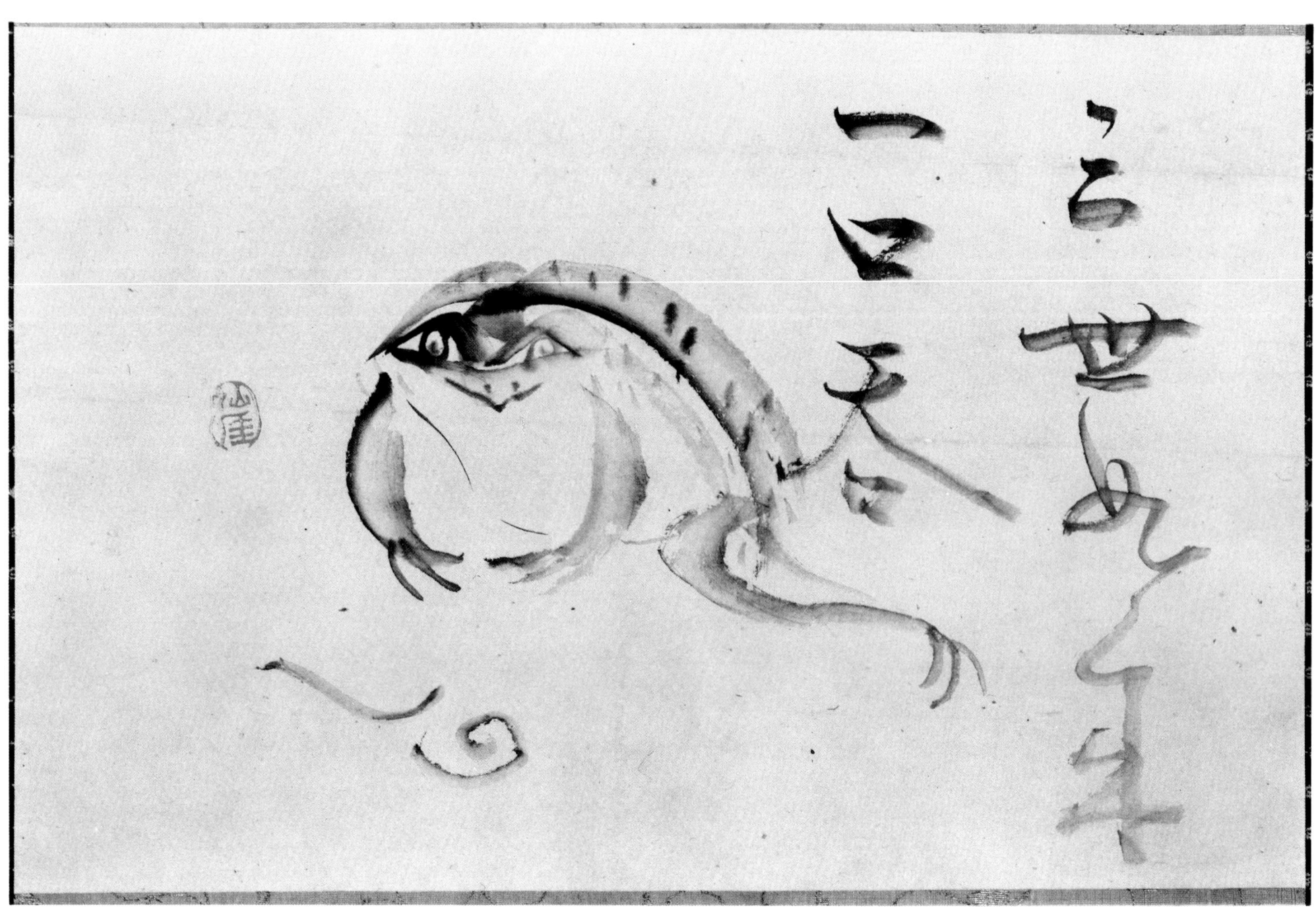

Sengai Gibon
1750–1837

36

Frog and Snail
(See color plate no. 36)

Hanging Scroll
Ink on paper
35.1 x 52.7 cm

Seal
Sengai

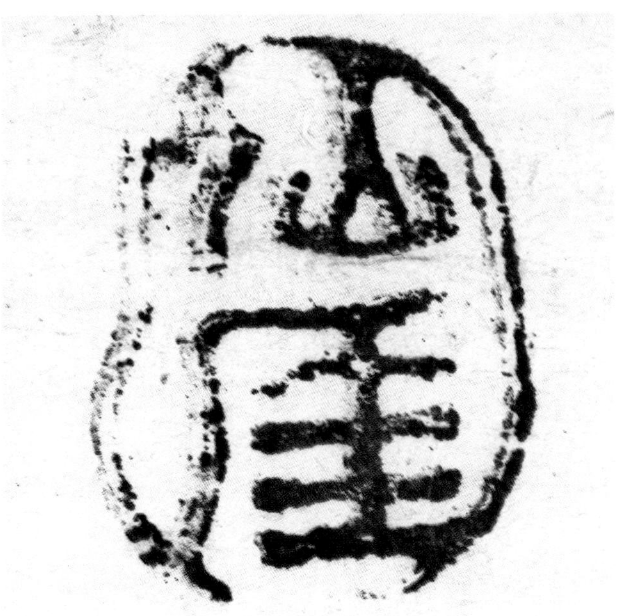

Detail

The brilliance of pictorial invention possible for an essentially untutored Zen painter appears in this deceptively simple composition of a frog about to leap upon a snail. The victim was depicted in only two curved lines; the back, eyes, and legs of the frog were established with katabokashi (rapid modeling strokes of a brush that was unevenly inked). The same direct, creative energy went into the writing of the simple Zen aphorism at the right:

The Buddhas of the Three Worlds [past, present, and future]
Gobbled up in one mouthful.

The motif of the frog absorbed Sengai, who painted it many times and with a wide range of symbolic nuances; here the significance seems to be that the lowly creature, real and immediately in view, surpasses in sanctity the deities of traditional Buddhism. Such apparent irreverence was part of Zen Buddhism's efforts to see the world of ordinary experience as a realm or path in which people may attain salvation, in contrast to the elaborate visions of paradise and the pantheon of deities who offer salvation to pious Buddhists on the basis of their faith alone.

In Sengai's vast oeuvre, many motifs from everyday life served the same symbolic purpose as the frog: a bullfinch, an eggplant, a morning glory, farmers going to the fields, a beggar, a flash of lightning. Sengai's purpose was always to shock the viewer into an awareness that Buddhist enlightenment lay close at hand, to be achieved by a person's own efforts and insights. However, he also depicted frogs satirically, going back to the ancient frolicking animal scrolls attributed to Toba Sōjō, in which a fat bullfrog was shown as a corrupt Buddha image worshiped by other frogs. Sengai, in one frog painting, used the creature to mock the notion that zazen (seated meditation) alone suffices to bring a person to salvation. In other paintings he referred to the frog in Matsuo Bashō's celebrated haiku, in which the sudden leap of the creature into a pond was, for the poet and perhaps for the frog itself, a stunning moment of self-realization.

Published
Birds, Beasts, Blossoms, and Bugs: The Nature of Japan, Stern, Harold P. (New York, 1976), no. 63.

References
Sengai, Furuta, Shōkin (Tokyo, 1966), pls. 124, 136.
Sengai, the Zen Master, Suzuki, Daisetz (London, 1971), pls. 40, 110.
Sengai Zenji Bokurin-satsu, Onshi Kyoto Hakubutsukan (Kyoto, 1931), pls. 52, 78.

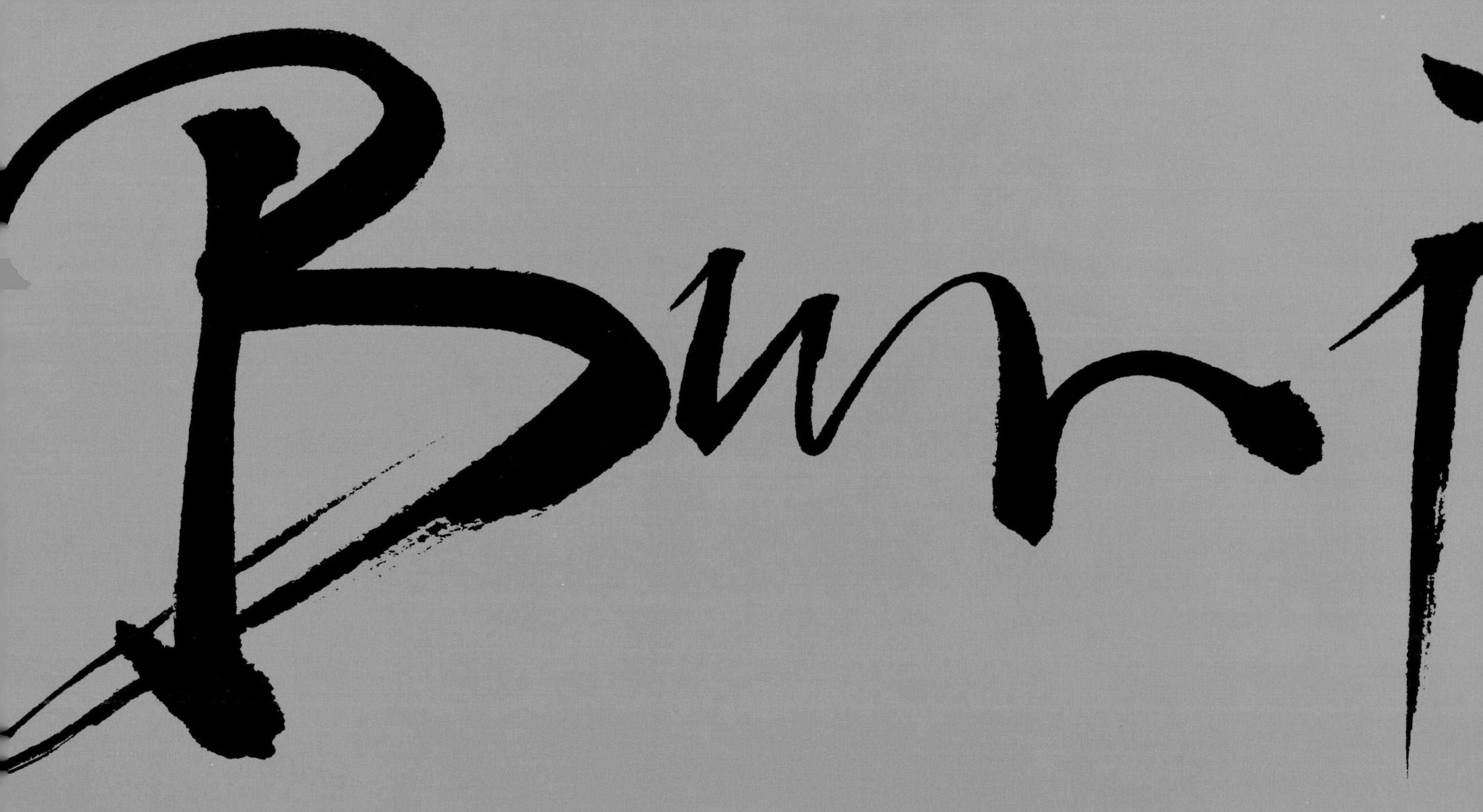

Part III

Bunjinga: Paintings of the Literary Men

In China, the art forms of the wen-jen (literati) had become such an integral part of the cultural fabric that their distinctive character was taken for granted. In Japan the bunjin (literati) movement was one of a dozen major trends that flourished in the relative stability and internal peace of the Edo period (1603-1867). In both lands, as well as in Korea, the cultural movement which centered on the literati became the leading vehicle of East Asian humanism, expressing a devotion to learning, to individualism, and to a life-style that was leisurely, tranquil, and closely attuned to a refined vision of nature.

In China, the wen-jen were members of traditional scholarly families. They delighted in learning, in painting and calligraphy, in the carving of seal stones, in poetry, in antiquarian research; they cherished, above all, the relaxed and informal companionship of like-minded friends. They were inspired by a major current in Chinese Confucian philosophy that applauded the sage, the man of lofty, incorruptible character and philosophic vision who devotes himself to scholarship and cultivation of the self as a model for others in society. Although such men, under traditional Confucianism, served the state as advisers and administrators, by the fifteenth century some of the finest artists among Chinese literati were choosing to avoid official life.

Among the leading Chinese literati artists of the fifteenth and sixteenth centuries were Shen Chou (1427-1509), Wen Cheng-ming (1470-1559), and Lu Chih (1496-1576)—a succession of painters linked as master and pupil who developed painting styles and modes of behavior in harmony with wen-jen ideals. In order to avoid subordinating their own inner motivations to the wishes of someone of wealth or high status, they refused to work for casual patrons or to accept financial rewards. They considered themselves amateur in the basic sense of the word, and, thus, were free from the professional artists' subjection to sophisticated technical training, a client's taste, and commercial transactions. They often painted extremely simple linear compositions: modest and small-scale depictions of landscapes and flowers and birds, avoiding the ostentatious techniques and elaborate calligraphic flourishes practiced by professional scribes and painters. On other occasions they considered themselves scholarly artists and attempted to recreate the effects of admired masters of the past. They viewed themselves as part of an artistic tradition dating back centuries, and singled out ancient poets and painters as their historical prototypes. Although the Chinese literati followed no single, unified style, they tended to paint modest, ingenuous, personal, and expressive imagery.

By the time the Ming dynasty fell in 1644, the ideals and styles of the wen-jen had become codified. This process is apparent in painting manuals such as the **Mustard Seed Garden Painting Manual** available in woodblock-printed editions and distributed throughout East Asia. The writings of Tung Ch'i-ch'ang (1555-1636), a high government official, collector, painter, calligrapher, and theoretician, were also available. Tung classified Chinese painting of the past into two traditions, employing the analogy of the history of the Ch'an sect of Buddhism in China, which had been divided into northern and southern branches. The northern schools of Ch'an emphasized obtaining enlightenment through methodical intellectual process, whereas the southern schools emphasized sudden, or instantaneous, enlightenment. Tung's northern school of painting (Pei-hua in Chinese) was composed of the more professionalized and rigorously academic styles, exemplified by the Sung masters Li T'ang (ca 1050-1130) and Hsia Kuei (ca 1190-1225). The southern school of painting (Nan-hua, or Nanga, in Japanese), which he preferred, comprised the more informal, supposedly amateur tradition which appealed to the wen-jen point of view and included the painters Wang Wei (699-759), Tung Yüan (active 937-975), and Chü-jan (active 960-980).

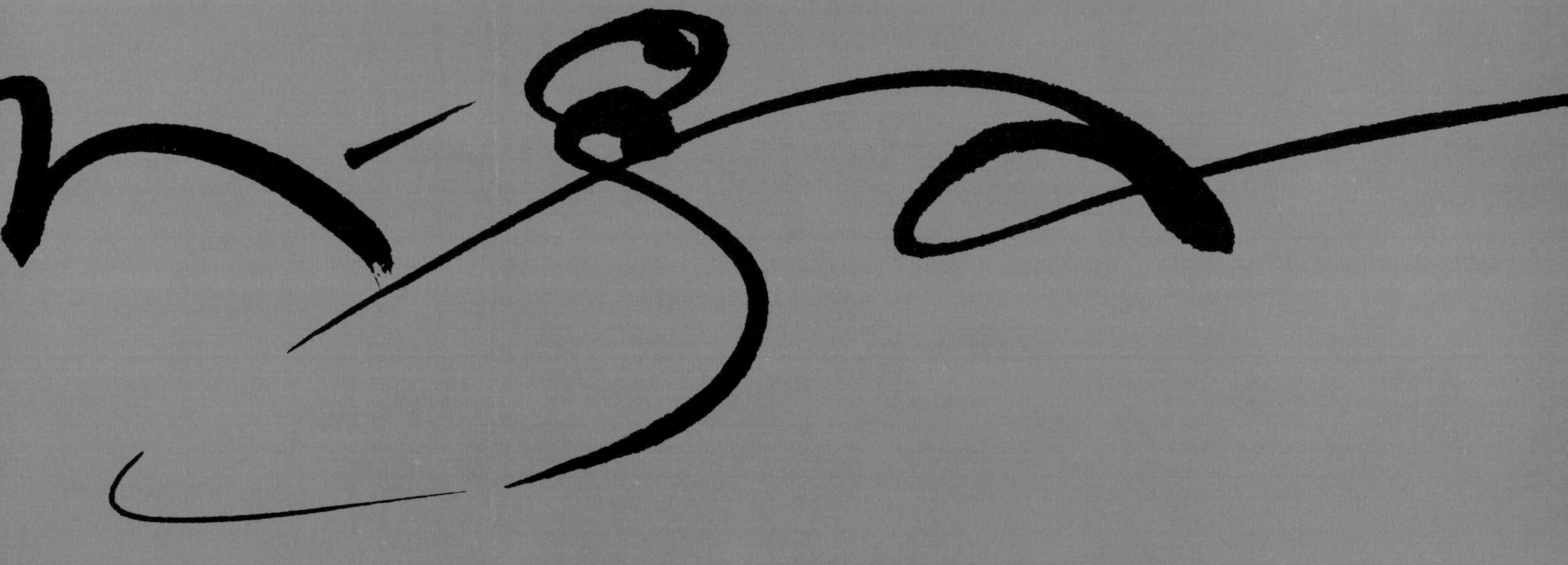

The writings of Tung Ch'i-ch'ang came to Japan in the seventeenth century along with painting manuals and rubbings of engraved paintings and inscriptions. They were part of the vast quantity of Chinese literary material imported into Japan as the Tokugawa regime sought to buttress the role of Confucianism as the basic ideology of its rule. In the opening decades of the eighteenth century, Japanese advocates of the literati tradition began to appear; by the last half of the century, hundreds of painters, calligraphers, scholars, and publishers were caught up in the movement. The literati became one of the most influential elements in the nation's cultural life, and successfully challenged the Kanō school as the most authentic expression of Chinese artistic values in Japan.

The Sansō Collection includes one of the finest selections of Japanese literati painting available in the West, with representative works from masters of the early, middle, and late phases of its development. To suggest the human circumstances out of which these paintings emerged, we have composed another hypothetical biography. As we did in the introduction to the suiboku paintings, we combined data from the lives of many men to suggest the career of a typical master of literati style painting. We have given him an appropriate artist's name, Kempō (literally, dry peak), and placed his career in the middle phase of the movement, suggesting that he was born around 1735 and lived until the early 1800s.

Kempō, our bunjin painter, was born into a high-ranking samurai family attached to one of the great clans governing a large fiefdom in western Honshu. Although some of the bunjin he later came to know were sons of prosperous farmers or educated professionals such as pharmacists or doctors, the majority were members of the hereditary warrior class that, in an era of relative peace and stability, acted as administrators rather than as soldiers.

Kempō's father was a close attendant of one of the most influential and wealthy of the regional lords and served him for many years, first as a clerk, then as a personal secretary. The martial traditions of the painter's family had faded, and the father was a sober, bookish man who worked long hours composing letters for the diamyo to send to lords in Edo, the modern Tokyo, or elsewhere. When seeking guidance on policy questions within the fief, he often studied the books of the Sung Neo-Confucian philosopher, Chu Hsi (1130-1200) in his personal library.

When Kempō was six years old, he was sent to a local Buddhist temple school where the priest taught him how to use the writing brush, how to form Chinese characters, and how to read simple texts. When he was nine, he began his studies at the hangaku, the fief academy established by the daimyo for the children of the fief's military and professional families. At the time, it was one of only ten such provincial schools. By the end of the Edo period, however, the number of such schools increased to over two hundred fifty.

The academy's cluster of substantial, tile-roofed buildings within a high-walled enclosure rather resembled a Buddhist temple. In it the young sons of the samurai, like the painter-to-be, received as many as five years of stern and detailed instruction intended to prepare them for a career in government and warfare and to impart lofty moral character and valor. The chief teachers had been trained in Edo at the Confucian academy founded in the Uenō district by Hayashi Razan (1583-1657), Confucian adviser to Ieyasu, the first Tokugawa shogun.

The painter-to-be proved to be an indifferent, occasionally rebellious student in every aspect of his training except calligraphy. In keeping with his father's bookish character, he refused to exert himself in martial exercises and was eventually excused from classes in archery and swordsmanship. He was bored by the long-winded Chinese texts and tiresome discussions on how li, the Principle of Heaven, produces social stability and harmony through the Five Relationships: the mutual obligations between father and son, ruler and subject, husband and wife, older and younger brothers, and between friends. He could barely keep a straight face during the solemn rehearsals for ceremonial occasions: family observances in honor of deceased ancestors, the semiannual rituals in honor of Confucius, or receptions at the courts of the local daimyo or the great shogun at Edo.

Calligraphy, however, intrigued him. His hand and eye seemed to be in close coordination, and he delighted in endlessly copying the four different styles of Chinese script in the **Thousand Character Classic,** the old Chinese poem in four-character verses used to train calligraphers. He also quickly excelled in the flowing script of the Japanese hiragana syllabary. His teachers concluded that he might make a satisfactory scribe or clerk. After graduation, he was assigned to sit and copy manuscripts in a gloomy corner of the office of tax records, while his classmates rode horseback into the countryside to supervise the rice fields, irrigation ditches, and culverts, or accompanied shipments of tax rice by bullock cart to the great warehouses at Okayama.

Despite the drabness of his clerical duties, young Kempō did not find life unbearable. He received a small but adequate stipend from the feudal administration. His father and uncle arranged a marriage for him with the daughter of a local samurai and, with her, he sired two sons. He was gregarious and fun-loving, and soon was part of a close circle of like-minded friends. This group included one of Kempō's teachers from the fief academy who shared his interest in Chinese calligraphy and poetry. Another member, Uzaemon, also worked in the clan administrative office. He played the shakuhachi (a long, vertical bamboo flute) and taught Kempō some simple tunes. The group leader was a cherished teacher, retired from the school, who specialized in Confucian doctrines but was also passionately devoted to Japanese poetry, particularly the Manyō shū.

On a hot summer evening, the group would spread a picnic by the shaded bank of a stream and, attended by a pair of servant boys, sing to the plaintive notes of the shakuhachi, gossip about how badly the daimyo was ruling his domain, and drink dozens of cups full of warm rice wine. When Kempō's father berated him for his intemperance and informal ways, the youth replied with a famous passage from a Sung poem: when the ancient wen-jen poet T'ao Yüan-ming drank wine, his heart remained as clear as a mirror, but the heart of the ordinary man, intoxicated with worldly concerns, is clouded with dust.

The father, perhaps to lure the son from indolent ways, arranged for him to join one of the daimyo's annual four-month stays in the shogun's capital at Edo. Each of the feudal lords was required to maintain a house in Edo and, together with his family, to spend a stipulated period of time there so that he would be subject personally and directly to the control of the shogun's regime. Although Kempō eventually made the trip five or six times, his first visit turned out to be one of the crucial experiences of his life.

The journey itself was a revelation. The daimyo, because of his high status, was entitled to assemble an enormous and impressive entourage: dozens of porters and pack horses to carry luggage, numerous palanquins to carry him and his close relatives, a large troop of foot soldiers and mounted horsemen, and a host of clan officials and servants. The procession slowly made its way through the cities of Osaka, Kyoto, and Nagoya until it reached Edo, the shogunal capital. There the main party entered the yashiki, the vast mansion compound built and maintained by the clan near the huge castle of the shogun. It was just one of dozens of such compounds built by the regional lords in a lavish competition to demonstrate their wealth and status.

Kempō was allowed to attend the audience held by the shogun for the regional lords who had come for their annual period of mandatory residence. In order to prepare himself, he desperately tried to recall the lessons about dress and protocol he learned at the fief school. He was awed by the size of the vast reception hall in the Edo castle, and by the stern solemnity with which dark-robed lords and their retainers filed into the room, kneeled row upon row before the shogun and his chief advisers, and listened, with heads bowed, to the stern address of welcome delivered by the head of the Council of Elders.

Kempō had few duties, apart from maintaining ledgers for the delegation, and he soon joined other samurai in exploring the delights of the Yoshiwara, the vast, licensed pleasure district less than three kilometers from the mansion. With the help of illustrated guidebooks to the district, he and his friend Uzaemon, the shakuhachi player, discovered a so-called Green House which they liked. They spent many evenings there dining, drinking, and playing their flutes accompanied by young women who strummed the samisen, sang, and occasionally slept with them.

Kempō became madly infatuated with an especially beautiful geisha but, unfortunately for him, so did a wealthy merchant from northern Japan. On his fixed income, Kempō could not afford much of the talented, expensive geisha's time. Although he spent what he could, he could not compete with the wealthier merchant. Bankrupt and broken-hearted, he turned his attentions elsewhere.

Kempō's father knew that a samurai was expected to seek out the pleasures of the flesh, but he also knew that a samurai was supposed to maintain balance and proportion. To further Kempō's moral and intellectual growth, he introduced him to some of the leading Confucian scholars in the capital. The son felt that most of the scholars were as tiresome as Pure Land priests constantly reciting ancient formulas about the Way of Heaven. He was, however, particularly drawn to one scholar, an advocate of the doctrines of the Ming Confucian philosopher Wang Yang-ming (1472-1529). Wang's ideas, which stressed individuality and subjectivity, appealed to many Japanese who were disenchanted with the cold rationalism of the Chu Hsi school officially advocated by the Tokugawa regime.

The old Confucian scholar operated a private academy for samurai sons intending to pursue a career in government administration and had gathered around him an informal circle of students and friends similar to Kempō's group at home. Kempō and Uzaemon were invited to join this group's evening gatherings in private homes or gardens. The men would drink and sing together; occasionally someone would bring out paper and brushes and an ink stone, and they would paint, for example, a picture of myna birds on a plum branch, each man adding one part of the picture and a verse above. The old teacher possessed an imported set of the six volumes of the **Mustard Seed Garden Painting Manual** which gave clear, step-by-step instruction in painting bamboo, orchids, plum blossoms, birds, landscapes, and the human figure. Kempō was allowed to take the books to the clan mansion, to spend hours copying the illustrations and poring over the text. He showed his drawings at an evening gathering and one of the group members, who was proud of his own abilities as a painter, took him and Uzaemon to his own house, where he kept several small albums of Chinese landscape paintings and a number of Chinese illustrated books. He criticized Kempō's brushwork, but for encouragement gave him Chinese paper, an ink stone, and a fine porcelain water dropper. He also showed Uzaemon how to carve seals in the Chinese fashion, a favorite avocation of the literati.

After the delegation returned from the capital, the young artist devoted increasing amounts of time to painting. That spring, after his drinking group had gone to view the local waterfall in full spate, he recreated the scene in a simple colored painting and presented it to the retired teacher. The old man liked it so much that he sent it to Osaka to be mounted with expensive Chinese brocade; when the painting came back, he showed it to the drinking companions, and he and our artist each inscribed a Chinese poem about waterfalls in the upper part of the picture and impressed their seals on it.

Kempō was not destined to play a major role in the administration of the fief due to his nonchalant ways. Nonetheless he and Uzaemon were sent to Osaka to check the records of the fief office that received and sold its rice and other produce and represented the daimyo to the Osaka money lenders. In Osaka they found a shop selling stationery, painting supplies, and illustrated books. The proprietor, a central figure in the circle of local bunjin who knew those who passed through town, invited the two men to his house where he showed them paintings by an artist living in the Bizen district not far from their own fief. On their way home, they stopped off to visit the painter and Kempō exchanged pictures with him. Uzaemon carved a seal for him. The Bizen painter worked in an extremely free, even eccentric style that Kempō had never seen before; it inspired him to become more relaxed and inventive in his own paintings.

On another occasion, Kempō was sent on clan business to Nagasaki, the only port open for trade with the Chinese and Dutch. He took advantage of this opportunity to visit a monk painter who had collected a large number of Chinese pictures and had studied with two Chinese painters in Nagasaki. Kempō was disappointed with the highly realistic flower-and-bird pictures he saw. He knew enough about Chinese art to realize that they had been done by journeyman painters who lacked the elevated spirit and ideology of the wen-jen; their work was highly competent and polished but lacked the engaging simplicity that marked the style of the literati. He was much more impressed with a book from Holland which he was shown in the office of one of the shogunal trade officials. It was illustrated with copper plate engravings of scenes of the great cities of Europe. The striking sense of roundness and the spatial illusion of the mountains and buildings astonished him. When he returned to his fief, he tried to recreate these effects with brush and ink, but he rarely succeeded.

Kempō's personal responsibilities increased when his father died and he became head of the family, but his official duties remained light. He continued to accompany the daimyo on the mandatory trips to Edo and to rejoin the circle of Edo bunjin who had become his warm friends. One year he was distressed to learn that the old Confucian had been ordered to close his academy because he had stressed the doctrines of Wang Yang-ming too enthusiastically; the military government wished that only the Chu Hsi school be taught. Another of the Edo Confucian teachers was imprisoned when he protested this imposition of ideological uniformity. His private savings were confiscated by the government, and his students were given stern warnings. The painter Kempō had met in Bizen told him of a close friend in Bizen who advocated the Wang Yang-ming tradition; the friend had been forced to resign from a fief academy and, as a result, had committed suicide. This series of events had distressed the Bizen painter profoundly, and he and our artist agreed that the political situation suggested the power of the regime was deteriorating. In the name of social harmony, the great Confucian ideal, policies were growing increasingly oppressive and in contrast to their intent, the regime seemed to be generating disharmony among the populace. Through his own work Kempō realized the government was having financial difficulties; he knew firsthand that the central government was crediting the tax rice delivered by the regionl lords at rates that were ludicrously low. As a result, his own master had fallen deeply in debt to the Osaka moneylenders, and had been forced to reduce the stipends of all who, like Kempō, depended on him. The daimyo had also been forced to increase the share of the produce which the farmers had to hand over to him as tax. For a while the farmers had protested these exactions; now they were beginning to rebel.

Even though these gloomy events preyed on his mind, Kempō spent increasing amounts of time at his table painting. When he became head of his family, he built a small detached study with a thatched roof, like a farmhouse, in a corner of the residence compound. With one simple room inside, his study was shaded by a grand old camphor tree in the summer, and his table looked out into a pleasant, informal flower garden inside a bamboo fence. He supposed that the Chinese literati like Wang Wei or T'ao Yüan-ming had made their gardens the center of their universe, and he delighted in tending morning glories and chrysanthemums, peonies and irises.

Kempō always seemed to find an appropriate occasion for a picture. When he learned Uzaemon's son was to be married, Kempō painted an album of flowers of the four seasons for the young couple. The Bizen painter came once a year for a visit and he and Kempō exchanged their best works. When the old daimyo died and was succeeded by his son, a former classmate, Kempō painted an album for him showing celebrated Chinese poets at leisure. He was disappointed, however, when he received only a perfunctory note of thanks from the new feudal lord. Apparently scenes of poets at leisure were not welcomed by a young ruler who had been instructed in Edo to strengthen the nation's moral and military fibre.

Fortunately for Kempō, not all officials were of the same mind. The daimyo of a remote district in the north of Honshu, who had seen his work while visiting the late head of the clan, invited our artist to come to his court to teach painting. Kempō was flattered by the invitation and, obtaining his own lord's permission after an almost intolerably long wait and forfeiture of part of his stipend, he went north accompanied by his second son. The youth, then fifteen years old, had pleased his father enormously by showing interest and talent for painting; he often helped his father by cleaning out the study and grinding ink. The northern daimyo received them with great honor and gave them chambers in his mansion. Kempō, in turn, gave calligraphy and painting lessons to a dozen officials who had been ordered by the daimyo to attend. He and his son spent nearly a year there until he was invited to perform a similar role at another provincial court, along the east coast of northern Honshu.

By now, Kempō's ties to his fief were weakened. He was beginning to suffer from stiffness in his legs and hips, and he longed for a permanent place to settle. Returning for what proved to be the last visit to his fief, he passed through Kyoto and, to his delight, found that his old friend Uzaemon had moved there and had joined a large circle of bunjin centered on a local Confucian scholar of immense prestige. Fortunately there were positions for teachers in small Confucian academies in Kyoto, and Kempō was able to secure a post teaching calligraphy and poetry which paid enough of a stipend to support his wife, his sons, and himself.

Although the nation as a whole was becoming increasingly disturbed by political dissension, economic difficulties and the arrival of European powers in the northeast Asian seas, the world of the Kyoto bunjin remained relatively tranquil. Thus, for the last decade of his life, Kempō was able to maintain the pattern of activities so deeply cherished by the literary men: the quiet drinking parties among close friends, the exchanges of poems and paintings, the brief excursions to view the autumn maple leaves at their peak, the exciting discovery of a rare Chinese volume in a book stall, the acquisition of an antique seal or a fine old ink stone. When he died he was mourned by the literati of Kyoto as one of the most gentle and admirable of men.

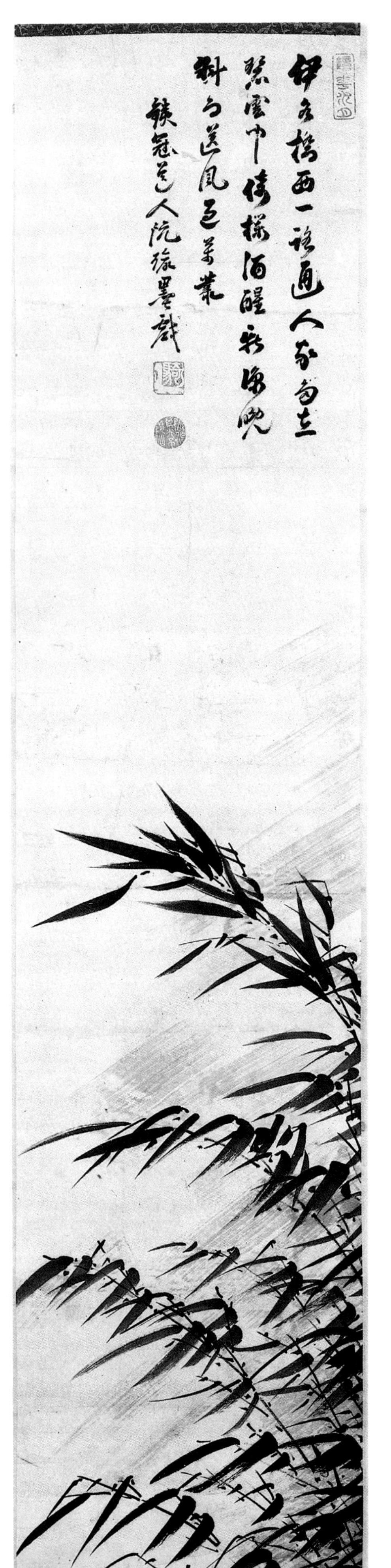

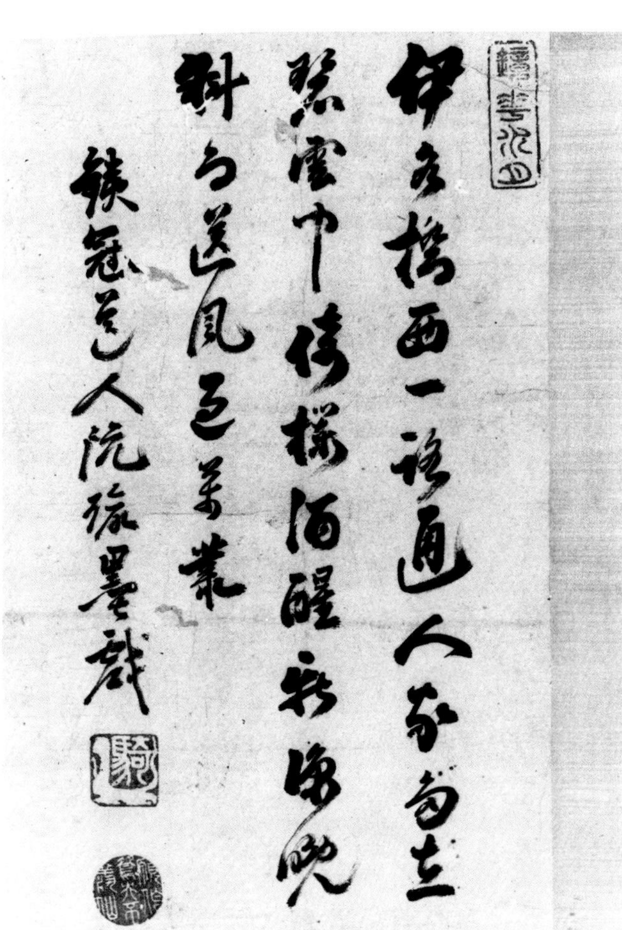

Detail

37

Bamboo in the Wind

Hanging Scroll
Ink on paper
129.6 x 27.3 cm

Signature
Tekkan Dōjin Genyu Bokugi

Seals
Kyōka Suigetsu
Kiryū
Gansaku Enō Fusensen

Gion Nankai
1676-1751

This painting of bamboo in stark, black ink is a demonstration of virtuosity in brush handling and calligraphy. The artist, Gion Nankai, one of the three pioneer masters of the literati movement in Japan, compressed the composition into the lower portion of the paper to leave empty space above for his inscription. Beginning with the leaves at the top of the tallest bamboo stalk, he worked with increasingly rapid strokes—a kind of serial imagery—until the paper was textured with modulated patterns of leaves set against the arching lines of the branches. Reinforcing the leaf shapes, the diagonal, slashing strokes express the force of the driving wind.

In the upper portion of the paper, Nankai wrote a long poem in a style of writing that reflects the calligraphy of the recently arrived Chinese monks of the Obaku sect of Zen Buddhism. The skillful blending of calligraphy, painting, and poetic sentiment into a harmonious entity was a basic concern of the literati artists. The poem itself, in Chinese, refers to the I-shui, or the I-ho, the river that flows near the old Chinese capital of Lo-yang and near the great Buddhist cave site at Lung-men:

To the west of the I-shui bridge
A road leads
To clustered houses
Amid blue clouds of kitchen smoke.
I rest against the rail,
Sobered by cool breezes after evening wine;
The sharp wind
Whips through dense thickets.

Playfully painted in ink by Tekkan Dōjin Genyu

Gion Nankai was born in Edo in 1676, the son of a physician in the service of the lord of Kii, in the present-day Wakayama prefecture. From the age of fourteen, he studied with Kinoshita Junan (1621-1698), one of the foremost Confucian scholars of the day. Later, in 1697, Nankai became the head of the local school, and was supported by the lord of Kii with a stipend of one hundred koku of rice. Nankai's early training in poetry and the Confucian classics is well-documented, but little is known about when and how he was introduced to the art of painting. He did note in his own writings that he studied woodblock-printed Chinese painting manuals, such as the **Mustard Seed Garden Painting Manual (Kaishien Gaden)** and the **Albums of Eight Types of Paintings (Hasshu Gafu)**. He paid particular attention to favored themes of the literati school: bamboo, pine, plum, orchid, and chrysanthemum.

More important than the study of instruction manuals was the opportunity to see original paintings. Chinese paintings had begun to enter the homes of wealthy samurai throughout Japan, but a more influential source for Nankai were the collections of Chinese painting at the Zen monastery of Mampuku-ji near Uji, a short distance from Kyoto. Chinese monks actually lived in Mampuku-ji, and Nankai, like his fellow Nanga pioneer, Yanagisawa Kien (1706-1758), was a follower of the Ōbaku sect of Zen and sought from the highly educated monks of Mampuku-ji instruction in the arts of calligraphy, poetry, and painting. In fact the Sansō picture by Nankai distinctly resembles the bamboo painting style of the Ōbaku priest, Taihō (1691-1774).

Nankai, like many other artists of Edo Japan, experienced difficulties with the law. For reasons that have never been made clear, he was stripped of his rank and stipend and banished in 1700 to an obscure hamlet in Wakayama, where he survived by teaching village children. After a decade in exile, he was recalled to the household of the lord of Kii and put in charge of preparing for the visit of an embassy from Korea the following year. Once again in favor, he was granted a yearly stipend, assigned to accompany the Korean embassy, and, in 1713, reappointed head of the clan school. For the rest of his life, he devoted his energies to the pursuits of the Bunjin. His collected poems were published in 1750; the following year he died, still in remote Wakayama but recognized throughout Japan as a major Confucian scholar and a fine calligrapher and artist.

References
Gion Nankai, Yanagisawa Kien, Katō, Shūichi and Nakata, Yūjirō, et al., Bunjinga Suihen vol. 11 (Tokyo, 1975).
Obaku: Zen Painting and Calligraphy, Addiss, Stephen, exhibition catalogue (Lawrence, KA, 1978).

Detail

Nakayama Kōyō
1717-1780

38

Wang Hui-chih at the Gate of his Friend

Hanging Scroll
Ink and light color on paper
82.8 x 49.5 cm

Signature
Kōyō Sanjin Sha [su]

Seals
Chū Teichū
Shiwa Shi

Executed in soft, lightly colored ink washes, this painting depicts one of the charming allegorical tales in which the literati movement expressed its ideals and values. In this rustic landscape beneath a layer of freshly fallen snow, the luminous reflected light of the moon sets the world shimmering. Leaning over a charcoal brazier in the wooden punt sits Wang Hui-chih, fifth son of the famed calligrapher Wang Hsi-chih (321-379), the man who sponsored the famous literary gathering at the Lan-t'ing pavilion in 353. In the present anecdote, the son, better known by his other name of Tzu-yu, set out in a boat to visit his friend Tai An-tao. The beauty of the scenery as the boat moved toward his destination so enraptured Tzu-yu that he abondoned his plan and ordered the boatman to return by the way they had just come, better to enjoy the moonlit landscape.

Tzu-yu is seated, leaning relaxed against an armrest, with a large jug of wine and a tiered food basket nearby. On shore is the garden gate at Tai An-tao's house, beyond which grows a bamboo thicket. The edge of the thatched roof rises over the bamboo. From the rocky shore a large pine thrusts skyward beside the still-closed gate. This detailed foreground acts as a focus for the broadly rendered landscape; in the middle ground, a spreading band of fog divides the wooded area.

In the background, moving across the upper half of the painting, a line of snowy peaks rises and falls in a sweeping rhythm, punctuated at intervals by tight angular turns. As much a signature of the artist as the written characters at the right, this strong linear and angular rhythm is echoed throughout the composition: at the edge of the wash above the trees in the middle ground, and again in the foreground rocks. The prominent rock, which seems to stand on top of the water at left of center, repeats in reverse the opening in the screen of peaks above. It also represents in a positive form the opposite of the moon, which is a circular shape left uncolored in the ink wash that forms the night sky.

Nakayama Kōyō belonged to the second generation of literati painters that included Ikeno Taiga (nos. 39-41) and Yosa Buson. He came from the castle town of Sakai in the province of Tosa on the island of Shikoku. His father was a merchant dealing in antiquities and Chinese objects; however, the family had once been samurai and the family lineage claimed a connection with a branch of the aristocratic Fujiwara. Kōyō studied Confucian thought and was attracted to the study of literature, painting, and calligraphy at an early age. A reference in one of his poems comparing Sakaki Hyakusen (1697-1752) to Wang Wei, the proverbial T'ang-period founder of the Southern school of painting, supports the usual contention that Kōyō knew and studied with Hyakusen. The two men surely shared a common interest in Chinese art and literature, but Kōyō was more single-minded about it. He preferred ancient Chinese literary forms to Japanese poetic styles, whereas Hyakusen was a leading haiku poet. Moreover, little in Kōyō's painting suggests a lasting influence from the older artist. Kōyō is known to have made numerous copies of illustrations of Sung and Yüan paintings, and to have copied a handscroll of the four seasons by Sesshū Toyo (1420-1506). Kōyō might well have studied independently the ancient texts and rubbings of calligraphic inscriptions that were then arriving from China.

His poetry and painting had gained Kōyō local prominence and had attracted the attention of the Tosa feudal lord Yamanouchi Toyonobu, who granted him permission to go to the shogunal capital. In the spring of 1759, Kōyō was in Edo working and painting regularly at the mansion maintained by the Yamanouchi clan. Clan records suggest that Kōyō held an official appointment as artist to the feudal lord; in 1761, as a mark of appreciation, he was granted permission to wear a sword and use a surname. He also received a generous stipend. Kōyō was at home among the intellectuals of the eastern capital and gained considerable renown. The publication in 1775 of his three-volume **Gadan Keiroku,** in which he attempted to distinguish Northern and Southern schools of painting, marked the beginning of aesthetic criticism among Japanese literati painters.

Kōyō's career moved into its full development in the mid-1760s. The names in the seals used on this painting, Chū Teichū and Shiwa, were first used in 1769, and thus help date the painting to the years when he had developed his own strong artistic identity and no longer repeated Chinese painting exercises. The emotional authenticity found in this painting may have been prompted by his seven-month visit to the north country in 1772. Kōyō had occasionally taken long walking tours, climbing mountains, sketching sights, and recording his experiences and impressions in diaries. Among Japanese Nanga painters of the eighteenth century, perhaps only Buson exhibited a stronger interest in, or more skillful treatment of, the effects of natural light and, in particular, the phenomena of night scenes, than Kōyō exhibits in this painting.

In the Kyoto area, Taiga and Buson shaped the development of Nanga; in eastern Japan, however, it was Kōyō whose long years of residence in Edo and whose work in publishing helped promote a regional standard for Nanga painting. Kōyō's oeuvre, generally less emotional than this painting, and his awareness of ancient Chinese painting ideals and formulas also helped establish a history of artistic eclecticism in the capital.

Published
Nakayama Kōyō Gafu (Kōchi City, 1971), pl. 47.
Tokyo Kokuritsu Hakubutsukan Kiyo, Hosono, Masanobu, "Nakayama Kōyō," no. 5 (1965), pl. 12.

References
Ikeno Taiga Gafu, vol. 4 (Tokyo, 1958), pl. 619.
Museum, Hosono, Masanobu, "Nakayama Kōyō—Sono shōgai to sakuhin," no. 222 (September 1969), pp. 4-24.
Shodō Zenshū, vol. 4 (Tokyo, 1960), p. 20.

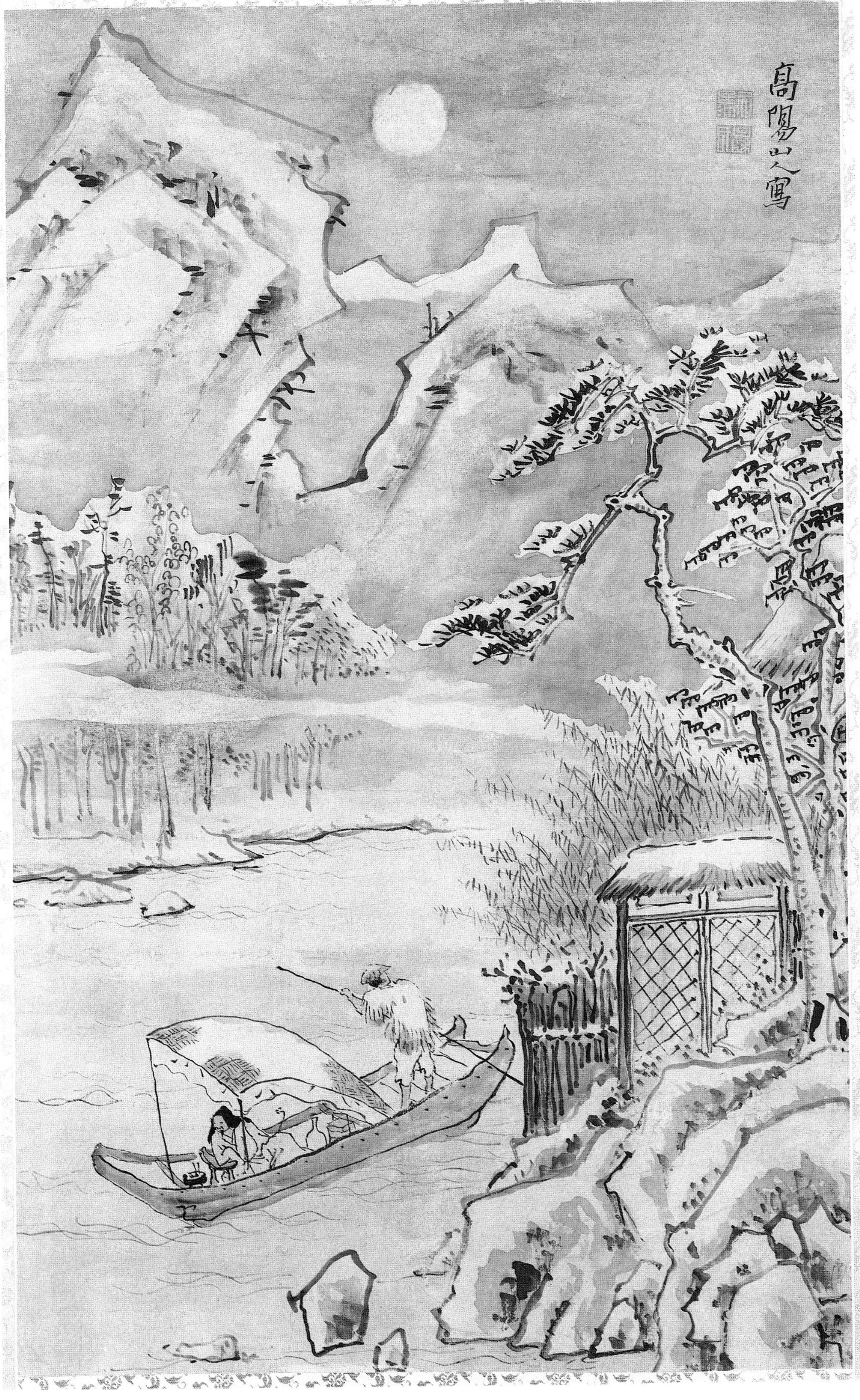

高陽山人寫

39

In the Spirit of Rain in the Hsiao-Hsiang District

Hanging Scroll
Ink and light color on paper
131.9 x 57.3 cm

Seals
Ka Shō
Zenshin Sōba Hō Kyūko

Ikeno Taiga
1723-1776
Datable to the fifth month of the year
corresponding to 1769

The jaunty, solitary angler wearing a straw rain hat and cape steps across the plank bridge. The bright colors lift the mood that the misting rain might otherwise dampen. Taiga has given a new interpretation to one of the eight traditional views of the Hsiao and Hsiang rivers, which were long considered a distillation of the scenic beauty of south central China. The themes were popular in poetry and painting, and as early as the Sung period, were standardized to the following motifs: Mountain Village on a Clear Day, Night Rain on the River, Distant Home-Bound Sails, Evening Glow over a Fishing Village, Autumn Moon over Lake Tung-t'ing, Wild Geese Alighting on a Sandbar, Evening Snow on the Mountains, and Evening Bell from a Distant Temple. The Northern Sung artist Sung Ti (eleventh century) is usually thought to have established the theme as a basic component of landscape painting. Chinese paintings of the Eight Views of Hsiao Hsiang were known in Japan from early medieval times. The concept of eight selected beauty spots was readily adaptable to the Japanese locale; in the Edo period, Eight Views of Omi and the Eight Views of Kanazawa were often painted.

Taiga has focused attention primarily upon the rustic fisherman without giving great detail to the landscape setting. The idea of rain is expressed by cloaking the fisherman in a rain cape, but also by suffusing the air with a humid mistiness imparting to the whole scene a shimmering sensation that recalls the tsuyu, or early summer rain.

Taiga was born in the fifth month of 1723, in northwest Kyoto. He must have been a precocious child, for it is said that he was studying the Chinese classics by the time he was five years old. Soon thereafter he received formal training in calligraphy from a priest at Seikō-in of the Dannō temple, Kyoto. It was perhaps through this priest, named Issei, that his talent for calligraphy came to the attention of the Ōbaku Zen priests at Mampukū-ji. According to the traditional story, Taiga, at about seven years of age, was brought to Mampukū-ji, center of Chinese-style calligraphy and painting, and amazed the priests with his command of the brush. His calligraphy training continued and a page with two poems inscribed by the eleven-year-old Taiga, still preserved today, attests to his skill. In 1738, during his early artistic training, he went to stay at the home of Yanagisawa Kien. Kien, as well as Gion Nankai (no. 37), was among the first in Japan to develop an interest in literati painting. Both men were to have an important effect on the development of Taiga's art, but Kien's influence came earlier and was perhaps more critical than Nankai's in establishing in Taiga a determination to direct his energies toward the Nanga movement.

The association with Kien brought Taiga professional opportunities and material advantages. Kien, related to one of the chief Confucian advisers of the shogunate, was wealthy and highly educated with wide associations and important contacts. As a mark of his debt to the master, Taiga eventually took as part of one of his own art names a portion of one of Kien's. Taiga had access not only to Kien's own paintings but also to his collection of books on painting. Taiga surely learned the bunjin art of finger painting from Kien and developed it with the Ōbaku priest Taihō (Ta-p'eng), twice abbot of Mampukū-ji and a renowned specialist in finger painting, particularly of bamboo. Taiga himself gained fame in this idiom, and when in 1748 and 1749 he traveled east and stopped over in Edo, he was a popular guest at parties where he demonstrated finger painting techniques.

His finger painting is but one instance of Taiga's limitless curiosity. Taiga had become acquainted with Chinese woodblock-printed books on painting at an early age, and the fans he made for sale when he was fifteen years old were said to have been modeled on the Chinese designs available in the **Hasshu Gafu,** a compendium of Chinese compositions. In the series **Six Sights of Kyoto,** done in his thirties, he ranged through the styles of such diverse Chinese artists as Fan K'uan, Mi Fei, Chü-jan, Li Kung-lin, Li-T'ang, and Hsia Kuei. But he studied Japanese modes as well. He found useful the Rimpa school technique of tarashikomi (dropping ink or color into still-moist areas to achieve special effects), and adapted to his own use the gold ground screens with opaque color designs that the Kanō and Rimpa artists had developed. He inscribed a screen painting with the notation that he was following the style of Soga Dasoku, a Muromachi ink painter. Little beyond the inscription connects the work with Dasoku, but Taiga's awareness of this name shows his familiarity with a wide diversity of painting, both Chinese and Japanese. He came under the influence of Hakuin (nos. 28-32) and his disciples, and incorporated some elements of Hakuin's style into his own.

In his calligraphy, too, Taiga was catholic in his tastes and reproduced poems and inscriptions by many different famous Chinese calligraphers. Dating from near the end of his life is a set of sixteen fans with the **Eight Views** and poems by Sung, Yüan, and Ming dynasty artists and scholars, including well-known names like Wu Chên and Tung Ch'i-ch'ang and less well-known names such as Hu Tsung-jên, Pao Hsun, and Wu Chun-shun of the Ming dynasty. This set of paintings offers examples of Taiga's seemingly limitless versatility. Among the **Eight Views,** for example, is the same scene shown here; the **Night Rain on the River** shows the same solitary angler crossing a footbridge to a bamboo setting. But the mood of that painting is totally different; Taiga compacted into the small format of a fan painting all the energy found in the more developed Sansō painting. The idyllic summer scene of this Sansō painting is transformed into an explosive force. The accompanying calligraphy, too, reflects the differing conditions. The inscription on the Sansō work is a relaxed, semiformal gyō, or semicursive, style appropriate to the large-scale highly developed work. The calligraphy of the fan version dissolves into an impressionistic blur or rapid sōsho, or cursive, script.

This painting and the next one (no. 40) were part of a set entitled **Twelve Landscapes of the Four Seasons** which were mounted on a pair of six-panel screens. One of the paintings was dated to the fifth month of Meiwa 6 (or 1769). When the **Ikeno Taiga Sakuhinshū** was published in 1960, four of the paintings had been converted into independent hanging scrolls; the remaining eight were then remounted into four two-panel screens, but have since been converted into hanging scrolls.

Published
Ikeno Taiga Gafu, vol. 4 (Tokyo, 1958), pl. 462, pp. 161-164.
Ikeno Taiga Sakuhinshū (Tokyo, 1960), pl. 462-2.

Reference
Nihon no Bunjinga, Tokyo National Museum (ed.) (Tokyo, 1966), pl. 49.

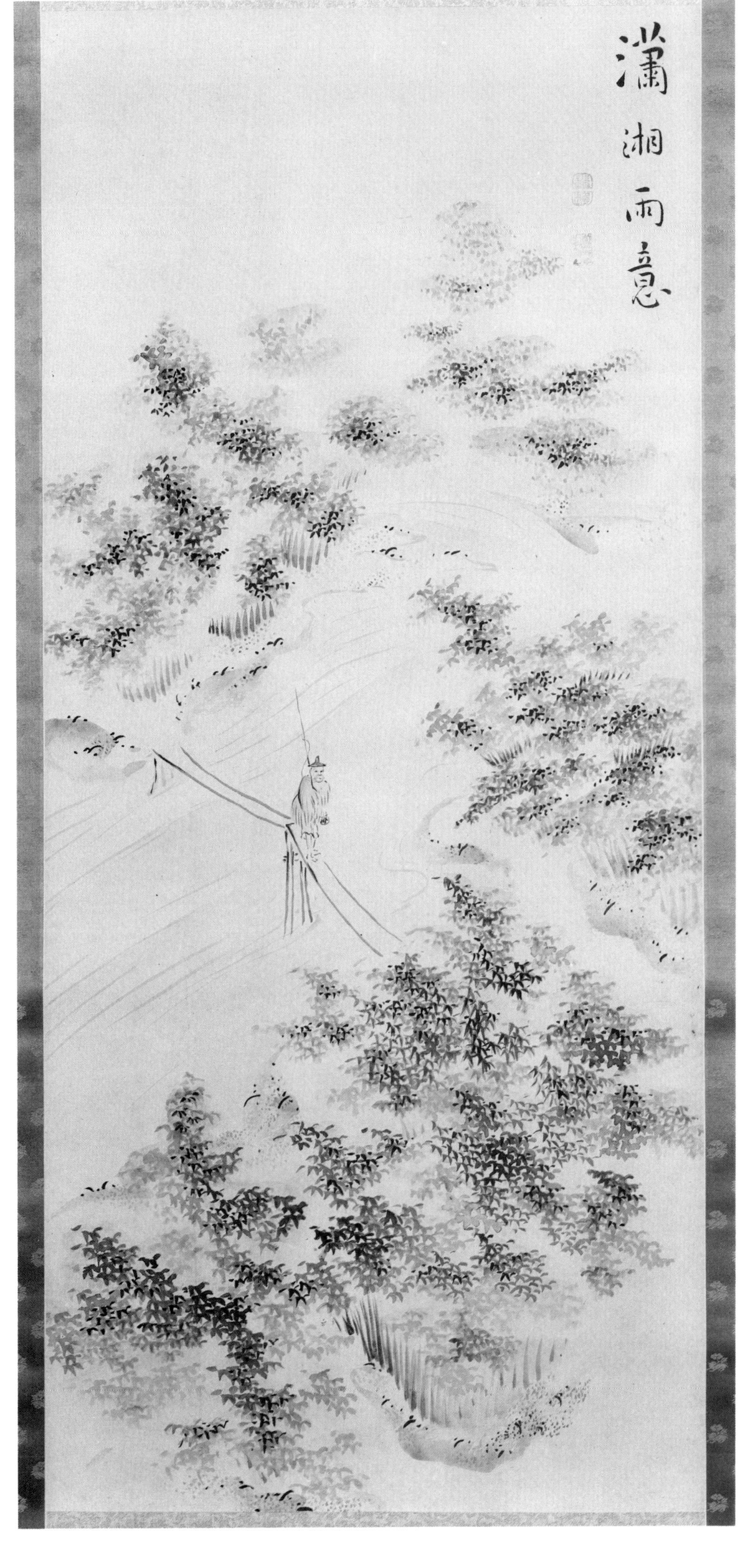
瀟湘雨意

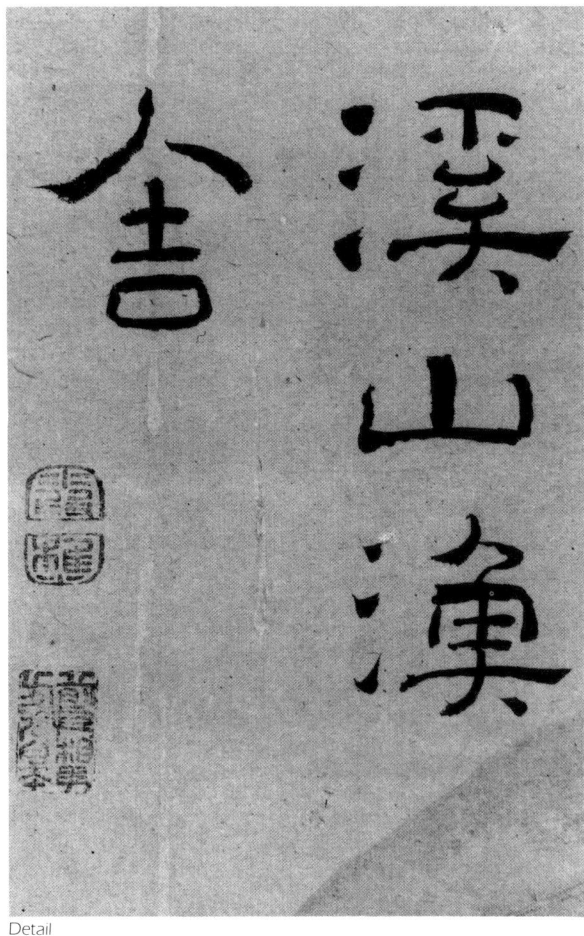
Detail

40

Fisherman's Hut by a Mountain Stream
(See color plate no. 40)

Hanging Scroll
Ink and light color on paper
131.9 x 57.0 cm

Seals
Ka Shō
Zenshin Sōba Hō Kyūkō

Ikeno Taiga
1723-1776
Datable to the fifth month of the year
corresponding to 1769

Taiga's sense of joy in nature and his sunny disposition are nowhere more evident than in this riotous, lightly colored landscape, which was originally part of the same set as the preceding painting (no. 39). After establishing vertical and horizontal axes in the foreground with willow, bamboo, and bridge, Taiga, in this painting, tipped the horizon and painted the background mountains wildly uphill with a torrent of water rushing in the opposite direction.

The usual Nanga treatment of this type of scene would be a rhapsodic, romantic image of the simple fisherman's life in the countryside. Taiga, however, imbues the imagery with such pictorial invention that he approaches pure expressionism. His daring knew no limits. He reversed the usual manner of manipulating brush strokes. For instance, he used the katabokashi (one-side modeling) technique to paint the foreground willow, describing the trunk conventionally in the lower portion and in the center at the left side. The rich pigment carried on the tip of the brush flowed to outline the dark edge of the trunk. On the right side he used the same technique, but, there, the dark line defines the outside edge and the watery pigment describes what in reality should be air. The inconsistency, however, worked well in Taiga's hands, and after only a slight hesitation, the eye accepts the image without objection. This same katabokashi technique was used in the standard fashion to define the brows of little hillocks, and to cap the high hill at the right.

Taiga's free handling of the landscape was not the result of a lack of familiarity with nature. He knew at first hand the stony roads of even the remotest parts of the country. Between 1748 and 1750 he climbed some of the most challenging mountains in Japan, twice ascending Mount Fuji. These climbs had spiritual overtones, for some peaks were sacred to both Buddhist and Shinto traditions, and throughout his life he continued to travel about the country. While stopping over in Edo in 1749, he was introduced to Noro Genjō (died 1761), a famous botanist who had become a high government official. Genjō had learned to speak Dutch, and the annual Dutch emissaries to the shogun's court reported to him. Through his contacts with the foreigners he came into possession of Western books and engravings that Taiga saw. Taiga admired Western pictures and on occasion made use of the principles of diminishing scale and shaded mass with good effect.

Taiga never hesitated to combine in one painting realistic Japanese scenes, pure fantasy and imaginary Chinese landscapes in the true literati manner. He might, as in this painting, mix these elements and add a humorous touch, such as the tipsy scholar who in this painting must hold on to his servant while crossing the bridge. Or, as in a set of fusuma paintings at Jishō-ji (Ginkaku-ji), he mixes Chinese conventions and Japanese scenery. He shows genial and rather portly Chinese scholars somewhat uncomfortably swaddled in voluminous robes and gathered in a pine grove in their pursuit of the four gentlemanly accomplishments: music, calligraphy, the game of gō, and painting. But, in the section describing the pursuit of painting, a young attendant holds aloft a scroll bearing an unmistakable view of Mount Fuji.

This painting and the preceding one were once a part of a group of twelve landscapes attached to a pair of six-panel screens. One painting in the group dates to the year 1769, which provides a reliable reference for the group as a whole. Even without this datable reference, however, Taiga's assured handling of the composition and his powerful and sweeping line declare this painting a superior example from his mature period.

Published
Ikeno Taiga Gafu, vol. 4 (Tokyo, 1958), pl. 462.
Ikeno Taiga Sakuhinshū (Tokyo, 1960), pl. 462-2.

Reference
Nihon no Bunjinga, Tokyo National Museum (ed.) (Tokyo, 1966), pl. 49.

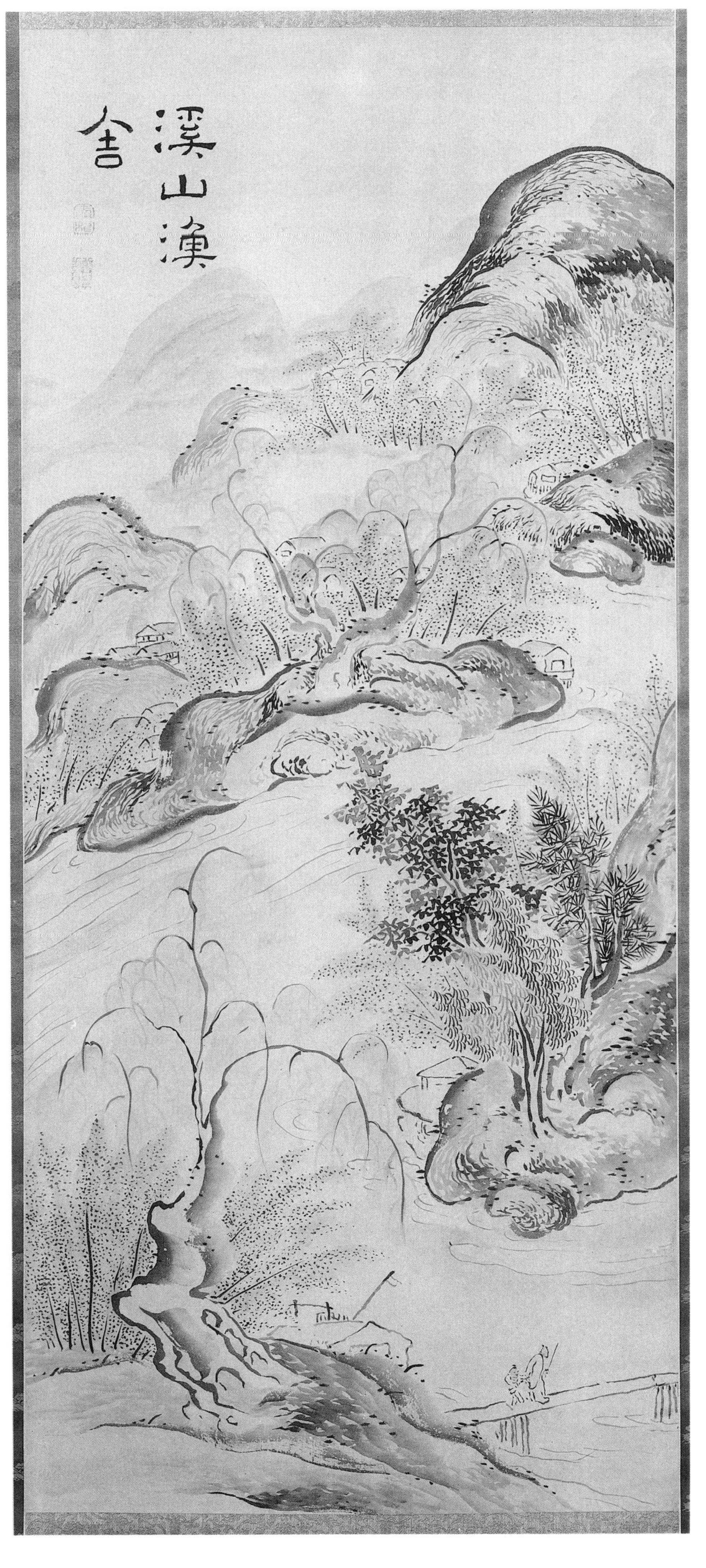

溪山漁舍

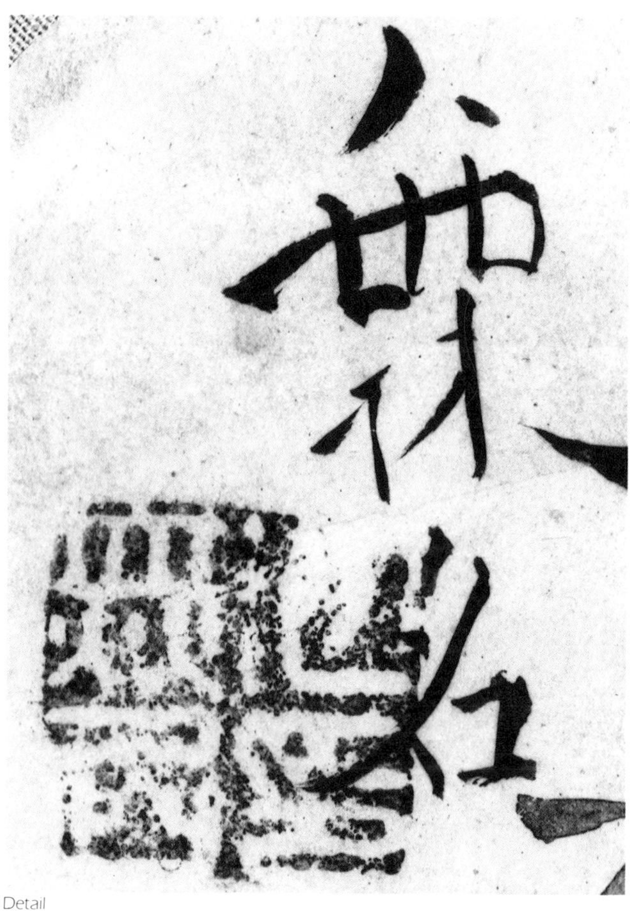

Detail

41

Cultivating and Weeding the Fields

Hanging Scroll
Mounted fan painting
Ink on mica-coated paper
25.8 x 27.6 cm (fan only)

Signature
Mumei

Seal
Ike Mumei In

Ikeno Taiga
1723-1776

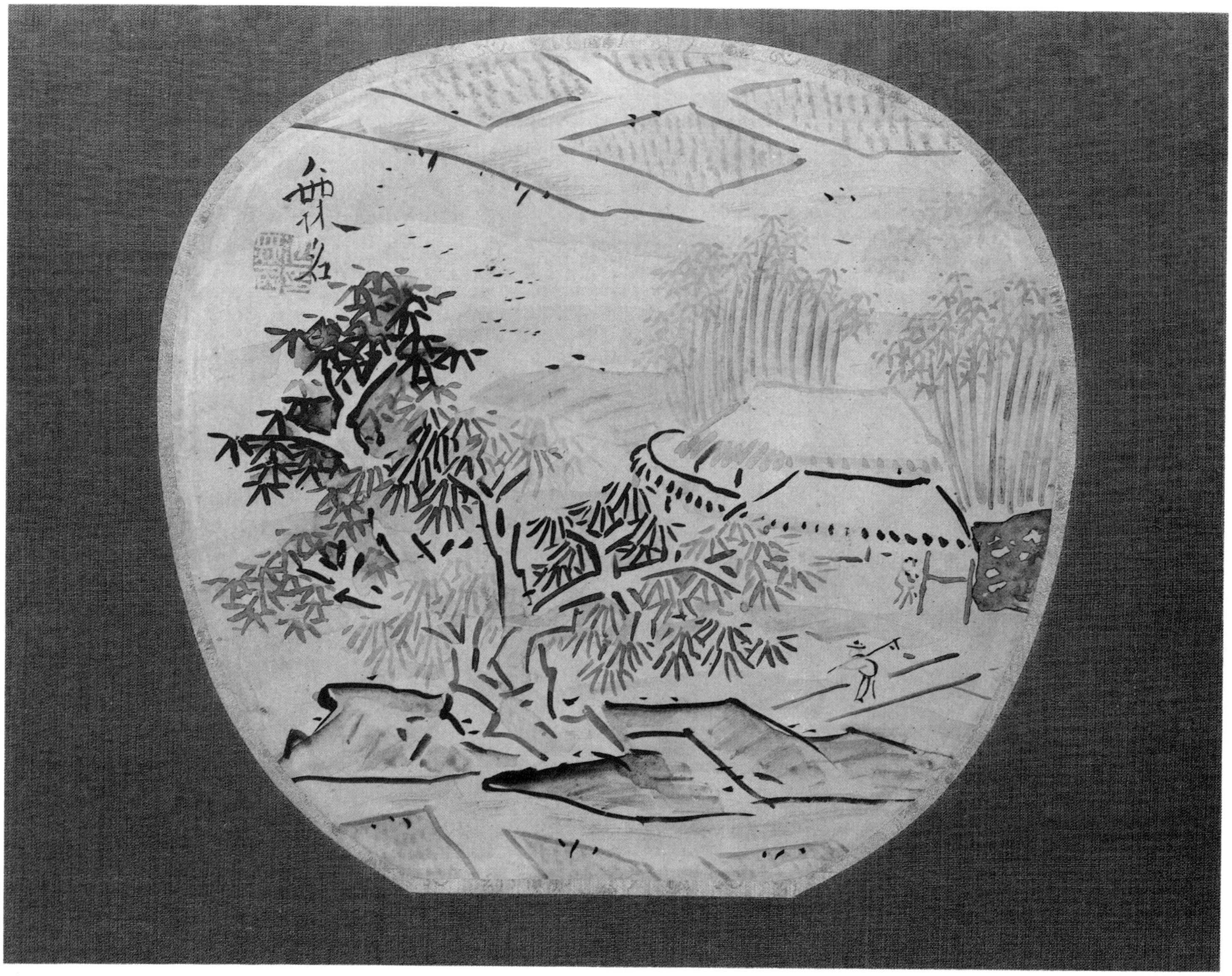

Taiga composed this landscape so that the distant fields appearing at the top balance the near fields at the bottom; he bound the two areas together with the spreading branches of the tree at the left and the swaying bamboo rising over the farmhouse at the right. The figures at the lower right, one on the bridge and one at the doorway of the house, are merely coincidental. The utmost skill in two-dimensional design has been put to use in this landscape.

This fan painting closely resembles Taiga's contributions to the famous 1771 **Jūben-Jūgi** albums done together with Yosa Buson (1716-1784). Taiga provided the illustrations and the text of the **Jūben,** or **Ten Conveniences of Living in the Country.** This piece is an even more abstract composition, but the motifs and techniques employed here—the system of structuring the bamboo, the roof lines, the laid-out rice fields—clearly point to a date close to that of the **Jūben-Jūgi.** It is thus probably a little later than the two other Taiga paintings (nos. 39 and 40) in the Sansō Collection. The **Jūben,** to be sure, is more developed in terms of coloring and detail. Fans like this were seldom intended for posterity; they were used for a season or two before being discarded. Nevertheless, because of his great reputation, many of Taiga's fans from late in his career have been preserved. In these small-scale, expendable items, Taiga reached perhaps the ultimate in spontaneity, with eager thrusting lines and roughly exciting abbreviations of natural forms that press to the edge of pure expressionism.

The fan format had been a favorite of Taiga's from the early days of his career. Taiga had, in fact, begun his professional career operating a fan shop. Kyoto's sultry summer heat made fans not merely a matter of fashion but a necessity of life. Taiga's fan shop did not flourish. Possibly the teenage Taiga, noted in later life for his eccentric behavior, was inattentive to business. More likely still, his designs did not catch the public fancy, for he was already following the Chinese woodblock-painting books known in Japan as the **Hasshu Gafu.** His designs must have appeared awkward to a public accustomed to the sensuous colors, curving lines, and familiar literary themes of Yamato-e and Rimpa compositions.

This late fan, however, also shows how far Taiga had come in his lifetime in developing Nanga into a distinctly Japanese idiom. Taiga's early fans show the Chinese Nanga style which artists such as Nankai (no. 37), Kien, and Hyakusen first employed in eighteenth-century Japan. Fifty years later, as this fan shows, Taiga and Yosa Buson had evolved a distinct Japanese Nanga idiom. Taiga was a gregarious soul who attracted many followers. Among them, men like Kuwayama Gyokushū (no. 43) and Kimura Kenkadō (no. 45) helped to shape the general acceptance of Nanga; and through their own painting and published art criticism promoted Taiga's aesthetic standards.

Published
Ikeno Taiga Gafu, vol. 4 (Tokyo, 1958), pl. 525.
Ikeno Taiga Sakuhinshū (Tokyo, 1960), pl. 525.

Reference
Ikeno Taiga, Bunjinga Suihen vol. 12 (Tokyo, 1973), seal no. 56, p. 144.

Ikeno Gyokuran
1728-1784

42

Landscape
(See color plate no. 42)

Hanging Scroll
Ink and color on silk
110.0 x 33.7 cm

Signature
Gyokuran

Seals
Gyoku
Ran

Gyokuran's husband and teacher, Ikeno Taiga (nos. 39-41), was perhaps the most dynamic personality on the literati painting scene. He is justifiably famous as one of the two artists (the other being Buson) in the second half of the eighteenth century whose art was directly responsible for defining the Japanese expression of the Nanga style. Any appraisal of Gyokuran's work, therefore, usually stresses how nearly successful she was at achieving the standards of Taiga's work. As with other students close to their teacher, Gyokuran's work reflects the master's vision of subject matter, composition, and palette. This painting in particular among Gyokuran's work is related to Taiga's landscapes of circa 1760.

In brushwork, however, Gyokuran and Taiga are clearly distinct personalities. More than Taiga's, Gyokuran's brushwork exhibits a tendency toward regular forms and patterned textures. Gyokuran's brush shows a restraint derived from years of submitting to the discipline of traditional cursive calligraphy. She was an accomplished traditional Japanese waka poet, and when these poems appear in her paintings, the calligraphy exhibits the same light, springing bounce and resilient profiles that the brushwork of her paintings demonstrates. Although the painting styles of Gyokuran and her husband resemble each other superficially, Gyokuran's painting exhibits a uniquely charming expressiveness derived from this restrained delicacy and sense of contained energy that Taiga's explosive showmanship obliterated in his own dramatic works.

Gyokuran was an art name; her family name was Machi. She was born in Kyoto in about 1727; the exact date is not known, but it is thought that she was about four years Taiga's junior. Perhaps her first teacher was Yanagisawa Kien, the pioneer Nanga artist, who was friendly with Gyokuran's grandmother, Kaji, and who praised Kaji's literary abilities. There is a tradition that the Gyoku of her art name was granted by Kien, from one of his own art names, Gyokukei (or Gyokkei). Taiga too shares one art name received from Kien: Gyokukai.

Gyokuran's grandmother had started a small tea stall in the Gion district of Kyoto. She became well known for her connoisseurship of Japanese poetry, and from the beginning, the shop developed literary associations. Gyokuran along with her mother, Yuri, continued to operate the shop, and they were known for their skill at waka poetry. It is thought that Taiga first approached Gyokuran and her mother regarding the study of poetry; soon, romance blossomed and Taiga and Gyokuran were married, perhaps around 1752.

It was rare for a townswoman in the mid-eighteenth century to be educated in poetry, calligraphy, and painting. It is only in recent decades that Gyokuran's skill at painting has come to receive the recognition it has well deserved, and her place established as an important Nanga artist.

Published
Kokka, no. 998 (March 1977), pp. 36-39.

Reference
Kobijutsu, no. 44, special issue on Taiga and Gyokuran (April 1974).

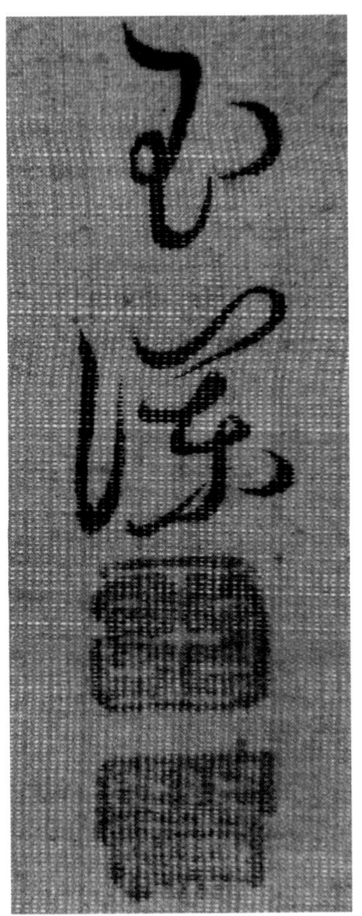

Detail

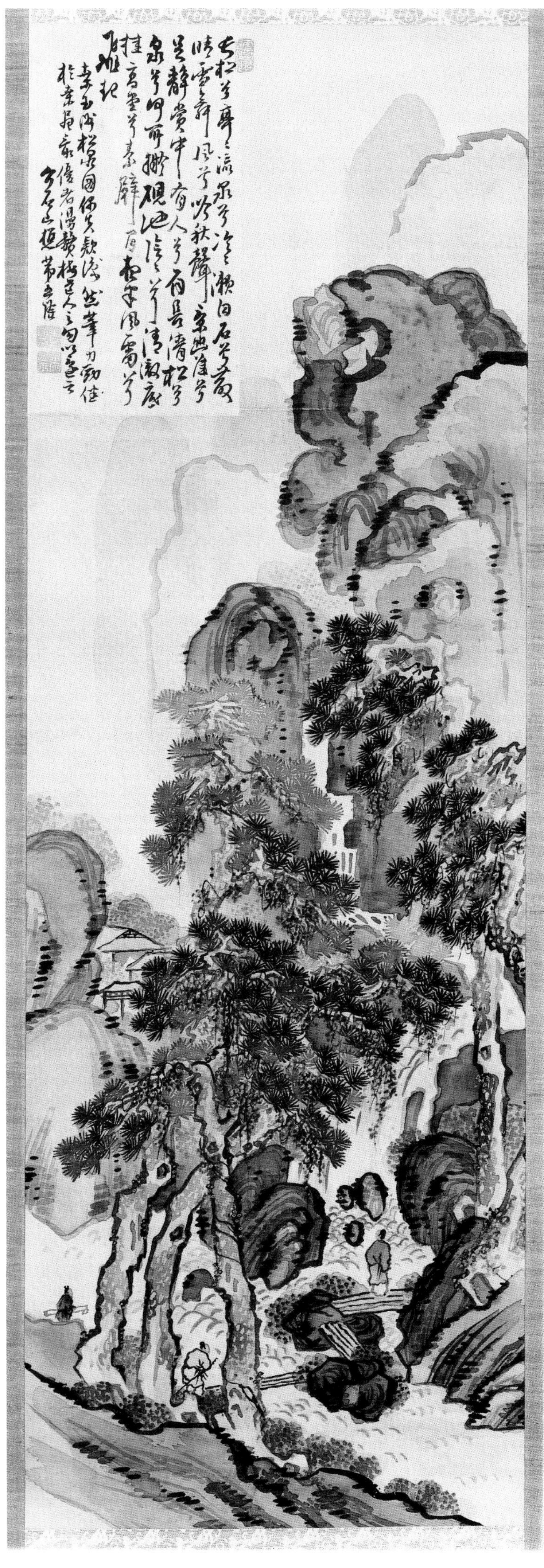

Kuwayama Gyokushū
1746–1799

Inscription
Noro Kaiseki
1747–1828

43

Pine Trees by a Spring
(See color plate no. 43)

Hanging Scroll
Ink and color on silk
98.5 x 32.8 cm

Inscriber's Signature
Kaiseki Sanshō Daigoryū

Inscriber's Seals
Daigoryū In
Kaiseki Koji
Ummu

This painting is more firmly structured than many paintings by Gyokushū, showing decorative coloration with unified composition and mannered brushwork. More commonly, Gyokushū's compositions are diffuse with languid though elegant brushstrokes. It is perhaps these other qualities that prompted his friend Noro Kaiseki (no. 44) in his long inscription to characterize this as "most excellent among Gyokushū's paintings." Gyokushū patterned his painting by dotting the surface with parallel horizontal Mi strokes that serve as a brake to the otherwise swift contour lines that cascade like the tumbling waterfall in the long vertical in the center. The rather nervous jumps his line makes with self-conscious repetition and ringing regularity impart an insistent, though pleasant, visual and psychological impact on the viewer. The richness of this painting's lush chromatics and active brushwork give it a visually powerful attraction.

Gyokushū's signature does not appear on the painting; it was perhaps originally where the paper with Kaiseki's long inscription was added at the upper left. Attesting to the picture's authenticity, Kaiseki titled the painting **Pine Trees by a Spring** and copied a long poem by the Yüan dynasty painter, calligrapher and poet Wu Chen (1280-1354). Kaiseki concludes the inscription with a remark that he returns the painting with these few lines, suggesting that he had been requested to authenticate the painting and in the process wrote a fine colophon that the owner then attached to it.

Kuwayama Gyokushū was from Kii, modern Wakayama prefecture, from a well-to-do merchant family. Because of the remoteness of the family home, he found his best models in the works of art and calligraphy that he collected. He may have studied briefly with a professional painter in Edo. He also came to know of the Nagasaki style of seminaturalistic, colorful flower-and-bird painting, but his own ingenuity brought him to an understanding of Nanga in terms of Japanese tradition in a way unmatched by other theoreticians. He found precursors to the Nanga movement in such diverse artists as Sōtatsu, Kōrin, Konoe Nobutada, and Shōkado Shōjō. For him, the Japanese landscape was well suited to Nanga ideals; he incorporated a local scenic spot in his painting of the **Peach Blossom Spring,** a standard Chinese theme depicting the legend of a fisherman who discovered an enchanted garden.

Gyokushū is more highly regarded as a critic and theorist than as a painter. He wrote a very influential essay on Nanga aesthetics, the **Kaiji Higen,** and wrote and published in 1790 the tale of his own artistic pilgrimage in the **Gyokushū Gashu.** The **Kaiji Higen** was published posthumously by his friend Kimura Kenkadō (no. 45) in 1800. From the **Gyokushū Gashu** we learn of his friendship with Noro Kaiseki. The two were from the same area and early in their youth formed a relationship that lasted throughout their lives. Kaiseki's inscription, attached to the painting subsequent to the initial mounting, clearly attests to their friendship. Gyokushū also tells in the **Gashu** of his association with Taiga and Taiga's good friends Kō Fuyō and Kimura Kenkadō. Kushiro Unsen (no. 46) was also numbered among his literati painter friends.

Gyokushū was acquainted with and studied painting under Ikeno Taiga during the last years of Taiga's life, and it was the influence from this period that seems to have marked Gyokushū's style the most. The verve in the brushwork and the fondness for color in this painting recall Taiga's painting style.

The inscription by Noro Kaiseki begins with a poem by the Yüan-period painter and poet, Mei Tao-jen, or Wu Chên, and ends with a tribute to Gyokushū's painting:

A tall pine tree towers alone,
With refreshing sound the flowing stream
Rinses stones white and scatters the fair-weather snow.
The heavenly wind, dancing, sings the sounds of autumn,
And the tranquil beauty of the scene is enough for
quiet appreciation.
Among them there are men whose eyebrows are long.
Noble pine and spring, how can they be compared?
The pool is calm and limpid to the bottom.
A building is suspended high up on the sheer walls of
the cliff.
At midnight a thunderstorm suddenly appears.

Sō Gyokushū's **Shōsenzu (Pine Trees by a Spring).** His signature happens to be missing but the power of his brush is vigorous, and this is the most excellent among Gyokushū's paintings. Although I have said unnecessary things [about this painting], I return it with Mei Tao-jen's lines.
Kaiseki Sanshō Daigoryū.

Published
Ryūsen Shūhō: Mayuyama Seventy Years, vol. 2 (Tokyo, 1976), pl. 483.

References
Bijutsu Kenkyū, no. 128 (January 1943), pp. 37-38.
Kokka, no. 962 (October 1973), pp. 28-29.
Kokka, no. 851 (February 1963), pp. 31-33.

Noro Kaiseki
1747-1828
Dated in accordance with
1826

44

Landscape

Hanging Scroll
Ink and color on silk satin
118.8 x 38.7 cm

Signature
Daigoryū

Seals
Daigo
Ryū
Shihekisai

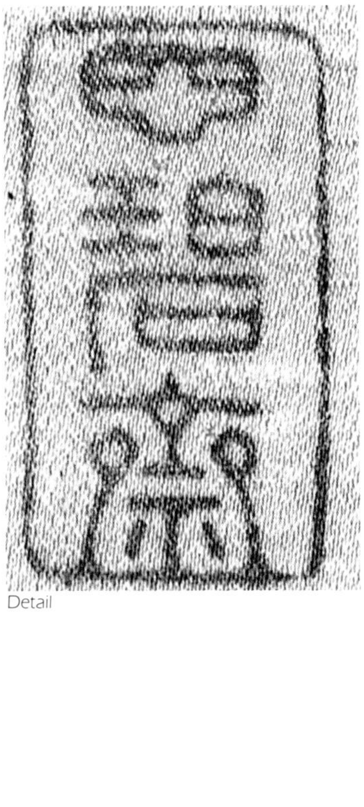

Detail

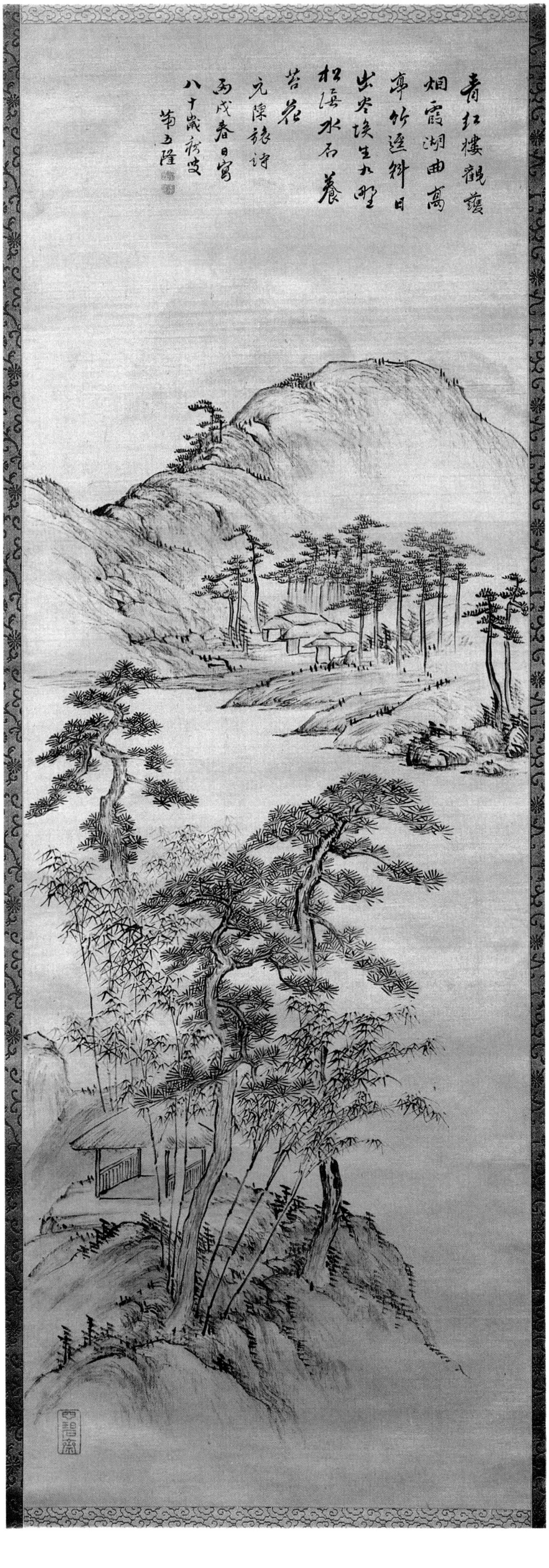

Noro Kaiseki was a prominent member of the generation of conservative literati masters who came to the fore in the first three decades of the nineteenth century. This painting and its inscription, done in his eightieth year, faithfully reflect the artistic and literary ideals that he cherished. The style of Ni Tsan (1301-1374) was the source of the empty middleground receding in a diagonal manner, as well as the hut and clump of trees in the foreground. Kaiseki himself inscribed the poem of a relatively obscure Yüan scholar and poet, Ch'en Lu (1288-1343); it describes the quiet mood of rural life preferred by the literati:

Blue and red watchtower sheltered by mist;
High pavilion by the lake; twisting path through
the bamboo.
The sun rises; dust and dirt emerge from the world.
Shaded by pine, stones in the water nourish the
flowering moss.

Poem by Ch'en Lu of Yüan

Painted on a spring day of Hinoe-inu [Bunsei 9-1826]
by the foolish, eighty-year-old man

[Signed] Daigoryū

This tranquil scene is not a verbatim reproduction of the one described in the verse but, rather, the artists's somewhat free interpretation of it. Many of the traits admired in Yüan painting are present here, such as the dry linearity and openness of forms; strong control and direction are also present in the painting, symptomatic of the precision and academic qualities of Ch'ing period orthodox literati painting. In contrast to the spatial qualities in the landscape style of Ni Tsan, the background mountain in this painting recedes into depth in a manner that makes the illusion of space more three-dimensional in quality.

Noro Kaiseki was born to a samurai family in Kii province, the modern Wakayama prefecture. He began to study painting under Kuwayama Gyokushū, also then a young artist in Kii, and the two remained life-long friends, as the inscription on the Gyokushū painting (no. 43) testifies. While in his teens, Kaiseki moved to Kyoto, where he may have studied under Taiga. His later paintings owe little to Gyokushū, but retain some reflections of Taiga's more Chinese manner. In 1797 he returned to his home, perhaps summoned, to become the official artist to the lord of Kishū. In 1799 and 1801 he was able to make trips to Edo, where he studied at first hand original Chinese paintings, particularly the work of I-Fu-chiu.

In his later years, dwelling in remote Kii province far from Japan's busy cities, Kaiseki was a prestigious exemplar of the literati ideal of the amateur gentleman-artist, freed from the aura of professionalism that enveloped the urban artists. He was sought out by younger contemporaries wishing advice and encouragement; Tanomura Chikuden (nos. 49, 50) visited him in 1811. Kaiseki's name is linked with that of Sō Aiseki (died ca 1837), one of his students, and Nagamachi Chikuseki (1747-1806). They are referred to as the three seki, or rocks, suggesting that they were the basis on which orthodox early nineteenth century Naga painting was built.

As a theorist, Kaiseki expressed a strong naturalistic viewpoint. He criticized those who followed Chinese pattern books, and to demonstrate his dedication to truth in nature, he did several well-known paintings of the sacred Nachi waterfall at Kumano, on the southern coast of his home province of Kii. A number of his other paintings depict the rugged, mountainous landscape of the Kii peninsula, one of the most picturesque regions in all Japan; and he kept a sketchbook at his side in order to record the scenery as he traveled about the country.

Nonetheless, the painting of Kaiseki exhibited here is surely a conventional landscape, with no attempt to represent a specific site. Kaiseki was not a revolutionary figure; his published admonitions to be true to nature and to avoid copying the pictures of other artists were intended to reinforce or invigorate traditional Nanga painting modes, not to challenge them seriously. He had no desire to provoke among Nanga artists the extremes of pictorial illusionism of Western-style artists like Shiba Kōkan or the expressionism of men like Gyokudō (nos. 47, 48). Yet, as in this painting, his works often have a sense of pictorial depth that is subtly informed by the techniques of Western illusionism, and he worked in a great number of stylistic idioms, true to the spirit of inquiry so prominent in the literati point of view.

References
Bijutsu Kenkyū, no. 74 (February 1938), pp. 21-28.
Bijutsu Kenkyū, no. 72 (December 1937), pp. 6-16.
Bijutsu Kenkyū, Mori, Senzō, "Kaiseki no Kenkyū," no. 71 (November 1937), pp. 26-35.
Kokka, no. 924 (July 1970), pl. 11, pp. 5-19.
Kokka, no. 353 (October 1919), pp. 148, 151-155.
Nagasaki-ha Shasei Nansō Meigasen, Onshi Kyoto Hakubutsukan (ed.) (Kyoto, 1939), pl. 102.
Shobi Shiryō Kōshū 8-3 (Tokyo, 1916), pl. 25.

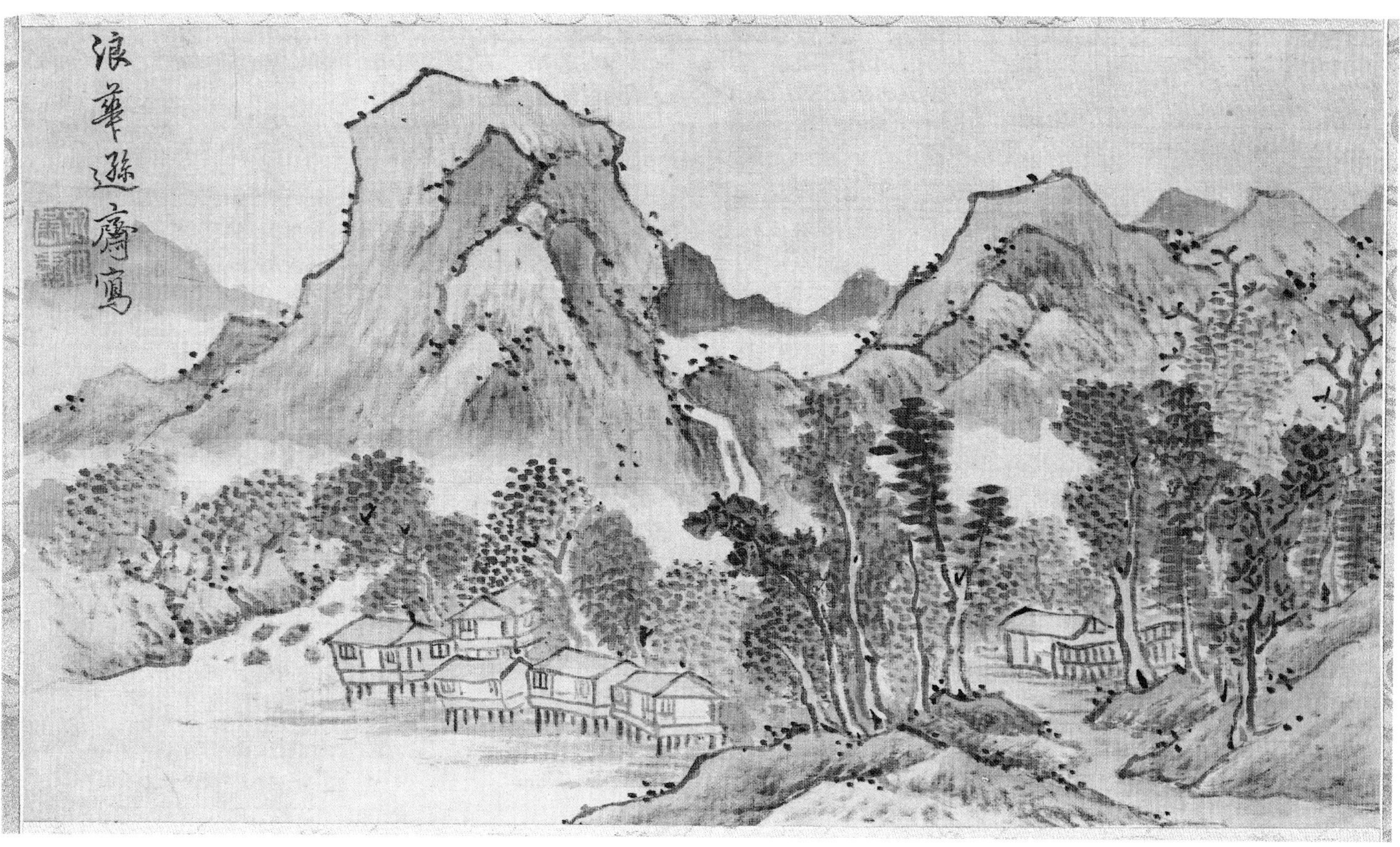

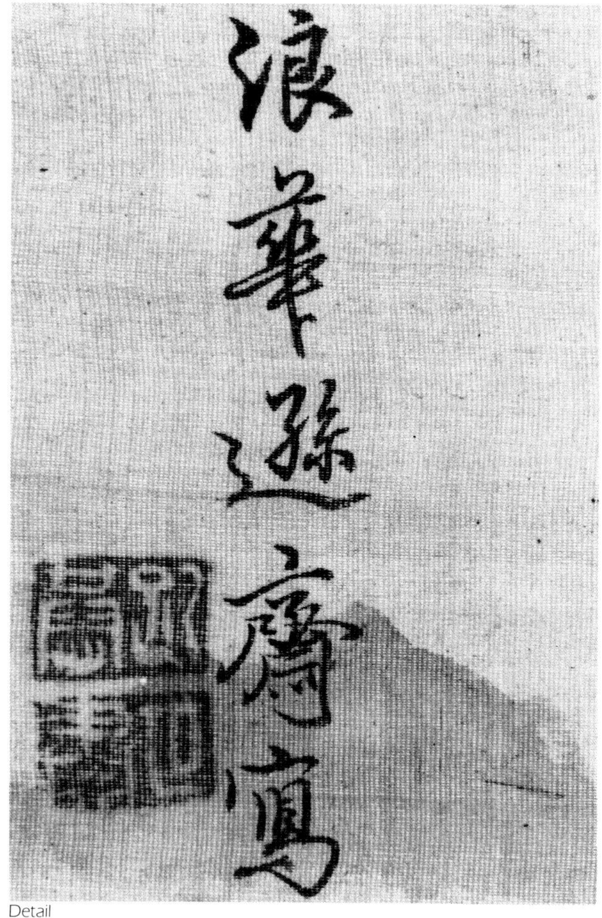

Detail

Kimura Kenkadō
1736-1802
ca 1800

45

Waterside Village and Mountain Landscape

Hanging Scroll
Ink and color on silk
21.6 x 36.2 cm

Signature
Naniwa Sonsai Sha[su]

Seals
Kokyo
Seishuku

This tiny, delicate landscape on silk, done in a manner related to that of Ikeno Taiga, is suffused with a sense of uncluttered innocence in keeping with the literati ideals of artlessness and direct simplicity. Thin washes of color and outlines of ink define the waterside cluster of houses and low background mountains. The crescent-shaped bay in the foreground is reflected by the rounded depression in the mountains to give the composition a harmonic focus. The simple schematic strokes used to define trees and houses belie the artist's reputation as a naturalist. When a child, Kenkadō suffered from a delicate constitution and was encouraged to develop an interest in honzō gaku (botany); his collection of animal and insect specimens grew to become one of the best-known of his day.

Kimura Kenkadō belonged to a well-to-do Osaka family of sake brewers. The standard biographies mention that he was discovered producing sake in excess of the allotted amount, a serious violation of economic controls that resulted in the confiscation of his fortune and virtual banishment. He moved from Osaka to Ise, where he became the guest of the lord, Masuyama Sessai. Sessai, himself a painter and art enthusiast, gave Kenkadō protection and supported him during a long stay. Kenkadō was eventually pardoned and returned to Osaka, where he opened an art goods and stationery shop and became familiar with such illustrious artists as Uragami Gyokudō (nos. 47, 48) and Tanomura Chikuden (nos. 49, 50), who had also come to break with the strictly regulated modes of feudal society. Kenkadō was a gregarious man; his shop soon became a lively center of literati activity, and every artist passing through the area was immediately welcomed. In 1788, Tani Bunchō (no. 55), on his way to Nagasaki, stopped to pay his respects to the older artist, and formed a relationship that was reflected in Bunchō's superb 1803 portrait of Kenkadō—one of the most striking and charming portraits to emerge from the literati movement. At Kenkadō's shop, Bunchō also met Kushiro Unsen (no. 46), who made such a deep impression on him that Bunchō was spurred to investigate Ming painting in the literati style.

Kenkadō's own art seems to have been the product of independent development of his rather strong innate talent. Yanagisawa Kien (1706-1758) had been a frequent visitor to the Kimura household; this pioneer literati artist might have been an inspiration to the young Kenkadō, but there is no clear evidence that Kenkadō followed any particular artist. He did study for a while with a minor Kanō school artist, Ōoka Shumboku (1680-1763).

Kenkadō's name is often connected with that of Ikeno Taiga, for there are undeniable reflections of Taiga's style in Kenkadō's work. However, the precise nature of his contacts with the Kyoto master remain unclear. Kenkadō, as a central figure in the Osaka literati circle, was well aware of the major personalities and styles of Japanese Nanga. His scholarly interests were capped in 1777 by his publication, with Kō Fuyō (1722-1784), of Sakaki Hyakusen's **Dictionary of Painters of the Yüan, Ming, and Ch'ing Dynasties (Genminshin Gajin Meiroku).**

References
Kokka, no. 697 (April 1950), pp. 107-109.
Nihon no Nanga, Yoshizawa, Chū, Suiboku Bijutsu Taikei, Bekkan no. 1 (Tokyo, 1976), pl. 9, pp. 154, 182.

46

Landscape

Hanging Scroll
Ink and slight color on paper
127.0 x 50.8 cm

Signature
Unsen

Seals
Unsen no In
Chūfu

Kushiro Unsen
1759-1811

This landscape twists with a vivacity far different from its Chinese prototypes, both ancient and contemporary, studied by Japanese literati painters. Unsen inscribed a very similar picture to indicate he believed that he was following in the style of the fabled landscape master, Chü-jan (active 960-980), and he may well have thought that this painting was in Chü-jan's style. It would seem likely, however, that his ideas of the Chü-jan style were derived from the work of such later artists as Ch'a Shih-piao (1615-1698) or Yun Shou-p'ing (1633-1690) of the Anhui group and had little to do with the grand and formal compositions of the Five Dynasty period. In this painting, Unsen clearly adhered to Chinese ideas and motifs, but he avoided the self-conscious sobriety that characterized the landscapes of his Kyoto contemporaries like Nakabayashi Chikutō (no. 52).

Kushiro Unsen was born at Shimabara on Kyushu, site of a historic Christian rebellion in the seventeenth century. He studied under Chinese painters in his native town and at the port city of Nagasaki. Nagasaki was the only place throughout much of the Edo period where foreigners—a few Dutch traders and a slightly larger number of Chinese—actually resided. The Chinese were, for the most part, either Buddhist priests or merchants who followed painting as amateurs; they had, however, been trained in China and had seen with their own eyes fine paintings of the Chinese literati tradition. It was therefore possible for Japanese students to gain from these men a more authentic feeling of the attitudes and ethos of the tradition than they could achieve from the study of book illustrations and handmade copies of Chinese paintings.

Unsen thus steeped himself in the lore and painting styles of the later Chinese literati, and even learned to speak Chinese. He came to Kyoto and joined the large, active group of Nanga artists there, but like others he also traveled throughout the country—as far as Edo in the east and the Japan Sea coast in the north. Later Unsen settled in the provincial center of Niigata on the rocky and stormy coast of the Japan Sea, where he worked and lived in virtual seclusion until his death at the early age of fifty-two years. Although he worked far removed from the chief cultural and political centers, he is increasingly recognized as one of the more original and accomplished Nanga artists of the late eighteenth century.

References
Bunjinga, Iijima, Isamu, Nihon no Bijutsu no. 4 (Tokyo, August 1966), pl. 141.
Koga Bikō, Asaoka, Okisada, vol. 2 (Tokyo, 1912), pp. 1147-1148.
Kokka, no. 356 (January 1920), pp. 266-267, 271.
Nansō-ha 2, Nihonga Taisei vol. 10 (Tokyo, 1930-1932), pls. 40-43.

Detail

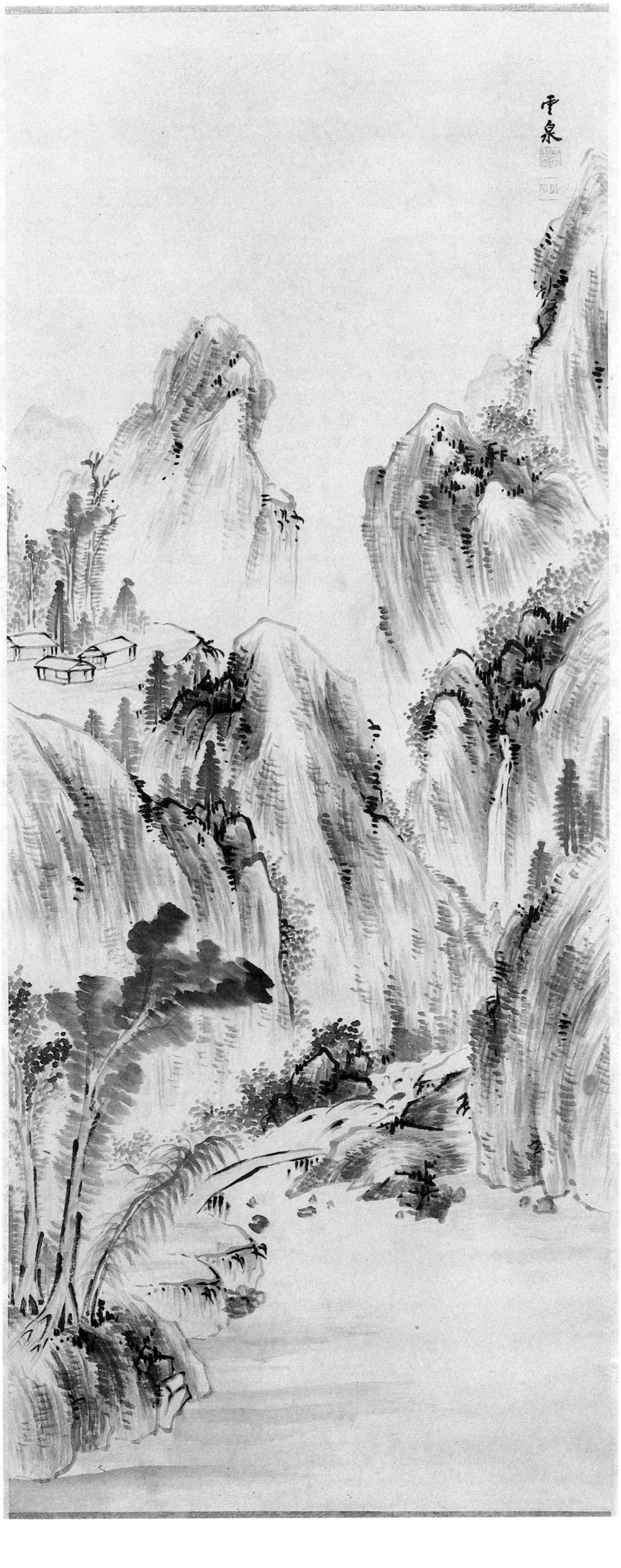

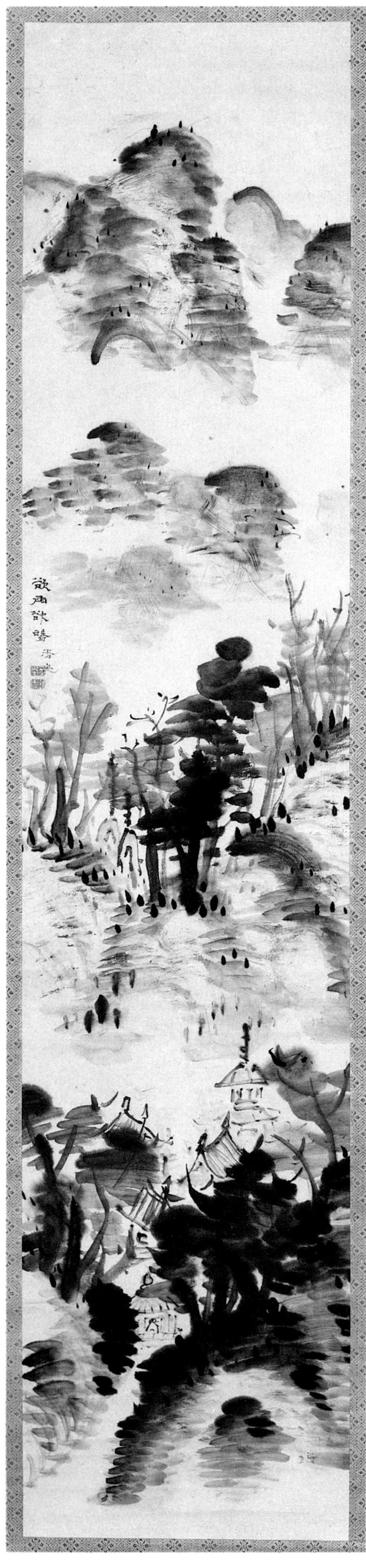

Uragami Gyokudō
1745-1820

47

Wishing for Rain,
Wishing for a Fine Day

Hanging Scroll
Ink and slight color on paper
122.0 x 26.7 cm

Signature
Gyokudō

Seal
Gyokudō
Ki no Hitsu

This landscape by Gyokudō contrasts strongly with the other work by Gyokudō in this exhibition (no. 48). Although the two share certain characteristics, they arise from different attitudes and techniques. In the other painting, Gyokudō structured his composition carefully so that an observer can walk through the landscape; in this painting, however, he has represented a narrow slice from nature to be taken at a single glance from a stationary position. This approach is reflected in the attitudes of the figures shown: in no. 48, an old man is active, crossing a bridge; in this painting, a man is passive, seated calmly by the window of a hut. Further, in this painting Gyokudō's brushwork is spontaneous and quickly executed, with bold contrasts of dark and light, lacking the delicate subtlety found in no. 48. Here, Gyokudō has placed one landform on top of another, and distributed foreground, middle ground, and background evenly in the composition. Spatial progression is suggested more by the intensity of the ink than by differences of scale or separation of the elements. He employed a full range of ink tones and brushwork, and a clear sense of structure, with counteracting diagonals of the land and carefully tilted trees that tie the composition together. A heavy mist weaves in and out of the landscape elements. In the upper portion, Gyokudō combined his favored Mi dots with drier, scratchier lines accented with dark dots to create a beautiful texture, and retain a convincing appearance of mass.

Unlike Taiga and Buson who excelled at abbreviated compositions painted with simplified but animated lines, Gyokudō was best at laboriously building up his paintings. Even though his bold and expressive ink tones often give the impression that Gyokudō worked in a quick and spontaneous way, a study of his paintings reveals his carefully insistent and intense layering of ink. Tanomura Chikuden (nos. 49, 50), one of the first to observe this quality in Gyokudō, wrote in his **Sanchūjin Jōzetsu** that Gyokudō "worked hard on lines and smearing." He praised Gyokudō's work by referring to the words of the Chinese painter Li Jih-hua: "Li Jih-hua says that painting must contain some uncertainty and intesnse thought. This is how an ancient painter reached his pinnacle…Gyokudō is the only one in Japan who understood this, and I learned that from him." (Translation by Hiro Kawasaki.)

The seal on this painting, Ki no Hitsu, appears often on works completed in Gyokudō's late forties, and the combination of the seals Gyokudō and Ki no Hitsu appears on his work at around fifty-four years of age. Ki no Hitsu means literally, "to aid the Ki family," and refers to Gyokudō's presumed descent from the poet Ki no Tsurayuki.

Reference
Gyokudō, Bunjinga Suihen vol. 14 (Tokyo, 1974), pls. 44, 79, pp. 109-122, 157-164.

Detail

Quietly Observing
Summer Mountains

Hanging Scroll
Ink on paper
28.9 x 64.0 cm

Signature
Gyokudō Kinshi Saku

Seal
Takeuchi Taijin no Son

Uragami Gyokudō
1745-1820

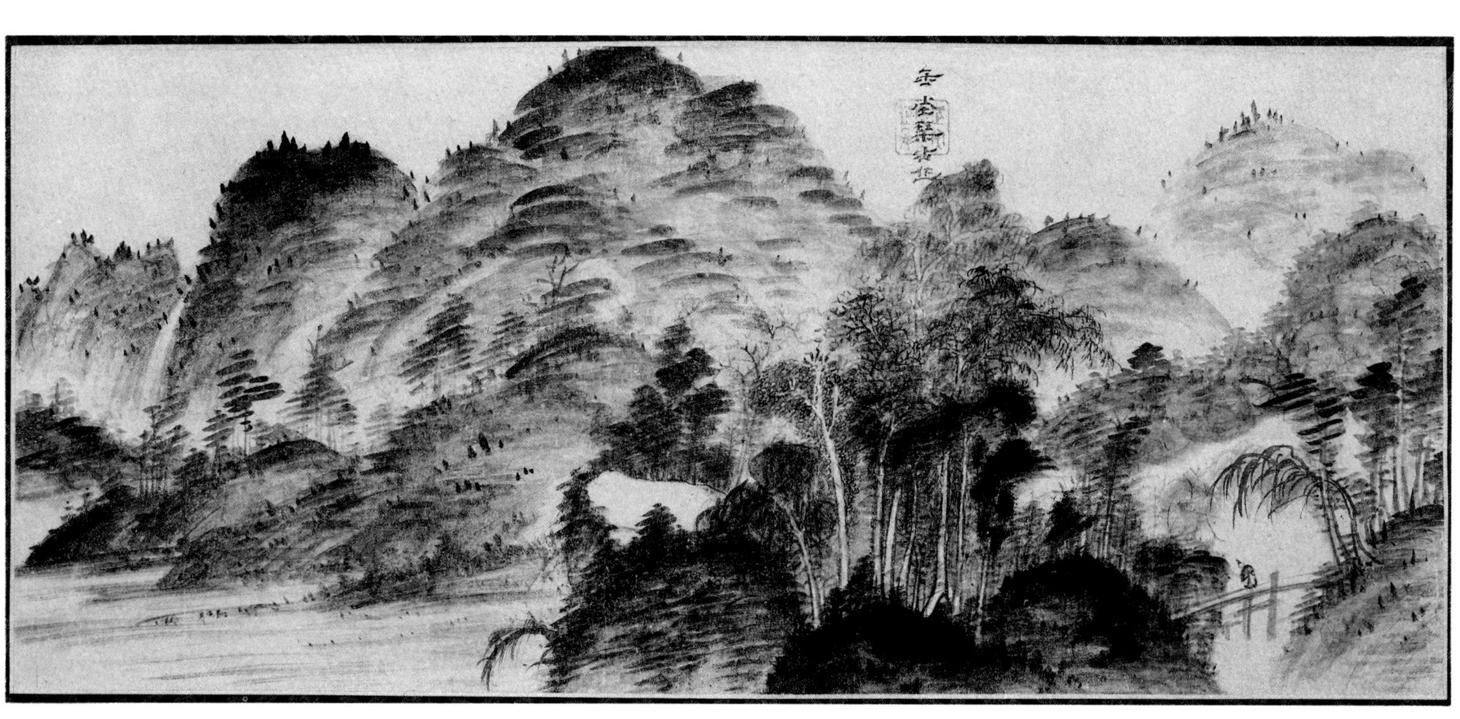

This landscape in horizontal format is an excellent example of Uragami Gyokudō's mature style, painted when he was in his late sixties. Like the majority of his works, it is in ink monochrome on paper, and the landscape elements are all brought relatively close to the picture plane, with only a restricted suggestion of receding space. Against a background of hillocks and water extending to the left, a grove of tall and spare trees rises in the foreground, suggesting an island. This island connects to the land at the right of the composition by a simple bridge, where we see a lone figure in Chinese robes. The figure's direction suggests that he is headed for the white clearing at the left. His position on the bridge gives him a view of the sharply receding river valley behind him, and in this manner, Gyokudō leads the viewer through the landscape.

Although the artist brings the entire scene close to the picture plane, he defines a clear spatial separation between foreground and background. Although he paints the trees and landmass in the foreground with short and closely laid strokes, he depicts those in the background across the river with longer strokes laid sparsely to permit the white of the paper to show through. The strokes he uses in the foreground are carefully differentiated through variations in the value of ink, giving a dramatic range of dark and light. In contrast, Gyokudō painted the mountains in the back with uniform strokes; only a few trees are distinctly recognizable. The softer contrasts in grays push them to the back, resulting in delicately undulating forms that retain their identities as masses. The whole composition, unified by the use of the so-called Mi dots or strokes, is characteristic of Gyokudō's imagery, unique in Nanga painting for its abstraction and dynamism.

Gyokudō's great artistic achievement grew from personal eccentricity and individualism, which often led him to a solitary life. Society seemed to excuse him from conformity with the usual standards of behavior. His contemporaries would encounter him traveling through the countryside or walking the crowded streets of Kyoto, wearing Chinese robes, his white beard flowing, and a Chinese ch'in (zither) on his back. He had a reputation for being fond of drink, and often played his music and painted his pictures while inebriated. During his life, Gyokudō's genius in painting was largely unappreciated; he was more famous as a musician and composer. In fact, his son Shunkin, was in greater demand as an artist. Gyokudō's paintings were probably of little help in gaining him a livelihood; they were painted mostly for his own enjoyment, or self-expression, or at most, as payments for lodgings he received on his journeys through Japan.

Gyokudō was born into a family of samurai, serving the lord of the Ikeda clan in Bizen province, modern Okayama prefecture. It is not clear when and how he came to study the art of painting. In his autobiographical essay, **Gyokudō Jidaiheiki,** he spoke of beginning his study of Chinese classics at the age of nine. Also, in a colophon he inscribed on a portrait of him by Shunkin, he mentioned that he began the study of poetry at the age of fifteen. Ikeda clan records, **Ikedake Rirekiryakuki,** express a concern about Gyokudō's artistic tendencies, and suggest that these tendencies were the main reason for his resignation from official service in 1794. Another reason may have been his involvement with Neo-Confucianism based on the Ming dynasty philosopher, Wang Yang-ming. The Tokugawa government prohibited the study of this heretical philosophy early in the Edo period, and prescribed severe penalties for it in the Kansei Reforms of 1792.

Most of Gyokudō's paintings date from the late phase of his life—his sixties and seventies. The few surviving early paintings show some characteristics of his mature style, but tend to conform to the general stylistic character of late eighteenth-century Nanga in the Kyoto area where the Taiga and Buson modes were being converted into more decorative forms in the hands of later painters.

Gyokudō's mature style possesses a strong formalistic appeal for the twentieth-century viewer. His brushwork is often bold and spontaneous, and the distribution of dark and light is exceptionally expressive as pure form. Most of all, Gyokudō landscapes communicate a sensitive, but intensely emotional interaction between an eccentric, lonely soul and his surrounding nature. His vision is immediate and intimate; it is filled with energy and is constantly changing in front of our eyes, reflecting the changes in the painter's subjective and spiritual responses toward nature.

The seal used on this painting, Takeuchi Daijin no Son, appears only once in the work of Gyokudō's sixties, but is common on the work of his seventies. Takeuchi Daijin (Minister) was a legendary figure in the court of Yamato. His descendants are said to have included many famous historical figures, one of whom is the poet, Ki no Tsurayuki. Gyokudō's family name, too, was originally Ki, but before his time, it was changed to Uragami. Therefore this seal designates lineage, claiming that Gyokudō was a descendant of the Minister Takeuchi.

Published
Kobijutsu, no. 32 (December 1970).

References
Gyokudō, Bunjinga Suihen vol. 14 (Tokyo, 1974), pp. 160-165.
Gyokudō, Mokubei, Yoshizawa, Chū, Suiboku Bijutsu Taikei vol. 13 (Tokyo, 1975), pp. 41-59, 176-180.

49

Conversation under the Full Moon
(See color plate no. 49)

Hanging Scroll
Ink and light color on silk
123.8 x 40.2 cm

Signature
Chikuden Sei

Seals
Isshō Senzan Sei
Kyūhō Mukai Nōsu

Tanomura Chikuden
1777-1835
Datable probably to 1832 or 1833

Tanomura Chikuden was born into a family serving the Nakagawa clan in Bungo province, modern Oita prefecture, on the island of Kyushu. Like Nankai before him, his father was a physician, and the father's profession encouraged Chikuden to pursue an academic life. His brilliance in Confucian studies convinced the clan administrator to allow him to abandon medical studies in 1798 and to teach at the clan school. During this period, Chikuden also participated in a compilation of the clan history. By this time, Chikuden seems to have begun a study of painting, working first under some local artists and later actively seeking out other sources for study. During the first decade of the nineteenth century, he found opportunities to visit Nagasaki, the Osaka and Kyoto area, and Edo. These visits had a lasting impact on the formation of Chikuden as a true literatus, for at Nagasaki he met Chinese painters and studied contemporary Chinese paintings. He also became acquainted with many Japanese scholars and artists such as Kimura Kenkadō (no. 45), Tani Bunchō (no. 55), Uragami Gyokudō (nos. 47, 48), and Noro Kaiseki (no. 44). About this time he also met Rai Sanyō, the great scholar, who was to become a very close friend.

During the eighteenth century, the Nanga painters had striven both to assimilate the literati tradition of China and to give it an expression suited to Japanese temperament. Until after the mideighteenth century, most artists, including Taiga and Buson, had only limited contact with actual literati paintings from China. They often pursued their study from woodblock-printed manuals of painting; therefore they gained little insight into the essential theory or into the qualities of the Chinese works themselves. The art of Taiga and Buson, for instance, is visually rooted more in Japanese than in Chinese aesthetics, literature, and history. Not until the time of Chikuden were the Japanese literati able to demonstrate a profound grasp of the subject of Chinese painting history and theory.

Chikuden's **Sanchūjin Jōzetsu**, first published in 1835, was a collection of essays that displayed his knowledge of Chinese art theories and reflected his direct observation of many fine paintings, both Chinese and Japanese. In addition, Chikuden has left writings on many other subjects: journalistic recollections about many of his friends, an anthology of poetry, and essays on flower arrangement, incense, and tea. He was the epitome of the literati man.

More than many literati painters, Chikuden utilized poetic inscriptions in his painting format. Many of his inscriptions, as this one, are lengthy and include much detailed observation beyond the poetry itself. Here, the theme of the painting is set by the poem: "In the west the sun dips down and the heat of the day retreats before the evening coolness…; the moon rises, breaking clouds; trees scatter shadows like a patterned net; visitors bringing wine and fish…" (Translated by Hiro Kawasaki.) The poem continues, describing how, although the wine and fish were not of the finest quality, having good friends, whom he had not seen for some time, contributed to the pleasantness of the party. As they ate and drank, they sat "happily, with their knees close together," discussing their poetry. The postscript tells us that these visitors were Tsunoda Kyūka and Takai Gentei, longtime friends and neighbors of Chikuden on Kyushu. It laments that the painter's "many good friends have passed away and [he] has been gradually losing such fine occasions as this," reflecting a touch of melancholy in the mood of the poet-painter toward the end of his life.

This towering landscape belongs to the late years of Chikuden's career. A group of paintings with similar composition and stylistic qualities bears a date corresponding to 1833, which provides a very probable date for this painting. Stylistically, these paintings share the particular motif that Chikuden created—adding broken darker ink lines along the trunks—to describe certain trees. His use of richly patterned foliage as a compositional device is also shared by other works of this period.

Chikuden often covered his compositions with small and densely laid brush strokes, carefully delineating each object, attaching a sense of dignity to the smallest things. His approach was well-suited to a small format and he was often at his best working in album leaf compositions. He succeeded, however, in transferring a similar lyricism and jewel-like quality to larger works such as this painting, in which pale earth tones and grayed blues impart a hushed intimacy to the moonlit landscape, inviting the viewer to share the artist's experience.

Deep lyricism is a major characteristic of Chikuden's mature work. A sensitive poet, Chikuden put into practice the ancient Chinese dictum that "poetry is a painting with words; there must be poetry in painting."

Published
Chikuden Meiseki Taizushi Ketteiban, Togari, Soshinan (ed.), vol. 2, pl. 141.
Nihon no Bunjinga, Tokyo National Museum (ed.) (Tokyo, 1966), pl. 130.
Ryūsen Shūhō: Mayuyama Seventy Years, vol. 2 (Tokyo, 1976), pl. 492.
Tanomura Chikuden, Bunjinga Suihen vol. 14 (Tokyo, 1975), pl. 24.

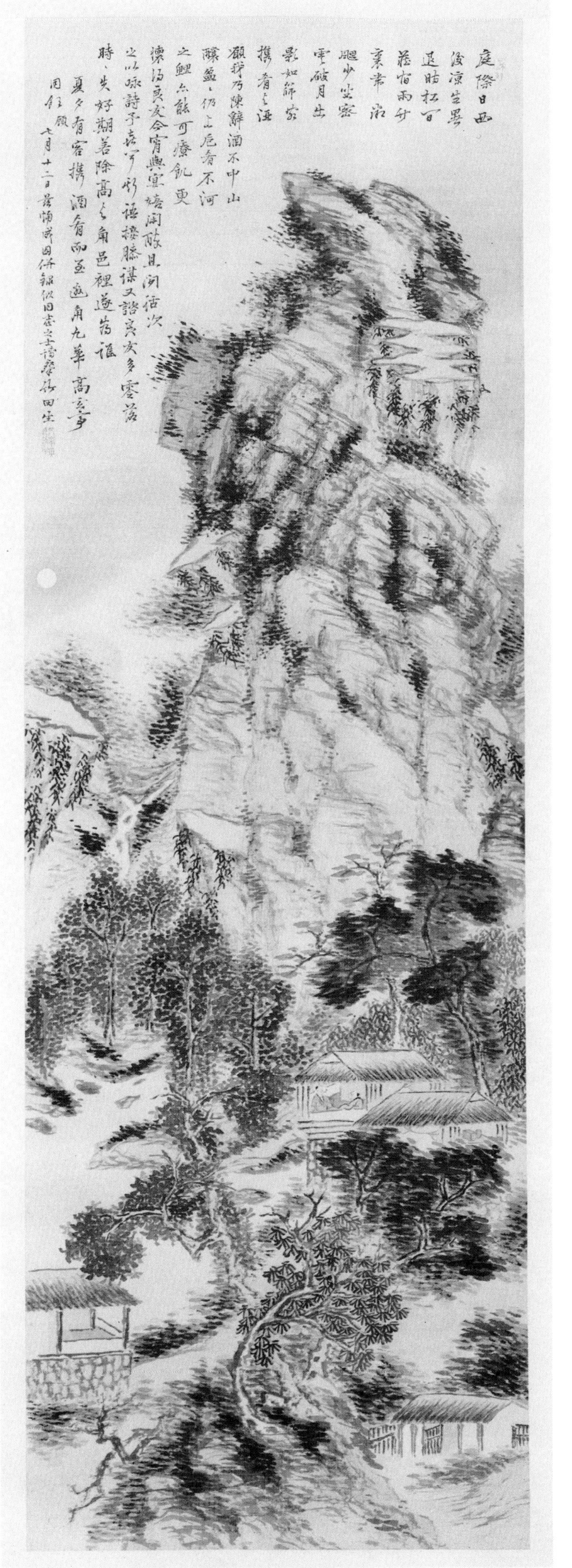

50

Scholar Gazing at the Mountains

Hanging Scroll
Ink and light color on silk
112.0 x 41.8 cm

Signature
Chikuden Sei

Seals
Ken In
Chikuden

Tanomura Chikuden
1777-1835
Dated in accordance with 1834

This landscape was painted in 1834 at a temple in Aki province (modern Hiroshima prefecture), probably Kichijōmitsu-in, where Chikuden stopped during one of his frequent trips about the country. The preceding landscape painting exemplified Chikuden's mature style with its romantic images and elegant and precise calligraphy. The present scroll, however, shows another view of the artist, ceaselessly probing for new ideas and experimenting with techniques for expression.

The scholar, shown standing in the foreground center and gazing upward to the right, most likely is T'ao Yüan-ming, the prototypical Chinese literatus (no. 4). T'ao was noted for his love of chrysanthemums, and the clusters of small spherical shapes massed at the edge of the path and in crevices among the crags overhead represent this flower, which, like the unique staff, usually appears in depictions of this poet. To the left, a tall pine tree spreads its branches above the figure, and behind a rock form rises sharply presenting an ambiguous relationship to the cliffs in the background. This ambiguity is further heightened by the overlapping of the branches and the foliage behind the trees. The rock forms curve around the shore as they rise to tall cliffs, which cast their reflections with that of the distant shore over the calm surface of the water at the right.

In contrast to Chikuden's typical late-period paintings of serene and stately pace, this work possesses a pulsating tension partially created by an unusually abstract use of ink values. In most of his late paintings he limits the often rhythmic and decorative moment to the surface of the picture plane. His land masses might swell and undulate, but they are structured for an understandable spatial progression. In this painting, however, the forms overlap sharply and create a staccato rhythm. The abrupt contrast of darks and lights contributes to this sense of ambiguity of spatial relationships, resulting in a tension and dynamic movement rarely found in Chikuden's painting.

Chikuden's inscription includes his own poem, a lyrical expression of bunjin values, and may be translated:

The tide ebbs, an embankment in the field casts an
even shadow,
The wind blows on the tips of the pine tree, starting
the crying birds,
Looking back at the mountain, standing and leaning
against a single staff of wisteria wood,
I myself see the mind of a superior man detached from
the mundane world.

This scroll painting was completed after nine years of hesitation, but is crude like this. However, people wanted it and my friend rejected the idea of my abandoning it; again I was tranquilly able to overcome.

Painted at a temple in Onomichi in Ryūgetsu fifth month of Kinoe-uma [1834.]
Chikuden-Sei

(Translated by Hiro Kawasaki)

Chikuden was a man of high moral purpose and strict discipline. His samurai sense of propriety, reinforced by Confucian ideals of resisting bad government and protecting the weak, brought him into conflict with his feudal lord, and Chikuden was forced to resign his position. Many other exsamurai painters left their positions purely as a result of unacceptable behavior, but Chikuden's retirement was partly an assertive act of political protest. Around 1808, in reaction to poor governmental administration, there was much unrest among the peasants of the province. This unrest was not isolated, but was one of many manifestations of dissatisfaction with the crumbling Tokugawa feudal regime. Chikuden wrote two proposals sympathetic to the peasants' plight, and his appeals for relief were rejected. This daring act of criticising authority—unthinkable in the social climate of the period—cost Chikuden his position.

The next twenty-five years of Chikuden's life were devoted to aesthetic pursuits. He was one of the most prolific of Japanese literati painters and writers. Although Chikuden had to resort to selling his paintings to earn a living, he maintained the independent attitude of the true literati.

Published
Chikuden, Takahashi, Kazuo (ed.) (Tokyo, 1976), p. 109.
Ryūsen Shūhō: Mayuyama Seventy Years, vol. 2 (Tokyo, 1976), pl. 489.

References
Kobijutsu, no. 52 (May 1977), pp. 149, 154-155.
Tanomura Chikuden, Bunjinga Suihen vol. 17 (Tokyo, 1975).

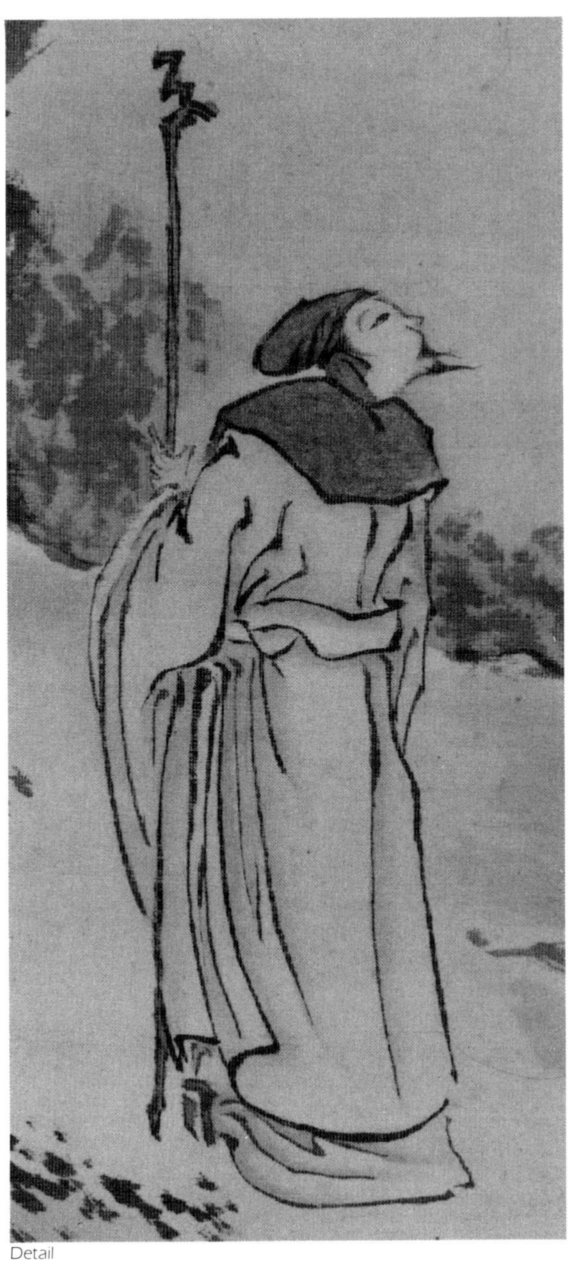

Detail

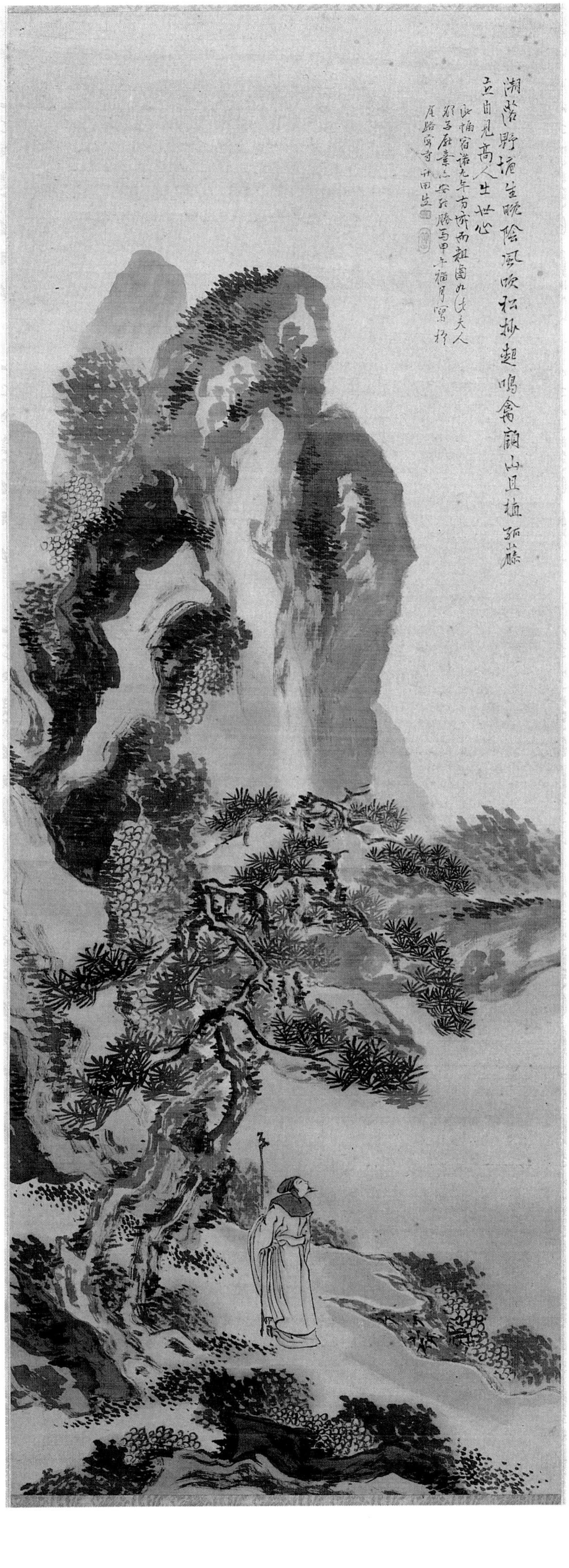

51

Mountain Landscape

Hanging Scroll
Ink and slight color on paper
139.5 x 28.6 cm

Signature
Hankō Denshuku

Seal
Denshuku no In

Okada Hankō
1782-1846
Dated in accordance with 1813

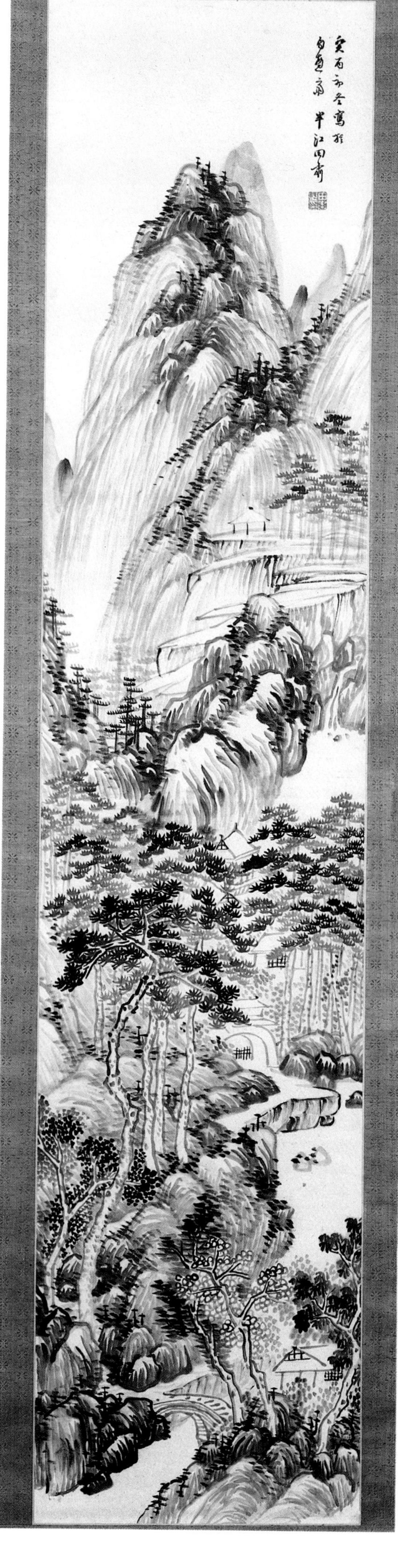

Detail

Hankō has presented an elaborate landscape of a gorge with mountains soaring in the background. In the foreground, trees push upward from a rocky stream bank; a footbridge leads to a gate and houses in the middle ground. The whole is tied together by a broad path leading in switchbacks to a pavilion part way up the mountain, leaving on the right side two cells of restful, flat water surface. This general format proved to be an archetypal one for Hankō, the leading Osaka master of bunjin-ga, and he continued to paint it in various styles and with different variations for many years.

Hankō and fellow-artists such as Kaioku, Chikutō, and Baiitsu (nos. 52-54), were well versed in contemporary Ch'ing painting, and even though the proportions for this painting are extreme for a Japanese painting of this period, the current taste in China was for a decidedly tall and narrow format. This generation, active in the second quarter of the century, remained increasingly faithful to mainland prototypes and were conservative in outlook and style. A generation earlier there was still room for experimentation, humor, and far less reverence for Chinese models. Gyokushū (no. 43) or Kenkadō (no. 45) could relax the rules or invent new ones if they chose; bright colors frequently appeared in the works of a Taiga or Kenkadō, but the next generation returned to a more sober mode, with meticulous execution and dignified authenticity.

Hankō's father, Okada Beisanjin (1744-1820) belonged to the more adventurous age in Nanga painting in the Kansai area; his paintings have a bravura that sometimes borders on parody. He was fond of working in a loose and energetic version of the hemp fiber stroke, highlighted by contrasting bare paper with strokes in a deep ink. He also characteristically used the horizontal Mi dots, hence his name Beisanjin, the Bei of which is the character used for the Mi in Mi Fu's name.

Hankō studied under his father, and many of Hankō's paintings bear inscriptions written by his father. Their close association is revealed in this rather early painting by Hankō with its echoes of Beisanjin's style. There is a hint of the father's style in the hemp fiber strokes, the horizontal Mi strokes, and the unexpected, enfolded small hilltops that pop out amid the major tall peaks. One might even expect to find one of the father's short inscriptions tucked unobtrusively in a lower corner but in his enthusiasm for the new taste, Hankō has filled the surface so densely there is scarcely space available for his own signatory inscription. Hankō's mature painting style often shows a softer, more atmospheric approach to landscape than here.

Painters of the late Edo period were not the only ones caught up in an urge for authenticity through faithfulness to a foreign or antique model. A general wave of Chinese influence and interest in the Bunka and Bunsei eras (1804-1830) extended, for instance, even to anonymous Arita porcelains, in which earlier styles, both Chinese and Japanese, became very popular. The potter and Nanga painter Aoki Mokubei (1767-1833) delighted in designing Ming style porcelains, adding touches of authenticity down to the cracks and chips. Also in Kyoto his teacher, the artist-potter Okuda Eisen (1753-1811) was recreating Ming style enamel decorated porcelains for the tea ceremony. All the arts flourished during this time, one of the last moments of cultural well-being before the collapse of the Tokugawa shogunate in midcentury.

References
Kobijutsu, no. 53 (July 1977), special issue on Okada Beisanjin and Hankō.
Kokka, no. 706 (January 1951), pp. 37-45.
Nansō-ha 3, Nihonga Taisei vol. 11 (Tokyo, 1932), pls. 20-24, 26, 27.
Okada Beisanjin, Bunjinga Suihen vol. 15 (Tokyo, 1978), pl. 54.

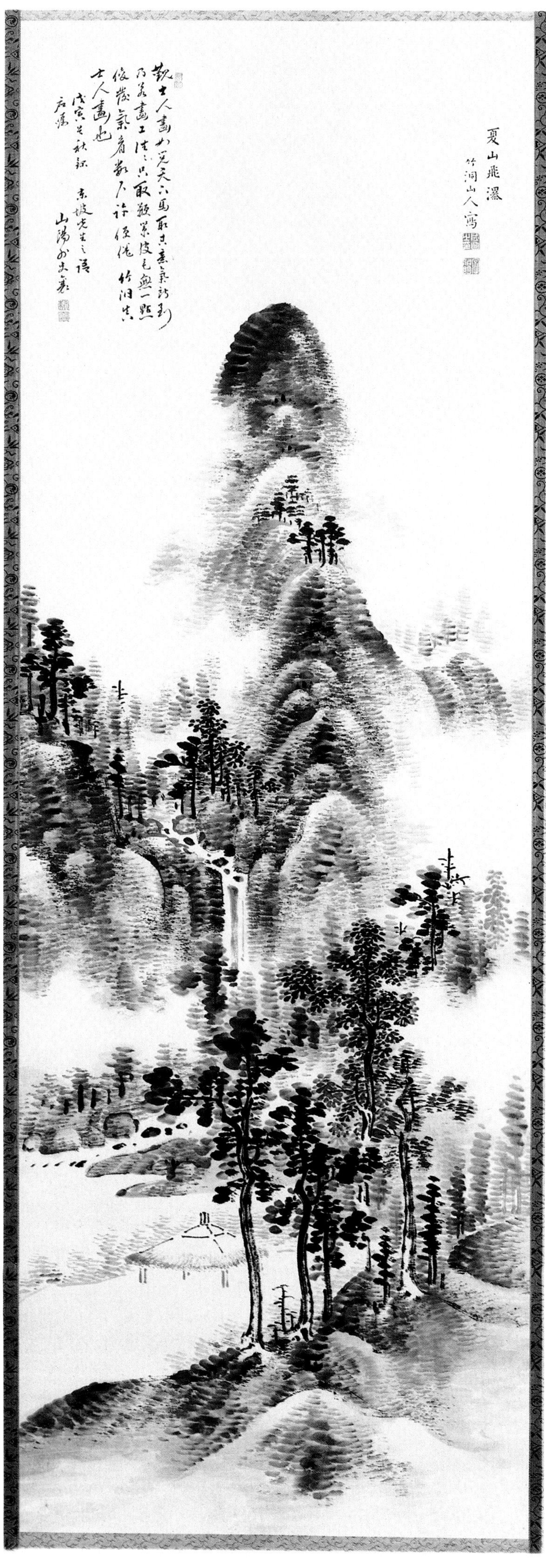

Nakabayashi Chikutō
1776-1853

Inscription
Rai Sanyō
1780-1832
Dated in accordance with 1818

52

Summer Mountains Enshrouded by Mist from the Waterfalls

Hanging Scroll
Ink on paper
139.7 x 47.6 cm

Signature
Chikutō Sanjin Sha[su]

Seals
Sei shō no In
Azana Hakumei

Inscriber's Signature
Sanyō Gaishi Yuzuru

Inscriber's Seals
Rai
Yuzuru

Nakabayashi Chikutō was born in Nagoya, the son of an obstetrician, in an environment that encouraged academic pursuits. At the age of 15 years, he became the protégé of a wealthy and enthusiastic connoisseur of Chinese art, Kamiya Tenyū, whose collection became an important inspiration for young Chikutō as well as for his friend Yamamoto Baiitsu (1783-1856). Their names, Chikutō (Bamboo Curtain) and Baiitsu (Plum Leisure) were given to them by Tenyū after the three of them had visited a temple and had seen fourteenth-century Chinese paintings of bamboo and plum. Chikutō and Baiitsu both received their early training in painting from Yamada Kyūjō, a local painter in Nagoya. At the age of twenty, Chikutō established his own studio in a Nagoya temple and became an important member of a society of local artists that sponsored art exhibitions. In 1802 Chikutō, accompanied by Baiitsu, went to Kyoto for further painting instruction. There they came into contact with a group of literati who were centered on Rai Sanyō (1780-1832). This group placed strong emphasis upon orthodoxy in all aspects of Chinese studies. This tendency is reflected in Chikutō's paintings as well as in a number of theoretical treatises he wrote on literati painting, including the **Gadō Kongō-shō** of 1802 and **Chikutō Garon** of 1812. Chikutō also published many illustrated books, such as the **Chikutō Gafu** of 1800 and the **Yusai Shikunshi Gafu** of 1850. In addition, he wrote essays on poetry and music.

Chikutō worked in a number of traditional Chinese styles; yet he rarely used them in an innovative fashion. Whether it was the Mi strokes or the systematically repeated squared form in the Huang Kung-wang manner, his landscapes seemed always to end in a similar compositional format. But he did exhibit the high technical sophistication of a professional painter and had an exquisite sensitivity to decorative surface quality. Many of his landscapes appear at first glance to be static and uneventful. Yet his patiently and delicately applied surface patterns soon begin to scintillate before our eyes.

This hanging scroll, entitled **Summer Mountains Enshrouded by Mist from the Waterfalls**, employs a simple vertical composition, a format often used by Chikutō. In such works, the upward vertical thrust is initiated by a few trees in the foreground and continued to the sharply piled-up mountains in the background. The waterfall in the middle ground, and the many trees on both sides of this central axis, also emphasize this direction. Against this axis, carefully constructed diagonals lead our eyes upward in a zig-zag motion, beginning at the lower left corner and following the diagonal contour of the hills toward the right. A counter-diagonal is then established by the contour of the foreground at the right, through the lower branches of the trees, to the shore of a stream in the middle ground. In this manner, more diagonals and counter-diagonals cross the central axis. Except for an occupied pavilion at the lower left corner, voids created by the criss-crossing diagonals represent the mist created by the waterfalls.

In spite of the pavilion and the clearing surrounding it, there is no indication of human presence in this painting. The foreground, therefore, does not hold our attention, as it should in this type of composition; consequently, our eye movement is propelled by the vertical and diagonal arrangements of motifs. The combination of these movements and the meticulously applied brush strokes tend to flatten the painting. In addition, the manner in which the texture strokes are used seems not to give substance to the hills and trees. However, Chikutō's skillful use of dark and light ink creates a sense of light flickering through the atmosphere. By the early nineteenth century, Japanese artists had a fairly thorough awareness of the role of light in landscape painting. Although Chikutō ignored systematic use of the principle of a single light source, he was still able to communicate the transient moods of nature through deft brushwork and lush ink tones.

The inscription by Rai Sanyō, the preeminent Kyoto Confucian scholar of his day, offers valuable insight into the criteria of literati aesthetic judgment:

Looking at a scholar's painting is like examining a world-renowned horse, and grasping its perfection of spirit. If a painter continually whips the hide and yet his steed shows no superior dynamic spirit, one becomes bored after looking at only a few feet of the scroll. Chikutō was a true scholar painter. Recorded by request in the seventh month of Tsuchinoe-tora. Su Tung-p'o's words.

[Signed] Sanyō Gaishi Yuzuru

(Translated by Hiro Kawasaki)

References
Kokka, no. 379 (December 1921), pp. 225-228.
Museum, no. 379 (May 1973), pp. 13-29.
Nansō Meigaen, Tajima, Shiichi (ed.), no. 24 (Tokyo, 1910), pl. 9.
Nihon no Nanga, Yoshizawa, Chū, Suiboku Bijutsu Taikei, Bekkan no. 1 (Tokyo, 1976), pl. 121, p. 196.

Yamamoto Baiitsu
1783-1856
Dated in accordance with 1845

53

Wild Geese and
Autumn Grass

Hanging Scroll
Ink and light color on silk satin
140.3 x 51.4 cm

Signature
Baiitsu Ryō Sha[su]

Seals
Ryō In
Baiitsu

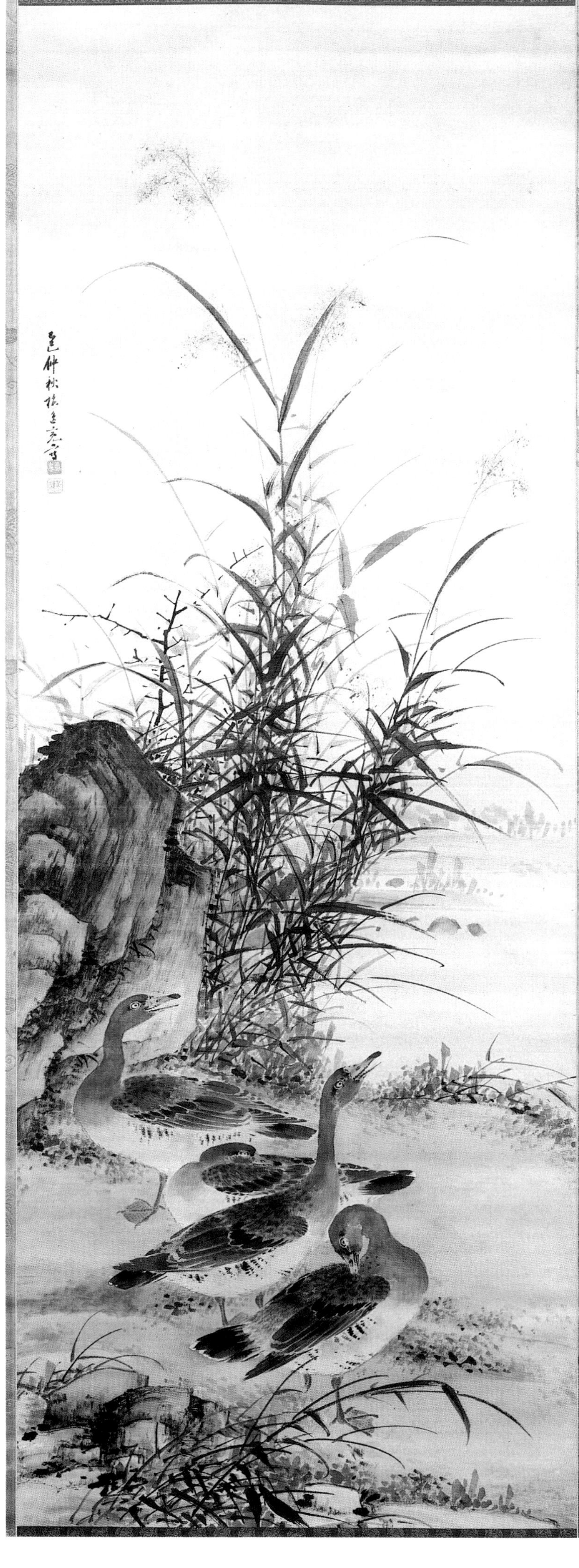

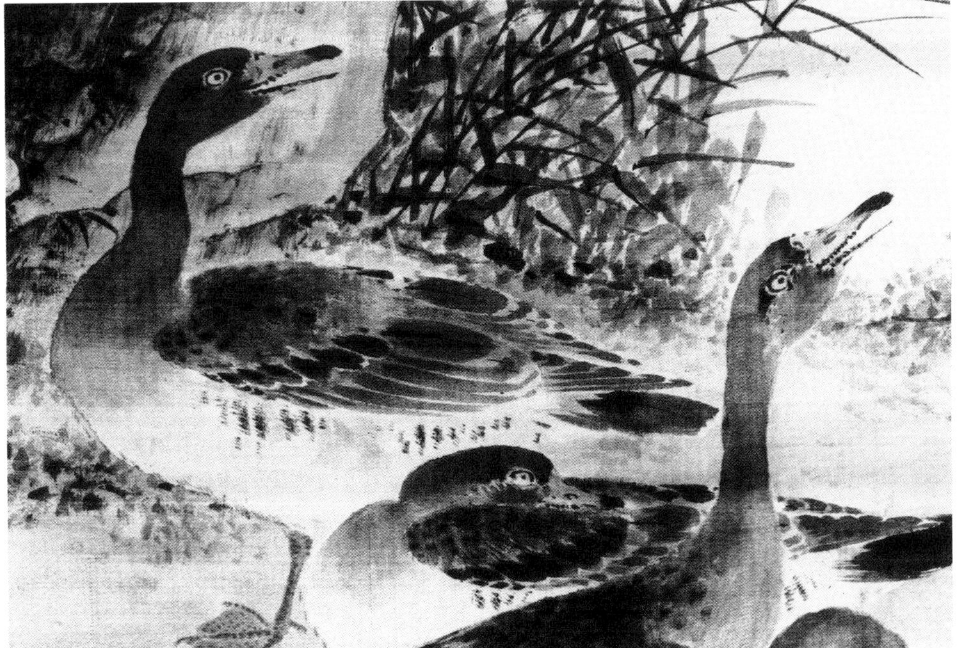

Detail

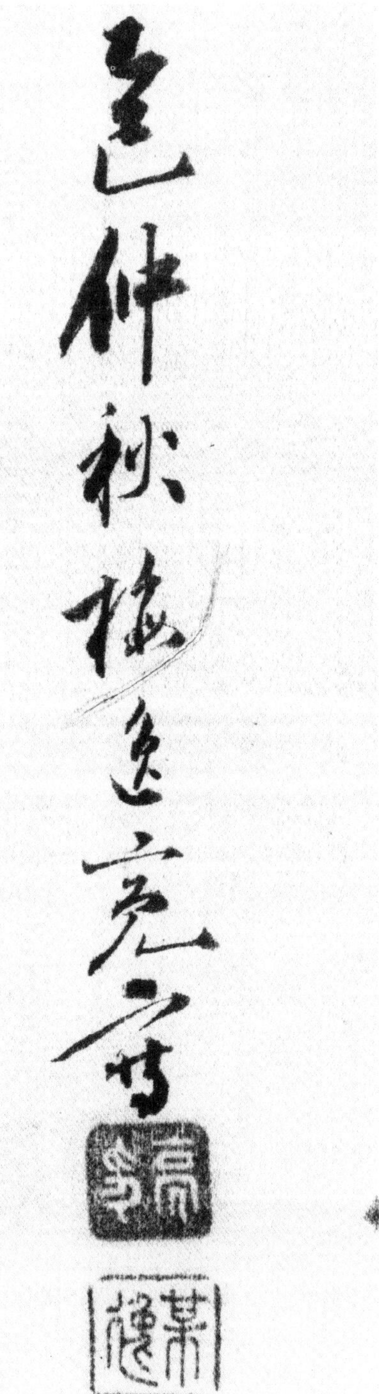

Detail

Baiitsu, in spite of his reputation as one of the finest of the conservative literati painters with a deep understanding of Chinese painting styles, worked here in strong affinity with the naturalistic style of the Maruyama-Shijō school. The painting was done in ink and light colors on silk satin, with delicately graduated ink washes on the birds and rocks. Absent is the usual emphasis on outline so prominent in literati painting; instead Baiitsu employed the so-called mokkotsu, or hidden bone manner, by which forms are defined through contrasting areas of light and shade. The four birds, overlapping one another, establish the spatial recession of the foreground. They were sensitively observed and defined in a manner reminiscent of the naturalistic studies of Maruyama Ōkyo (1733-1795). Also enhancing the sense of three-dimensionality are the skillful juxtapositions of ink intensities in the reeds and rocks, as well as the low distant horizon.

The composition is a masterful interplay of formal elements. Two of the birds face to the right, and two to the left; the turning and outstretched necks create a rhythmical pattern, one that is not repeated elsewhere. The two birds whose necks stretch toward the right direct their attention outside of the picture and suggest that this scroll was meant to be hung to the left of another painting of a continuing scene.

As the son of a Nagoya woodcarver, Baiitsu was familiar with flower-and-bird designs as a child. In his early teens, he and his friend Nakabayashi Chikutō (no. 52) came under the patronage of a wealthy collector of Chinese paintings, Kamiya Tenyū, and was initiated into the traditions of the literati movement. Together with Chikutō he studied under local Nagoya painters such as Yamada Kyūjō and Yamamoto Rantei, the latter of whom permitted Baiitsu to adopt his surname. Baiitsu later extended his association to Tani Banchō and other painters of the Edo school. Although most noted as a painter, Baiitsu shared with many of the literati artists interests in other aesthetic pursuits. He was a skilled musician, especially able with the bamboo flute. His taste in Chinese ceramics and tea utensils was famous in Kyoto, and a certain popular style of tea drinking came to be associated with his name.

Baiitsu emerged from the artisan class and, in spite of his literati inclinations, was an accomplished professional painter. When he returned from Kyoto to settle in Nagoya, one of his patrons, the lord of Owari province, permitted him to wear swords, signifying that the painter had joined the samurai class. As a professional artist, Baiitsu was extremely versatile and prolific. Like Chikutō, he adhered to orthodox Nanga (Southern School) doctrines. Although remaining within the limited stylistic range of that tradition, Baiitsu experimented with far more complex and varied compositions than did Chikutō. He was a technical virtuoso in the handling of ink and brush, and often displayed a brilliance and finesse that easily matched the most skillful among the academically trained artists.

References
Birds, Beasts, Blossoms, and Bugs: The Nature of Japan, Stern, Harold P. (New York, 1976), no. 72.
Kokka, no. 978 (March 1975), pp. 27-31.
Kokka, no. 885 (December 1965), pp. 23-27.
Nanga Kanshō, Takeuchi, Baishō, "Chūkyō Nanga no Ni-Meika: Chikutō to Baiitsu ni tsuite," 3-10 (October 1934), pp. 30-33.
Shōbi Shiryō Kōshū (later edition), 1-3 (Tokyo, 1918), no. 24.

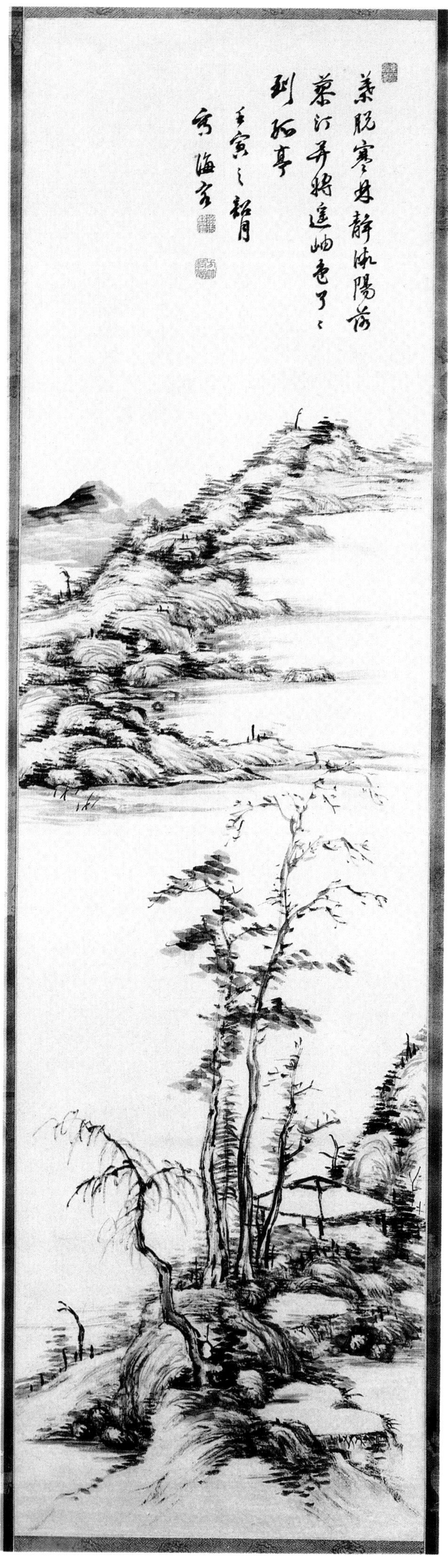

Nukina Kaioku
1778-1863
Dated in accordance with 1842

54

Winter Landscape

Hanging Scroll
Ink on paper
121.9 x 32.7 cm

Signature
Sha [su] Kaikyaku

Seals
Kaioku Shiga
Raku Yūkyo
Hōchiku Shinsha

The composition of this painting, like that of Noro Kaiseki of two decades earlier (no. 44),
evokes the spirit of Ni Tsan, the Yüan-period pioneer of literati painting. Hallmarks of the
Ni Tsan manner are the clustered trees and hut in the foreground, the diagonal recession
of a flat and empty middle ground, the use of short strokes of a relatively dry brush, and
the tenor of lyrical melancholy that pervades both the image and the poem above,
inscribed by the artist himself. Nonetheless, like Kaiseki's, this picture is a product of its own
age and historical circumstances. The treatment of deep spatial recession of the low
sandbanks, with the ambiguous location of the most distant mountains at the left, would
never have occurred in Ni Tsan's highly rational and abstract compositions. Kaioku's
painting also has a certain personal warmth and buoyant mellowness that is absent in
the more aloof and introverted works of Ni Tsan known to modern scholars.
The poem, in Chinese, can be translated as follows:

Leaves fallen, the forest cold and silent,
The faint sun setting behind smartweeds lining the shore,
As the color of distant mountain peaks
Finally approaches the lonely pavilion.
A splendid month in Mizunoe-tora [1842].

Painted by Kaikyaku

Nukina Kaioku was born to a family of archery instructors in Awa province on the island
of Shikoku, and was trained as a bowman in the tradition of his family. He failed to
distinguish himself in the martial arts, but his training, typical of young men of the
provincial warrior classes, included tutoring in calligraphy and in painting, especially in the
officially recognized Kanō style. In these endeavors he did distinguish himself, and he was
eventually recognized as one of the best calligraphers of the late Edo period and a
scholar of the history of Chinese writing styles. He assiduously collected and copied
rubbings taken from famous engraved calligraphies in China. An uncle, who was a priest
of the great Shingon sanctuary of Kongōbu-ji on Mount Kōya, stimulated his interest in
the powerful writing style of Kūkai (774-835), founder of the monastery and reputedly
the man who invented hiragana, the cursive Japanese phonetic syllabary.
Japanese literati painters of Kaioku's generation were often deeply indebted to Ming
Chinese taste in Nanga. In fact, tradition has it that Kaioku was inspired to adopt the Ming
style by a painting of the Suchou master, Ch'ien Ku (1508-ca 1574), pupil of the famous
Wen Cheng-ming. Kaioku made three trips to Nagasaki, the only place in Japan where
contact with Chinese nationals was relatively easy. There he studied Nanga painting and
calligraphy with Hidaka Tetsuō (1791-1871), abbot of Shuntoku-ji, a Zen temple. Tetsuō, a
fine painter, had studied with an immigrant master Chiang Chia-pu and gained deep
insights into conservative literati styles. Through contacts and experiences such as these,
Kaioku became a leading embodiment of the Chinese-style scholar, painter, and
calligrapher. He eventually opened his own academy for Confucian studies in Kyoto, the
Shūsei-dō, in what is now the Okazaki district.
Kaioku was also a stalwart traveler, not only in the Kyoto-Osaka region and in the
Takayama district, near Gifu, where he lived for three years, but in other parts of Japan as
well. He often made sketches of the places he visited, and was once arrested while
sketching by the seashore. Local officials, suspicious of strangers, feared that he was a spy
recording coastal defenses.

Published
Kinsei Nanga Gojūnen-ten, Kansai Koshugakkai, (ed.) (Kyoto, 1976), pl. 75.

References
Kokka, no. 939 (September 1971), pp. 25, 29-31.
Kokka, no. 295 (December 1914), pp. 167-168.
Nukina Kaioku, Ueda, Sōkyū and Nakata, Yūjirō (eds.) (Tokyo, 1962).

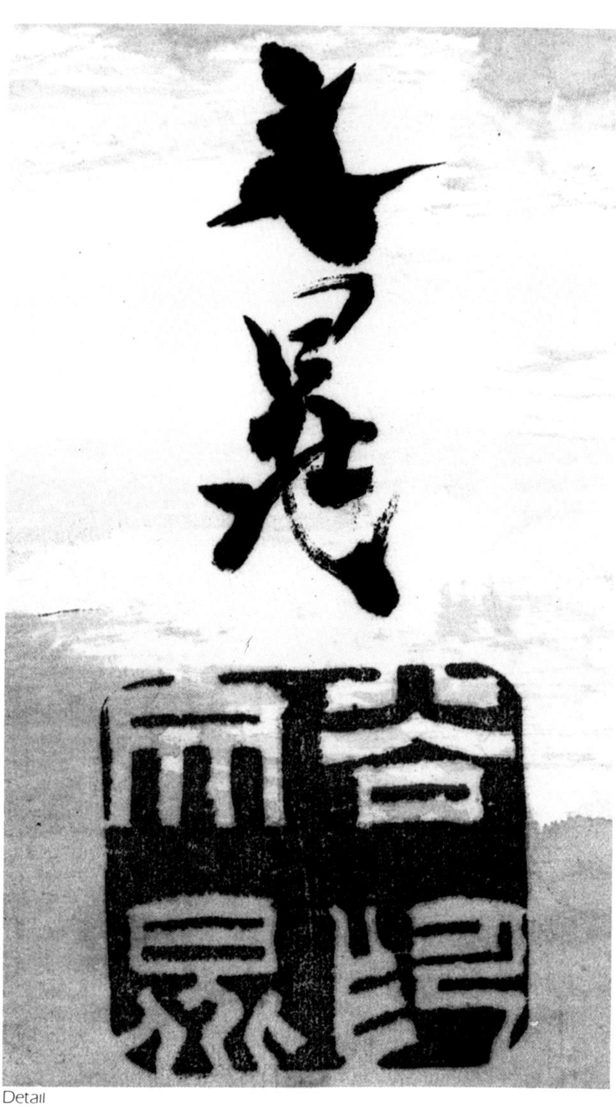

Detail

55

Plum Tree in the Moonlight

Hanging Scroll
Ink on paper
156.8 x 76.2 cm

Signature
Bunchō

Seal
Tani Bunchō In

Tani Bunchō
1763-1840

Bunchō's interpretation of the plum tree, blossoming freshly even in its hoary age, is an emotional and dynamic burst of calligraphic energy. Here the trunk of an ancient plum tree is painted as though by moonlight; the dark night sky, hiding the early spring moon, is shown as a gray wash that leaves the plain white paper to represent the brilliant purity of the blossoms. The whiteness of these blossoms—forced jubilantly by nature from the gnarled branches of the aged tree—is accented by hard, black ink dots and strokes repeated more broadly in the massive, twisted trunk and limbs.

Tani Bunchō carried into the nineteenth century the Nanga tradtition which Nakayama Kōyō (no. 38) had established in Edo. Bunchō studied for a while with Watanabe Gentai (1749-1822), the only known student of Kōyō. Gentai left no great mark in the world; yet he served as a link between two of the most important painters in the Eastern Capital.

The leading Nanga painter in Edo, Bunchō was one of the most influential talents of his day. The impact of his art, both directly and indirectly through his numerous students, lasted well into the last decades of the nineteenth century. Students like Watanaba Kazan (no. 58) transmitted the power and vitality of Bunchō's imagery as reflected in this painting. Later commercial artists emphasized the almost photographic, Western-style approach Bunchō employed in works like his topographic landscapes of the late 1790s.

Bunchō also helped to compile and illustrate the important inventory of national treasures, the **Shūko Jisshū**, an elaborate record of about eighty-five volumes surveying antiquities preserved in temples and shrines throughout the country. Bunchō returned to Edo from Nagasaki, where he studied Chinese and Western painting, and was employed by Matsudaira Sadanobu (1758-1829), the leading figure in the shogun's administration, to assist in making a thorough record of such holdings. This fateful experience lasted several years, providing Bunchō with an ideal opportunity to examine countless artistic wonders and to copy them directly. The exact dates for the compilation of the **Shukō Jisshū** are not known, but in 1796 Bunchō visited Kyoto, probably in pursuit of antiquities, where he saw and copied Mu-ch'i's tiger and dragon paintings at Daitoku-ji. During this same trip he may also have copied a Yüan-period picture published in the great compendium on which he modeled this plum blossom painting.

Bunchō's illustrations for the **Shūko Jisshū** were completed and published in woodblock-printed books probably in 1800 (Kansei 4), the date noted in the preface. Bunchō was still an impressionable twenty-seven-year-old, and the enforced discipline of illustrating this book in a naturalistic style obviously affected his development as an artist. More important for his artistic future was the exposure to great works of art of different types, styles, and periods. This work may be one of the main sources of the notable eclecticism in his own art. In his late years he returned to producing woodblock-printed books, which helped widen and perpetuate his already legendary influence on the art world of late Edo Japan.

Published
Birds, Beasts, Blossoms, and Bugs: The Nature of Japan, Stern, Harold P. (New York, 1976), no. 52.

References
Nansō-ha 2, Nihonga Taisei vol. 10 (Tokyo, 1930-1932), pls. 22-26, 28, 30.
Nihon no Nanga, Yoshizawa, Chū, Suiboku Bijutsu Taikei, Bekkan no. 1 (Tokyo, 1976), pls. 96-99, pp. 193-194.
The Poet-Painters: Buson and His Followers, French, Calvin, et al. (Ann Arbor, 1974), no. 33, pp. 108-109.

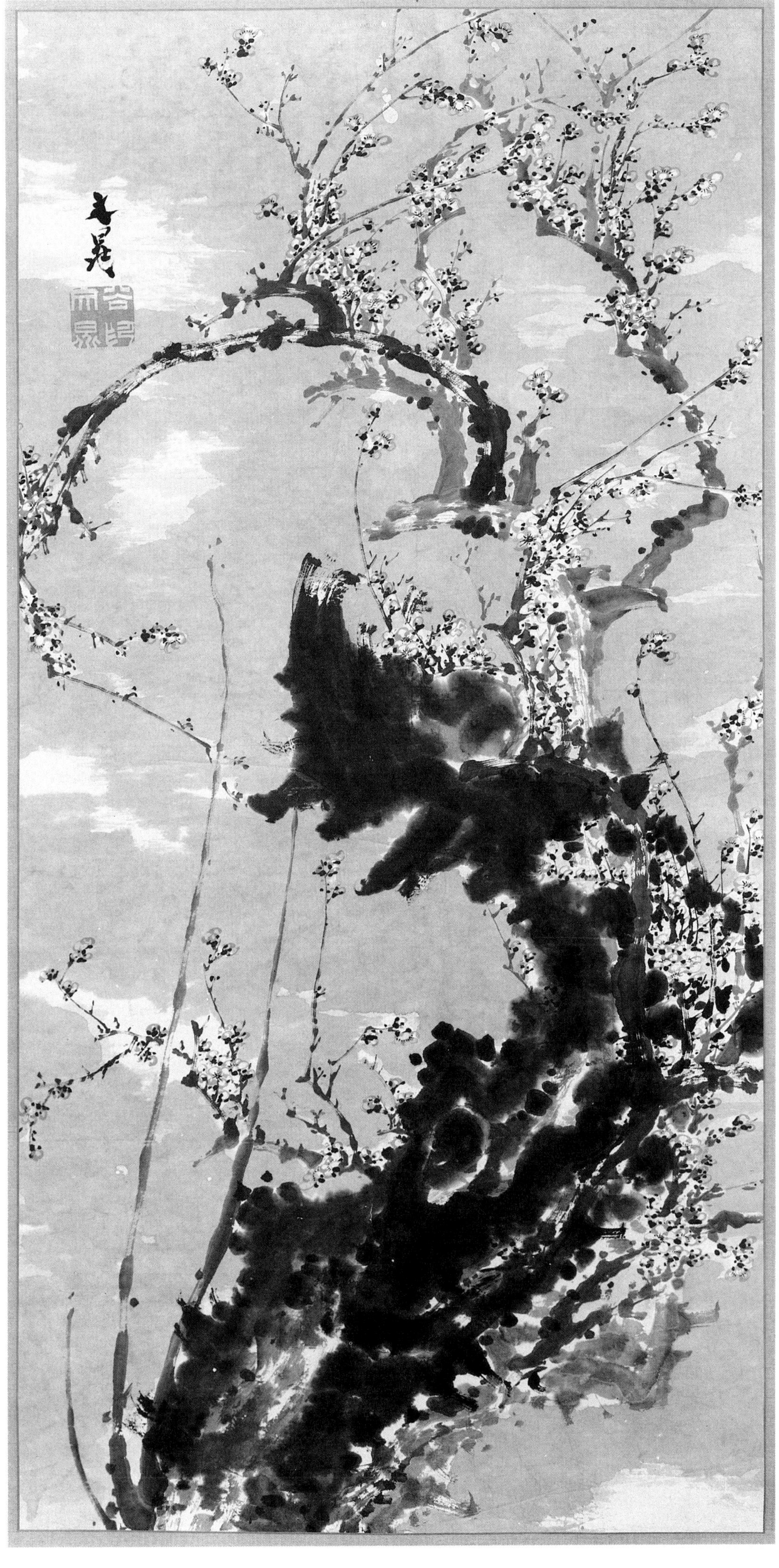

56

Grapevine and Bamboo

Hanging Scroll
Ink on paper
138.5 x 60.3 cm

Signature
Nin Hitsu

Seals
Tachihara Nin In
Nin

Tachihara Kyōsho
1785-1840

Three of the better-known students of Tani Bunchō—Kyōsho, Aigai, Watanabe Kazan—are represented in the present exhibition. The oldest, Tachihara Kyōsho, is the author of this almost calligraphic study of entwining grape vines and two stalks of bamboo with its sharply contrasting tonal values. Kyōsho came from a samurai family, and all his life was a loyal retainer who held a position as Master of Pages in the shogun's castle in Edo. Painting, however, was his true vocation. He enjoyed the patronage and trust of his feudal master, who eventually arranged a well-paid sinecure so that Kyōsho could devote more time to painting.

Kyōsho, who was of a studious nature, had gained a reputation as a calligrapher and a connoisseur of art works. His interest in scholarship led him to join a band of unofficial students of rangaku (foreign learning). The government wished to have strict control over the number of people who had access to foreign scientific texts, which were brought in by the Dutch merchants. Uncontrolled contact with such ideas was fraught with potential for seditious activities; therefore the government raided homes and meetings to sweep up people who were unofficially involved in the study of this foreign knowledge. Kyōsho escaped any serious consequences, but only through his intervention was the death sentence for Watanabe Kazan (no. 58), his friend and a fellow student of Bunchō, successfully converted to house arrest.

Kyōsho studied originally with local artists of widely varied backgrounds. Bunchō, as the leading artistic personality in the Edo area, attracted many followers, and Kyōsho's experience as Tani Bunchō's student considerably influenced his later painting. In keeping with Bunchō's eclectic approach, Kyōsho painted in no one style, but this briskly brushed study reveals Kyōsho's Nanga training and his fine talent for calligraphy. The composition moves into the space from the right, the vines rise swiftly in a sweeping arc. Two bamboo stalks stand at the left, turning the arc back into the painting space, and firmly anchor the composition. The elements, first stated in one ink tone, are repeated in a lighter or darker shade. The leaves are grouped on either side of the vines as large mottled masses, accented with sharp black veins, sometimes tinged with deep tones. The compact forms of the spherical grapes act as smaller accenting clusters, whereas the bamboo stalks and leaves repeat the same varied shapes and accented ink tones. The whole painting is a skillful and pleasing array of sumi play. The flow of brushwork ends in the pair of tendrils which balance the composition and reach out into the lower space, toward the initial brush stroke.

The verse inscribed by Kyōsho is taken from one by the T'ang poet Liu Yü-hsi and describes grape wine, a novelty that appealed to the Chinese taste for exotic customs:

The taste of wine, after fermenting for ten days,
Equals that of the Five-Cloud Potation.

References
Bijutsu Kenkyū, no. 96 (December 1939), pp. 407, 439-440.
Nansō-ha 2, Nihonga Taisei vol. 10 (Tokyo, 1930-1932), pls. 140, 141, 143, 144.
Nihon no Nanga, Yoshizawa, Chū, Suiboku Bijutsu Taikei, Bekkan no. 1 (Tokyo, 1976), pls. 29, 113, 114, pp. 184, 195.

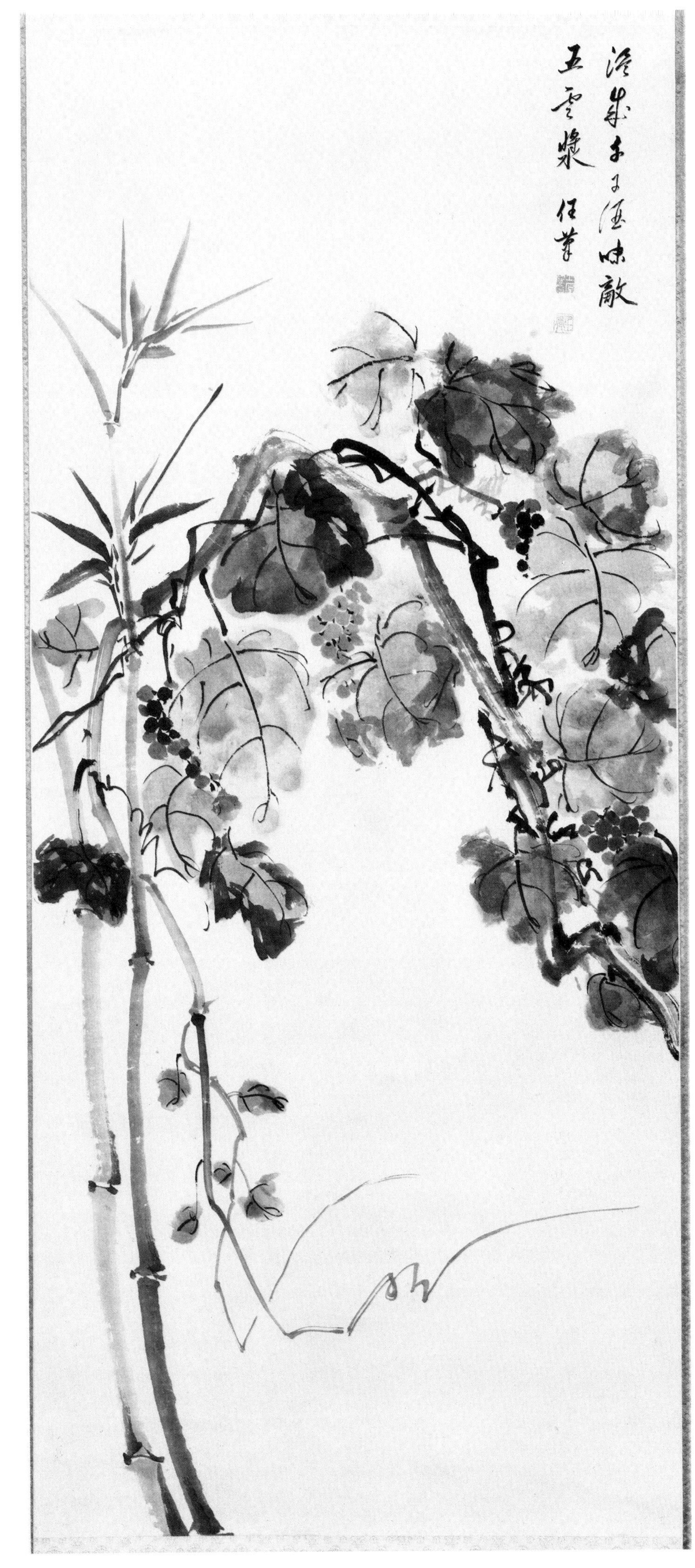
淡茶本味敵五雲漿
任薰

57

Landscape

Takaku Aigai
1796-1843

Hanging Scroll
Ink and slight color on paper
171.1 x 91.4 cm

Signature
Sorin Gaishi sha-i

Seals
Takaku Chō In
Sekiso

Takaku Chō, better known as Aigai, was born in 1796 in the province of Shimotsuke, modern Tochigi prefecture, northeast of modern Tokyo. He studied calligraphy and painting locally while a young man. After his painting teacher died, he studied the works of other artists, especially Ikeno Taiga and I Fu-chiu, a Chinese who had visited Nagasaki in the eighteenth century and whose works were very popular. Both painters were long dead, but by the time Aigai was growing up, Taiga was a much admired artist and his works were well known.
In his twenties Aigai moved to Edo, where he met Tani Bunchō (no. 55) and came under this great artist's influence. Aigai seems to have had an almost insatiable appetite for studying and copying antique Chinese paintings, and is said to have had a special fondness for the styles of Wu Chen and Shen Chou. By the nineteenth century, however, collections of recent and contemporary Chinese painting had begun to grow in Japan, and Aigai had opportunities to examine many authentic Chinese works.
Aigai like many other Nanga artists traveled about the country. He made a prolonged tour of the north country, crossing over to the Japan Sea side. He gradually made his way to the Kyoto area, where he continued his search for Chinese paintings to study and copy. Eventually he returned to Edo, where he maintained an establishment at Nihombashi.
As an artist Aigai gained a reputation as a landscape painter, but his continued research on actual Chinese paintings was equally important for the history of Japanese Nanga. He was popular as an artist, and along with Tachihara Kyōsho and Watanabe Kazan he was one of the preeminent students of Bunchō. Through his own students and the popularity of his works, he engendered a knowledgeable orthodoxy among later Nanga painters.
According to Ming literati painting standards, the vocabulary of this landscape is highly accurate, from the horizontal strokes in the mountains to the types of foliage and the motifs for pine bark and needles. The scholar and attendant crossing the bridge round out the inventory of painting manual correctness. This large-scale work's air of indisputable authenticity is evident in the deft distribution of compositional elements and the modulation of the ink. Early Japanese painters often signed their painting to indicate that they were copying the style of earlier Chinese masters, but frequently their work bore no resemblance to the intended style. This is not the case with Aigai. Aigai's accuracy and sense of orthodoxy indicate a major shift from the attitude of artists like Gyokushū and his friends who found Nanga themes close at hand and who made a virtue of painting actual scenes in the Japanese countryside. Aigai and some of his contemporaries still knew how to balance restraint and orthodoxy with a profound attachment to landscapes. And Aigai, as this painting shows, boldly displayed his powers as a Nanga artist. With Aigai, however, Japanese Nanga painting—which had begun as a revolt against the stifling orthodoxy of the Kanō academy—had itself become accomplished, academic and orthodox.

References
Kokka, no. 228 (May 1909), pp. 288, 291, 293.
Nansō-ha 2, Nihonga Taisei vol. 10 (Tokyo, 1930-1932), pls. 66-69.
Nihon no Nanga, Yoshizawa, Chū, Suiboku Bijutsu Taikei, Bekkan no. 1 (Tokyo, 1976), pl. 115, p. 196.

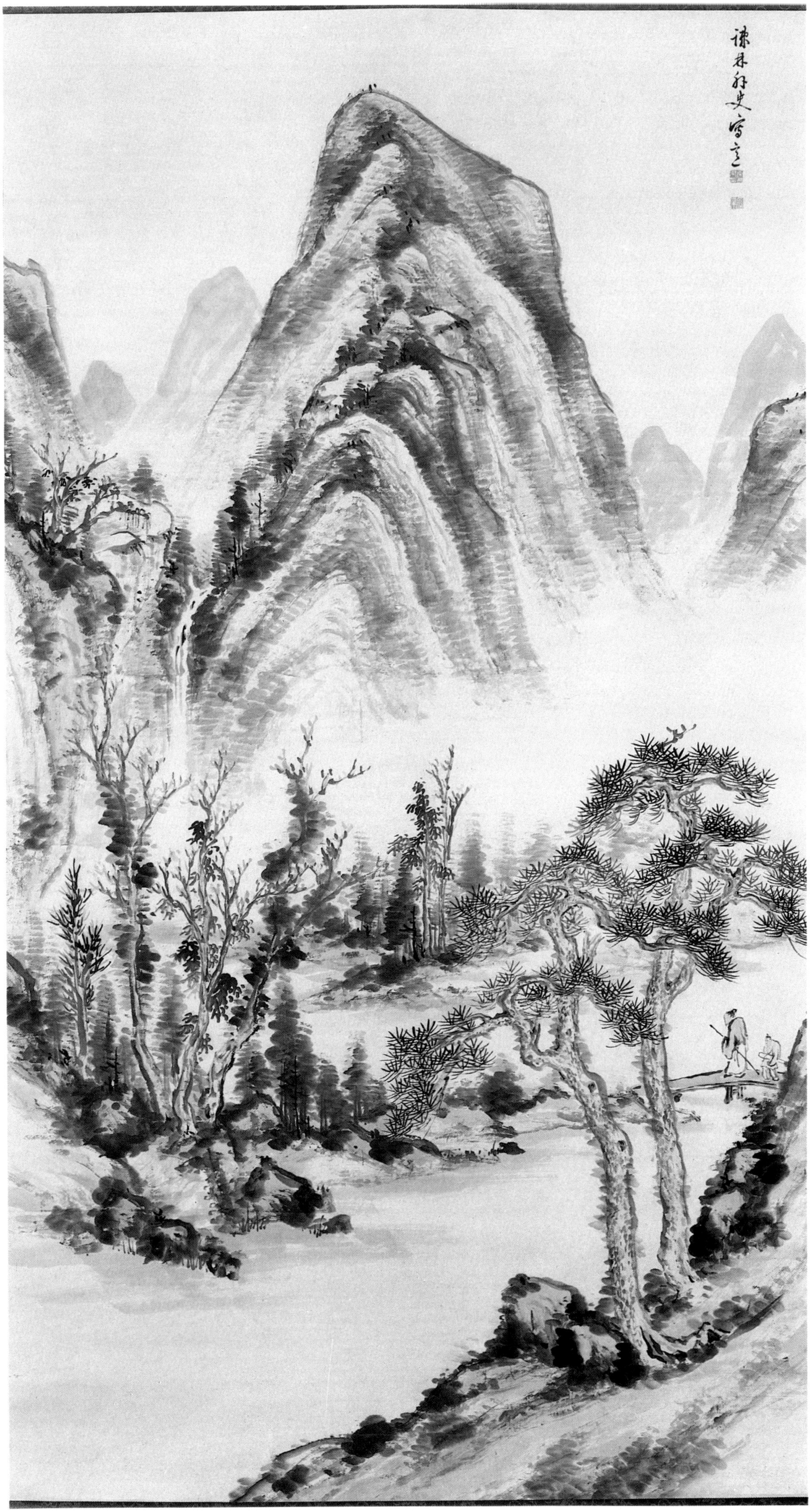

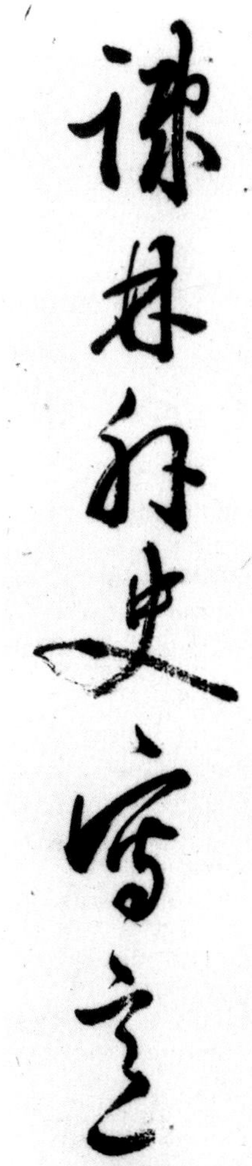

Detail

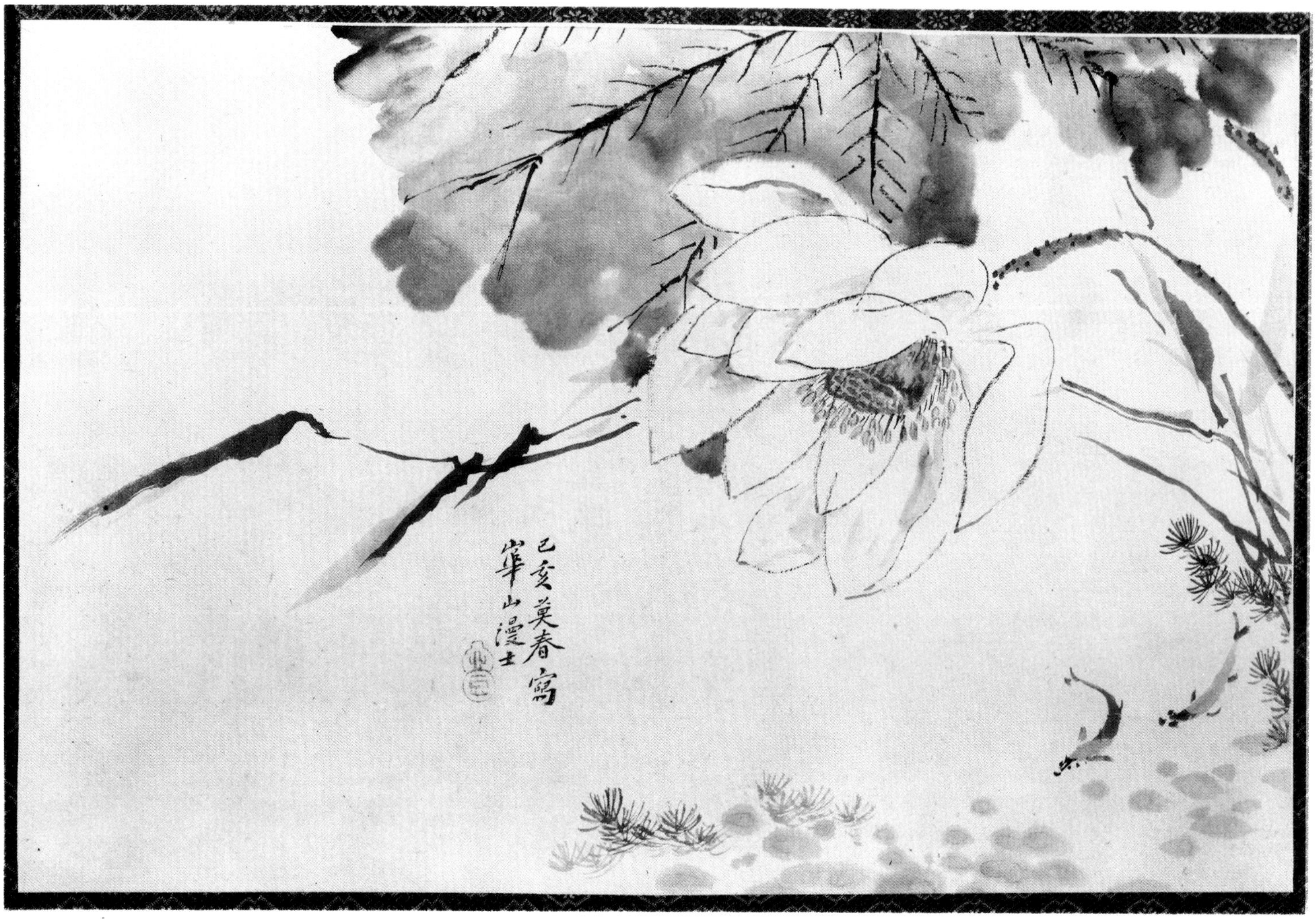

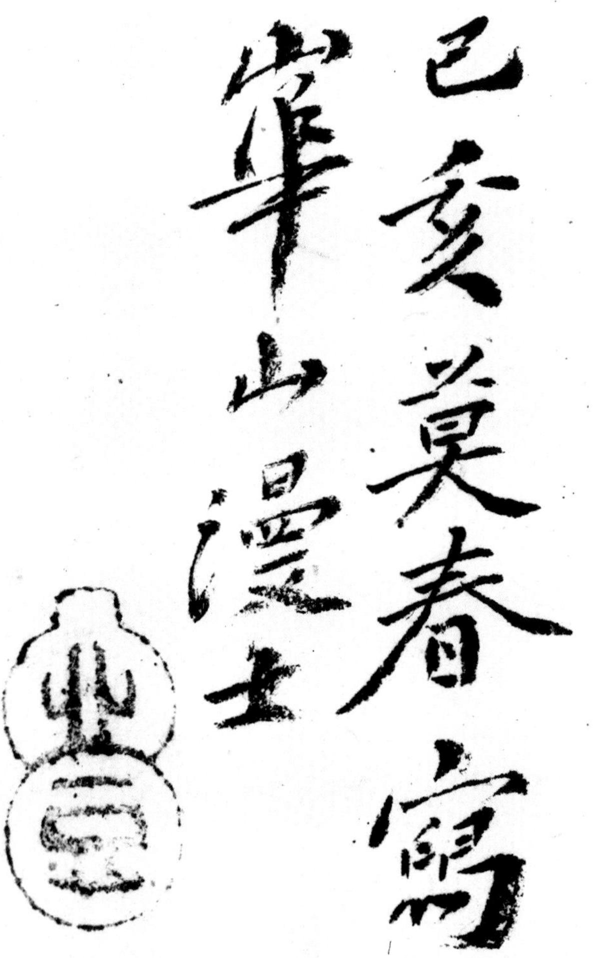

Watanabe Kazan
1793-1841
Dated in accordance with 1839

58

Lotus Flower and Swimming Fish
(See color plate no. 58)

Hanging Scroll
Mounted album leaf
Ink and light color on paper
30.5 x 45.6 cm

Signature
Kazan Mashi

Seal
Noboru

Detail

The artist has perched the viewer in midair to observe the playful fish darting among water plants, safe in their cool, unfettered world beneath the swaying lotus blossom. Moving off the picture at the top, the massive leaf spreads a protective umbrella over the scene. On the left, young leaf-shoots reach across the painting, echoing the dashing little fish on the right, anticipating their movement and repeating, in variation, the shapes of the lotus petals.

Kazan was, by birth, the chief retainer of the Tawara clan, which had its fief near the present Nagoya. This position of very high rank in the feudal system was one of great privilege, even though the Tawara clan was almost totally impoverished. Kazan was born in Edo in the clan residence, and lived most of his life in Edo in dire poverty. The Tawara clan had become a victim of the mismanagement of the late Tokugawa shogunate, which stubbornly held on to the rigid conventions that its founder had imposed on the Japanese society and economy in the early years of the seventeenth century. The regime could neither accept the realities of a changing time nor change them. Economic power had slipped out of the hands of the military clans, like the Tawara, and into the hands of the merchants, rich farmers, and small craftsmen-manufacturers in the large urban centers. Increasingly the clans and their samurai retainers became beggars who tried to maintain the appearance and estate of nobility.

From the beginning, Kazan had painted to make money to provide the necessities of life for himself and his family. He studied with various local artists, but inevitably was drawn into the orbit around Tani Bunchō, the dynamic and overpowering artist in Edo. Even more than Bunchō, however, Kazan was intrigued by Western art and the resolution of spatial problems. In his work, Kazan used shading for mass and naturalistic appearance in the Western manner.

The subject matter and themes of Kazan's paintings reflect his interest in the culture and scientific learning of foreign countries. Particularly interesting is the scientific realism of his portraits, which he was able to invest with human emotion. His strongly affecting portraits reproduce the countenances of artists, scholars, and military and governmental leaders, especially those close to Western learning. One of his first portraits was of Takami Senseki (1785–1858), a samurai whose particular interest was geography and who collected maps and illustrations of foreign countries. Among many other superb examples, is a preparatory sketch for a portrait of Tachihara Suiken, a great Japanese historian, and father of Kazan's friend, Kyōsho (no. 56).

In contrast to any sense of depth, the colors and the brushwork of this painting, although reflecting nature, are purely traditional in their application. This tension between Western scientific techniques and the traditional Japanese modes posed a true dilemma for Kazan. His samurai training and sense of patriotic duty battled with his urge to involve himself, and by extension his country, in the proscribed Western science and culture. He attempted to assuage his anxious desires by associating with physicians and scholars, like Takami Senseki, who were sanctioned by the government to gain this Western knowledge. Finally, against all regulations, he began to study on his own, and the power of personality soon placed him at the center of a group. Kazan, as high-ranking samurai, received the brunt of the official wrath when his group was apprehended in 1839 by a government intent on controlling the dissemination of this knowledge. Kazan was taken prisoner in the spring and was incarcerated until December. He was then sent to his feudal master's fief away from Edo and kept under strict house arrest. The intervention of friends like Tachihira Kyōsho and Tsubaki Chinzan had effected a reduction in the original death sentence to imprisonment.

The inscription on this painting gives the date of 1839 and Kazan was indeed using this seal at that time. Under the terms of his confinement, however, he was prohibited from selling any of his new paintings. Kazan was desperate for funds to support his family, and as a way of circumventing this prohibition, he would add earlier dates to his newly completed works and smuggle them out of the house with visiting friends. The subdued coloring and the shorthand descriptive nature of the images in this work correspond to other similar works which, although they bear earlier dates, scholars believe Kazan produced during these years. These facts, plus references in Kazan's letters, lead modern scholars to believe that this painting also comes from those calamitous years.

The humiliation and frustration of arrest and confinement at last proved unbearable. This man who foresaw the dangers implicit for his country in a confrontation with the European nations, and who glimpsed the need for Japan to develop the strengths of her potential aggressor, was damned for his vision. Finally, on the eleventh day of the tenth month of the year corresponding to 1841, Kazan released his troubled spirit by committing suicide.

Published
Kazan, Kamimura, Masurō and Takamizawa, Tadao (eds.), Kinsei Nihonga Taikan vol. 10 (Tokyo, 1932), pl. 112.
Ryūsen Shūhō: Mayuyama Seventy Years, vol. 2 (Tokyo, 1976), pl. 496.
Watanabe Kazan Sensei Kinshin Zufu, vol. 2 (Tokyo, 1941), pl. 329.

References
Kazan, Suganuma, Teizō (ed.), exhibition catalogue, Tokyo Chunichi Shimbun (Tokyo, 1962), pls. 68, 69.
Kazan no Kenkyū, Suganuma, Teizō (Tokyo, 1969).

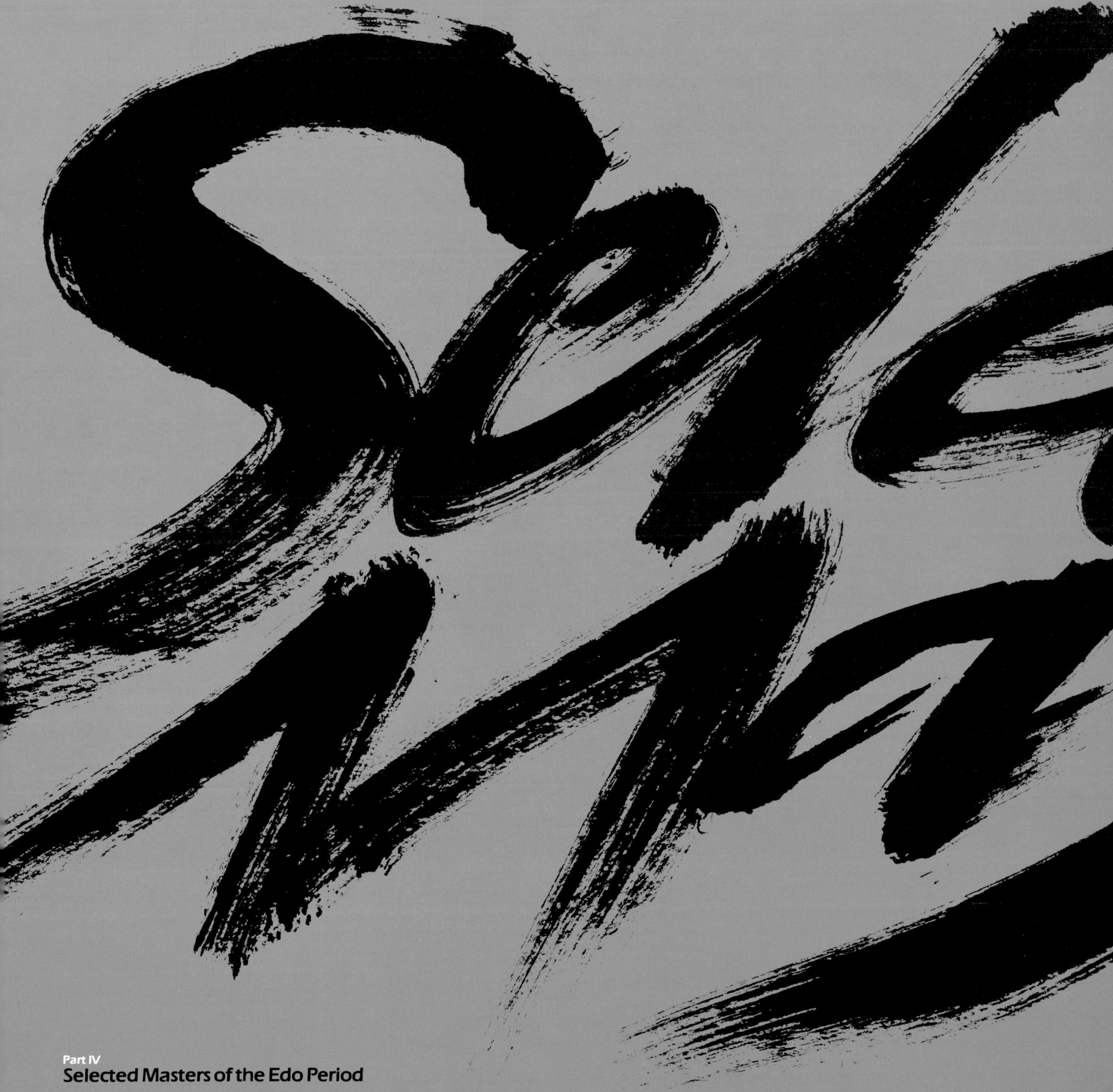

Part IV
Selected Masters of the Edo Period

Japan during the Edo period (1603-1867), self-contained and essentially closed off from the outside world, fostered more artistic diversity and plurality than any other country at that time. By the year 1810, for instance, painters of half a dozen or more different schools and traditions worked in Kyoto alone. The Kanō and Tosa schools, for example, which had started out in the late fifteenth century, were still officially sponsored by the military government and the imperial court, respectively. Though these schools had ceased to produce great artists, they still produced self-confident, competent craftsmen. The so-called Rimpa school, started by the calligrapher and designer Honami Kōetsu (1558-1637) and the painter Tawaraya Sōtatsu (active ca 1600-1636), produced Ogata Kōrin (1658-1716), the school's last great master painter. The Zenga painters had lost the towering personality of Hakuin Ekaku (1685-1768), but by 1810 Sengai Gibon (1750-1837) retired as abbot of Shōfuku-ji in Hakata and became an independent Zenga master in his own right.

In 1810 when the Nanga tradition of literati painting was in a vigorous and productive stage, many masters of the school were at the peak of their careers: Uragami Gyokudō (1745-1820), Tanomura Chikuden (1777-1835), and Kushiro Unsen (1759-1811); and the younger Nanga painters including Okada Hankō (1782-1846), Nukina Naioku (1778-1863), and Yamamoto Baiitsu (1783-1856) were reaching artistic maturity and reformulating an aesthetic vision that was simultaneously secular and profoundly spiritual. Among the Kyoto-based painters were such great individualists as Soga Shōhaku (1730-1781), Nagasawa Rosetsu (1754-1799), and Ito Jakuchū (1716-1800). The newly founded Shijō school, begun by the virtuoso painter Maruyama Ōkyo (1733-1795) and continued by Matsumura Goshun (1752-1811), had risen to great prestige largely because of its appeal to the so-called kamigaka, the old-fashioned aristocratic and artisan families of the imperial capital. Also reflected in Kyoto was the vigorous school of Chinese professional flower-and-bird painting based in Nagasaki, the port city of Kyushu, where direct contact with both Chinese and Dutch foreigners was possible. The remarkable school of Western-style artists, which produced for example Shiba Kōkan (1747-1818), was painting and making prints of Italian cities and Dutch quaysides.

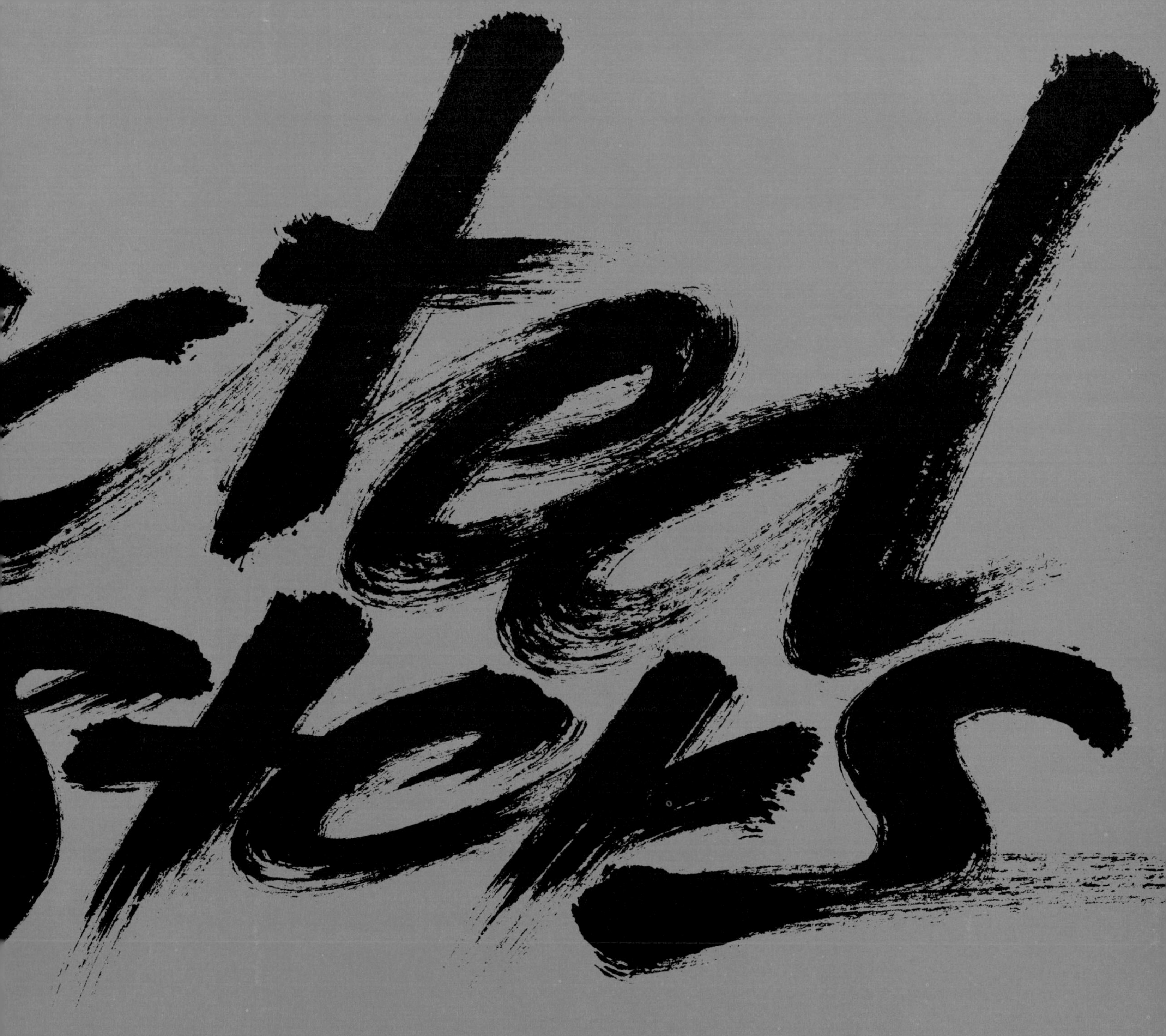

Even though painters and painting schools with divergent and seemingly incompatible aesthetic beliefs and techniques were active in various parts of Japan, Kyoto remained the artistic center of the nation. In Kyoto, all the artistic schools were recognized; painters of the different schools visited each other, drank with each other, commented each other's work, and tolerated each other. Outside the circle of well-established, respectable artists, the painters and the woodblock print designers of the Ukiyo-e, "floating-world," school flourished, producing their popular prints of courtesans and actors; after 1800, in a last outburst of creativity, the Ukiyo-e school produced the great landscape masters of Edo, Katsushika Hokusai (1760-1849) and Andō Hiroshige (1797-1858).

The same artistic energy characterized every other phase of the Edo period. In the mid-1600s, for instance, Sōtatsu's followers actively pursued his vision, Kasumi Morikage (active during the last half of the seventeenth century) broke away from the authority of Kanō Tanyū, his kinsman by marriage, and Iwasa Matabei (1578-1650) went back to the older Japanese painting foundations for Ukiyo-e. In the early 1700s, the encounter with Chinese literati painting vastly enriched the expressive range of Japan's cultural elite and produced such pioneering Japanese Nanga artists as Gion Nankai (1676-1751) and Nakayama Kōyō (1717-1780).

Two major traditions in Edo period painting—Zenga and Nanga—are represented in the Sansō Collection by enough high quality paintings to deserve separate mention. Major figures from the Kanō school are included among the ink painters in Part I of this catalogue: Kanō Sanraku (1559-1635), head of the Kyoto Kanō school, and Morikage. Other artists are represented in this Part IV by carefully selected examples. From the Rimpa school come paintings attributed to Sōtatsu and Kōrin. Of the individualists there is one painting by the eccentric Shōhaku and two by the inventive and introspective Rosetsu.

59

Child Holding a Spray of Flowers

Hanging Scroll
Ink on paper with faint color
92.8 x 40.0 cm

Attributed to
Tawaraya Sōtatsu
Active 1600-1636

Seal
Taiseiken

This painting, which is said to have been paired with a picture of two puppies, shows a seated child, probably a girl, wearing a short coat and grasping a branch. The lack of a background, as well as the darkness of the hair, painted with extremely fine black lines, immediately directs attention to the child's face and to the eyes, which are fixed upon the branch. Fine, wet strokes are used to delineate the facial features whereas broad, pale lines are used for the drapery folds and the rest of the figure. The painting is unsigned, but bears a seal impression in red ink reading Taiseiken (literally, house or studio facing green forest or hills), a seal frequently employed by the famous seventeenth-century master of decorative painting, Tawaraya Sōtatsu.

Sōtatsu seems to have had a special affinity for themes of children playing, particularly in conjunction with puppies. These were so important a part of his oeuvre that the motifs were repeated by the so-called Rimpa artists, men of later generations who continued the tradition of his distinctive imagery and painting techniques; children, usually labeled as Chinese, and puppies are thus found in the work of Ogata Kōrin and Sakai Hōitsu (1761-1828). Virtually identical to the Sansō painting of the child is one in a private Japanese collection bearing Sōtatsu's signature as well as the Taiseiken seal.

Sōtatsu had been a faithful student of earlier Japanese narrative painting, and had copied older versions of the Saigyō scrolls. Several children depicted in one of the Saigyō scrolls are similar to the child here, especially a little girl playing outside Saigyō's cottage, who has both hands holding a toy and one foot upraised. Sōtatsu did not, however, uncritically borrow motifs from the past; he utilized them in his own compositions and imbued them with an animation of their own.

Very little is known about the life of Nonomura Sōtatsu, who is also known as Tawaraya Sōtatsu. Literary references and a few dated works give us a sketchy biography of this leading personality in early Edo period painting. The time and place of Sōtatsu's birth are still unknown, though he is said to have been born around 1560 and to be from Noto province. His father is thought to have been a wealthy merchant of the Nonomura family who owned a shop in Kyoto called the Tawaraya, which made and sold painted fans.

A more specific note comes from the genealogical chart of the Kataoka family, listing Sōtatsu as having married a cousin of Honami Kōetsu (1558-1637). This would account for Sōtatsu's close collaboration with Kōetsu in the elegant handscrolls of poetry on decorated paper. However, the most direct reference to Sōtatsu as a painter is a colophon found on the fourth scroll of the **Saigyō Ekotoba** in the Morikawa Collection. It was written by the nobleman Karasumaru Mitsuhiro (1579-1638), who ranked as one of the preeminent calligraphers and patrons of his day. Mitsuhiro stated that the set of the Saigyō scrolls in the imperial collection was copied by Sōtatsu at the request of Honda Tomimasa, the lord of Izu. The date of the inscription is early in the ninth month of the seventh year of the Kanei era (1630). It gives Sōtatsu the title of Hokkyō, the highest priestly rank accorded an artist, usually in his advanced years, indicating that Sōtatsu was a well-known and accomplished painter in the later part of his career. A key commission that would account for his receiving this honorific title was the successful completion in 1621 of the doors and screens for Yōgen-in in Kyoto. Sōtatsu's career came to an end sometime between 1639 and 1642.

Sōtatsu is best known for his bold screen paintings, fan paintings, and decorations on poetry scrolls done in collaboration with Kōetsu, who brushed the calligraphy. Stylistically, as well as aesthetically, Sōtatsu's attitude was a return, after a century and a half of political and social unrest, to cultural patterns of Japan's past. The calligraphy scrolls hark back to the highly decorative literary classics of the Heian and Kamakura periods. He also mastered the techniques of Muromachi period ink painting, as revealed in his famous pair of scrolls depicting black bullocks and inscribed by Mitsuhiro. His ink paintings also include flower-and-bird scenes as well as paintings of children and puppies from which the Sansō surely derives.

Reference
Koetsu, Sōtatsu, Kōrin, Yamane, Yūzō. Suiboku Bijutsu Taikei, vol. 10 (Tokyo, 1975), pl. 70, figs. 92, 93, 94, 96.

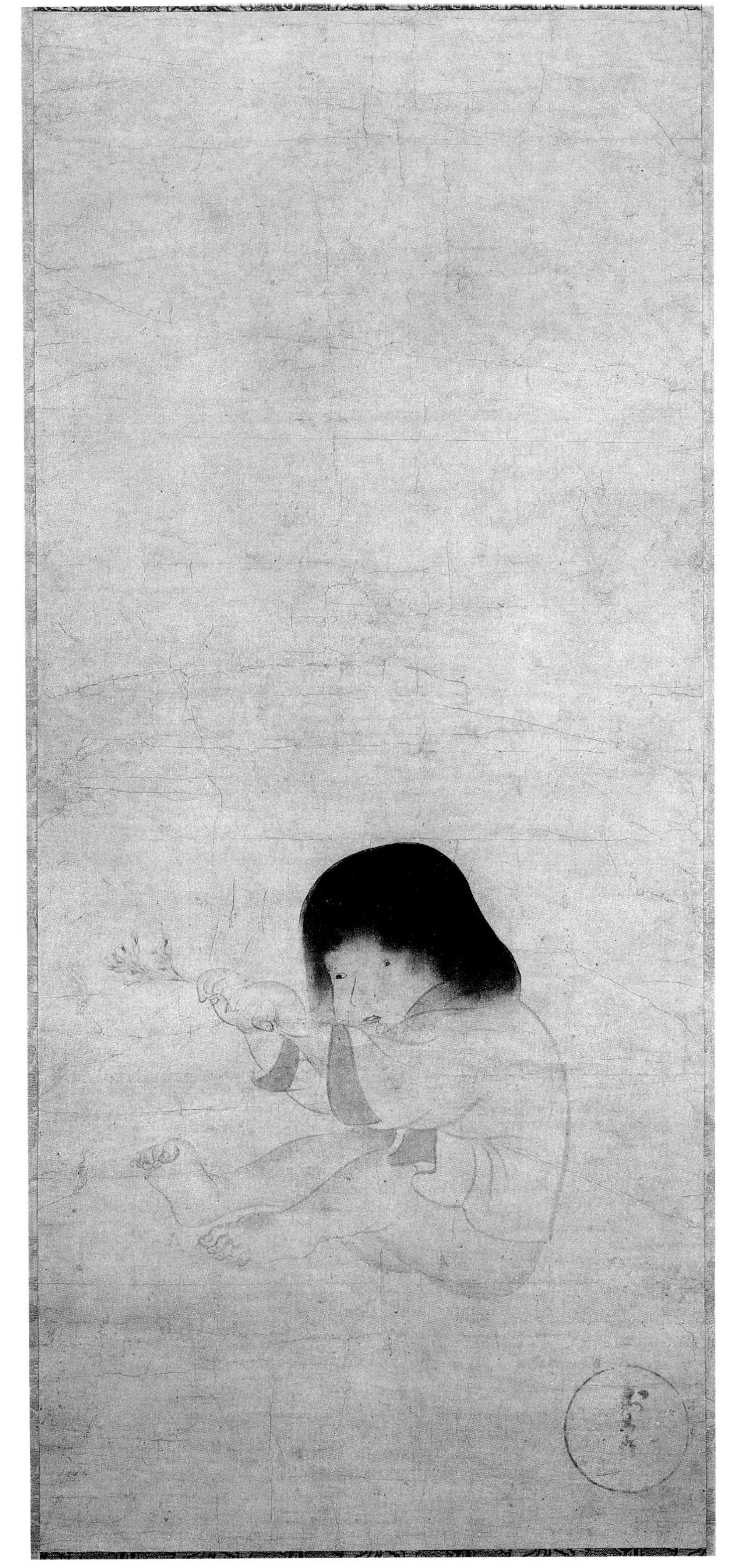

60

Autumnal Ivy Leaves with Bamboo
(See color plate no. 60)

Hanging Scroll
Mounted fan painting
Ink, color, gold, and silver on paper
22.7 x 28.2 cm

Seal
Kōrin

Ogata Kōrin
1658-1716

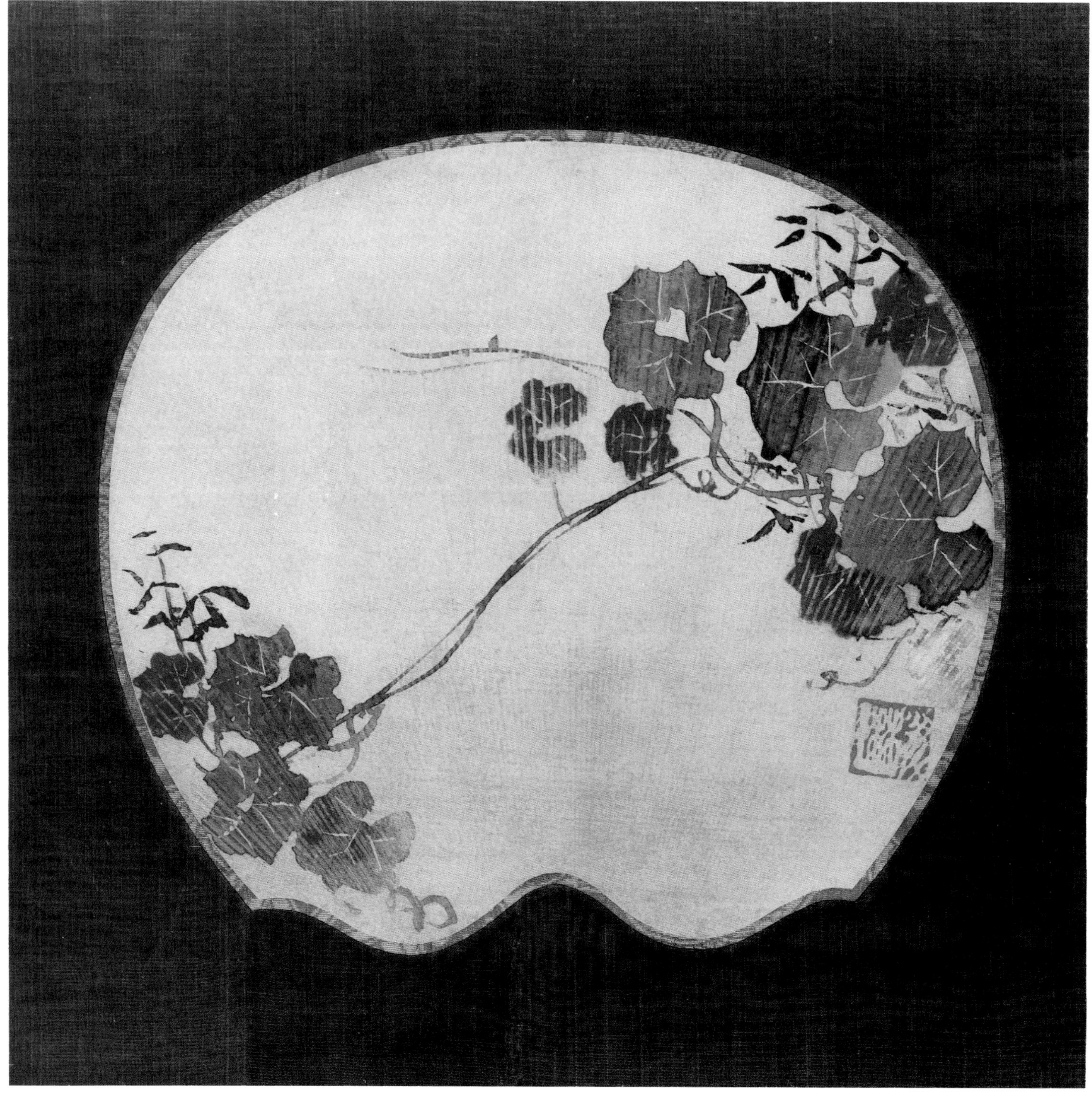

The motif of ivy was popular with Sōtatsu and his followers of the Rimpa school. Here, Kōrin is no longer faithfully copying Sōtatsu's style but has dramatically yet delicately portrayed the ivy vine among bamboo shoots. The asymmetrical composition is tied together by the spontaneous, calligraphic strokes of the entwining vines. The pattern of the leaves, though organic, denotes an adherence to simple forms that might be found in a textile pattern. The swift, agitated strokes of the bamboo complement the soft, languid grace of the ivy. In the ivy leaves, the artist made effective use of tarashikomi, the technique of placing ink or color on a surface that has already been painted and that is still wet so that they blend and splotch together. Beginning with Sōtatsu, this was a favorite method among Rimpa artists. Kōrin has used his colors more or less monochromatically to evoke the wide range of tones in the ivy rather than to establish a contrast of vibrant colors.

This fan typifies the Rimpa school's indebtedness to the literary classics. It illustrates an episode from the tenth-century book, the **Ise Monogatari (The Tale of Ise)**. The passage is "Utsu no Yama," where the hero, Narihira, journeys with his companions to the province of Suruga. The road they are on at Mount Utsu is dark and overgrown with ivy vines and maple. On it they encounter a former acquaintance to whom the hero gives a message to convey to a lady in the capital. Sōtatsu portrayed this same theme, one of his most dramatic versions being a pair of screens showing simply a road of ivy. Kōrin eliminated the landscape elements to depict only the ivy; the back of the fan, which is now separated, shows brilliant red maple leaves and represents another motif from the literary source.

Among the artists of the Rimpa school, Ogata Kōrin is by far the best known. The son of Ogata Sōken, the wealthy proprietor of the textile shop called the Kariganeya, Kōrin was born in Kyoto and was trained in the literary accomplishments requisite for a gentleman. Kōrin is said to have studied Kanō school painting with Yamamoto Soken (died 1706) and was also a pupil of Kanō Tsunenobu (1636-1713) and Sumiyoshi Gukei (1631-1705). His initial learning, though, was undoubtedly under the tutelage of his father, who, in addition to being a well-established businessman, was also an avid student of calligraphy and painting, the tea ceremony, and the Nō theater. Ogata family ties with the aristocracy can be traced as far back as the twelfth century, and when the Kariganeya was founded in 1590 by Kōrin's great-grandfather, Dohaku, the shop had an impressive list of clients, including Yodogimi, the wife of Hideyoshi and later the wife of the Tokugawa shogun Hidetada, and her daughter, who became Empress Tōfukumon-in.

A more important fact that would throw light on Kōrin's artistic development is that Dohaku married Hoshu, the elder sister of Honami Kōetsu. Furthermore, Kōrin's grandfather Sōhaku (1571-1631) lived in the art colony of Takagamine that Kōetsu had established; his house faced Kōetsu's across the road. Sōken was known to have excelled in the Kōetsu style of calligraphy, and his interest in the arts has to be counted as a factor in the formation of Kōrin's talents. It is in this environment of financial affluence, social and cultural refinement, and artistic tradition that Kōrin and his younger brother Kenzan, a potter, were able to become leaders of the decorative arts.

Kōrin's early interest was not in painting but in dancing, music, and dramatic poetry. He lived the life of a playboy, extravagantly spending money as he moved in aristocratic circles. In 1687 Sōken died, leaving the family textile business to the eldest son, Tosaburo, while Kōrin inherited a large fortune, which he proceeded to squander over the next ten years. During this time the patronage of the Kariganeya shop suffered as prosperity shifted from the aristocracy to the new middle-class merchants. Kōrin found himself deeply in debt; he could no longer continue to borrow heavily from his brother Kenzan or sell the family heirlooms.

Throughout this entire period, Kōrin had made sketches and drawings of nature. However, when he was struck by the economic realities of his situation, he turned to a career as a painter. It was around this time, 1692, that Kōrin changed the characters of his name, though retaining the same pronunciation, which meant "shining gems." This was perhaps an indication of his resolve to improve matters. Kōrin began to collaborate with Kenzan by decorating his pottery. Kenzan had studied under Ninsei, the master potter of Kyoto. In 1699, Kenzan opened his own kiln in Narutaki, in the northwestern suburbs of Kyoto, and Kōrin continued to execute his black designs on the white pottery. By 1701, Kōrin had sufficiently distinguished himself as a painter to merit the title of Hokkyō, a priestly title given to highly regarded artists.

Kōrin left for Edo in 1704, in hopes of an expanding market there—or, as the story goes, was banished from Kyoto by the angered authorities for his continued excesses and extravagance. He returned in 1705 but again left in 1707; he returned home in 1709, remaining in Kyoto among the declining aristocracy until his death in 1716.

Little is known about Kōrin's paintings of before 1701, but his early training in the Kanō and Tosa styles had an undeniable influence on his own style, developing the form and brush techniques of the Kanō school and combining them with the color and design qualities of the Tosa school. His ultimate source of inspiration lay in the Yamato-e of the eleventh century and later, drawing from ancient works as did the founders of the Rimpa school, Kōetsu and Sōtatsu.

Sōtatsu, aside from being distantly related to Kōrin, must have impressed him at an early age from the very fact that his works were available in the Ogata household. Although Kōrin studied the art of Sōtatsu through the traditional method of faithful copying, his own paintings show greater boldness and more dramatic compositions owing in part to his experience as a textile designer. His designs are more abstract and startling; the innovative themes that the Kariganeya created for the fashion-conscious ladies of the aristocracy paved the way for the powerful graphic designs and varying color combinations seen in Kōrin's paintings.

Published
Kobijutsu, no. 47 (January 1975), pp. 69, 76, 77.
Kōrin, Takamizawa Mokuhansha (Tokyo, 1940), pl. 121.
Kōrin, Tanaka, Ichimatsu (ed.) (Tokyo, 1959), fig. 84.
Sōtatsu Kōrin-ha Zuroku, Tokyo National Museum, exhibition catalogue (Tokyo, 1952).

61

Winter Landscape

Hanging Scroll
Ink on paper
129.5 x 52.0 cm

Signature
Soga Kiyō Zu [su]

Seal   **Soga Shōhaku**
Dasokuken Shōhaku   1730-1781

An atmosphere of breathless tranquillity is conveyed by soft rounded mountains. Pure white snow sits on the tree branches and mountain slopes, blanketing all things. The feeling of cold, crisp air is expressed in the bands of mist obscuring the lower slopes of the distant mountains. The landscape is alive with a sense of contained energy; tree branches and reeds, beneath the weight of the snow, are bent with a buoyancy of life. A gentleman and his servant make their way across a snowy bridge to the mountain village nestled on the cliff. A servant sweeps the path to the entry gate, and a boat glides silently through the water past empty pavilions along the shore.

This description of the scene could be readily applied to a Muromachi ink painting. In fact, it is from earlier suibokuga that Soga Shōhaku drew his inspiration for this work. The composition is characteristic of the older landscapes—strong asymmetry, evocative empty spaces, deep recession, and a high vantage point. Yet the painting is very much the product of the eighteenth century. Shōhaku conceived it as a series of broad ink washes superimposed one on the other, with the white areas established by the paper left untouched. The composition thus has a remarkably powerful light and dark structure and sense of consistent spatial recession; it is a tour de force of careful planning and brush handling.

Soga Shōhaku along with Itō Jakuchū (1716-1800) and Nagasawa Rosetsu (1754-1799), (nos. 62, 63) have been termed the "three eccentrics" of the eighteenth century. Shōhaku was the most extreme, a highly unorthodox man who openly flouted the mores of Kyoto polite society. He was arrogant and overbearing by some accounts, and was said to drink excessively. The phenomenon of the wildly eccentric artist in the East has begun to attract scholarly attention, for it was also prevalent in China, and seems to have been an Asian manifestation of some of the cultural factors that, in the West, created French and German expressionism—an exhaustion of the authority of classical painting styles, an urban atmosphere in which eccentricity was attractive to patrons and collectors and thus encouraged among artists.

Shōhaku's origins are still a matter of speculation, but the latest research of Tsuji Nobuo indicates that he may have been born in Kyoto as the son of a local merchant family by the name of Miura; he chose the surname Soga only later in life, identifying himself with that ancient family, the story of whose sufferings at the hands of Minamoto Yoritomo and his allies became a tragic epic of loyalty and revenge in Edo popular literature. Bearing the same surname, however, was an important monk painter of Daitoku-ji, Soga Dasoku, whose style served as the basis of an informal lineage of ink painters through the sixteenth and seventeenth centuries. Shōhaku attempted to affiliate himself with that line, incorporating Dasoku's name in signatures and seals, as in this landscape painting, where the signature reads Soga Kiyō Zu (painted by Kiyo—literally, bright hawk—of the Soga family), and the seal is Dasokuken Shōhaku (Shōhaku of the Dasoku studio). In other signatures, Shōhaku claimed to be the tenth-generation heir to the Muromachi period master. The notion of a lineage of Soga Dasoku school painters had remained alive until Shōhaku's time. Kanō Sansetsu (1589-1651) is known to have used the Dasoku signature himself; the same is true of Sansetsu's grandson, Kanō Eikei (1662-1701) who in turn was the teacher of Takada Keiho (1674-1755), Shōhaku's own painting teacher. Keiho was a minor Kanō artist from the Ōmi region near Kyoto, and perhaps Shōhaku felt his relationship, no matter how tenuous, was sufficient grounds to claim membership in this lineage.

Soga Shōhaku's paintings show both Kanō influences and elements from Muromachi ink painting. Yet he incorporated them into a style that was distinctly his own, showing many individualistic and eccentric mannerisms and often bursting with energy. The most erratic paintings, however, date from his early period. His later works, which include this painting from the last decade of his life, show a great deal more control, forethought, and restraint.

References
Kinsei Itan no Geijutsu-ten: Jakuchū, Shōhaku, Rosetsu, Suzuki, Susumu (Tokyo, 1971), pls. 79, 83.
The Paintings of Soga Shōhaku, Hickman, Money, 2 vols., unpublished doctoral dissertation, Harvard University, September 1976.

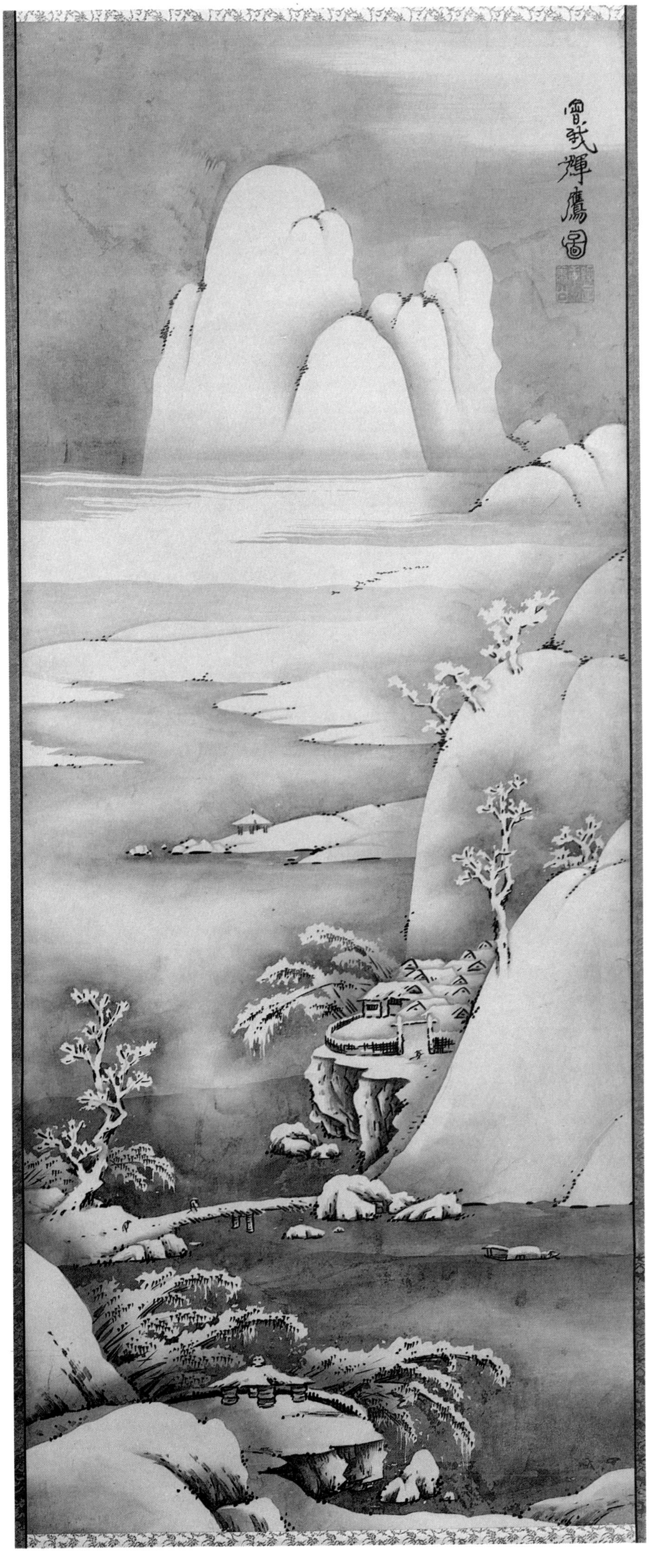

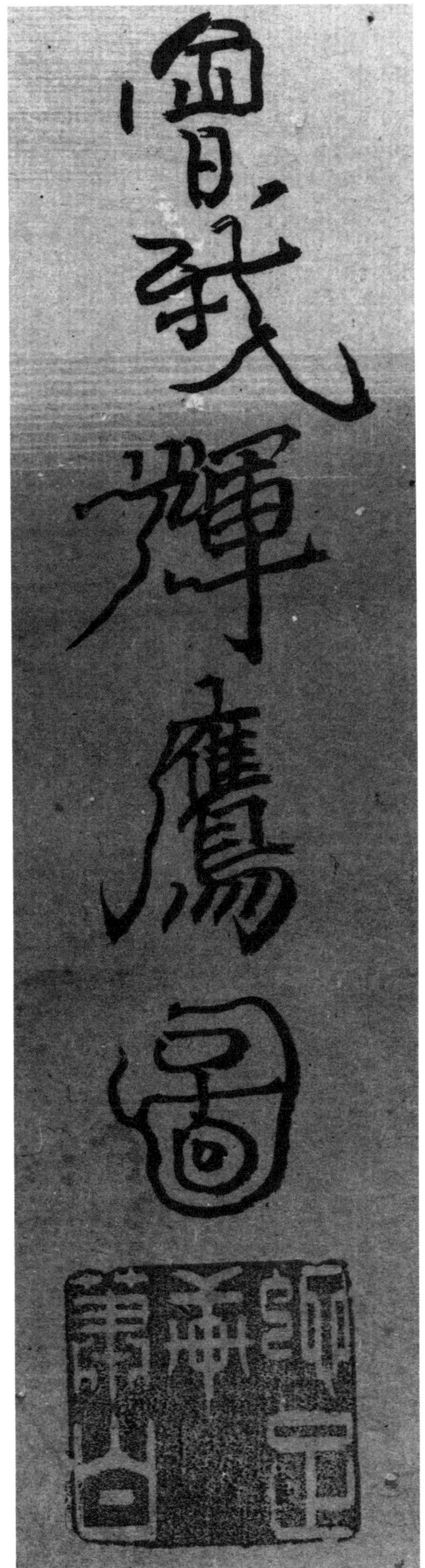

Detail

62

The Temple Bell at Dōjō-ji

Nagasawa Rosetsu
1754-1799

Hanging Scroll
Ink and light color on paper
111.8 x 56.7 cm

Signature
Rosetsu Sessha[su]

Seal
Gyo

This large, rapidly brushed painting amply illustrates the whimsy and imagination of the painter. Rosetsu allotted three-quarters of the scroll to an extremely small section of a huge bronze temple bell, which dominates the entire painting surface. The lower section of the composition reveals a portion of a kimono sleeve trailing out from beneath the bell.

The painting is derived from the popular legend of the Dōjō-ji, which is performed as a Nō drama and a Kabuki play and which revolves around events of the 1250s, when an innkeeper's daughter, Kiyohime, suffered from unrequited love for a monk named Anchin. Anchin made pilgrimages to Kumano, and would stay at the inn at Masago, befriending the little girl. As Kiyohime grew up, her love for Anchin became more ardent and pressing, and his refusals eventually turned her passion into wrath. She prayed to the deities of hell to help her destroy Anchin, but his recitations of the Buddhist prayer formula Namu Amida Butsu warded off the evil spirits. The incensed Kiyohime pursued him into his temple, the Dōjō-ji in Wakayama, and Anchin tried to evade her by hiding under the ten-foot-high bronze bell. Her fury was so great that she changed into a dragon that emitted flames from all over its body. The dragon coiled itself around the bronze bell, and the heat was intense enough to melt the bell, destroying the monk and the dragon in the process.

Rosetsu has provided a capricious touch to this well-known story. He has depicted the crucial moment when Anchin is under the bell being hotly pursued by Kiyohime as a dragon. However, instead of being incinerated by her, a happy ending is intimated. Kiyohime is following Anchin underneath the bell and only the sleeve of her woman's kimono peeks out, the light red spot of flame on the right corner of the sleeve identifying the wearer as Kiyohime.

The huge bell was defined in a light ink wash, the horizontal brushstrokes being applied with a broad flat-edged brush. The lower bands of ornamentation on the bell were swiftly added over the wash while it was still wet, achieving a blurred effect. A seal employing the character gyo, meaning fish, was used by Rosetsu throughout much of his career. It is said that Rosetsu had a dream in which he saw a fish frozen in the stream; the sun came out and melted the ice, whereupon the fish swam away. Rosetsu interpreted this as a sign that he should break away from the academic style of Ōkyo. From 1787 on, a large gyo seal with the wavy outline shape of a tortoise shell appears on many of his paintings. Sometime between 1792 and 1794 the upper right corner of the border was broken off. One account says that the seal was dropped and broke; another states that Rosetsu purposely broke a section to emphasize his independence from the Ōkyo influence. The seal with the section broken off appears in this painting as well as in the following one, which would then place both pictures in his late period. This dating is confirmed by the striking composition and the novel twist to the subject matter, as well as the signatures in a semicursive style.

Published
Kinsei Itan no Geijutsu-ten: Jakuchū, Shōhaku, Rosetsu, Suzuki, Susumu (Tokyo, 1971), pl. 20.
Rosetsu, Moes, Robert (Denver, 1973), no. 42.

Reference
Jakuchū, Shōhaku, Rosetsu, Suiboku Bijutsu Taikei, vol. 14 (Tokyo, 1973).
Legend in Japanese Art, Joly, Henri (London and New York, 1908).

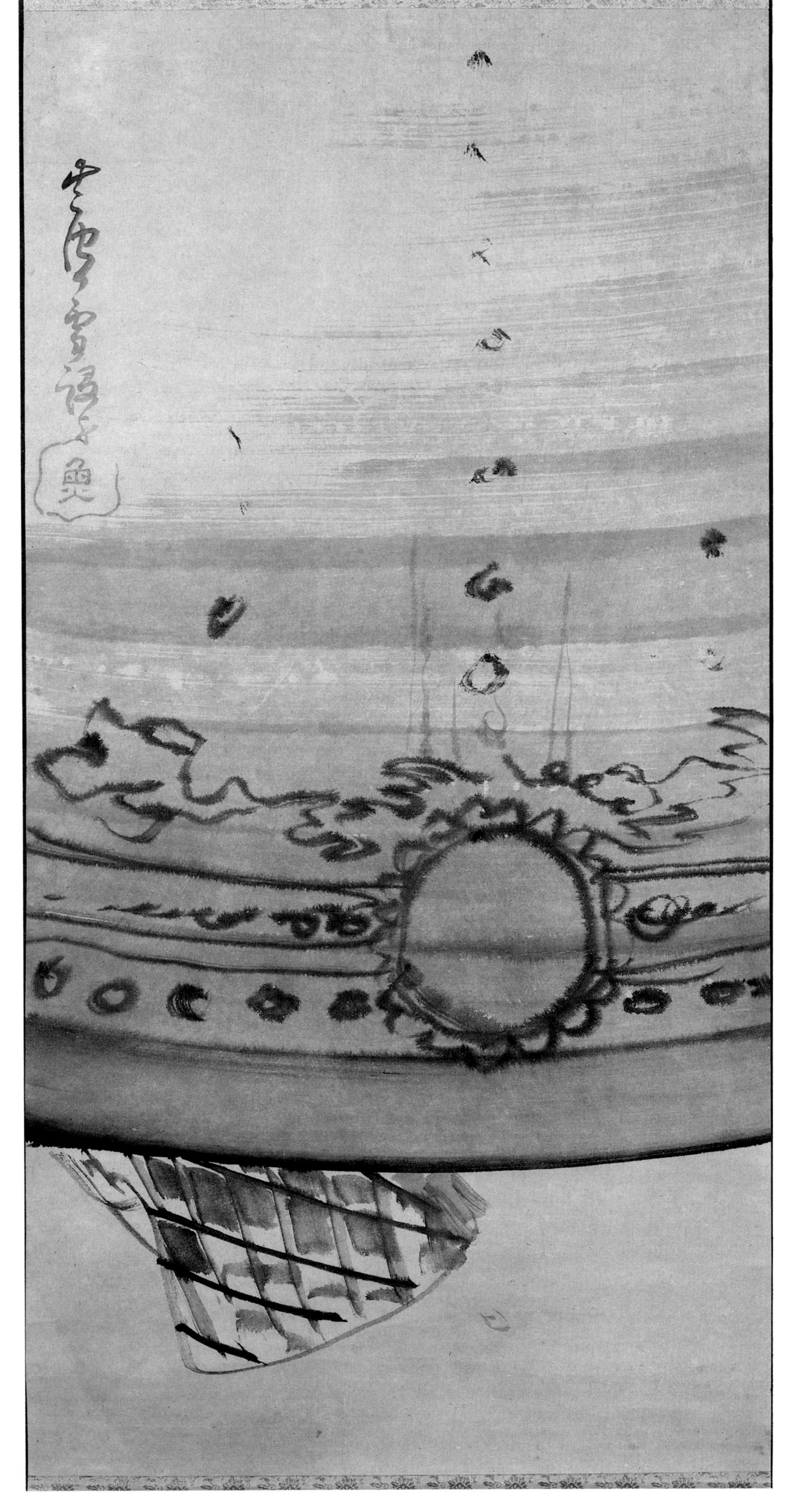

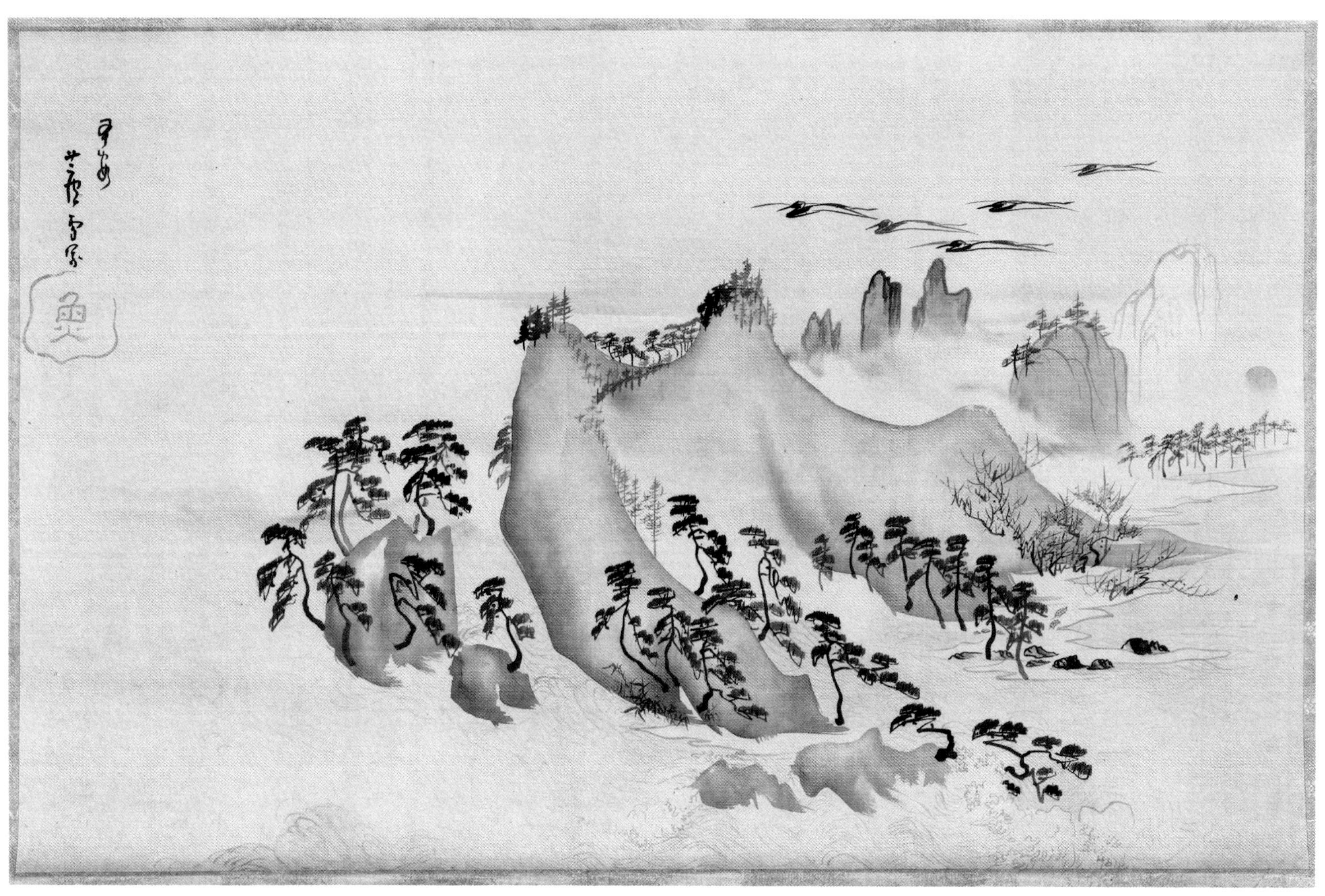

Nagasawa Rosetsu
1754-1799

63

Mount Hōrai, Island of Immortality
(See color plate no. 63)

Hanging Scroll
Ink and light color on silk
58.0 x 85.5 cm

Signature
Heian Rosetsu Sha[su]

Seal
Gyo

Shown here rising from the mist and crashing waves is one of the three islands in Chinese Taoist mythology where immortality may be attained. Called P'eng-lai (Hōrai in Japanese), it was supposed to lie off China's east coast and to be inhabited by immortal demigods and tortoises, cranes, and stags—all symbols of longevity—as well as auspicious plants: pine, peach, plum, and mushroom. In the Sansō painting, Rosetsu has shown tiny tortoises on the beach and large cranes sweeping overhead. The pine trees that cling to the cliffs are delineated in Rosetsu's characteristic dark, swift, and controlled strokes. Soft velvet-like ink washes define the solid masses of the near mountains and the amorphous mists behind them, whereas the distant peaks are executed with a flat-wedged brush and strong outlines. The tonal contrasts and overall sense of movement from right to left combine with the delicate images and fanciful theme to create a landscape of ethereal beauty.

The theme of the Isle of the Immortals is one that appealed greatly to Rosetsu; and it is believed that most of his Hōrai paintings were done in 1794 during his stay at the Itsukushima Shrine on the island of Miyajima in Hiroshima Bay. He may well have likened that tranquil, mist-shrouded island, sacred to both Shinto and Buddhist traditions, to the Taoist P'eng-lai.

Nagasawa Rosetsu was indeed a strongly imaginative and individualistic artist; along with Soga Shōhaku (no. 61) and Itō Jakuchū, he is considered one of the strongest eccentrics of his age. He came from a family of low-ranking samurai from Sasayama in Tamba province (modern Hyōgo prefecture). His father, Uesugi Hikouemon, was in the service of the Aoyama clan, governors of Shimotsuke, but Rosetsu seems to have been adopted by the more prosperous Nagasawa family in the Yodo fief, south of Kyoto. There he also served as a feudal retainer to the Inaba clan, rulers of Tango. His early life is somewhat sketchy, but he appears to have gained the patronage of the Yokoyama family in Yodomachi, who were instrumental in sending him to Kyoto, during his twenties, where he became a student of Maruyama Ōkyo (1733-1795), the leading realist painter.

Many stories describe the relationship of the headstrong, volatile pupil with the dignified, mild teacher. Rosetsu is said to have been expelled from Ōkyo's studio, but their association appears to have lasted most of their lives. By 1790 Rosetsu had completed, in Ōkyo's stead, a series of commissions for screens and wall paintings in Buddhist temples in the Kii area (modern Wakayama prefecture). Rosetsu was already an established painter in his own right by the year 1782, when he was ranked as the fourth artist in Kyoto, under Jakuchū, Ōkyo, and Buson, in the **Heian Jimbutsu-shi (Record of Kyoto Personages)**. Thus his collaboration with Ōkyo in the temple projects as well as in carrying out a commission for paintings in the Summer Palace of the Kyoto Imperial Palace compound along with Kanō and Tosa painters would point to a close friendship.

Rosetsu traveled extensively in Kii province in 1786 and 1787, establishing a reputation there. In 1796, however, he began exhibiting his works in the Higashiyama Exhibition of New Calligraphy and Painting organized by his good friend, Minagawa Kien. The exhibition was held twice a year from 1788 to 1801 and was the first public exhibition in Japan where talented artists could display their works. Kien has suggested in his **Collected Writings** that the bold, innovative style characteristic of Rosetsu's later works was the result of his attempts to catch the eyes of the public for these exhibitions. Rosetsu died at the age of forty-six years while visiting in Osaka. The circumstances surrounding his death are unclear, but the stories that have been related reinforce the image of a personality who was introspective and eccentric in behavior, attributes to which many of his more subjective paintings bear witness.

Scholars have separated Rosetsu's stylistic development into three major periods. The early works of Rosetsu closely follow the style of Ōkyo, who combined the academic painting of the Kanō school with a realism or naturalism derived from Western art. Even his calligraphy at that time, done in a neat, formal, precise kaisho, is similar to Ōkyo's. However, Rosetsu imbued his works with greater energy through his use of the brush, giving his subjects much more life and animation.

The middle period spans the years 1785 to 1794. During this time Rosetsu's calligraphy underwent a change from the neat, academic kaisho to a sharp, quick, semicursive style, gyosho. His paintings as well as his calligraphy became more expressive; they were endowed with a personality that is often whimsical and exaggerated. Rosetsu departed from the naturalism learned from Ōkyo and concentrated on the witty characterizations and brushwork that is more reminiscent of Zenga. During the latter part of this period, Rosetsu became more lyrical and this style was expressed through softer lines and more romantic subject matter.

The paintings from his late period, beginning around 1794, generally show softened brushstrokes and a highly personal view of life. The subject matter expresses his more introspective attitude and the portrayal becomes more exaggerated. His calligraphy is also at its freest, usually written in an abbreviated grass style, sōsho, or continuing in the semicursive style. Mount Hōrai falls into this later group of works.

Published
Kinsei Itan no Geijutsu-ten: Jakuchū, Shōhaku, Rosetsu, Suzuki, Susumu (Tokyo, 1973), pl. 90.
Kobijutsu, no. 54 (December 1977), pp. 111-112, 115-117.

Reference
Kokka, no. 536 (July 1935), pp. 179-188.

Part V

A View of Japan through Japanese Art

Peter F. Drucker

Japan, as everybody knows, is a country of rigid rules and of individual subordination to a collective will. It is the country where the young college student goes hiking in the mountains, but turns boots and pack over to a younger brother or sister upon graduation. It is a country where the student is a radical in college but becomes a faithful conservative upon being hired by the Mitsubishi Bank or the Ministry of Finance. It is a country where the young woman wears one kind of kimono until the day of her wedding, and then puts on the married woman's kimono for the rest of her life.

Japan is a country where junior high school graduates become manual workers, high school graduates become clerks, and college graduates become managers and professionals—all three thus slotted for the rest of their lives by the school-leaving diploma. It is a country where there is lifetime commitment to one employer. Japan is also, as everyone knows, the country of mutual obligations in which even speech is minutely regulated by social relationship and status. It is the country of Japan Incorporated, where conflicting interests pull together for the greater glory of the common economy. The best-known—and best—book on Japanese social organization and institutions, **Japanese Society** by Chie Nakane (Berkeley: University of California Press, 1970), depicts the ie, the community of the clan or tribe, as the organizing reality within which the individual exists as a member rather than as a person. Whenever Japanese and Western (especially American) scholars meet, in any discipline and on any subject, the Japanese at once contrast Japanese cooperation with the excessive competition and rampant diversity of the West.

Yet the most pervasive trait of all Japanese art is the individualism. In every major period of artistic activity in the West there has been one universal style; we speak of the Hellenistic, of the Romanesque and the Gothic, the Renaissance and the Baroque. But every period of great artistic activity in Japan has been characterized by diversity. Indeed in the arts, and especially in painting, the contrast is properly between Western conformity and the excessive diversity of Japan. During the Edo period (1603-1867) the Japanese tendency to diversity reached its apogee. In painting alone, over a dozen major schools flourished, along with countless sub schools. There is nothing comparable in other cultures to the flamboyant diversity of the last great artistic era of premodern Japan. The Japanese scholars and experts who castigate American excessive competition, and who contrast it to its disadvantage with Japanese cooperation, think of competition among businesses in the marketplace or of competition for promotion within the management group in a company. They never, it seems, think of the Japanese school system. Yet every American recoils in horror when told that a Japanese schoolboy, ten years old, will applaud with joy upon hearing that his best friend is ill and will have to miss a week or two of school. The friend will thus fall behind in the competition for the examination that will decide on the few who will make it into the prestigious junior high school.

And as to Japan Incorporated, there is no commercial rivalry and competition in the West that compares with the fierce ruthlessness with which the major Japanese industrial groups, the zaibatsu, fight one another. If Mitsubishi goes into a new field, be it synthetic fibers or electronics or shipbuilding—Mitsui and Sumitomo have to go in too— never mind that overcapacity already exists in that industry worldwide. And Japanese political parties are not disciplined monoliths; they are not an ie. They are loose congeries of fiercely competing factions.

The Japanese are probably the world's best animal painters. In the West, the few animal painters are specialists, a Rosa Bonheur or George Stubbs, for instance. In Japan almost every painter painted animals. The Japanese took some traditions of animal painting from the Chinese: the kachōga (flower-and-bird) painting, for instance, which is represented in the Sansō Collection by the pair of paintings attributed to Kantei (no. 19) or the Unkei Eii painting of two myna birds (no. 11). The latter is, I think, one of the most satisfying paintings—so simple, so right, so good-humored. But upon closer analysis the apparent simplicity dissolves into the most carefully controlled and balanced composition and sophisticated handling of the brush. Another example is the Sengai **Frog and Snail** (no. 36) with its ingenious calligraphy—I don't know who enjoyed himself more: the frog about to fulfill his Buddha destiny by swallowing the snail, or Sengai painting it.

Nothing I know expresses one basic trait of the Japanese as well as these bird paintings do: the capacity for pure enjoyment. It is the same capacity one gets at a Japanese picnic or at a simple folk dance in an empty lot on a summer's night. It is the capacity for pure enjoyment that makes pompous company presidents and grave scholars play the silliest children's games at a party, without embarrassment or reticence. It is the capacity for pure enjoyment that can be seen in parks on Sundays where young Japanese fathers romp with their children. It is a quality of immediacy that is present in the most sophisticated Japanese artwork or novel, and that is the essence of the haiku. Unkei Eii's **Myna Birds** and Sengai's **Frog and Snail** are done with complete control of brush, ink, and composition, but they also express the artists' intuitive, immediate projection of their own selves into the spirit of the birds or frog. These Japanese paintings are a hymn to diversity and spontaneity in keeping with the modern English poet, Gerard Manley Hopkins, who sang, "Glory be to God for dappled things."

And yet the cooperation, the mutual obligations, the lifetime commitment to one employer, the ie, and even Japan Incorporated, are not myths. Central to Japan is constant and continuing polarity between tight, enveloping community—supportive but demanding subordination to its rules—and competitive individualism demanding spontaneity.

Japanese artists of the eighteenth century were highly individualistic, yet most considered themselves as belonging to a school—Nanga or Rimpa or Shijō for instance. The few who did not—Shōhaku, Rosetsu, Jakuchū— are called eccentrics in Japan. And if an artist starts in a school and then outgrows it and develops his own style, Japanese propriety demands that there be a violent break, like the confrontations of a Kabuki drama. Nagasawa Rosetsu, for instance, is reported to have broken violently with Maruyama Ōkyo, whose student he originally was, though the record shows unambiguously that the two actually kept on working together and that Ōkyo entrusted Rosetsu with important and confidential commissions. Similarly, a century earlier, Kusumi Morikage was reported to have been excommunicated by, and exiled from, the atelier of Kanō Tanyū when he went his own way, even though the record shows a close and continuing family relationship between the two artists.

Even today, in a modern, Westernized Japan, it is not considered proper for a young man to be on his own and not to belong to an organization, an ie. My interpreter on my first lecture tour in Japan, twenty years ago, was a young Japanese who had gone to graduate school in the United States and who had then established his own marketing consulting practice in Tokyo. He was, I found out, not welcome in his father-in-law's house. When I met the father-in-law, who was dean at a university where I lectured, I asked him what he had against his son-in-law. "He is barely thirty," he replied, "and on his own; that's quite improper. He has no organization to back him up, no boss to bail him out when he gets into trouble. What's worse, he is successful and thus sets a dangerous precedent." The point of the story is that the father-in-law was known all over Japan as the Red Dean, who delivered himself every Saturday evening on national radio of a violent philippic against the remnants of feudalism in Japanese family life and against the evils of the organization man.

Art history (or art anecdote) may provide the answer to the paradox, and a key to understanding the relationship between the right community of the ie and the spontaneity and individualism that characterize so much of Japanese art as well as of Japanese life and society. Sakai Hōitsu, the last of the great Rimpa masters, started out studying under a Kanō painter. He then became the pupil of a distinguished Nanga artist, Kushiro Unsen. Then he apparently went for career advice to Tani Bunchō, the recognized Nanga master in the city of Edo, Japan's political capital. Bunchō did not tell the young Hōitsu to stick to Nanga, but counseled him to study Kōrin and to become a Rimpa painter. A great teacher in the West might have said to such a highly gifted young man: "Find the style that fits you." Bunchō said, in effect, "Find the school that fits you."

The tension between the pressure to belong and to conform and the stress on spontaneity, independence, and individuality is one, but only one, of the polarities that characterize Japanese art and Japanese culture. The Sansō Collection contains three works by famous seventeenth-century masters: **Two Wagtails,** attributed to Kanō Sanraku (no. 22); the **Child Holding A Spray of Flowers,** attributed to Tarawaya Sōtatsu (no. 59); and a circular fan, **Autumnal Ivy Leaves with Bamboo,** by Ogata Kōrin (no. 60). Each epitomizes the Japanese talent for simplicity refined to the point of austerity. Yet Sanraku's best-known paintings, such as his screens of birds and trees and flowers, are ornate and sumptuous with gold and silver and ostentatious colors. Sōtatsu founded the decorative Rimpa school with its strong lyricism and colorful elegance, and Kōrin perfected it with his rich designs. Thus the three paintings in the Sansō Collection may be called atypical of their painter—and yet each is also completely typical of him.

Similarly, in this exhibition there is a landscape by Kantei (no. 18) that simplifies and makes more austere the already simplified and austere style of the Shūbun landscape; but there is also a pair of flower-and-bird paintings by the same master that is ornate, decorative, almost sumptuous (no. 19). This exhibition presents examples of the stark, austere style of the Sesshū circle—for example, the Unkei Eii or the Bokusho haboku (broken ink) landscapes. But Sesshū and members of his circle also painted highly decorative and colorful flower-and-bird paintings. Almost two hundred years later, in the early nineteenth century, the austere Neo-Confucian Watanabe Kazan painted the lush, sensuous **Lotus Flower and Swimming Fish** shown in this exhibition (no. 58).

To a Westerner, these seem to be contradictions. To a Japanese, they are polarities. A Westerner may feel that an artist should be attracted either to the austerity and empty space of a Muromachi haboku landscape or to the colorful, decorative design of a Kantei flower-and-bird painting or a Sanraku bird screen, but not to both. To the Japanese, however, these are necessary tensions; these are poles of expression within the same person.

Any visitor to Kyoto sees examples of this tension within a few miles of each other: Nijō Castle—ornate, sensuous, boastful, the official Kyoto residence of the military dictator, the Tokugawa shogun; and Katsura Villa—simple to the point of being austere, exquisite, without ornaments and totally disciplined, the summer villa of an imperial prince. Both were built within the same generation and by the Japanese ruling classes. And there is Nikkō, north of Tokyo, the great seventeenth-century mausoleum of the Tokugawa shogun Ieyasu with its extreme ornateness, almost too much even for baroque tastes. But the same shogun, in his castle, lived in restrained austerity. To the Japanese, the two belong together. The tension is not one of opposites but one of poles; and where there is a North Pole there has to be a South Pole.

This tension, this polarity extends through all of Japanese culture. It is found in the tension between the official ultra-Confucian male supremacy, which dictates that in public the woman is invisible and subservient, and the reality of family life, where the woman holds the power and the purse strings, and where a recent prime minister could say in parliament: "I have no position on this measure yet; my mother-in-law has been sick and I could not get her guidance." And the opposition spokesman nodded and said: "Please convey my wishes for a speedy recovery to your respected mother-in-law."

A similar polarity is found in the upbringing of children. Until they reach school age, children are indulged in a way that goes beyond any American permissiveness; and then they go to school and on the first day there is discipline and the children are expected to behave—and they do. There is a remarkable tension between the genius of the Japanese language in which everything focuses on human relationships, and the nature of Chinese ideographs, which are built up of representations of objects. The Japanese very early invented syllabaries in which the sounds of Japanese can easily be written. Every Japanese learns the two national syllabaries in the elementary grades. But then the syllabaries are used mainly as auxiliaries to Chinese ideographs. To the Japanese the tension between the Japanese language and the Chinese ideograph is essential, no matter how heavy a burden it puts on learning and literacy.

There are strict rules for proper behavior that tell every Japanese what form of address to use when talking to his aunt and to his uncle's boss and to his cousin's mistress. But there is also the encouragement of the eccentric, who is given almost infinite leeway. Sengai, for instance, was the most respected cleric, the abbot of an ancient and most sacred temple—but at the age of eighty-five years he was also a free spirit who traveled around the country, often in low company, and satirically painted frogs to look like the Buddha.

This polarity can be found today in Japanese industry and its human relations. To a Westerner an organization can be either autocratic or democratic, but the Japanese organization is both. Surely no more perfect example of the autocratic personality exists than the head of a big Japanese organization, whether government agency or business. Yet decision-making is by consensus and participation, and starts at the bottom rather than at the top. In every Japanese organization from ancient times to the present, the word of the chief has been absolute law; this chief could order a retainer to commit suicide or to divorce his wife. And yet no chief could make one step without the consent of his retainers, and indeed without active participation of the clan elders in a decision. Similarly, today the top people in a company or in a government agency are obeyed without argument or reservation—and yet every decision comes up from below and is an expression of a general will. Every Japanese organization is in Western terms both an extreme of autocracy and an extreme of democratic participation.

The tension is not dialectic, and resolved in a higher synthesis, nor does one principle overcome the other. It is not the dualism of the Chinese yin and yang. The Japanese do not mix their principles any more than one mixes North Pole and South Pole. For the Japanese tension is not contradiction or contrast or conflict—the tensions of the analytical mind. It is polarity—the tension of perception, of configuration, of existence. To understand Japanese art and Japanese life, one has to accept the polarity between the ornate and the austere; between male supremacy and female power; between spoiled indulged brats and disciplined scholars; between the Japanese language with its inflected verbs and syllabary script and the complexities of the Chinese ideograph. Even though the Koreans too developed a syllabary of their own, centuries after the Japanese, such polarities are essential to Japan and, to my knowledge, to Japan alone.

It is this tension, this polarity, that has made Japan throughout its history a country of contrasts, of sharp and sudden swings—from wide-open receptivity to foreign cultures and foreign commerce to self-imposed isolation, for instance, in the seventeenth century. But it is also this polarity that gives Japanese art, Japanese literature, and Japanese industry their dynamics and creativity.

A Westerner who has business in Japan—the professor who goes there to lecture or the businessman who negotiates a contract—soon becomes familiar with the phrase Wareware Nihon-jin, which means: "We Japanese." But whenever it is used—and it is used all the time—it conveys: "We Japanese are so different that you will never understand us."

To understand what a Japanese friend or business partner, or the student in the audience who gets up and asks a question, means when he starts out with Wareware Nihon-jin, one needs to look at Japanese landscape paintings: perhaps at the Nyosui Sōen and the Unkei Eii landscapes (nos. 7, 10) in the Suibokuga section of this exhibition, or at the paintings of Ikeno Taiga, the small Uragami Gyokudō landscape (no. 48) and the Tanomura Chikuden paintings (nos. 49, 50) in the Bunjinga section. But where in these landscapes are the people—the Nihon-jin? Yet it is precisely their absence, or their subordination to the land, that is the point. For Nihon-jin does not just mean Japanese. It means: "We who belong to the land of Japan." The landscape painting is the soul of Japanese art because the Japanese landscape has formed the soul of Japan.

Some of the features of these landscape paintings the Japanese took from the Chinese—the bizarre rock formation of the eroded Chinese karst limestone that can be seen in the small Shūtoku landscape in this exhibition (no. 8) is an example. But most of the features of these landscapes can be found in Japan; indeed, a Japanese friend of mine claims that he knows the valley, someplace near Gifu, that Gyokudō painted in his small lyrical landscape in the Sansō Collection (no. 48). The Japanese landscape looks like the landscape of the Japanese painters, as everyone knows who has traveled in the Japanese countryside. And yet the Japanese landscape does not look a bit like the landscape of the Japanese landscape painter, nor does any landscape on earth. The landscape of the Japanese painter is a spiritual landscape, a landscape of the soul.

The Japanese feeling for this landscape is included in Shinto. What Shinto really means, probably no Westerner has ever been fully able to understand. It surely does not mean a religion in the Western sense; it becomes a religion only after 1867, when the Meiji Restoration created a monstrosity known as State Shinto because it felt it had to emulate the way religions are set up in the West. Far more ancient and pervasive are the many Shinto shrines and rituals; but there is, above all, a Shinto feeling—the feeling of the uniqueness of Japan as an environment. I did not write human environment; it is far more than that. It is an environment fully as much for the supernatural, for the forces that control the universe, as it is an environment for man and beast, plant and rock. It is unique and it is complete. And it is different: and this is the point of Wareware Nihon-jin. Underlying the phrase is the feeling that Japan is unique; that Japan is by itself. What this means is expressed in the landscape paintings. Their hills and trees are the visible surface, the skin, of a spiritual landscape that is invisible and unique. There may be landscapes elsewhere that look like it. Taiwan has similar hills, and so does Korea. But there is no landscape, to a Japanese, that **means** the same thing. A painting of the Japanese landscape can be a realistic image that serves as a valid legal document to determine the boundary lines of a Shinto shrine, as some of the earliest Japanese landscape paintings were intended to do; and it means an inner space, a landscape of the soul that is the center of gravity of Japanese existence. This landscape is, so to speak, Japan an sich.

I am not saying that the Japanese are in fact unique; I am saying that the Japanese feel that they are. It is not that they feel superior; nationalism has been a Japanese vice only in rare, short moments of aberration. They feel different because they feel at home only in this landscape of their soul. This may explain why of all the foreign students in the United States or in Europe, the Japanese are the only ones who, with very few exceptions, cannot wait to go back home.

I now come to what I would call "Japanese aesthetics" or the "topological approach," or "What makes the Chinese so uneasy when they look at a Japanese painting?"

Almost any landscape in the Sansō Collection could be used to demonstrate Japanese aesthetics—good examples are the Unkei haboku (broken-ink) landscape (no. 10) and the two Chikuden landscapes (nos. 49, 50). Both painters deliberately set out to follow the Chinese and both ended up with paintings that are quite un-Chinese and distinctly Japanese.

The haboku style in which Unkei painted had been mastered by Unkei's great contemporary, Sesshū, and was clearly seen by the painters of Sesshū's circle as distinctly Chinese. The Unkei landscape in the Sansō Collection (no. 10) is probably a Chinese subject—one of the Eight Views of the Hsiao and Hsiang District. Unkei, by using the recently imported Chinese technique for a traditional Chinese subject, surely aimed at painting a "Chinese" painting.

Chikuden, three hundred years later, was deeply versed in Chinese styles and Chinese painters, and wrote learned treatises on Chinese techniques, Chinese aesthetics, and Chinese motifs. In both of the Chikuden paintings in the Sansō Collection (nos. 49, 50), the inscriptions invoke the spirit of the Chinese literati painters and scholars whom the Japanese tried to emulate. And yet, put a Chinese connoisseur or a Chinese art historian in front of these paintings, and he will be uneasy. "Yes, these hills here in Unkei look like so-and-so in China. And yes, this rock in Chikuden looks like some other painter in China. And the brushwork is this or that technique. And the haboku, of course, follows a Chinese example. And yet, and yet, and yet..." What he is saying, if he is candid, is: "And yet these are definitely not Chinese paintings. They make me very uneasy and I do not understand why. But I do not want to have them around."

One only has to put these works next to Chinese paintings to understand his feelings. I am not saying that one cannot mistake a Chinese painting for a Japanese one, and vice versa. The technique is the same, the brushstrokes are the same, the ink values are the same—and the painting is different. What makes it different is the Japanese sense of beauty.

The Japanese paintings are dominated by empty space. It is not only that so much of the canvas is empty. The empty space organizes the painting. This is opposite to what most Chinese would do, but it is basic to Japanese aesthetics. The same aesthetics are found, for instance, in the Sansō Collection's small fan painting by Ogata Kōrin (no. 60)—a painter who did not go to school with the Chinese—or in the very late painting by Kazan (no. 58).

If I were to try to define these aesthetics in contrast to those in Western and Chinese painting, I would say that Western painting is basically geometric. It is no coincidence that modern Western painting begins with the rediscovery of linear perspective, around 1425, that is with the subordination of space to geometry. Chinese painting, on the other hand, is algebraic. In Chinese painting, proportion governs, as it does in Chinese ethics. Japanese painting is by contrast topological—that branch of mathematics that began around 1700 and that deals with the properties of surface and space in which shapes and lines are defined by space, so that there is no difference between a straight line and a curve, such as a hyperbola. Topology deals with angles and vortices and boundary lines. It deals with what space imposes rather than with what is imposed on space. The Japanese painter is topological in his aesthetics. He sees space and then he sees lines. He does not start out with the lines.

It has been commonplace for Western art critics and art historians for almost a hundred years to say that painters do not see objects but configurations. But the Gestalt that the Japanese painter sees is what we today would call a design rather than a structure. This is what the topologist means when he says that, topologically speaking, it is space that determines the line rather than the line that determines space.

In discussions of Japanese painting one usually finds a reference to the Japanese tendency to become decorative. The Nanga painters abhorred the decorative as totally incompatible with the values and aesthetics of their Chinese literati models; and yet, we are told by all authorities, that they always became decorative, as witness in the Sansō Collection the paintings by Nukina Kaioku and Tani Bunchō (nos. 54, 55), or the two big landscapes by chikuden (nos. 59, 50). Like so many words in art criticism, decorative is misleading; the right word might be "designed." And this irrepressible tendency towards design—the tendency that explains why, in Japanese art, ceramics, lacquer, and painting tend to be closely allied, while the Chinese kept them strictly separate artistically and socially—is based on the Japanese vision that is neither perspectival, i.e., geometric, nor proportional, i.e., algebraic, but design that is topological.

Both suiboku painters, such as Unkei, and Nanga painters, such as Chikuden, looked to the Chinese as models and masters. Both learned techniques from the Chinese, but also motives and style and form. But both transmuted Chinese algebra into Japanese topology. This ability to receive a foreign culture and then to Japanize it, is a continuing thread in Japanese history and experience.

Around 500 AD, Buddhism, and with it the highly advanced and most refined civilization of China, swept into Japan. At first, the impact seemed to inundate Japan completely. Everything was brought from China or Korea, including monks and architects and artists and artisans and scribes and poetry and art works and textiles. After only two centuries, by the Nara period, Japan produced religious sculpture which is completely Buddhist and yet deeply Japanese, even though the techniques are still those of the Chinese and Korean sculptors. But Japan equally transmuted China's governmental and social structures. It made both Buddhism and Confucianism serve a tribal, and soon thereafter, a warrior society. It made Chinese concepts of land tenure, grounded in family ownership of soil, serve a system in which there was no ownership of land at all, except by temples and the throne. There were only graduated rights to the product of the land—that is graduated rights to tax and tribute rather than ownership rights in land as such. The same thing happened in ceramics, in poetry, and in architecture.

It is happening again today; only it is the West rather than China that is the foreign culture that is being Japanized. Forms, techniques, and concepts are used very skillfully. As Sesshū did, and Chikuden, the Japanese rapidly improve on the techniques. There are few Chinese painters whose control and command of the brush equal Sesshū's. There are few Western companies that have the control and command of the corporate form and of managerial techniques that the large Japanese trading companies possess. But the essence is Japanese. The Japanese are not unaffected by the foreign influence; it becomes part of their own experience. But they distill out of the foreign influence what serves to maintain and strengthen Japanese values, beliefs, traditions, purposes, relationships. The result is not a hybrid. It is, as the Muromachi paintings or the Chikuden paintings show, all of one piece. This is a truly unique Japanese characteristic.

Japan has again and again lived through periods when it was wide open to foreign influences. But then it closes in again and digests, transmutes, and transforms almost alchemically. What is considered base metal in the foreign culture sometimes becomes gold in Japan, as with the Chinese Zen painters Mu-ch'i or Yin T'o-lo, who became the ancestors of Japanese ink painting in the fourteenth and fifteenth centuries. But sometimes the metal in a foreign culture may become dross in Japan, as happened in this century to the idea of the national state, imported from the West and transmuted into a poisonous parody of an old and peculiarly Japanese political form, the shogunate, or military government. Yet the shogun had always before served to eliminate fighting, to make war both unnecessary and impossible and, above all, to prevent foreign adventure.

The Japanese aesthetics are a way to understand, or at least to perceive, a fundamental and central element: the very special—I would say unique—relationship between Japan and the outside world; a relationship of receptivity, ability to learn quickly and to improve on what is being taught, while at the same time accepting, or at least retaining, only what makes Japan more Japanese; what fits topology rather than geometry or algebra; what fits Japanese human relations; what fits the inner experience of the uniqueness of Japan; what fits what might be called, with a Western term, Japanese spirituality. We are talking here of an existential phenomenon; and by the way, the best translation of the peculiar word Shinto is probably spirituality.

Whether it can maintain these abilities is the great question ahead of Japan, I think. Japan is now becoming integrated into the outside world, and not just economically—perhaps least of all economically—in a way which neither the Japan of the sixth century, that of the Buddhist and Chinese tidal wave, nor the Japan of Sesshū's time around 1500, nor perhaps even the Japan of a hundred years ago, could have imagined. Is it still possible for Japan to encapsulate and transmute into Japan-ness the foreign, the non-Japanese, culture, behavior, ethics and even aesthetics? I dare not even speculate—but there are a few straws in the wind. If one looks at the visual arts that today prosper in Japan—the modern Japanese woodblock print; the Japanese movie; modern Japanese sculpture and ceramics; and perhaps one could add Japanese architecture—one would say that there is a possibility, perhaps a probability, that the Japanese are again Japanizing the imported culture. The Japanese woodblock print is modern and Japanese very much the way in which Nara sculpture was Buddhist and Japanese. And so, to a large extent, are the ceramics of Japan today. I can hope only that the Japanese will do again what they have done before so many times. The world needs a culture that is both modern and distinctly, uniquely, non-Western. It needs a Japanese Japan rather than a Japanese version of New York or Los Angeles or Frankfurt.

"Ten minutes and eighty years," Hakuin Ekaku is said to have answered when asked how long it took him to paint one of his paintings of Daruma. Of course, Rembrandt might have given the same answer when asked how long it took him to paint the self-portraits of his old age, Claude Monet when asked how long it took him to paint one of the hymns to light in his paintings of Reims Cathedral that now hang in New York's Metropolitan Museum, or Pablo Casals when asked how long it took him to play one of Bach's Unaccompanied Suites For Cello. But Hakuin's answer has two levels of meaning beyond that of the Western artist—it expresses a Japanese view of the nature of man, and a Japanese view of the nature of learning.

These may be seen in a dimension in Japanese figure and portrait painting for which the West has no real parallel, nor does China: the spiritual self-portrait. If the Westerner says that it takes eighty years to be able to do what Rembrandt's last self-portrait represents, or Monet's pure light and Casals' Bach, he talks of the decades of practice needed to attain the skill. But the "eighty years" of the Japanese saying refer, above all, to the spiritual self-realization needed to become the person who can paint Daruma. An old Zen saying has it that "Every painting of Daruma is a (spiritual) self-portrait." The Zen painter who has not worked for decades on control of the self will not be the person to paint Daruma. Daruma is not a god, he is not a saint. He is a man, but one who has realized man's full spiritual potential, who has attained man's full spiritual power, and who has transformed himself into a spiritual being. And only the painter who has himself become the spiritual man which Daruma represents can then paint a portrait on which he can inscribe, as Hakuin did on the earliest of his Darumas in the Sansō Collection, "This is the Buddhist Law!" The spiritual power, the spiritual qualities of Daruma cannot be faked. No matter how great a painter's skill, if he lacks these qualities, his Daruma will lack them too.

Both Kanō Tanyū and Rosetsu, both very great masters and without peers in painting skill, painted Daruma. Tanyū's Daruma looks like an elderly bureaucrat or a successful banker; Rosetsu's like the urbane and witty chairman of a university graduate department. Both are excellent paintings—but neither has spirituality, power, total compelling control. But the Daruma painted by a painter who himself has the spiritual power will have that power even if, as in the case of the Daruma in the Sansō Collection painted by Hakuin in his extreme old age, the body is weighed down by the physical infirmity of advanced old age, the legs have given out, and death is very close.

Daruma is mortal. He is a sentient being. But unlike the saints of Christianity or of Buddhism, he is not dependent on divine grace, on a Supreme Being, or on redemption. He had attained spiritual perfection through his own efforts and by fulfilling the divinity within him.

This is not a "humanist" view of man but a spiritual and existential one. It is a view that focuses on wisdom rather than on knowledge; on self-control rather than on power; on excellence rather than on success.

The Zen saying of "ten minutes and eighty years" also expresses a uniquely Japanese concept of continuous learning. Both in the West and in China, one learns to do better what one already does well. One keeps on painting Daruma until the control becomes completely spontaneous. One draws, as did Konoe Nobutada, a picture of Tenjin every morning—the same picture, but with ever-increasing mastery (no. 25). Or, like Nakabayashi Chikutō, one paints more or less the same landscapes over and over again (no. 52). Of course, in the West the artist does that too—Casals practiced the Bach cello suites until his death, well past ninety years of age. But in the West—and in China—only the artist does this; the rest of us are like Confucian scholars who pass one examination to be qualified to sit for the next, and for whom one promotion is the stepping-stone to the next.

In Japan there is to this day the specialist in the trading company, the specialist on cotton, for instance, or on woodworking machinery, who gets more money and a bigger title but stays the specialist on cotton or on woodworking machinery all his working life, becoming more accomplished with every year. There is the continuous learning process in the Japanese factory, where employees get more money with seniority but keep on doing the same job, and meet every week to discuss how they can do their present jobs better. And there is the uniquely Japanese concept of the Living National Treasure, the great craftsman or artist who has excelled through doing the same work. The Western theory of the learning curve is not accepted in Japan—the theory that people reach a plateau of accomplishment after a certain time and then stay on it. The Japanese learning curve has them break out of that plateau again by continuing to practice—until they reach a new plateau when they again, after a time, start learning and growing, and so on, always approaching perfection. The Japanese learning curve, like the Zen master's ten minutes and eighty years, sees learning as an act of spiritual perfection and personal self-development as much as an acquisition of skills. It is a way of changing the person and not just a way of acquiring performance capacity.

Again this is but one strand. Japanese history and Japanese society are as full of climbers, of ambitious schemers, of people on the make, and people on the take, as any other history or society. But there is also the counterpoint—the ten minutes and eighty years of continuous learning to do better what one already does very well.

The Japanese or Zen concept of learning is not without dangers. It can degenerate into imitation and repetition. This is what happened to the Kanō school of painting, which degenerated into mechanical copying after the middle of the seventeenth-century—and which was still at mechanical copying when the Meiji Restoration opened Japan to the West more than two centuries later. But though capable of degenerating into mechanical copying and mindless repetition, the Zen tradition is closer to being a genuine theory of learning than the Western and Chinese concept of learning for the sake of advancement, promotion, or moving on. With its focus on developing the strengths of a person, it anticipated by hundreds of years modern theories of the person and of self-realization. There is indeed profound wisdom in the insight that work is an extension of personality and personality a distillation of work, so that one cannot paint Daruma's spiritual qualities without having them oneself, but so that one becomes Daruma by painting him every day for decades.

The insight and wisdom that lies in the Zen conception of the person and of learning are endangered in today's Japan. The Japanese educational system has opted for an extreme of the Western and Confucian position, which sees the purpose of learning in getting ready for the next examination, the next promotion, the next external reward. Infants are drilled to pass the entrance examination to the right nursery school, so as to be admitted to the entrance examination to the right kindergarten, which in turn leads to the entrance examination to the right elementary school and on to high school, the university, and the corporation. Is there still room for the emphasis on learning to become, on learning to be, on learning to say "This is the law!" when painting Daruma as a spiritual portrait?

I have so far used Japanese painting to look at Japan. Now I shall use—or abuse—Japanese painting to look at the West and at Western modern art. Rosetsu painted the Sansō Collection's **The Temple Bell at Dōjō-ji** (no. 62) in the 1780s. It is virtually an abstract, nonobjective painting, painted a century and a half before there were abstract painters in the West. Yet it is by no means Japan's oldest abstract painting. In fact, such painting can be traced back to the Heian period, to the tenth century.

The Tani Buncho **Plum Tree in the Moonlight** (no. 55) in the Sansō Collection was done shortly after 1800. It anticipates what Turner or Monet tried to do half a century later in the West: to make light the subject of painting. The Hakuin **Bodhidharma**, also known as **Daruma** (no. 29), is an expressionist painting, like those of Klimt, Schiele, and Kubin, and Picasso in his expressionist years, and Matisse, but with a power very few of them had. The Sengai **Frog and Snail** (no. 36) anticipates the late Picasso by almost one hundred fifty years. Modernism in Western art is thus anticipated by the Japanese tradition.

Yet, of course, Westerners had never laid eyes on the Japanese originals or even heard of them. Other than Ukiyo-e, the woodblock prints, Japanese art was virtually unknown in the West until fairly recent years. The West, in other words, has developed within the last century elements of a modern vision and sensibility that have ancient manifestations in Japan. The West has learned to see in somewhat the same way that the Japanese have seen all along. The West has shifted from description and analysis to design and configuration.

Marshall McLuhan has announced that the electronic media have changed our ways of seeing and interpreting the world and are making us perceive rather than conceive. But the view of Western perception, informed by an understanding of Japanese art, would lead to the conclusion that this shift began much earlier and owed nothing to electronic technology. On the contrary, it would appear more probable that the West became ready for the electronic technology and receptive to it because its perception had shifted from traditional description and analysis to the perception of design and configuration that Japan had known all along.

A distinguished historian of modern Western painting, Robert Rosenblum, in his recent **Modern Painting and the Northern Romantic Tradition: Friedrich to Rothko** (New York: Harper & Row, 1977), asserts that modern Western painting has its roots in the northern, mostly North German, painters of the early 1800s—Caspar David Friedrich and Otto Runge— who shifted from description to design. But this, it could be argued, is precisely what had occurred in Japan far earlier: perception as against conception, design as against description, topology as against geometry, and configuration as against analysis, have indeed been continuing characteristics of Japanese art from the Heian period on.

Edwin O. Reischauer, the former American ambassador to Japan and foremost authority on Japanese history and society, wrote in his recent book **The Japanese** (Cambridge, Massachusetts: The Belknap Press of Harvard University Press, 1978), that Japan has never produced a great or original thinker of the first rank. This has been read as severe criticism, especially in Japan, but Reischauer's point was that Japan's genius is perceptual rather than conceptual.

The towering achievement of the high Middle Ages in the West was Thomas Aquinas' **Summa Theologica**, perhaps the boldest conceptual and analytical feat in human history. The proudest achievement of Japan's classic Heian era is the world's first novel, Murasaki Shikibu's **Tale of Genji**, filled with intimate description of court men and women in life and love and illness and death. Japan's greatest playwright, Chikamatsu Monzaemon (1653-1724) had neither camera nor screen, but his Kabuki and Bunraku (puppet) plays are highly cinematic. They are song, dance, costumes, and music as well as the spoken word. The characters are defined not so much by what they say, but by how they appear. People rarely quote a line that Chikamatsu wrote. But no one ever forgets a scene. Chikamatsu was not a dramatist but a scriptwriter of genius. And without benefit of cinematic tools, his Kabuki theater invented cinema techniques; the mie in which the actors freeze, is, for instance, the equivalent of the movies' close-up.

The perceptual in Japanese tradition largely underlies Japan's rise as a modern society and economy. It enables the Japanese to grasp the essence, the fundamental configuration of the foreign, the Western, whether an institution or a product, and then to redesign. The most important thing to say about Japan, as viewed through its art, may well be that Japan is perceptual.

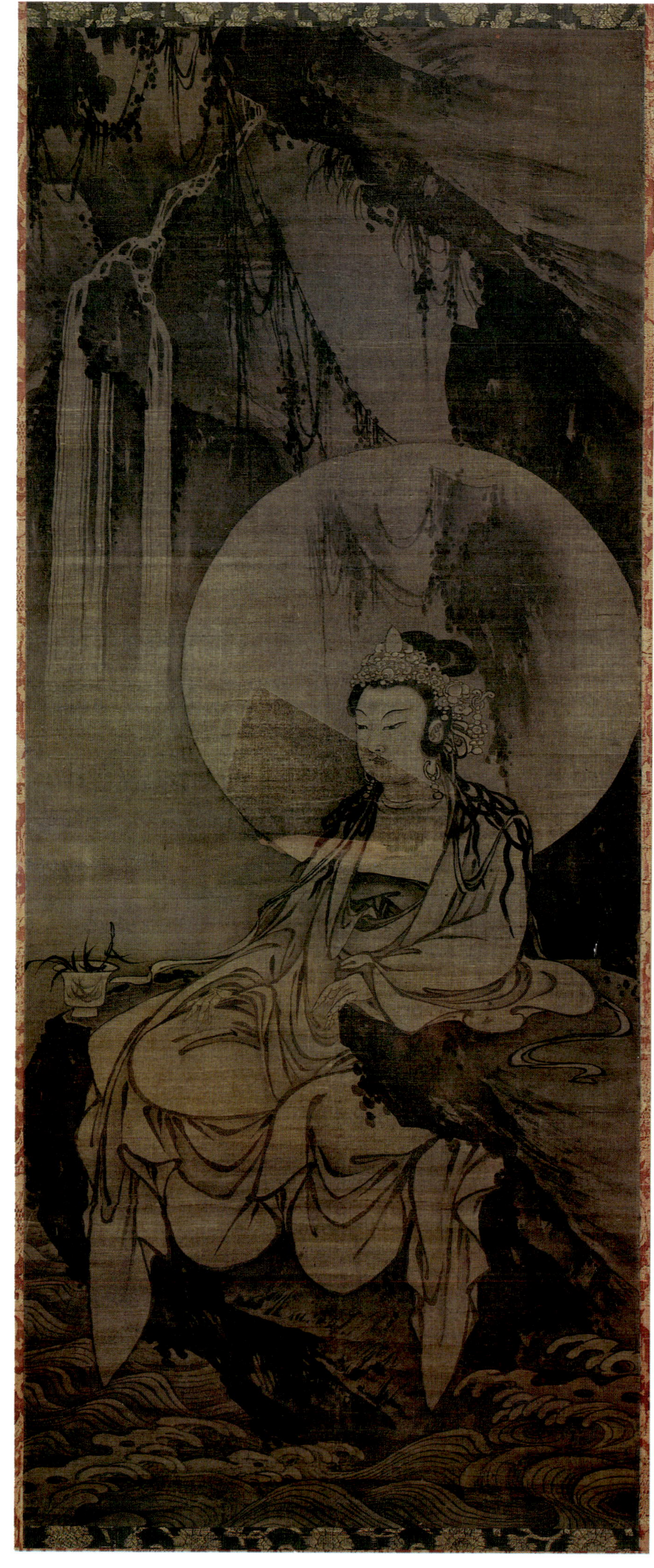

3

**The Byaku-e
(White-Robed)
Kannon**
Attributed to Isshi

19 ▶

Diptych
Blossoming Peach and Sparrow; Peonies and Butterfly
Kantei

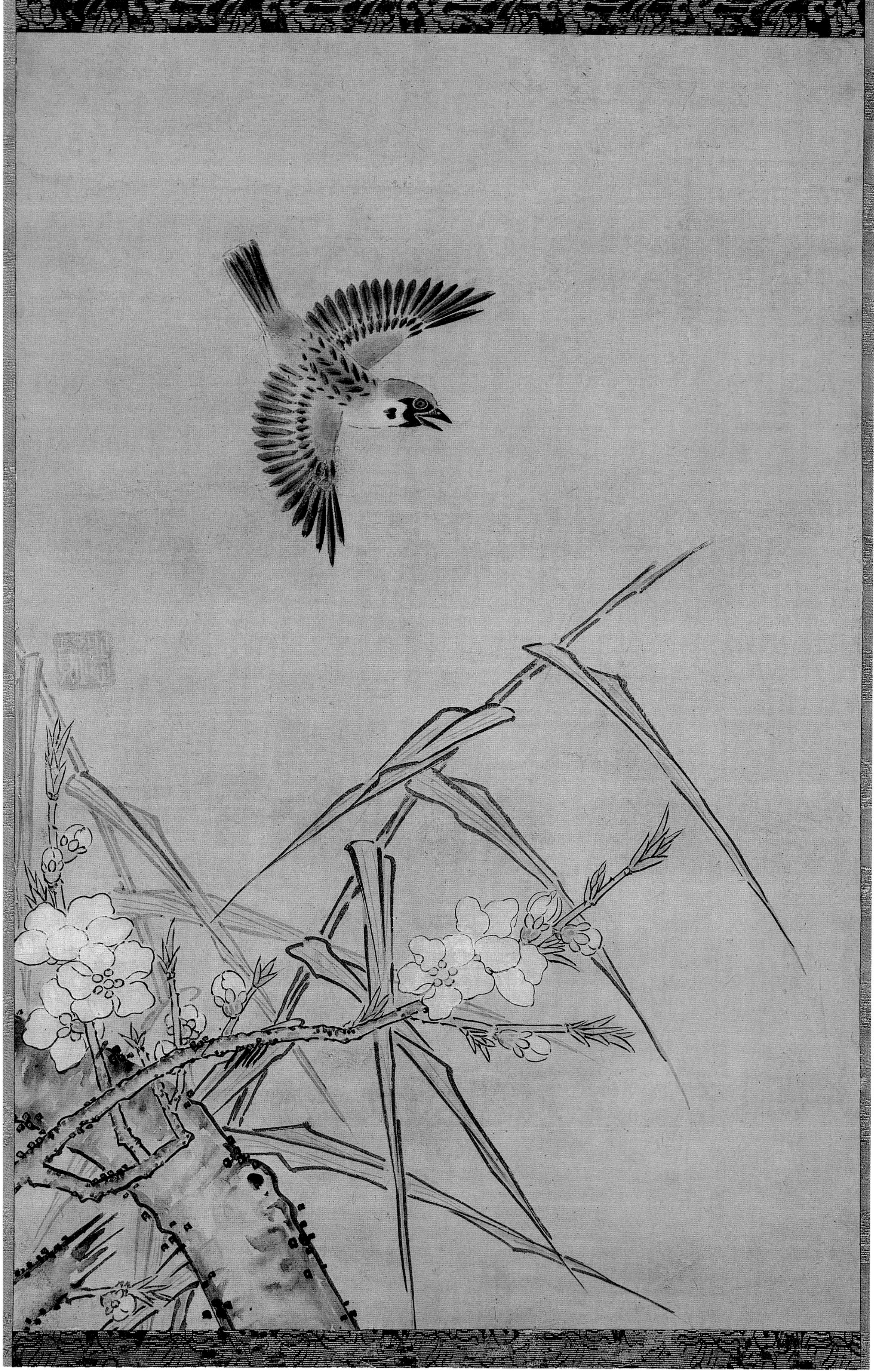

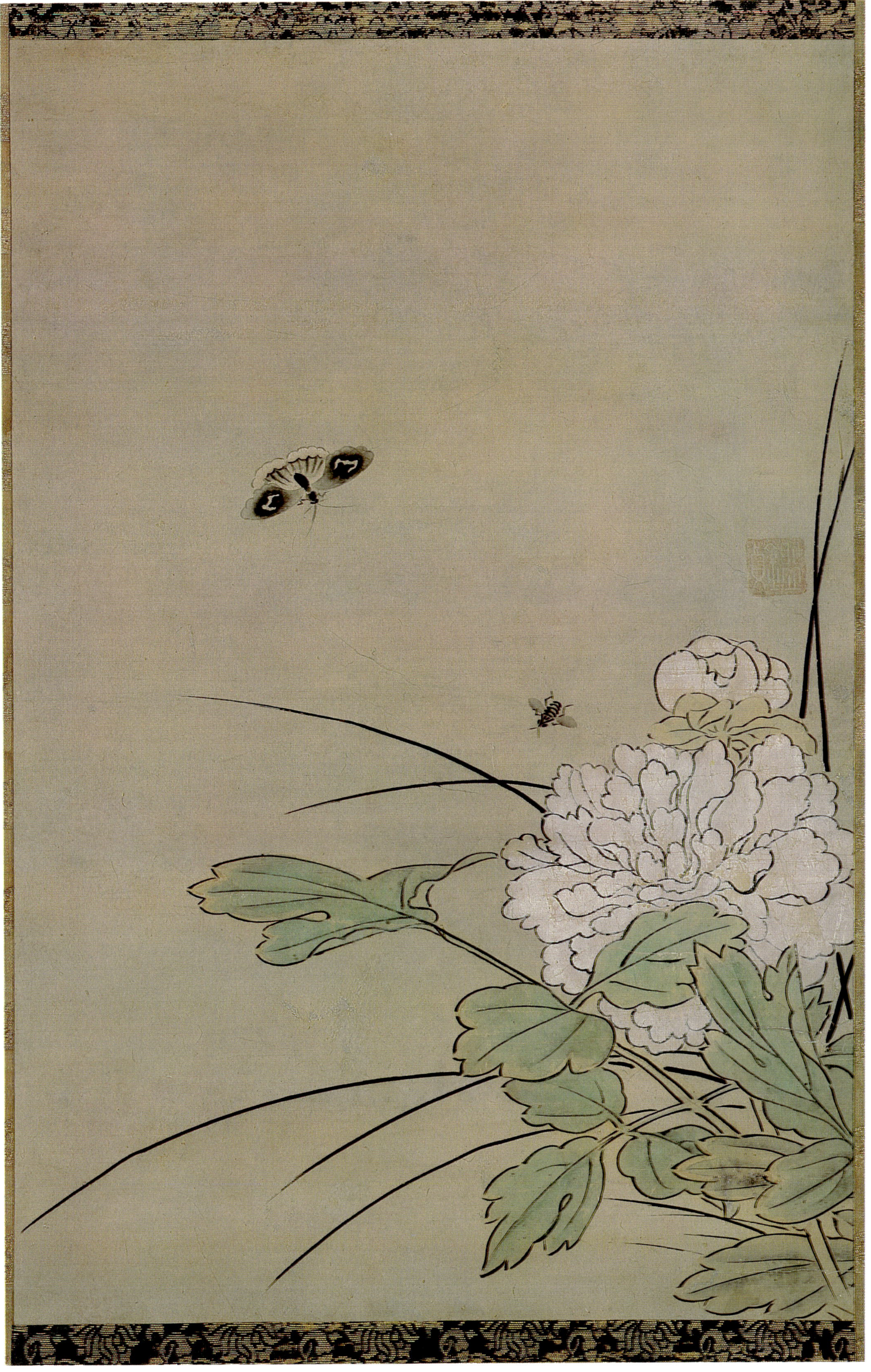

21

Fisherman and Windswept Coast
Sesson Shūkei

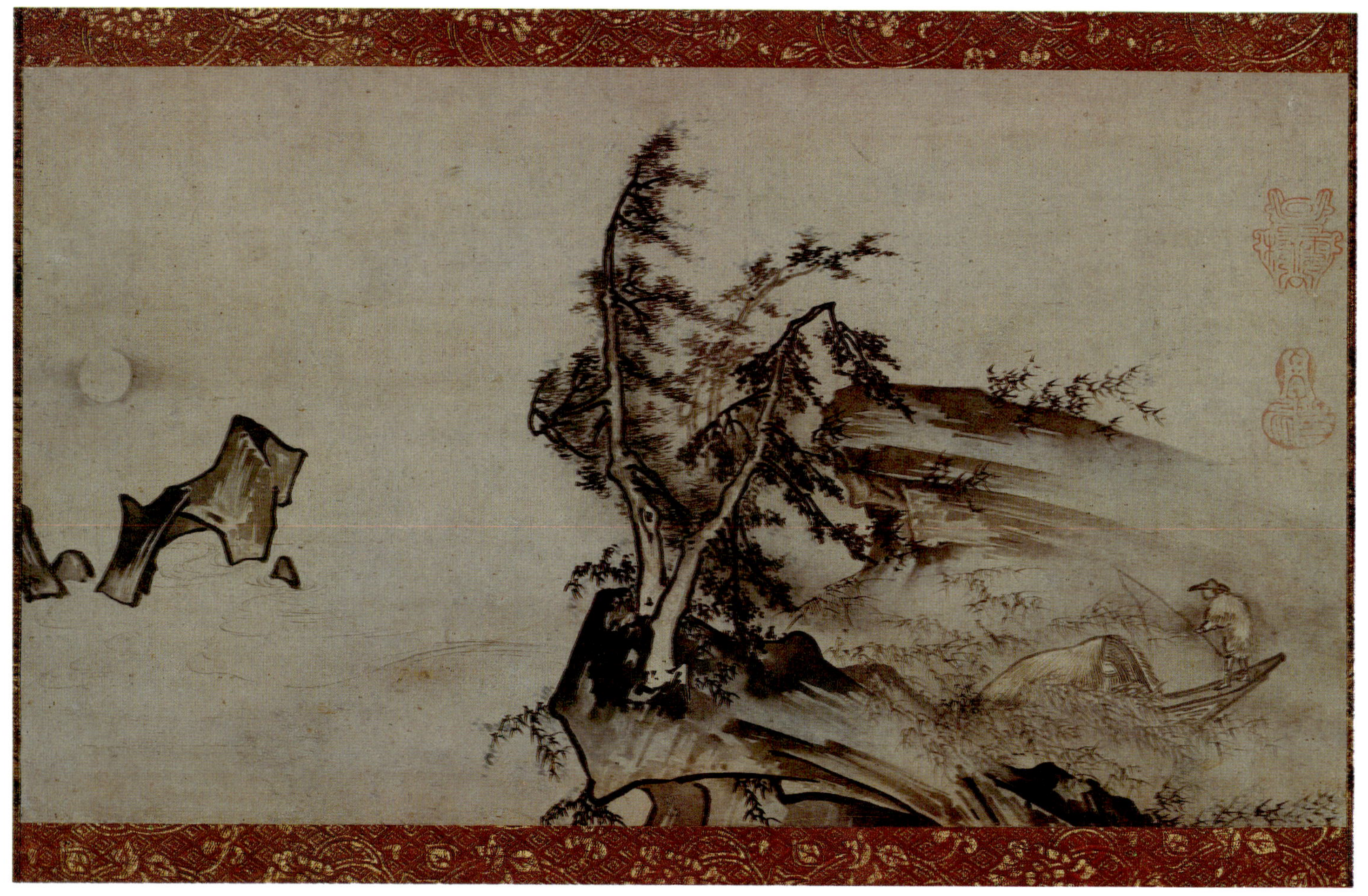

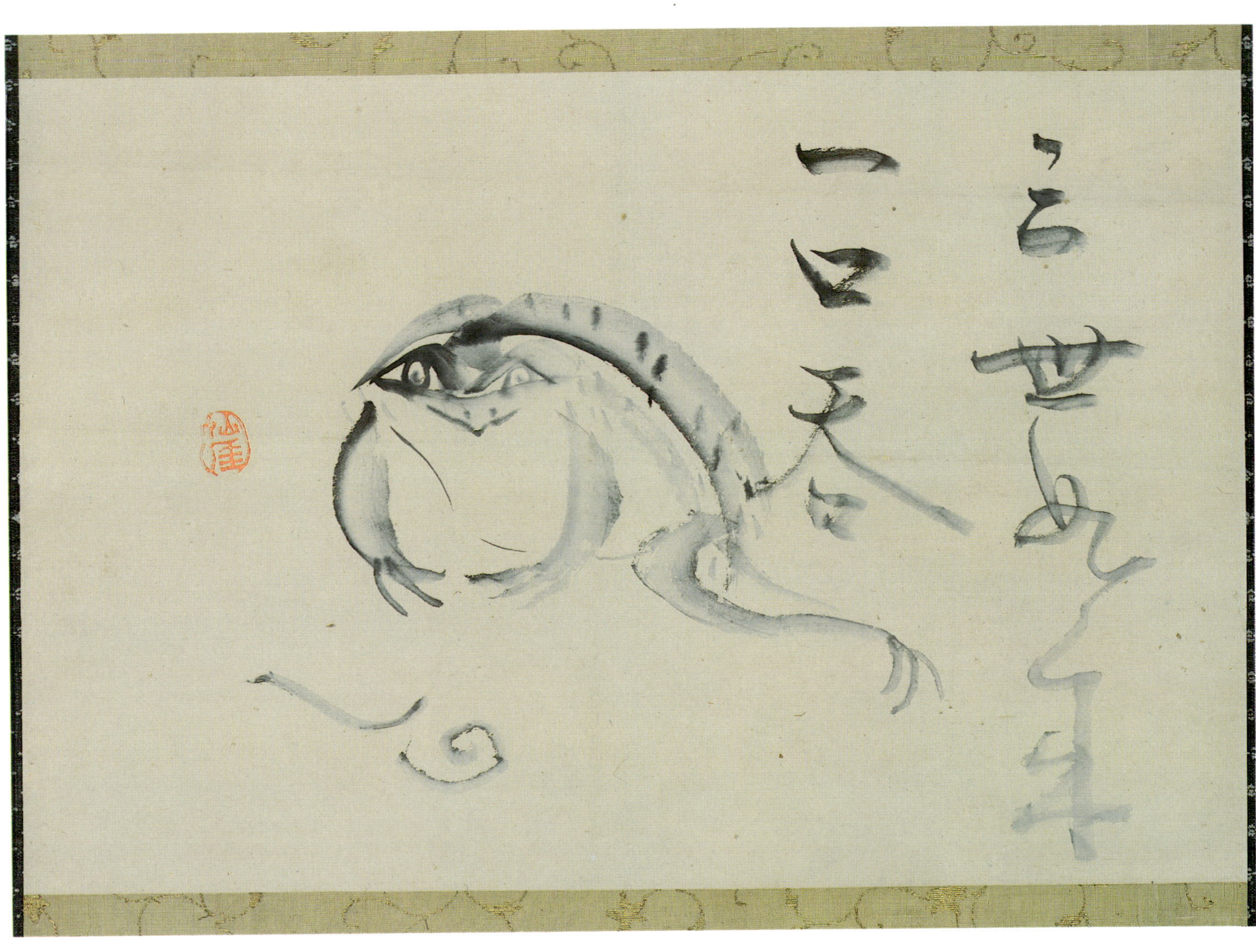

36

Frog and Snail
Sengai Gibon

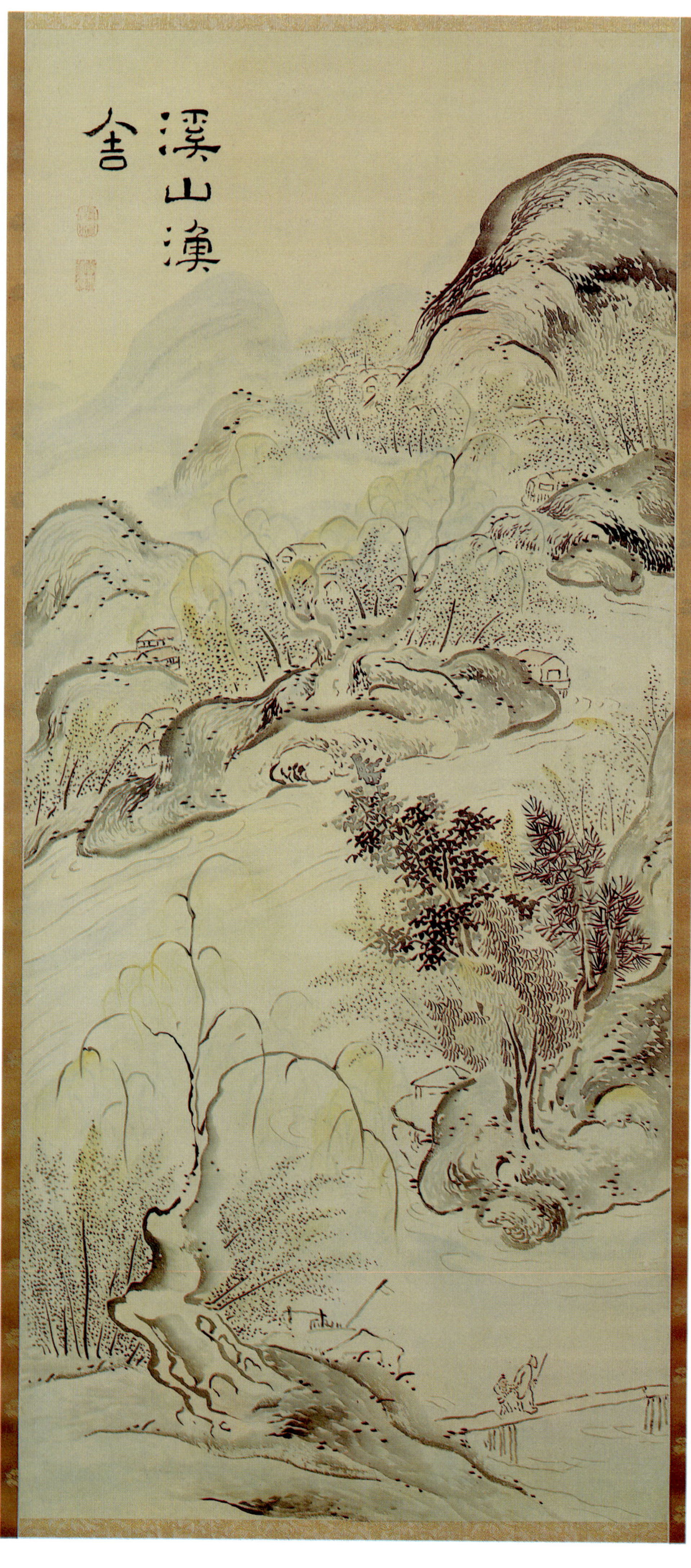

40

**Fisherman's Hut by a
Mountain Stream**
Ikeno Taiga

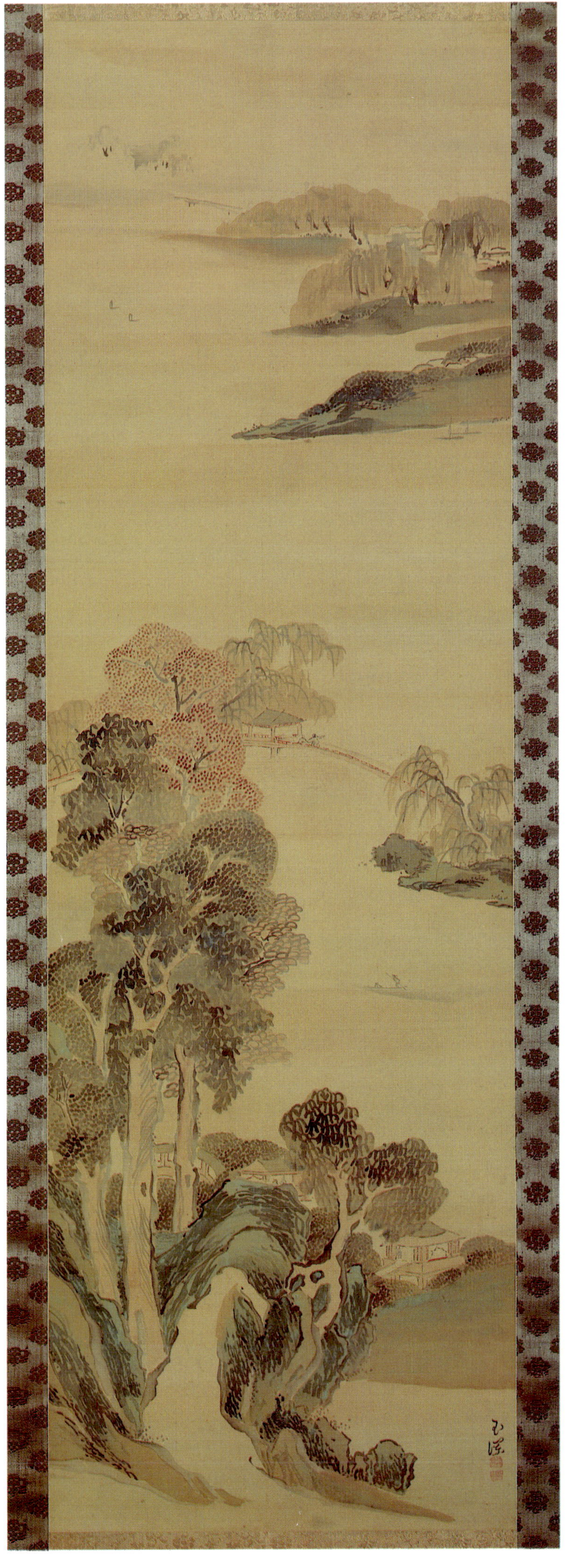

42

Landscape
Ikeno Gyokuran

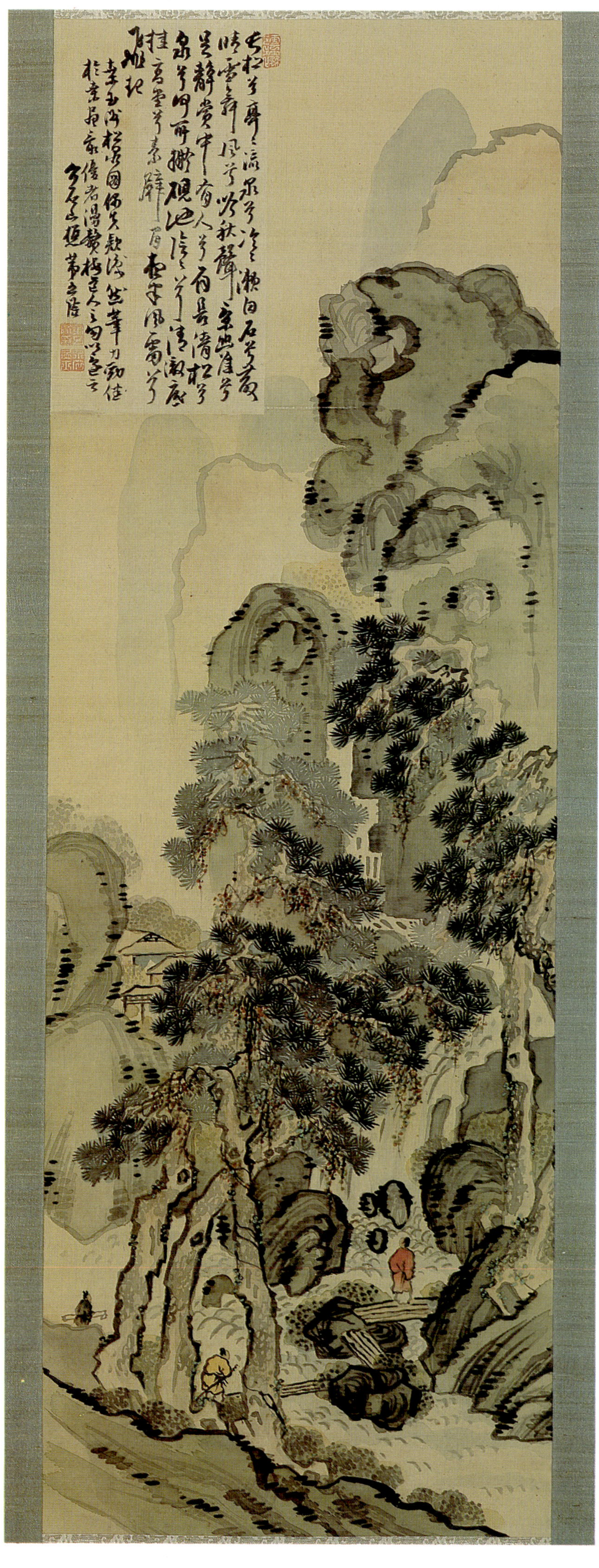

43

**Pine Trees by a
Spring**
Kuwayama Gyokushū

49

**Conversation under the
Full Moon**
Tanomura Chikuden

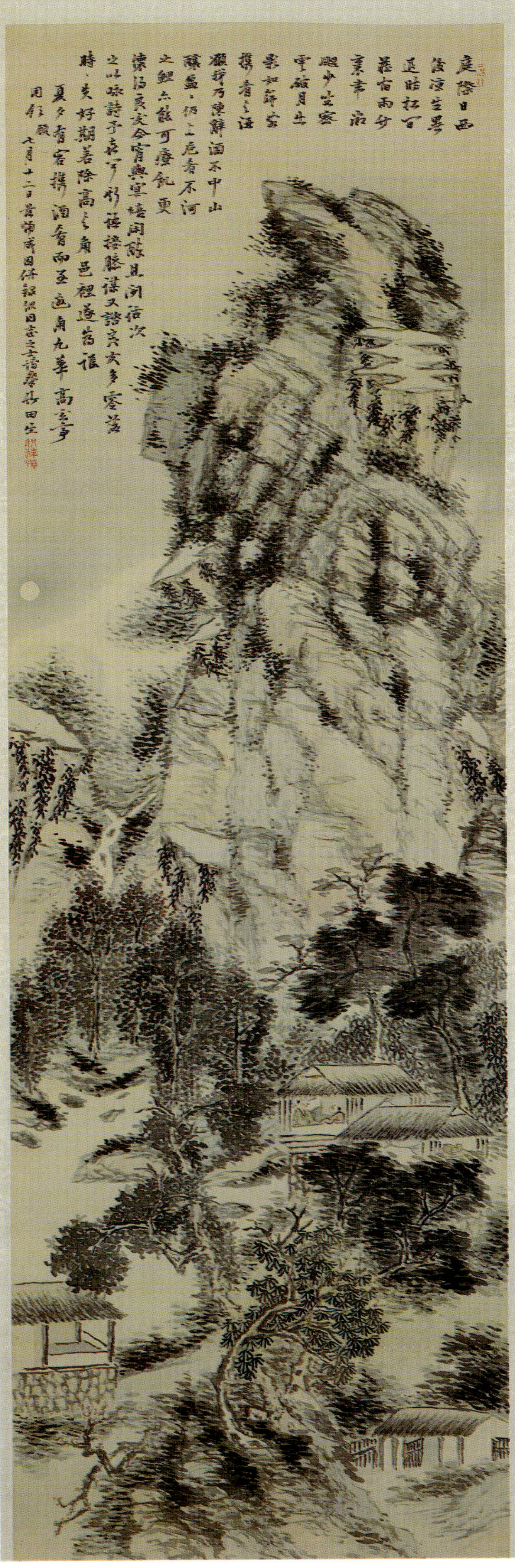

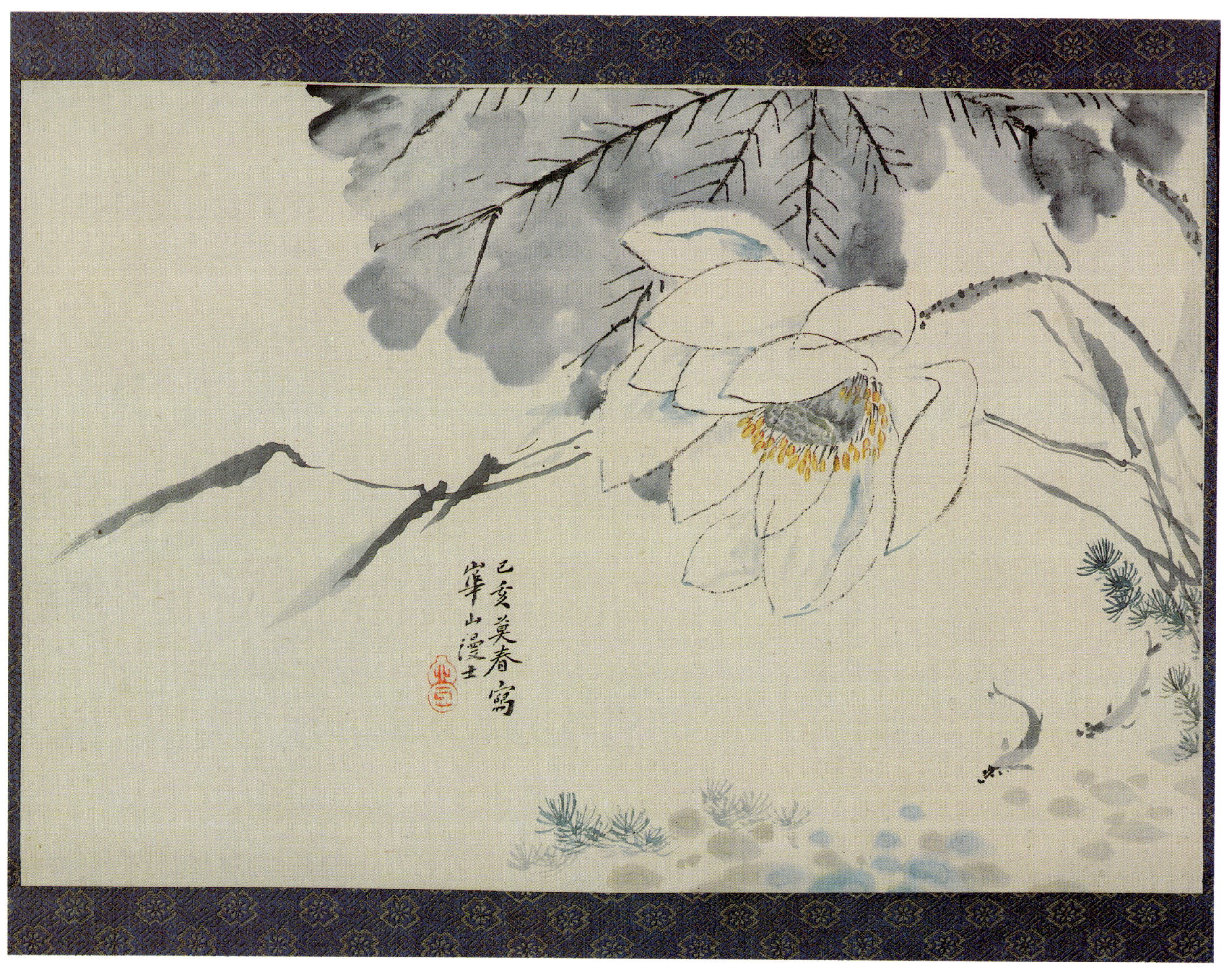

58

Lotus Flower and Swimming Fish
Watanabe Kazan

Autumnal Ivy Leaves with Bamboo
Ogata Kōrin

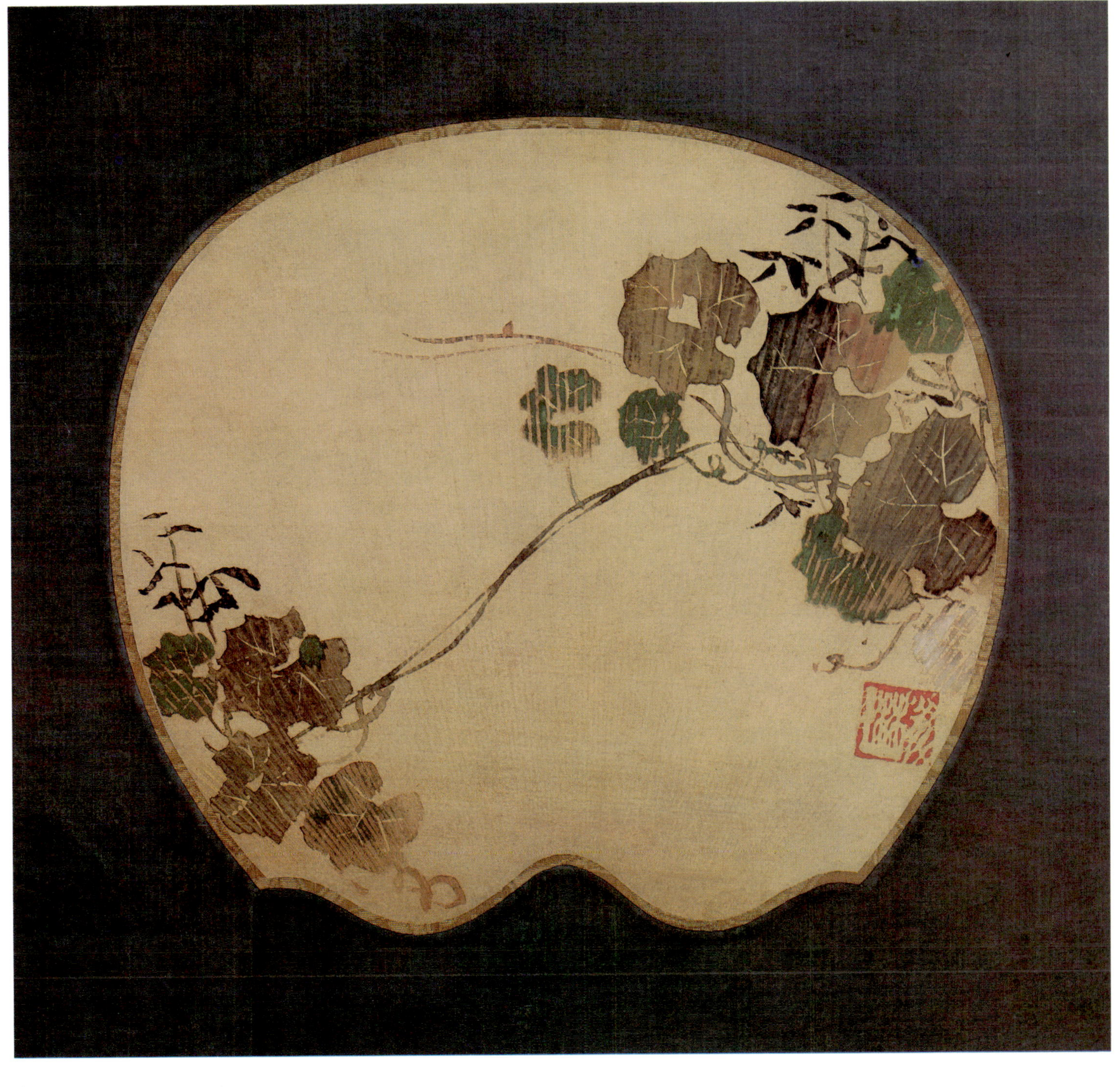

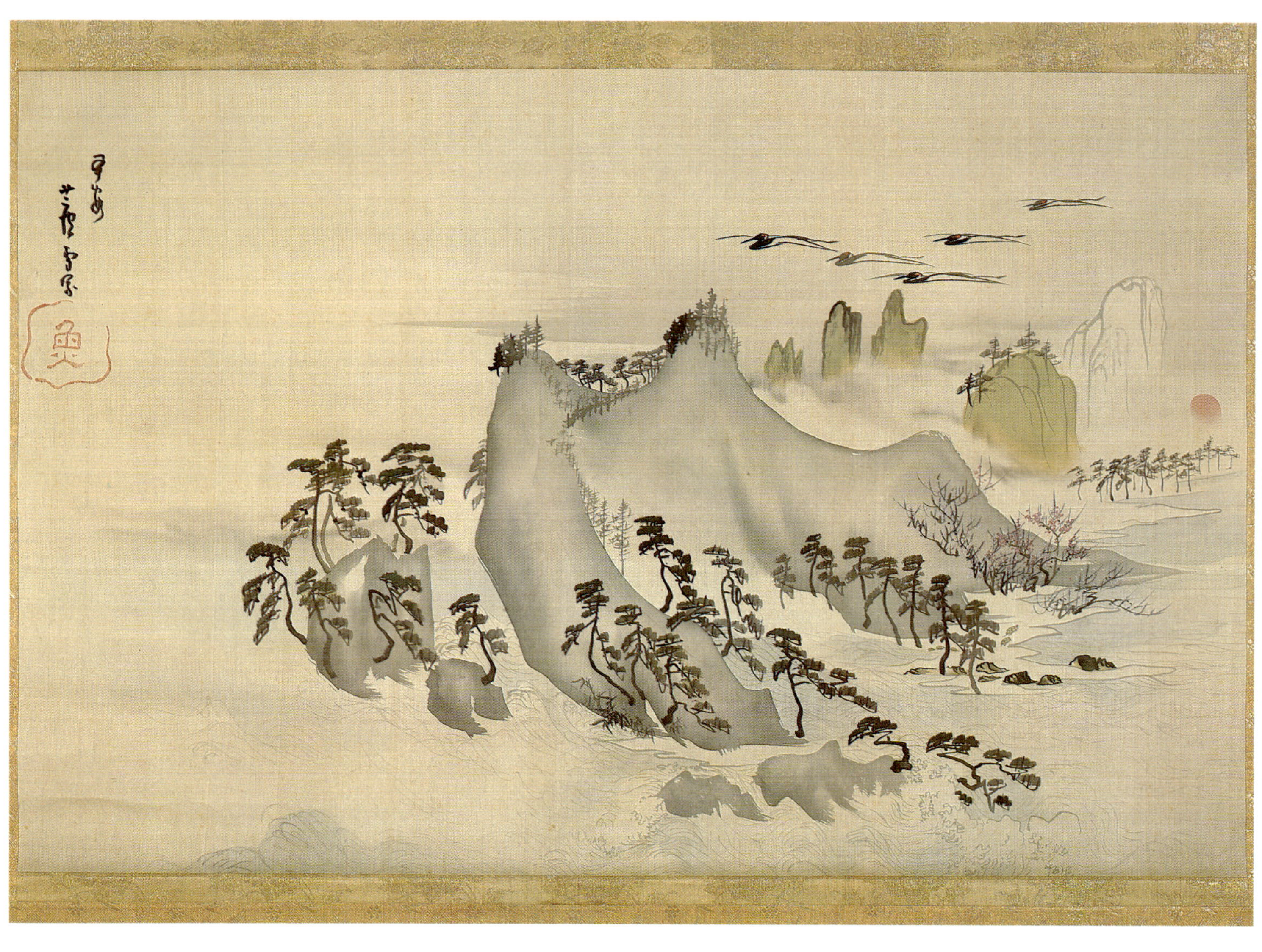

63

Mount Hōrai, Island of Immortality
Nagasawa Rosetsu

Selected Bibliography

Addiss, Stephen. **Obaku: Zen Painting and Calligraphy.** The University of Kansas, Lawrence: 1978.

Addiss, Stephen. **Zenga and Nanga.** New Orleans Museum of Art, 1976.

Akiyama, Terukazu. **Japanese Painting.** Lausanne: 1961.

Asaoka, Okisada. **Koga Bikō.** 4 volumes. Tokyo: 1912.

Bokubi. no. 101, October 1960, and no. 104, February 1961. (special issues on Fūgai Ekun).

Cahill, James. **Scholar Painters of Japan: The Nanga School.** New York: 1972.

Dumoulin, Heinrich. **A History of Zen Buddhism.** New York: 1963.

Fontein, Jan and Hickman, Money. **Zen Painting and Calligraphy.** Boston: 1970.

Furuta, Shōkin. **Sengai.** Tokyo: 1966.

Grilli, Elise. **The Art of the Japanese Screen.** New York and Tokyo: 1970.

Heibonsha Survey of Japanese Art. various volumes of 31 volumes. Tokyo and New York: 1972- .

Higashiyama Suibokuga Shū. 10 volumes. Tokyo: 1934-36.

Joly, Henri. **Legend in Japanese Art.** London and New York: 1908.

Kanda, Kiichirō, et al., eds. **Bunjinga Suihen.** 20 volumes. Tokyo: 1972- .

Kobijutsu. Quarterly review of the fine arts. Sansai-sha, publ., Tokyo: 1964- .

Kokka. Various volumes. Monthly magazine of Japanese art. Tokyo: 1890- .

Matsushita, Takaaki. **Muromachi Suibokuga (Suiboku Painting of the Muromachi Period).** Tokyo: 1960.

Moes, Robert. **Rosetsu.** The Denver Art Museum: 1973.

Murase, Miyeko. **Japanese Art: Selections from the Mary and Jackson Burke Collection.** New York: 1975.

Nakamura, Tanio. **Sesshū.** Nihon Bijutsu Kaiga Zenshū vol. 4. Tokyo: 1976.

National Museums of Kyoto, Nara and Tokyo, eds. **Nihon no Bijutsu.** Tokyo: 1966- .

Nihon no Bunjinga. Tokyo Kokuritsu Hakubutsu Kan. Benridō, Tokyo: 1966- .

Okabe, Hisashi. **400 Years of Zen Painting.** London: 1976.

Roberts, Laurence. **A Dictionary of Japanese Artists.** Weatherhill, Tokyo and New York: 1976.

Rosenfield, John and Shimada, Shūjirō. **Traditions of Japanese Art: Selections from the Kimiko and John Powers Collection.** Harvard University, Cambridge: 1970.

Ryūsen Shūhō: Mayuyama Seventy Years. vol. 2. Tokyo: 1976.

Shimada, Shūjirō. **Sesshū.** Kyoto National Museum. Kyoto: 1956.

Shimada, Shūjirō, and Narazaki, Muneshige, eds. **Zaigai Hihō: Japanese Paintings in Western Collections.** 3 volumes. Tokyo: 1969.

Shimizu, Yoshiaki and Wheelwright, Carolyn, eds. **Japanese Ink Paintings** Princeton, N.J.: 1976.

Stern, Harold P. **Birds, Beasts, Blossoms, & Bugs: The Nature of Japan.** New York: 1976.

Stern, Harold P. **Rimpa: Masterworks of the Japanese Decorative School.** Japan Society, New York: 1971.

Suzuki, Daisetz. **Sengai, the Zen Master.** London: 1971.

Umezawa, Seiichi. **Nihon Nanga Shi (History of Japanese Nanga Painting).** Nanyōdō, Tokyo: 1917.

Yonezawa, Yoshido, and Tanaka, Ichimatsu, eds. **Suiboku Bijutsu Taikei.** 15 volumes. Tokyo: 1972- .

Index of Japanese and Chinese Names and Seals

The following list includes the Japanese and Chinese names of artists, monks, other figures as well as the names on the seals. The numbers refer to catalogue entries and essays. The numbers followed by an asterisk (*) denote an entry about that artist.

A
Anchin 62
Andō Hiroshige 34, IV
Aoki Mokubei 51
Azana Hakumei 52

B
Bokkei 18, 19
Bokushō Shushō 5,* 10, V
Bunson 15,* 27

C
Ch'a Shih-piao 46
Chao Yung 4
Ch'en Lu 44
Chiang Chia-pu 54
Ch'ien Ku 54
Chikamatsu Monzaemon V
Chisokuken 2
Chiyū 16*
Chu Hsi III
Chŭ-jan 39, 46, III
Chū Teichū 38
Ch'ü Yüan 1, 2
Chūan Shinkō 3, 4,* 15, 33
Chūfu 46

D
Daigo 44
Daigoryū In 43
Dasokuken Shōhaku 61
Denshuku no In 51
Dohaku 60
Donkei Tōshitsu 23*

E
Eisai 32

F
Fan K'uan 39
Fūgai Ekun 26,* 27*
Fūgai Honkō 26
Fusō Shūkō 14

G
Gansaku Enō Fusensen 37
Genhan 22
Gessen 33
Gidō Shūshin 1, 2
Gion Nankai 37,* 39, 41, 49, IV
Gomizunoo II
Gyo 62, 63
Gyokuen Bompō 1, 2*
Gyokuenshi 2

H
Hakuin Ekaku 28,* 29,* 30,* 31,* 32,* II, IV, V
Hakuun Egyō 4
Hayashi Razan III
Hidaka Tetsuō 54
Hideyoshi 60
Hōchiku Shinsha 54
Honami Kōetsu 25, 59, 60, II, IV
Honda Tomimasa 59
Hoshu 60
Hsia Kuei 5, 21, 39, I, III
Hsien-tzu 12
Hsüeh-ch'üang P'u-ming 1, 2
Hu Tsung-jen 39
Huang Kung-wang 52
Hui-neng 31
Hui-tsung I
Hung-jen 31

I
I Fu-chiu 44, 57
I-lung I-she 12
Ieyasu II, III, V
Ike Mumei In 41
Ikei Shūtoku 8,* 9,* 10, 17, V
Ikeno Gyokuran 42*
Ikeno Taiga 38, 39,* 40,* 41,* 42, 43, 44, 45, 47, 48, 49, 51, 57, II, V
Ikkyū 31
Issan Shūshō 5
Issei 39
Isshi 3,* 4, 33
Issho Senzan Sei 49
Itō Jakuchū 61, 63, IV, V
Iwasa Matabei IV

J
Jonan Etetsu 13*
Josetsu 2, 7

K
Ka Shō 39, 40
Kaiseki Koji 43
Kaji 42
Kamiya Tenyū 52, 53
Kanō Eikei 61
Kanō Eitoku 22
Kanō Motonobu 22
Kanō Sanraku 22,* IV, V
Kanō Sansetsu 61
Kanō Seisen-in Yasunobu 19
Kanō Tanyū 6, 24, IV, V
Kanō Tsunenobu 60
Kantei 18,* 19,* V
Kaō 12
Karasumaru Mitsuhiro 59
Katsushika Hokusai 34, IV
Ken In 50
Kenkō Shōkei 4, 19
Ki no Hitsu 47
Ki no Jakenchi 47
Ki no Tsurayuki 48
Kidetada 60
Kimura Kenkadō 41, 43, 45,* 49, 51
Kimura Nagamitsu 22
Kinoshita Junan 37
Kiryū 37
Kiyohime 62
Kō Fuyō 43, 45
Kokani 28, 31
Kokyo 45
Konoe Nobutada 25,* 43, V
Kūkai 54
Kushiro Unsen 43, 45, 46,* IV, V
Kusumi Morikage 24,* IV
Kuwayama Gyokushū 41, 43,* 44, 51, 57
Kyōka Suigetsu 37
Kyuho Mukai Nosu 49

L
Li Jih-hua 47
Li Kung-lin 39
Li Po 4, I
Li T'ang 5, 39
Liang K'ai 12, 15, 23, I
Liu Yü-hsi 56

M
Ma Yüan 21
Machi 42
Maruyama Ōkyo 53, 62, IV, V
Masuyama Sessai 45
Matsudaira Sadanobu 55
Matsumura Goshun IV
Matsuo Bashō 35
Mi Fei (Mi Fu) 39, 51
Minagawa Kien 63
Mitsu 22
Mu-ch'i 13, 15, 55, I, V
Murasaki Shikibu V
Musō Soseki 1, 2, I
Myōan Eisai 33

Colophon

Design
Robin Rickabaugh

Photography
Paul Macapia

Calligraphy
Tim Girvin

Duotones and Color Separations
Wy'east Color

Typesetting
Schlegel Typesetting Co.

Lithography
Durham and Downey, Inc.

Binding
Lincoln and Allen

Paper
Vintage Velvet text in an edition of 5,000 softbound and 1,000 hardbound
Cover and jacket printed on Strathmore Grandee